English G 21

A5

für Gymnasien

Lehrerfassung

Abschlussband für die
5-jährige Sekundarstufe I

Cornelsen

English G 21 • Band A 5 Abschlussband für die 5-jährige Sekundarstufe I

Lehrerfassung

Im Auftrag des Verlages herausgegeben von
Prof. Hellmut Schwarz, Mannheim
Jörg Rademacher, Ilvesheim

Erarbeitet von
Laurence Harger, Wellington, Neuseeland
John Eastwood, Street, England
Susan Abbey, Nenagh, Irland
Barbara Derkow Disselbeck, Köln
Allen J. Woppert, Berlin
sowie Claire Lamsdale, Llangybi, Wales

unter Mitarbeit von
Wolfgang Biederstädt, Köln
Joachim Blombach, Herford
Helmut Dengler, Limbach
Dr. Annette Leithner-Brauns, Dresden
Jörg Rademacher, Ilvesheim
Jennifer Seidl, München
Sabine Tudan, Erfurt
sowie Uwe Chormann, Eiselthum; Udo Wagner, Voerde; Heike Wirant, Jena

in Zusammenarbeit mit der Englischredaktion
Dr. Christiane Kallenbach (Projektleitung);
Dr. Christian v. Raumer (verantwortlicher Redakteur);
Susanne Bennetreu (Bildredaktion); Britta Bensmann; Christiane Bonk; Dr. Philip Devlin; Gareth Evans; Bonnie S. Glänzer; Mara Leibowitz; Uwe Tröger; Klaus G. Unger *sowie* Ulrike Berendt

Beratende Mitwirkung
Ingrid Becker-Ross, Krefeld; Peter Brünker, Bad Kreuznach; Helga Estor, Darmstadt; Katja Fabel, Freiburg; Anette Fritsch, Dillenburg; Patrick Handschuh, Köln; Ulrich Imig, Wildeshausen; Bernd Koch, Marburg; Thomas Neidhardt, Bielefeld; Wolfgang Neudecker, Mannheim; Birgit Ohmsieder, Berlin; Gunthild Porteous-Schwier, Moers; Albert Rau, Brühl; Angela Ringel-Eichinger, Bietigheim-Bissingen; Dr. Jana Schubert, Genf/Leipzig; Sieglinde Spranger, Chemnitz; Marcel Sprunkel, Köln; Harald Weißling, Mannheim; Monika Wilkening, Wehretal

Illustrationen
Silke Bachmann, Hamburg; Roland Beier, Berlin; Carlos Borrell, Berlin; Dylan Gibson, Pitlochry; Christian Görke, Berlin; Graham-Cameron Illustration, UK: Eoin Coveney; Alfred Schüssler, Frankfurt/Main

Layoutkonzept
Aksinia Raphael; Korinna Wilkes

Technische Umsetzung
Aksinia Raphael; Korinna Wilkes; Stephan Hilleckenbach; Rainer Bachmaier; Heike Schuster (Lehrerfassung); Ellen Nonnenmacher (Lehrerfassung)

Legende zur Lehrerfassung

magical	**Lernwortschatz** (produktiv zu lernen) (► Vocabulary, SB-Seiten 181–210)
°barbie	**Situativer Wortschatz** (nicht produktiv zu lernen) (► Dictionary, SB-Seiten 211–264)
Yarra [1] 1 ['jærə]	**Aussprachehinweis** bei Eigennamen und schwierigen Wörtern
Box: Voc., S.182	Verweis auf **blue box** im Vocabulary
There was no one to help us.	**Neue grammatische Struktur**
... he can get a job.	**2. neue grammatische Struktur**
L S R W V S R W	**Schwerpunkt des sprachlichen Skills-Training** (*listening, speaking, reading, writing, viewing*) hier: *listening, reading* bzw. *viewing, speaking*
1.02	**CD-** und **Track-Nummer** (neben den Listening-Texten auch für alle Haupttexte)
Whiteboard Beamer ✓	**Interaktive Präsentationen** für **Whiteboards** oder **Beamer**
► KV 25 ► VAS 3A ► Folie 7	Zusatzmaterialien: **Kopiervorlagen, Vocabulary Action Sheets** in den Handreichungen für den Unterricht; **Folien**
Web-Code: EG21-A5-A-008	Zusatzangebote der **Cornelsen-Website**. Die Eingabe dieser Web-Codes unter **www.EnglishG.de** führt direkt zu den jeweiligen Materialien.
○ / ●	leichtere Übung / schwierigere Übung
Lektüre A Prayer for Blue Delaney	**Empfohlene Lektüre in der Reihe *Cornelsen English Library (CEL)***

Umschlaggestaltung
Klein & Halm Grafikdesign, Berlin

www.cornelsen.de
www.EnglishG.de

Die Internetadressen und -dateien, die in diesem Lehrwerk angegeben sind, wurden vor Drucklegung geprüft. Der Verlag übernimmt keine Gewähr für die Aktualität und den Inhalt dieser Adressen und Dateien oder solcher, die mit ihnen verlinkt sind.

Dieses Werk berücksichtigt die Regeln der reformierten Rechtschreibung und Zeichensetzung.

1. Auflage, 1. Druck 2010

Alle Drucke dieser Auflage sind inhaltlich unverändert und können im Unterricht nebeneinander verwendet werden.

Druck: CS-Druck CornelsenStürz, Berlin

ISBN 978-3-06-032172-8 – broschiert

Inhalt gedruckt auf säurefreiem Papier aus nachhaltiger Forstwirtschaft.

Dein Englischbuch enthält folgende Teile:

Units 1 2 3 4	die vier Kapitel des Buches
Getting ready for a test	Hier kannst du dich gezielt auf einen Test vorbereiten.
EXTRA: Text File	viele interessante Texte zum Lesen (passend zu den Units)
Skills File (SF)	Beschreibung wichtiger Lern- und Arbeitstechniken
Grammar File (GF)	Zusammenfassung der Grammatik
Vocabulary	Wörterverzeichnis zum Lernen der neuen Wörter jeder Unit
Dictionary	alphabetisches englisch-deutsches Wörterverzeichnis zum Nachschlagen

Die Units bestehen aus diesen Teilen:

Lead-in	Einstieg in das neue Thema
Part A, B, C, D	neuer Lernstoff mit vielen Aktivitäten
Practice	Übungen

In den Units findest du diese Überschriften und Symbole:

Exploring language	Hier lernst du anhand von Beispielen, neue sprachliche Strukturen zu verstehen und richtig anzuwenden.
STUDY SKILLS	Einführung in Lern- und Arbeitstechniken
Dossier	Schöne und wichtige Arbeiten kannst du in einer Mappe sammeln.
SPEAKING COURSE	Sprechkurs in vier Kapiteln mit nützlichen sprachlichen Hilfen
EVERYDAY ENGLISH	Übungen zum Bewältigen wichtiger Alltagssituationen
MEDIATION	Hier vermittelst du zwischen zwei Sprachen.
VIEWING	Aufgaben zu Filmausschnitten
Now you	Hier sprichst und schreibst du über dich selbst.
REVISION	Übungen zur Wiederholung
WORDS	Übungen zu Wortfeldern und Wortverbindungen
Extra	zusätzliche Aktivitäten und Übungen
	Partnerarbeit / Gruppenarbeit
	nur auf CD / auf CD und im Schülerbuch
	Filmausschnitte auf DVD

Contents

Die folgenden Angebote sind nicht obligatorisch abzuarbeiten. Die Auswahl der Übungen und Übungsteile richtet sich nach den Schwerpunkten des schulinternen Curriculums.

Australia	The road ahead	Stand up for your rights	Teen world

6 Unit 1 Australia

Lead-in Blog from Oz
Part A Australia
Part B Two Australian teenagers
Part C The Aboriginal people of Australia
Part D TEXT: In the outback

Grammatical structures
- REVISION infinitive constructions (verb + object + *to*-infinitive; after question words)
- REVISION tenses
- *to*-infinitives instead of relative clauses

Word fields
- weather
- animals
- sports
- teenage life
- travelling
- small talk

STUDY SKILLS
Talking about statistics
Reading literature (1–3): plot, setting, atmosphere, characters
SPEAKING COURSE (1)
Having a conversation
EVERYDAY ENGLISH
Writing an e-mail
VIEWING
Rabbit-proof fence (scene from a film)

26 Extra Revision – Getting ready for a test 1

32 Unit 2 The road ahead

Lead-in Young people's plans and expectations
Part A Personality quiz
Part B A year abroad
Part C The Business: A reality TV show
Part D TEXT: How to be a teenage millionaire

Grammatical structures
- REVISION gerunds (as subject/object of verbs; after phrases with prepositions; after prepositions)
- REVISION aspect
- gerund with its own subject
- gerund vs. infinitive
- phrasal verbs

Word fields
- personal qualities
- describing people
- interests
- qualifications
- education
- hobbies, interests
- work experience

STUDY SKILLS
Writing formal letters
Using a grammar
Visual aids in presentations
SPEAKING COURSE (2)
Asking for, confirming, giving information
VIEWING
The interviews (scenes from a reality TV show)

50 Unit 3 Stand up for your rights

Lead-in Human rights
Part A TEXT: First Amendment
Part B Running for office
Part C Free and equal?

Grammatical structures
- REVISION active and passive
- REVISION participle clauses instead of relative clauses
- participle clauses instead of adverbial clauses
- participles to provide extra information and for linking
- verbs of perception + object + present participle
- compound participles

Word fields
- human/civil rights
- politics
- economy
- the media
- immigration

STUDY SKILLS
Summarizing a non-fictional text
SPEAKING COURSE (3)
Giving an oral summary
EVERYDAY ENGLISH
Talking about politics
VIEWING
'That's enough debate' (scene from a film)

70 Extra Revision – Getting ready for a test 2

78 Unit 4 Teen world

Lead-in Teenagers – interests, activities, problems
Part A Mobile life and love
Part B Teens in trouble
Part C Get involved
Part D TEXT: The caller

Grammatical structures
- REVISION indirect speech
- REVISION conditional sentences
- REVISION modal verbs
- *should, had better, be supposed to*
- *the* + adjective
- English verbs instead of German adverbs

Word fields
- you and your mobile
- teenage language
- youth culture
- agreeing and disagreeing
- growing up

STUDY SKILLS
Argumentative writing
Online dictionaries
Reading literature (4): suspense
SPEAKING COURSE (4)
Having a discussion
EVERYDAY ENGLISH
Asking someone out
VIEWING
High school boot camp (scenes from a documentary)

98 Partner B

101 Extra Text File

102 **TF 1:** Project: The magic of Australia (zu Unit 1)
104 **TF 2** **Bilingual module** Ecosystems in Australia (zu Unit 1)
106 **TF 3:** Australian signs (zu Unit 1)
107 **TF 4:** The right advice? (zu Unit 2)
108 **TF 5:** Going to school in England (zu Unit 2)
109 **TF 6:** Checks and balances (zu Unit 3)
110 **TF 7:** The monarchy and Parliament (zu Unit 3)
112 **TF 8:** Luuurve debate (zu Unit 4)
114 **TF 9:** Who's guilty? (zu Unit 4)
120 **TF 10** **Bilingual module** A different kind of justice (zu Unit 4)

123 Skills File
153 Grammar File
179 Grammatical terms
181 Vocabulary
211 Dictionary (English–German)
253 List of names
254 Countries and continents
256 Irregular verbs
258 Classroom English
260 Acknowledgments
263 Key to *Getting ready for a test 1* and *2*
264 English-speaking countries

Whiteboard Beamer ✓

°Down under in Australia

Judith in Oz

About me

I'm Judith, 15. Born & grew up in Cologne, Germany. Now live in Melbourne, Victoria, Australia. °Yay! Mum's German and Dad's an °Aussie, so I'm half German and half Australian. That's cool °coz I speak both German and English.

- Subscribe to this blog.
- °View my complete profile.
- Click here for my photos.
- Click here for my sound file to go with the photos.
- Please write to me here.

LATEST:

19th November

It's getting hot now! Just back from a '°barbie' – that's a barbecue, not a dolls' party ;-) – at my friend Ella's house. There's a party nearly every weekend here coz we're too young to get into bars and clubs. Riley came too. He called me Jude, like my friends do.

OLDER BLOGS:

Box: Voc., S.182

14th October

All Aussies are sports-mad and it's catching! I used to be a °couch potato and now I'm learning to surf. It's hard but so cool how the waves carry you to the beach – and you have to surf if you want to be a °fair dinkum Aussie. Also, the surf instructor, Riley, is seriously gorgeous!

30th September

I know, I know – I haven't written for ages. Sorry! It's spring holiday and I've just come back from a 5-day hike in the bush. Amazing, but a bit scary too. One evening a °kookaburra (the weirdest bird!) stole a sausage from my plate and the next day a snake fell out of a tree onto another girl's arm. She really freaked out!

24th July

Life is less magical now – school has started! The school year has four terms in Australia and this is Term 3. We begin at 8.30 – no worries, but then we have to stay at school until 3.15! And after that there are lots of extracurricular activities like sport, music or debates – I have a piano lesson tomorrow. And there's homework too. School is going to fill my days now. :-(

22nd July

1 ['jærə]

Melbourne is very beautiful and very big: pop. 3 million. My first view of the city was awesome – the Yarra [1] River, the skyscrapers, the sea – magical.

1

09th July

Just arrived. My first night in my dad's home town in Oz – too excited to sleep so I'm beginning this blog. (I promised it to my mates and English teacher back in Cologne.) As we flew across Australia for hours, south towards Melbourne, I looked out of the window. The land seemed to °go on forever. It was mainly flat and red dirt roads cut across the endless, dry outback. It looked so huge and empty and I suddenly felt very, very small – and a bit scared. When I got off the plane I got a shock. I'd left Cologne on a hot July day, but here 'down under', on the other side of the world, it was a cold °winter's day.

2

3

4

5

6

1 Life in Australia 1.02

L S R W

a) *Read Judith's blog and write down five things that are new, interesting or surprising to you.*

b) *Now listen to Judith's sound file. What sounds can you hear?*

c) *Listen again and take notes on what you find out about the photos. Compare your notes with a partner's.*

d) **Extra** *Imagine you're in one of the photos and tell your group about it. How do you feel? What are you doing? Who are you with? What can you see, smell and hear?*

e) *Explain why you would/wouldn't like to go to Australia. Collect all the pros and cons in class.*

f) **Extra** *Write a comment for Judith's blog.*

2 Extra Australia project

L S R W

Choose one of the project topics from TF 1 on pp. 100–101. As you go through the unit, collect useful ideas, information, words and phrases for your project. (You might even do it in a blog.)

▸ **Text File 1** *(pp. 102–103)* • *SF Project skills (pp. 132–133)*

Background File AUSTRALIA

L S R W

1 Australian geography

Take notes while you work.

Quick facts

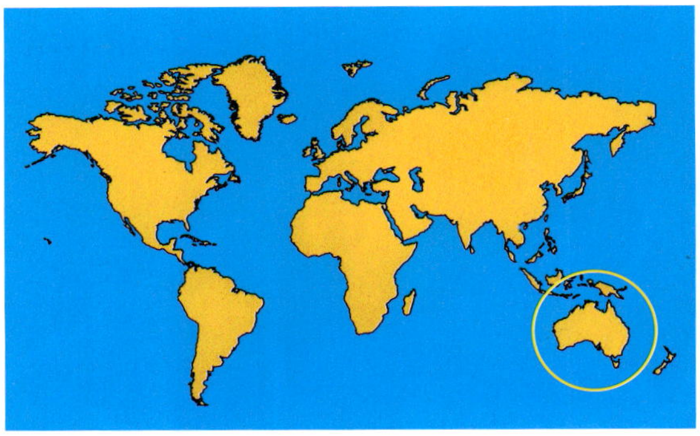

Flag:	
Area:	7,686,850 sq km
Population:	21.2 million
Capital:	Canberra (334,000)
Largest city:	Sydney (4.3 million)

a) *Look at the Australian flag. What other flag is in it? Why do you think that is? What could the stars mean?*

b) *Explain why Australia is often called 'Down Under'.*

c) *Look at the map of Australia on the front inside cover. Use the map and the Quick facts box to compare Australia and Germany (size, population, type of landscape, time zones, transport, ...).*

d) **Extra** *Discover another interesting piece of information on the map of Australia.*

2 Three °aspects of Australia

Work in groups of three. Each student works on a different section – A, B or C.
Read your section and take notes on it so that you can pass on information to the others in your group.

L S R W

A

A short history of Australia

Over 40,000 years ago, humans first started to arrive in Australia from Asia. They spread all over the huge continent and created trade routes for stone, wood, shells and other goods. These Aborigines changed the landscape with fire and developed the oldest rock art in the world. Their stories of the '°Dreaming' told how they thought the world had begun.

Nobody knows how many Aborigines were living in Australia when the first Europeans came in the 16th century, but the figure was probably between 300,000 and 1 million. Despite that, in 1770 Captain James Cook °claimed the world's largest island for Britain. In 1788 the British started a colony for convicts in what is now Sydney. Over the next 80 years, Britain brought over 160,000 convicts to Australia.

Other immigrants arrived and together with the former convicts, they started colonies in different parts of the continent. The colonies became states, and in 1901 Australia was founded and became independent.

During all this time, many Aboriginal people were killed, either by the Europeans or by the diseases the Europeans had brought, until at the beginning of the 20th century there were only about 150,000 left. Today their numbers have risen again to 455,000, but they have always had to fight hard for equal rights.

In the 20th century Australia kept its close links to Britain and fought with the British in both world wars. Since the 1970s Australia has done more and more business with Asia, and large numbers of immigrants now come to Australia from Asian countries.

B

°Be sunsmart

Australia has the highest rate of skin cancer in the world. Why is that?

- Most Australians are of European origin so their skin is fair. But Australia is much closer to the equator than Europe, so it has a different climate and the sun is stronger.
- Australians like to spend lots of time outside, at the beach, at barbecues, by the pool and doing sport.
- A suntan is seen as cool and healthy.
- Australia is not far from the Antarctic ozone hole, which means that more ultraviolet rays get through the earth's atmosphere.

Take five steps to protect yourself from the sun:

°Slip on some protective clothing.

°Slop on some sunscreen.

°Slap on a hat.

Seek shade.

°Slide on some sunglasses.

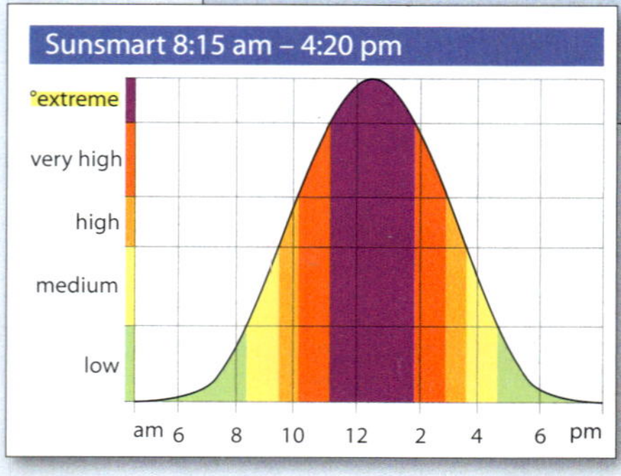

C

The natural sights of Australia

Australia is a country of wonderful natural sights, from rainforests to deserts, and unique wildlife like the kangaroo, koala and emu.

One of Australia's most famous natural sights is the Great Barrier Reef, the largest °coral reef in the world and the only °living thing on earth that can be seen from space with the naked eye. More than 2,000 km long, the reef is home to about 1,500 species of fish, 200 species of birds and 400 species of corals. Dolphins, whales, °sea snakes and °saltwater crocodiles can also be seen there.

Sadly, the reef is in danger. The oceans around Australia – like the rest of the world – are getting warmer and the corals will die if the water temperature rises by more than a few degrees. Other dangers to the reef include pollution from rivers, farms and cities on the coast, more and more tourists, the °crown-of-thorns starfish and °overfishing. If they are not °stopped, almost all the corals will have died by 2050.

► **Text File 2** *(pp. 104–105)* • **Text File 3** *(p. 106)*

3 Information exchange

a) *Use the notes you have taken and give the others in your group the important information from your section. Try to make your talk interesting.*

b) *Take notes on what the others tell you. Ask questions if anything is unclear.*

L S R W

4 Australian facts and figures

STUDY SKILLS Talking about statistics

A chart or table's title tells you what it is about. Tables show detailed figures clearly in columns. Bar charts are often used to compare the number or size of things. Pie charts help you to compare the different sections that make up the pie. Make sure you know what the figures mean – percentages or numbers. Look at them carefully and explain what they show. If possible, compare or contrast different figures, or say how they are connected.

Table:

Country	Population (2008)
USA	304,721,000
Germany	82,400,996
UK	60,776,238
Australia	21,373,760

Bar chart:

Land area in million sq km

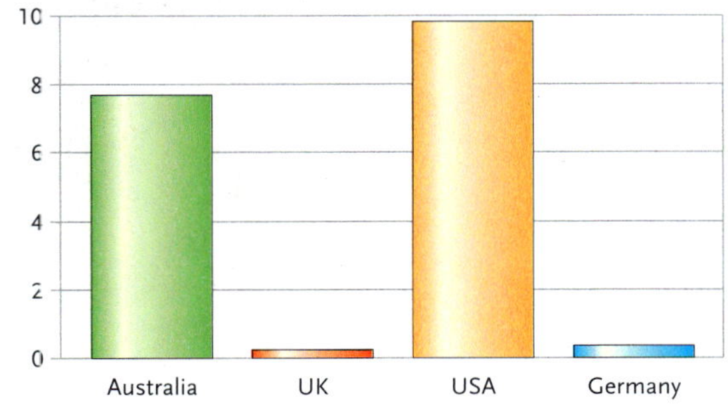

Pie chart:

Ethnic groups in Australia

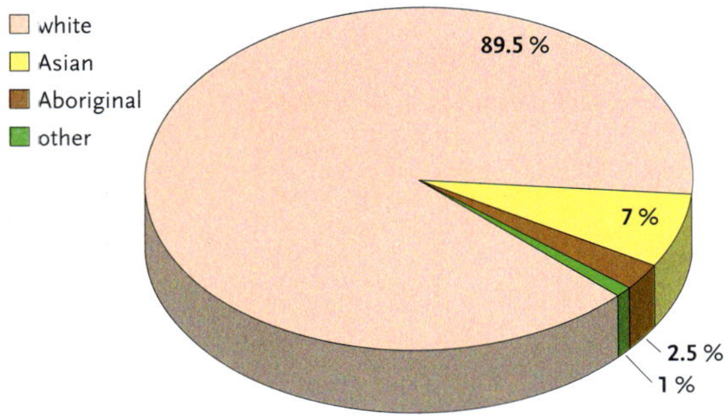

a) *Partner A: Explain the table to your partner.*
This table shows ...
Partner B: Explain the bar chart to your partner.
This bar chart compares ...

b) *Look at the table and the bar chart and explain what they tell you.*
The table shows ... and the bar chart gives us ...
From these figures we can see ...

c) *In writing, explain what the pie chart shows. Give details. Finish with a conclusion.*
The pie chart shows ...
There are ... main ...

Useful language
- The (pie) chart/table is about ...
- It shows the different ... in/of ...
- It compares the size/number of ... with ...
- It is divided into ... sections which show ...
- The figures show that ...
- ... has the largest/second-largest/smallest ...
  ... is twice/three times/... as big as ...
- A huge majority/small minority is ...
- They make up ... % of ...
- There are more than/nearly twice as many ... as there are ...
- You can see that ... is ... but/while ...
- So that shows that ...
- To conclude, you can say ...

d) **Extra** *Look for more statistics about Australia on the internet (temperatures, fires, largest cities/rivers, sport, ...). Find a chart or table and explain it to your partner. Present your findings to the class.*

▸ SF Talking about statistics (p. 127)

P1 REVISION A small town in South Australia (Tenses)

Put each verb into the correct form: simple present, present perfect, simple past, past perfect or will-future.

On 28th December 1838 the Zebra *reached* (reach) Adelaide, capital of the new British colony of South Australia. The ship ... (sail) from Hamburg on 12th August with 199 passengers. They ... (be) °Lutherans who ... (leave) their home for religious reasons. After landing, the captain, Dirk Hahn, ... (help) the settlers to find land for their farms. If today you ... (drive) along the South-Eastern °Freeway from Adelaide, you ... (come) to the place that the immigrants ... (choose) as their home. Hahndorf ... (be) a small town about 25 minutes from the city. Only 1,800 people ... (live) there, but many more people ... (hear) of Hahndorf. Now the town ... (become) a tourist attraction, with its buildings in the German style, its art galleries, its souvenir shops and its restaurants which ... (offer) traditional German food.

Of course not everyone in Hahndorf today ... (have) a German background. But there are still families who ... (be) there from the beginning. Try to visit Hahndorf if you ever ... (get) the chance. You ... (find) something to interest you.

► *GF I: The tenses (pp. 154–158)*

P2 WORDS Time phrases

a) *Read 'A short history of Australia' on page 8. Write down all the time phrases you can find.*

– *over 40,000 years ago*

– ...

b) *Read them aloud to your partner and make sure you understand what all the phrases mean. Add more time phrases you know. Many begin with words like:*

after, before, on, at, in, since, for, until, while, during, ...

– *After we moved to Berlin ...*

– *Before the 20th century ...*

– *Since 2006 ...*

– ...

c) **Extra** *Write your 'family history'. Use as many time phrases as possible. Be careful with your tenses. You could start like this:*

My family has lived in ... since ...

When my great-grandfather moved from ... in ...

P3 STUDY SKILLS Talking about statistics

Write about the bar charts below. Explain what the charts are about, what they compare, how they are connected and what the connection tells you.

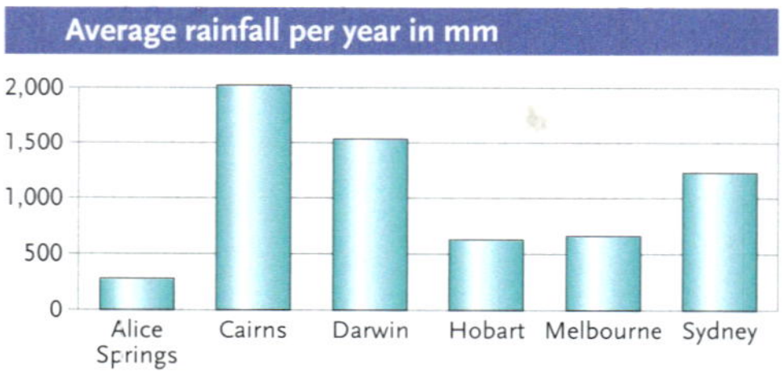

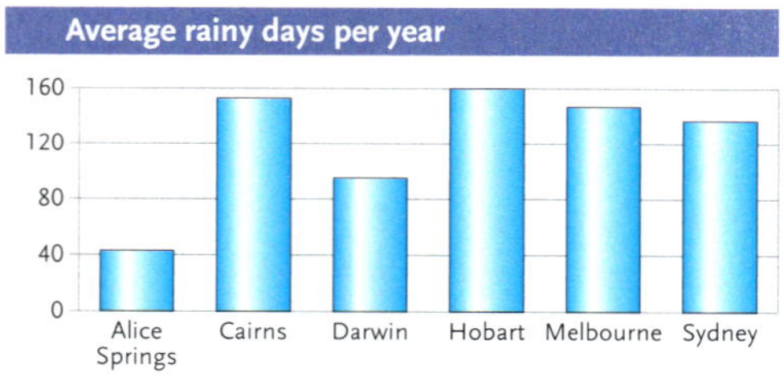

TWO AUSTRALIAN TEENAGERS

1 Jeannie – in the middle of nowhere

L S R W

Read Jeannie's e-mail. Then write captions for the photos.

Hi Cath,
It was great to get your e-mail. Yes, I'd love to be your online friend, although I don't honestly think my life in western Queensland is as exciting as your life in Hong Kong.

My dad works here on a °sheep station, so we live in the middle of nowhere. There are only twenty other people on the station but thousands and thousands of sheep. The nearest town is 300 miles away, so we don't have a local cinema, or doctor or even a school! But I still have school. My school is the Alice Springs School of the Air. It's cool! It comes to me through my computer. That means I don't have to sit in a classroom all day! (I can even take my laptop outside and do my work under a tree!) But I can talk to the teacher and class every day. Although Alice Springs is 800 miles away, my teachers are in a studio so I can even see them. A lot of our class have webcams, so we can see each other too. We're good friends although we only meet about three times a year at one-week courses. The next one is in Alice next month.

You talk about your sports and hobbies – dragon boat racing, tennis and discos. Well, mine are a bit different! There's no one here at the station my age, so I have to do things on my own a lot. I ride every day – which is great. (I have my own horse, Sally.) And I'm allowed to drive a dirt bike – that's great fun.

I'm attaching some photos. Please mail again soon.
Your new online friend,
Jeannie

A

B

C

2 Now you

L S R W

a) *Make a table and compare your school with the School of the Air. Headings could be:* times, teacher, lessons, rooms, students, ...

b) *Think: What are the advantages and disadvantages of the School of the Air?*
Pair: *Compare with a partner.*
Share: *Discuss with another pair*
– It would be boring/fun/...
– I would miss/hate/love/...
– Studying would be easier/harder because ...

3 Extra Royal Flying Doctor Service

L S R W

Isolated sheep stations in the outback don't have local doctors, but people can call the Royal Flying Doctor Service (RFDS). Find out more about the service and how it works.
Write a short report, illustrate it and put it in your DOSSIER.

▸ SF Research (p. 128)

4 Rob – sports-mad in Sydney 1.03

a) *Listen to Rob. Make a list of the sports he talks about. Which ones are not on this page?*

b) *Listen again. What are Rob's three favourite sports? Take notes so that you can give reasons for your answer.*

c) *Which of the sports in your list interest you most? Why? Have you ever done any of them? Can you do them where you live?*

A: I'd love to learn how to surf. It must be so exciting. But how can I? I live 600 km from the sea!

B: I'm not sure about surfing, but ...

5 Now you

a) *Work in groups of four. This is your topic: 'Differences between city or country life in Australia and Germany.'*
On a piece of paper, write a statement or question on the topic, then pass it on clockwise. On the next piece of paper you get, write a reaction, answer the question, or write a new statement.
Go on till you get your first piece of paper back. Now discuss your results. One student presents your group's results to the class.

b) **Extra** *If you could visit Jeannie or Rob for a week, who would you choose? Explain why.*

Web-Code: EG21-A5-A-013

SPEAKING COURSE Part 1

P1 SPEAKING Good to meet you (Having a conversation) 1.04

2:17

a) *If you want to talk to somebody you don't know, you may have to*

1 find a way to start the conversation,
2 introduce yourself,
3 ask the person questions and answer theirs,
4 ask the person for help if you need it,
5 react when you don't understand something,
6 end the conversation.

Match these things to the phrases below.

Sorry, I didn't get that. • Sorry, can you say that again, please? • The/A ...? What's that?/ What does that mean?
Bye! • See you tomorrow.
By the way, my name's ... • How are you? • Good to meet you.
Hi! • Excuse me, ...
Have you ever ...? / Have you ... yet? • What about you?
Can you tell me ...? • Do you know where ... ?

b) *At the beach last week, Rob met Anna, an English tourist. Listen to their conversation. Which of the phrases in a) can you hear?*

► *SF Speaking Course (pp. 142–143)*

c) *Role play*
With your partner act out a short conversation. Use the flow chart below and phrases from a).

Partner A:
– You want to sit down in a café.
– You'd like to see the film *Batman*, but don't know where it's on.

Partner B:
– You're sitting alone at a table in a café.
– You're reading a magazine with cinema tips.

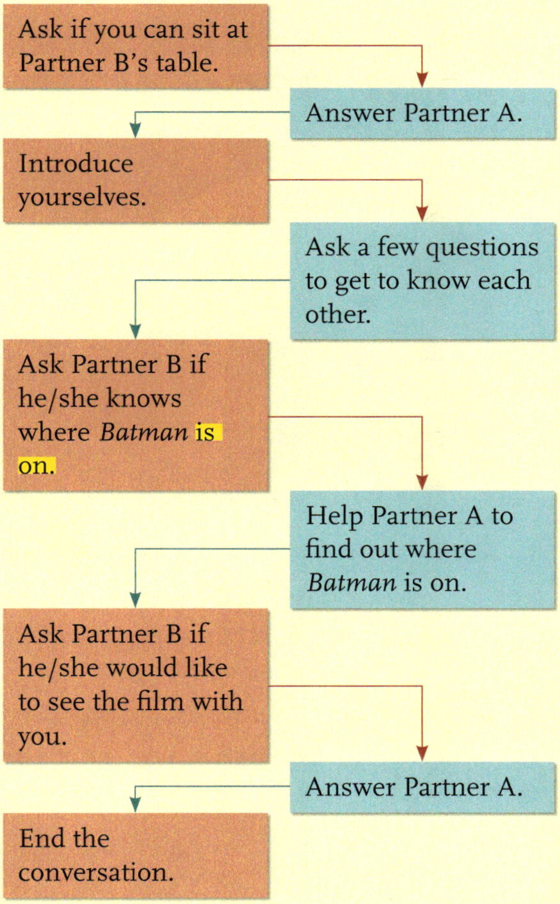

d) Extra *Role play*
In groups of three, act out a short conversation.

Situation:
The three of you are on holiday in Australia. You can't speak German. You meet in a hostel. Talk to each other about your holidays so far.

P2 LISTENING Learning to surf 1.05

a) When Anna got to the surf school, there were so many people there that she decided to phone them later. Listen to the conversation and complete the information below.

Easysurf – Let's go surfing!
Lessons: Beginners
Easysurf Courses
– When?
– How long?
– Group size?
– Equipment (wetsuit, surfboard)?
– Cost?
Private Lessons

b) Role Play
Partner B: Go to page 98.
Partner A: Use the role card below and act out the telephone conversation.

Name: Jenny
– You'd like to learn to surf.
– You've never gone surfing before.
– You're a good swimmer.
– You'd like to learn with other girls.
– You've got your own equipment.
– You want to know the price.

P3 WORDS Tricky translations

Some German words have different English translations. Find the right translations for the words in brackets and complete the sentences. If you are unsure, check in a German–English dictionary.

1 *(tragen)* When Rob goes surfing in winter he wears a wetsuit. He loves the way the waves carry him to the beach.
2 *(bringen)* ... me my paper please, and then could you ... this letter to the post office?
3 *(groß)* The African elephant is between 3.5 and 4 metres ... and is known for its ... ears.
4 *(während)* We met some nice guys ... we were waiting for the train and chatted with them ... our journey to Melbourne.
5 *(brauchen)* The bus from the station to the airport ... about ten minutes. And it's free, so you don't ... a ticket.
6 *(machen)* What are you ... this evening? – Well, I have to ... dinner for my family.
7 *(fahren)* My mum can't ... a car, so she ... her bike to work. It if rains, she ... by bus.
8 *(vor)* Two weeks ..., I went to see a film. I met my friends ... the cinema. ... the film we bought some popcorn.

P4 EVERYDAY ENGLISH WRITING Our lives (Writing an e-mail)

Look at pages 12 and 13 again. Write an e-mail to Jeannie or Rob.

– Use their names. Say what you find interesting or surprising about their lives. → I was really interested to read/hear about ... • I think it's great that you can/have ... • I was really jealous when I read that you ...

– What else would you like to know about their lives? Ask some questions. → I have some questions for you. • Are you allowed to ...? • What's your favourite ...? • Where/When/How often do you ...?

– Tell them something about your life, e.g. your school day, your favourite subject, the sports you enjoy, ... → My life in Germany is (a bit/very) different from yours. • For example, ...

– Find a good way to finish. → That's all from me for now. • Best wishes, ... / All the best, ... / Yours, ...

THE ABORIGINAL PEOPLE OF AUSTRALIA

L S R W

1 The Dreaming

For Aboriginal people, Tjukurpa – the Dreaming – explains why the world exists and helps them to lead their daily lives. It is passed on in dance, song, stories and art. Here's the story of how the world began:

In the beginning the world was flat and empty. But the ancestors of all living things were asleep in the ground. One day the ancestors rose, °gave birth to their children and called out their own names: I am Red Lizard, I am °Mulga-tree. Then they travelled across the land and the tracks they left are the world we see today. The paths they walked along became rivers. When they put sticks into the ground, trees were formed. When they died, their bodies changed into mountains. They ate, made love, laughed, played and fought. And when they had made the whole world, the ancestors sank back into the earth.

But the Dreaming is more than stories about the past: it links the past and present and shows Aborigines how to take care of the world today.

a) What other stories about how the world was created do you know? How is the Dreaming similar or different?

b) **Extra** *From what you have learned about the Dreaming, explain what attitude Aboriginal people probably have to the natural world.*

1 [ˈˌuːləruː, kætə, ˈtjuːtə]

L S R W

2 In Uluru-Kata Tjuta [1] National Park 1.06

6:45

Uluru at sunrise

Holes on Uluru made in the Dreaming by Tatji, the red lizard

a) Look closely at the photos of Uluru-Kata Tjuta National Park. Explain what they tell you about the place. Think of:
climate – landscape – the Dreaming – ...

b) Listen to the radio programme. What is your strongest impression? Exchange your thoughts in your group. Then write a short summary of what happens in the programme.

c) Listen again and take notes on two of the following. Then share your ideas in class.

tourists • colours • weather • Aboriginal culture • respect • sounds/music

Cave painting

► SF Listening (p. 134)

Web-Code: EG21-A5-A-016

3 The 'stolen generations'

L S R W

Children were stolen for a racist ideal. Now a nation says sorry

1 [zi:tə]

Zita[1] Wallace still remembers the day she was stolen from her Aboriginal family and taken to a home for orphans. The home was run by white nuns. She was seven years old.

Wallace and four other girls were tricked into leaving the place where they had been living with their families. One day some nuns arrived and said that the girls could go shopping with them. 'They put us in the back of a truck and took us to a home hundreds of miles away.'

At her house in Worita, 160 km from Alice Springs, Wallace spoke about her first night with the nuns. 'There were lots of children in one big room. On the floor there were hard mattresses to sleep on. I was terrified because there was no one to help us.'

She told us that she would never forget those first hours. 'There was a 4-year-old girl who just cried and cried. I put my head under my blanket and cried too.'

Wallace belongs to the 'stolen generations', the thousands of mixed-race children with fair skin who were taken from their families. The government wanted them to forget their traditions and grow up like white children. 'They used to hit us if we spoke our language,' Wallace told us. 'And there was always cooking and cleaning to do. We only got enough education to read and write.'

The stealing of children ended after 60 years in 1970. In

Zita Wallace with her mother's sister Aggie

1997 a government report said it was time to apologize. Now, eleven years later, Australia is finally saying sorry.

Wallace doesn't care about getting money from the government. 'I'll be listening to the speech tomorrow,' she said. 'And I can't wait to hear that word tomorrow: *sorry*.' ■

a) *Say how you feel about what happened to Zita Wallace.*

b) *Summarize what the article tells you about the 'stolen generations'. Why does the headline talk of 'a racist ideal'?*

c) **Extra** 1.07 *On 12th February 2008, the Australian prime minister, Kevin Rudd, at last said sorry to the 'stolen generations'. Listen to part of his speech. Imagine Zita Wallace wrote a letter to Kevin Rudd after she heard the speech. Write the letter.*

1:23

4 °VIEWING Rabbit-proof fence

V S R W

Rabbit-proof fence tells the true story of three Aboriginal girls who are 'stolen'. They escape and walk 1,900 miles through the outback of western Australia to get home.

a) *Watch part of the film. Describe what happens.*

b) *What do you find out about*
1 the man repairing the fence,
2 the fence,
3 the children's mother?

c) **Extra** *Watch again. Take notes on how the acting and the music help you to understand*
– the mother's feelings,
– the children's feelings.

– When the music gets louder you think …
– The way the mother looks when the car arrives shows …

▸ SF Taking notes (p. 135)

P1 REVISION 'Stolen generations' (Verb + object + *to*-infinitive)

In English, some verbs can be followed by an object + *to*-infinitive:
The Dreaming helps Aboriginal people to lead their daily lives.
The government wanted them to forget their traditions.

Use a verb from box A in the right tense and an infinitive from box B to complete the sentences.

A force • tell • not want (2×) • want (2×)

B to apologize • to get into • to give • to go shopping • to learn • to speak

1 Zita Wallace remembers how she was stolen. 'They **told** us **to get into** the truck.'
2 'They ... us ... with them. But it was a trick.'
3 'They ... us ... our language. They beat us if we did.'
4 'They ... us ... their language and the white man's way.'
5 Many Australians ... their government ... to the 'stolen generations' and in 2008 the government did.
6 Zita ... the government ... her money. Hearing them say sorry was enough for her.

► *GF 8.1: Verb + object +* to*-infinitive (p. 172)*

P2 REVISION On holiday in Australia (Question word + *to*-infinitive)

Partner B: Go to page 98.

a) *Partner A: You're on holiday in Australia and need some help. Look at the boxes on the right and tell your partner what your problems are. Start with 'I don't know/I'm not sure ...', add a question word and an infinitive construction and finish with 'Can you help? / Any ideas? / Do you know?'.*

I don't know I'm not sure	who where when how what	be at the meeting place bring on the tour get to the meeting place meet for the tour see about the Uluru tour

A: I don't know who to see about the Uluru tour. Can you help?
B: Yes, why don't you see the people at the tour desk?

b) *Listen to Partner B and decide what to say. You can use phrases like 'Why don't you ...?' or 'You should ...'.*

► *GF 8.2: Question word +* to*-infinitive (p. 172)*

1 Ask at the tourist office.
2 Check out by 11 am.
3 Go by plane.
4 Wear a pullover. It's often a bit cold.
5 Send one to your mum.

P3 Exploring language *to*-infinitives instead of relative clauses

a) *Look at these two sentences from page 17.*
1 On the floor there were hard mattresses to sleep on.
2 I was terrified because there was no one to help us.

You could also write them like this:
1 On the floor there were hard mattresses that we could sleep on.
2 I was terrified because there was no one who could help us.

What do we call the clauses in blue print?

b) *How else could you say the following?*
1 Zita wasn't the first girl to cry.
2 Your teacher is the person to ask about difficult grammar.
3 The Grammar File is the place to go to if you need answers.

► *GF 8.3: The* to*-infinitive instead of a relative clause (pp. 172–173)*

P 4 In the children's home (*to*-infinitives instead of relative clauses)

Here is some more of what Zita Wallace said about the children's home she was taken to. How else could you say the same thing?

1 In the children's home there were some hard mattresses that we could sleep on.
There were some hard mattresses to sleep on.
2 There was tea we could drink and bread we could eat.
3 There was lots of work that we had to do for the nuns.
4 There were clothes we had to wash, dinners we had to cook and rooms we had to clean.
5 There was nobody who could help us.
6 We had no families who could protect us.

P 5 The Aboriginal people (*to*-infinitives instead of relative clauses)

Use to-*infinitives and expand the notes to full sentences.*

1 Aborigines – first humans who arrived in Australia
The Aborigines were the first humans to arrive in Australia.
2 who will be the last people who live there? – nobody knows
Nobody knows who will …
3 Want to know more about the 'stolen generations'? *Rabbit-proof fence* is the film you should see.
If you want to know more …
4 Visit Uluru for more information on Aboriginal culture.
Uluru is the place …

Australian Aboriginal flag

P 6 MEDIATION An early morning walk at Uluru [1] (Spoken English to German) 1.08

a) While on holiday in Australia with a friend, you think you'd like to take an early morning tour of Uluru, so you call the tour company for more information. Your friend, whose English isn't so good, has lots of questions. Listen and find out the answers. Take notes.

1 Was können wir bei dieser Tour alles sehen?
2 Wann müssen wir aufstehen?
3 Wie kommen wir da hin?
4 Sind da Leute, die uns führen?
5 Müssen wir weit laufen?
6 Wie viel kostet uns die Tour?
7 Wie können wir buchen und bezahlen?

b) Answer your friend's questions in German.

1 [ˌuːləruː, ˈuːləruː]

Lektüre
A Prayer for Blue Delaney

In the outback (°adapted from the novel *A prayer for Blue Delaney* by Kirsty Murray)

This story is set in the outback. Before you read it, with a partner look at the photos, then use what you have already learned and make notes on what you think the atmosphere must be like in the outback. Some important new words are explained in the footnotes at the bottom of each page.

The story so far
During the 1950s Australia wanted to add to its population, so orphans were sent from the UK to children's homes there. Colm is one of these orphans. He is living in a home for boys, but the people at the home are very cruel and Colm decides to run away. He gets to know an old man, Bill, and his dog Rusty. When the police start to look for Colm, Bill offers to take him with him in Tin Annie – his old pickup truck (ute)[1] – as he travels through the Australian outback. Bill is hoping to get work on the Dog Fence, which runs from south to north-eastern Australia.

As they drove out of Ceduna, Bill said, 'I heard from an old mate that there's work on the Dog Fence. Thought I might take it. No one will follow us in that lonely[2] country. '

The Victoria Desert began to stretch out in front of them as they left town. They drove north towards the Dog Fence, through a wide, open landscape of earth and sky.

It was slow and hot travelling along the Dog Fence. The more they drove inland, the hotter the air became until Colm felt he was breathing fire. He and Rusty tried sticking their heads out the window, but it was worse than the burning heat[3] inside the car. The sandy air hurt Colm's skin and made his eyes sore. He pulled his head back inside. There was nothing to see except scrub[4] and tough little grasses in the rock and sand, and the fence stretching like a thin grey scar[5] across the landscape.

'What if we break down[6]?' asked Colm.

'Don't you worry about that. They used to do the fence on camel, but these days they use jeeps. Tin Annie here, she's part camel part jeep, so she'll be fine.'

'But what if we get lost?'

Bill smiled. 'We'll follow the fence, mate. It's more than three thousand miles long and there's no way we can lose it.'

Bill stopped next to the fence where an emu had crashed into[7] it. They both climbed out of the ute.

Bill shook his head. 'She's hit the fence very fast, this one. Looks like she broke her neck.'

In the distance another emu was running across the desert. 'See, they're so fast. They can go 30 miles an hour but they don't see the fence until they've hit it.'

Colm helped Bill as he looked for the tools he would need for the job and then climbed back into Tin Annie to wait

[1] pickup ['pɪkʌp], ute [juːt] *(AusE) kleiner Geländewagen mit offener Ladefläche* [2] lonely ['ləʊnli] *einsam* [3] heat [hiːt] *Hitze* [4] scrub [skrʌb] *Gebüsch, Gestrüpp* [5] scar [skɑː] *Narbe* [6] (to) break down [ˌbreɪk 'daʊn] *eine Panne haben* [7] (to) crash into sth. [kræʃ] *gegen etwas fahren/laufen*

while Bill repaired the fence. Later they stopped to fill in a hole made by a wombat[8]. The day dragged on[9]. They drove so slowly that Colm got tired looking at the fence. When he closed his eyes he saw the endless fence moving along in his head. Despite the flies[10] and the heat, he fell asleep[11]. When he woke up, it was to the sound of Bill repairing a fencepost[12].

Colm's shirt was wet with sweat. He went round to the back of the ute and took a long drink from the billycan[13]. The water was as warm as tea, but it was good to wet his throat. Flies buzzed around his face and although he tried to swat them away, they came back. Colm felt as if he was inside a strange and frightening[14] dream.

The days dragged on, long and boring. Colm's neck was sore from always turning his head one way to watch the fence. After a few days he took over the job of filling the wombat holes while Bill repaired the holes in the fence. They filled up the billycans at every dam or tank, and ate tins[15] of beef and vegetables until Colm felt he couldn't take another mouthful[16] of them. The nearest town was hundreds of miles away.

One morning, Rusty wasn't in camp when they woke up. Colm helped Bill to pack up the breakfast dishes, and all the time he scanned the scrub and looked for a sign of movement.

'Where is that dog?' said Bill. He put two fingers in his mouth and whistled. Nothing moved.

'I'll find her,' said Colm. He walked out into the scrub. If he closed his eyes and willed[17] it, then he should be able to feel Rusty wherever she was. He was sure she was quite close.

When he opened his eyes he saw something move in the dust. Rusty was lying under a bush: she was shaking violently.

'Bill,' called Colm. 'Bill, here, I've found her! But something's wrong! Hurry!'

Bill knelt[18] beside[19] the dog. When he touched her body, Rusty shook even more violently.

'What is it?' asked Colm.

'Snakebite[20], maybe. Then again, maybe not.'

Rusty started shaking uncontrollably, as if there was electricity running through her. Colm was cold with fear.

'What's wrong?' he cried, feeling tears in his eyes.

[8] wombat ['wɒmbæt] *Wombat (kl. Beutelsäuger)* [9] (to) drag (on) *sich hinziehen* [10] flies *Fliegen* [11] (to) fall asleep *einschlafen* [12] fencepost ['fenspəʊst] *Zaunpfahl* [13] billycan ['bɪlikæn] *Kochtopf* [14] frightening *erschreckend* [15] tin *Dose* [16] mouthful *Bissen* [17] (to) will sth. *etwas herbeiwünschen* [18] knelt [nelt] *kniete sich hin* [19] beside [bɪ'saɪd] *neben* [20] snakebite *Schlangenbiss*

'I think she's taken dingo bait[21]. Poison[22]. It might be better for her if we killed her.'

Colm walked beside Bill as he carried Rusty over to the ute and put her on her blanket in the back. Bill picked up the knife he used to kill rabbits.

'No! What are you doing!' Colm grabbed Bill's hand. 'We have to save her.'

'Get out of my way,' said Bill. He pushed Colm away and held Rusty's head. Quickly he made cuts on the side of Rusty's ears. Blood poured[23] down.

'Now go and fill the billycan.' Bill pushed it at Colm and then looked for something in the food bag.

When Colm returned[24], Bill threw two handfuls of salt[25] into the water. He took Rusty in his arms. 'Now I'll keep her mouth open. I want you to pour[26] the salty water straight down her throat.'

The salt water made Rusty throw up. When Bill put her down, she staggered[27] around the ute, and threw up again and again. As soon as they could, they poured more water down her throat. Finally, when she'd finished, Bill carried her over to a bush and put her on her old blanket. Bill and Colm knelt beside her and massaged her.

'Here, you need a break,' said Bill. 'Go get yourself a drink and sit in the car. I'll call you if I need you.'

'What are you going to do? You can't shoot her, Bill. You can't.'

'I'm hoping it won't come to that.'

Colm walked back to Tin Annie, fighting back tears.

The morning grew hotter. Colm fell asleep and then, when he woke, he prayed as hard as he could. He was still praying when he heard Rusty bark – a weak bark, but a bark. He ran across to where she lay.

'I prayed for her,' said Colm. 'Maybe it helped.'

'Maybe it did,' said Bill. 'Between your prayers and my hard work, she'll be better in no time.'

****

After several adventures Bill finds work and accommodation for the three of them with an old friend at Tara Downs, a cattle station up in the Northern Territory.

'C'mon. I've got a job to do. Can't just sit around and talk all day. A wild boar's[28] been making trouble just south a bit. They mess with[29] the dams and the fences. Get in the ute and you can help.'

They drove out into the landscape where the old trees looked like burnt bones. Tin Annie struggled over[30] the dry creek[31] beds and Rusty put her head out the open window, watching the fine red dust fly up around the sides of the ute.

'This is the place. We'll look for the bugger[32] on foot from here. You stay close by me.'

---

[21] bait [beɪt] *Köder* [22] poison ['pɔɪzn] *Gift* [23] (to) pour [pɔː] *strömen* [24] (to) return [rɪ'tɜːn] *zurückkehren* [25] salt [sɔːlt] *Salz* [26] (to) pour [pɔː] *schütten* [27] (to) stagger ['stægə] *schwanken, torkeln* [28] wild boar [ˌwaɪld 'bɔː] *Wildschwein* [29] (to) mess with sth. [mes] *mit etwas herumspielen* [30] (to) struggle over ... ['strʌgl] *sich über ... kämpfen, mühen* [31] creek *(AusE)* [kriːk] *Bach* [32] bugger *(infml, rude)* ['bʌgə] *Kerl*

Colm followed Bill through the scrub. A hot, foul smell was in the air. As the smell got stronger, Rusty put her head down and walked in front, as if she was following something. She led them to what was left of a steer[33]. A cloud of flies flew up in the air.

Bill knelt down beside the dead steer. 'He's had a great time with this steer. He hasn't been gone long.'

They climbed up a nearby[34] hill and scanned the countryside. Apart from[35] a family of wallabies[36], they could see nothing.

'Damn, he heard us coming and left.'

Bill turned to walk back to the steer. There was a noise in the scrub and the black boar was on them.

Colm jumped behind a rock as the boar hit Bill and sent him flying[37]. It ran at the old man with its tusks[38], tearing his boot and ripping open his leg. Bill let out a cry of pain.

Blood poured from Bill's leg as the boar attacked again, and the old man struggled free. Rusty sank her teeth into the boar's leg, but it turned and tore her with its tusks. Rusty yelped[39] and fell.

Colm jumped out from behind the rock. He had to do something.

Bill's face was scared. 'Run, Colm, get out of here,' he shouted. 'Get help!'

Colm turned and ran down the path. He had nearly got to Tin Annie when he heard a terrible cry, more animal than human. He stopped and turned. What if Bill was killed before he could get help? What should he do? Run back to Tara Downs? Try to save Bill himself? Suddenly he realized there was only one answer and there was no time to lose.

He ran back to Bill. On the way he picked up a stick. As he came over the hill, he ran at the boar, hitting it again and again. It turned to face Colm. There was blood on its tusks.

Bill tried to pull himself away, leaving a trail of blood behind him. Colm raised the stick high and brought it down on the boar's head. The boar snorted[40], but instead of running at Colm, it turned back to Bill.

Colm threw the stick down and grabbed Bill's gun. He was shaking as he raised the gun to his shoulder. Colm knew that if he shot the animal in the back, it would only make it wild. He let out a scream, a long, loud scream. The boar turned round. For a moment it stared at him with its small black eyes. Then it lowered[41] its head and ran towards him. Colm aimed straight between the eyes.

The kickback from the gun made Colm stagger. He fell in the sand beside Rusty.

'Colm, my mate,' said Bill. He held out one bloodied hand and smiled. Then he lay back in the red dust and passed out[42].

Suddenly, everything was quiet. Blood soaked into the dry earth around Bill in a dark circle. Colm could see the bones of his leg where the boar had ripped open the flesh. He would have to stop the blood flow or Bill would bleed to death. Colm ran back to the ute and grabbed an old shirt to tie up the wound[43]. Then he took off his own shirt and tore it up for Bill's hands. When he was sure the bleeding was slower, he sat back and tried to think. He had to get help, but how? The flies were collecting. He would have to get Bill into the car.

Colm took Bill's arms and put one over each of his shoulders and then tried to pull the old man up. It was almost impossible. He'd never be able to go far like this. He laid Bill down again and ran to Tin Annie. Colm took a deep

---

33 steer [stɪə] *junger Ochse* 34 nearby [ˌnɪəˈbaɪ] *nahegelegen* 35 apart from [əˈpɑːt] *außer* 36 wallaby [ˈwɒləbi] *Wallaby (kleine Art von Känguru)* 37 (to) send sb. flying *jn. zu Boden schicken* 38 tusk [tʌsk] *Hauer (Eckzahn eines Wildschweines)* 39 (to) yelp [jelp] *aufjaulen* 40 (to) snort [snɔːt] *schnauben* 41 (to) lower [ˈləʊə] *senken* 42 (to) pass out [ˌpɑːs‿ˈaʊt] *ohnmächtig werden* 43 wound [wuːnd] *Wunde*

breath and turned the key. Tin Annie started. He had no idea how to drive backwards, so he moved forwards carefully, bringing the car as close to Bill as he could. Somehow he found the strength[45] to pull Bill back on his shoulders and put him into the car. Then he ran and picked Rusty up. He could just hear the dog's heartbeat and it gave him hope.

The dust flew up around the car as Colm raced along the track. Every time they hit a stone Bill cried out with pain, but at least that meant he was still alive.

When they drove across a dry creek bed, Tin Annie first struggled, then stopped. Colm tried to start her up again. But even as his foot pushed to the floor, he knew it was a mistake. The old ute died completely.

They were just at the top of the hill and he could see Tara Downs, but there was still at least a mile to go. He tried to start the car again and again, but it was no good. He would have to go on foot and leave Bill and Rusty in the car.

Colm wished the old man was conscious[46] and could tell him what to do next. Then he began the long run to Tara Downs.

Colm's heart pounded[47] and his head hurt, but the ground flew beneath him. He took the steps up to the house two at a time.

'It's Bill. An accident. He's bleeding, real bad. A boar ripped him up.'

Then Colm sank down on his knees. People appeared from nowhere. They ran, a car started up and strong arms helped Colm to his feet and took him into a bedroom. For a moment he struggled against them. 'I have to be with Bill.'

'It's all right.'

'Bill needs me,' said Colm.

'They're getting the Flying Doctor out here. We don't know if the old man will make it if we have to drive him down to the hospital in Katherine. Best to fly him to Darwin.'

Colm felt the blood drain from his face. 'He will make it. He has to make it.'

---

[45] strength [streŋθ] *Kraft, Stärke* [46] conscious ['kɒnʃəs] *bei Bewusstsein* [47] (to) pound [paʊnd] *(wild) pochen*

Working with the text

1 What do you think?

Give your opinion of the story. Say which parts were especially exciting or boring. Give reasons.

2 The plot

Divide the story into parts – look for changes of time, place, characters, or just events that start and finish. Make a flow chart like this:

Bill and Colm drive into the Victoria Desert ... (ll. 1–29)	→	... repair the Dog Fence where an emu ... (ll. 30–...)	→	...

Find a part of the story where something that happens causes something else.

STUDY SKILLS Reading literature (1)

When you read literature, you'll enjoy it more and understand it better if you try to follow how the story develops (**plot**), get into the feeling of the story (**atmosphere**), and think about the **characters**.

Plot
The plot is the action and events that take place in a story. These events often happen because one event causes another. Stories also often use flashbacks in their plots.

▸ SF Reading literature (pp. 138–139)

L S R W

3 The atmosphere

a) *Look at what you wrote about the atmosphere of the outback before you read the story. How does it compare with the atmosphere of the story?*

STUDY SKILLS Reading literature (2)

Setting and atmosphere
The setting is the place and time of the story, e.g. the Australian outback in the 1950s. Atmosphere is the feeling created by the setting or by a situation in a piece of literature. This can be done through imagery, such as a simile (a comparison), e.g. "the water was as warm as tea" (ll. 63–64), or a metaphor, e.g. "the days dragged on" (l. 69).

b) *Look at lines 5–20. Find out how atmosphere is created in this part of the story. Look at the adjectives. Find metaphors or similes.*

L S R W

4 The characters

a) *Who are the characters in the story? Make a network of their names and describe the connections between them. What do they think of each other?*

STUDY SKILLS Reading literature (3)

Characters
The author can present the characters of a story in many ways. He or she may describe them or show the reader what they are like through their language and way of speaking, their actions, feelings, thoughts, words and their connections to other characters.

b) *Choose adjectives from the box below on the right or your own adjectives and describe Bill or Colm to your partner. Give examples from the story for your choice. Listen to each other's descriptions. Do you agree? Give reasons.*

brave • clever • difficult • easy-going • friendly • helpful • honest • nervous • old • stupid • violent • young

L S R W

5 Creative writing

a) *Write an ending for the story.*
What do you think will happen next?
– Will Bill survive?
– Will Colm try to follow Bill? Or will he go into the bush alone? Or back to the children's home?

Remember

Follow these steps of writing:
1. *Brainstorm your ideas. Make notes.*
2. *Write your text. Use linking words, adjectives and adverbs to make it more interesting.*
3. *Revise your text.*

b) **Extra** *Choose one of the following:*
1. *Imagine you are Colm. Rewrite part of the story from your point of view, using 'I'.*
2. *What would you need to do if you wanted to change the story into a film? Write down ideas for a screenplay.*

Lektüre A Prayer for Blue Delaney

1 WORDS Travelling

Complete the sentences with the correct words and phrases. Use the verbs in their correct forms. There are two more words/phrases than you need.

change planes • (to) check in • city centre • departure area • flight attendant • (to) land • meal • receptionist • rucksacks • (to) take off • (to) take a taxi • ticket • ticket machines

You're flying to Australia for a wonderful holiday! At the airport, you first (1) *check in*. Then you go to the (2) … For your flight it's gate D21.

Now you're on the plane. The flight to Australia is very long and on the way you need to eat and drink. The (3) … offers you a hot meal. There are lots of nice things on the menu today.

After you (4) … at Singapore Airport, you finally (5) … in Sydney. Of course, you hope that your (6) … arrive too! If not, you'll have to go to the lost luggage office.

So how do you travel from the airport into the (7) …? Well, the quickest and easiest way is to (8) … , but it's also the most expensive one: it costs about 50 Australian dollars. So you decide to take a train instead. The (9) … are easy to use and a (10) … to the city is only 15 Australian dollars.

Now – tired but happy – you're at your hotel. The (11) … gives you the key to your room. She also tells you about the hotel – for example, the times when you can have breakfast.

2 Judy's job (Simple present and present progressive)

a) *Judy is the flight attendant that you can see in the photo above. Finish these sentences about her job. Use the **simple present** or **the present progressive**.*

1 Judy's job is exciting. She often … (travel) to different countries.
2 Right now, she … (fly) to Australia.
3 A typical day for Judy starts early. She usually … (get up) at 5 o'clock. Then she … (have) her breakfast and … (drive) to the airport.
4 It is 10 o'clock now and Judy … (work). She … (bring) coffee and tea to the passengers on her plane.
5 Now it is 10 o'clock the next morning. Judy … (just / arrive) at her hotel.
6 Judy always … (stay) at a hotel when she is in another country. She … (sleep) at the hotel – then the next day she … (fly) home again.

b) *Write sentences about things that you often do and some things that you're doing right now.*
I often surf the internet. Right now, I'm chatting with my friends.

► GF 1.2: Talking about the present (p. 154)

3 Australia's most dangerous animals (Simple past and past progressive)

Read the text about Australia's most dangerous animals on the right, then complete the two stories below. Use the simple past or past progressive of the verbs in brackets.

AUSTRALIA is home to some of the world's most dangerous animals. There are snakes, spiders and sometimes sharks. The most dangerous of all, however, are crocodiles. Two or three people die every year in crocodile attacks. Here are two stories about people who were attacked.

There's a crocodile in our tent!

In January 2005, two young Australians went camping near the Pentecost River in the north of Australia. At about 2 o'clock in the morning, they (1) were sleeping (sleep) when suddenly a crocodile (2) ... (come) into their tent. They (3) ... (run) to their car and (4) ... (climb) onto it. The next morning at 11 o'clock, they (5) ... (still / sit) on their car when some hunters (6) ... (arrive) and (7) ... (save) their lives.

Smile please!

In 2008, a tourist in Queensland was stupid – but lucky. He (8) ... (sit) in a boat on a river when a crocodile (9) ... (swim) towards the boat. The man's friend (10) ... (stand) on land. 'Put your hand in the water and play with the crocodile!' he (11) ... (shout). 'I'm going to take a photo.' Seconds later, the crocodile (12) ... (try) to bite the man's hand. 'It was a scary moment!' he (13) ... (say) afterwards.

► *GF 1.3: Talking about the past (p. 155)*

4 WORDS It was scary! (Words that describe experiences)

a) *Look at the box with adjectives. Find five pairs of adjectives that mean (almost) the same: great – ...*

b) *Find at least eight pairs of adjectives that mean opposite things: awesome – boring; dangerous – ...*

c) *Write about ten things you have done (or invent them). Use adjectives from the box:*

1) Yesterday I played table tennis against my younger brother and lost 11–2. It was depressing!

2) ...

amazing • awesome • awful • boring • cool • crazy • dangerous • depressing • different • difficult • easy • excellent • exciting • fantastic • frightening • funny • great • horrible • interesting • laughable • lovely • mad • sad • safe • scary • shocking • silly • strange • surprising • terrible • unbelievable • wonderful

5 WRITING One day last year ...

a) *Below is a very short story! Can you make it more interesting? Write the story again. Use some ideas from the table.*

Jake was riding his bike in the mountains. He fell off and broke his leg. He called for help on his mobile phone. Some people saved him. He went to hospital. He met Anne, a doctor. They fell in love. They got married.

When?	one day last year, last September, first, then, next, after that, finally, ...
Who?	the man/woman/person/people who ...
How?	quickly, slowly, suddenly, ... (really) amazing/awful; (feel) wonderful/depressed, ...
Linking words	that's why, however, so (that), although, when, despite, ...

b) *Compare your story with a partner's.*

► *SF Writing Course (pp. 144–145)*

1 LISTENING Travelling to Australia 1.09–1.13

Listen to the announcement and conversations. While listening, answer the questions below in one to five words.
– You will hear the recordings only ***once****.*
– You will have 10 seconds at the end of the recordings to complete your answers.
– You now have 40 seconds to look at the task.

1 At which gate does your flight to Sydney depart? ...

2 What can you choose for dinner? *Roast chicken or* ... What drinks can you have? (Name two.) ... / ...

3 What is opposite the lost luggage office? ...

4 How much is the airport toll for taxis? *AU $* ...
How much is the taxi from the airport to the city all in all? *AU $* ...

5 What's your room number on the second floor? ...
When can you have breakfast tomorrow? *From* ... *to* ...

2 LISTENING Shark attack! 1.14–1.15

Listen to a radio report about a shark attack in which Jon Kerry, a young Australian, was badly hurt. The report is in two parts.
While listening, note down the correct answer: A, B, C *or* D.

Part 1

- *You will hear the recording only **once**.*
- *You will have 10 seconds at the end of the recording to complete your answers.*
- *You now have 15 seconds to look at the task..*

1 A shark attacked a ...
A diver.
B snorkeller.
C surfer.
D swimmer.

2 The attack happened near a beach in ...
A New South Wales.
B South Australia.
C Western Australia.
D Queensland.

3 The shark caught Jon's ...
A arm.
B leg.
C foot.
D shoulder.

4 The shark left a wound of ...
A 25 cm.
B 30 cm.
C 35 cm.
D 40 cm.

Part 2

- *Now listen very carefully. You will hear the next part of the radio report **twice**.*
- *You will have 15 seconds after you have heard the report for the first time and another 15 seconds after the second time to complete your answers.*
- *You now have 50 seconds to look at the task.*

1 When Jon swam back to the beach he was ...
A angry.
B depressed.
C terrified.
D tired.

2 His friends saved his life because they ...
A called the sea rescue.
B chased the shark away.
C pulled him out of the water.
D took care of the injury.

3 His doctors are sure that he ...
A won't be able to move for some time.
B will need future operations.
C will be fine despite a scar[1].
D won't even see a scar.

4 Experts want to ...
A ask people to report shark attacks.
B calm people despite past shark attacks.
C help people to survive shark attacks.
D warn people against new shark attacks.

5 To avoid shark attacks, people should ...
A not feed sharks.
B not go after sharks.
C swim with friends.
D swim in the morning.

[1] scar [skɑː] *Narbe*

3 LISTENING Young Australians and the internet 1.16–1.21

Listen to six students talking about the internet. While listening, match each of them with one of the statements A to G. There is one more statement than you need.
- *You will hear the recording only* ***once****.*
- *You will have 5 seconds between each recording and 10 seconds at the end to complete your answers.*
- *You now have 30 seconds to look at the task.*

A Older people know very little about the internet.
B Teenagers need to learn more about internet safety.
C You can do different activities on the web at the same time.
D People can create and define their identities on the net.
E Some teenagers waste a lot of time on the internet.
F Adults should stop warning about internet risks.
G You can have unpleasant experiences when you are online.

Student 1	Student 2	Student 3	Student 4	Student 5	Student 6
E	C	A	F	G	D

4 WRITING An online magazine for young Europeans

You often read an online magazine for young Europeans. This week, the magazine wants readers' ideas about the internet and it has a story competition. Write about 200 words on one of the topics below.

Topic 1: The internet and me
When and where do you usually use the internet? What do you do online? Which activitiy do you do most often? What are your ideas about being safe online?

Topic 2: A scary moment!
Finish this story in your own words.

It was a Saturday afternoon in September. I was bored, so I decided to go for a bike ride. After about an hour, I was on a small road in the country ...

Self-evaluation

Check your answers to tasks 1–3 on page 263.

About the test

This test gave you the chance to try some of the kinds of tasks that you have to do one day in your exam. If you found some tasks difficult, don't worry. You've got lots of time to practise. Remember: 'Practice makes perfect!'

Listening

The first three tasks in the test were listening tasks. The following questions will help you to think about how you did. Read the questions – which answer is right for you?

1 How hard or easy was each task?

	easy	OK	quite hard	very hard
Task 1				
Task 2				
Task 3				

1 What was difficult in the tasks?

a) People spoke quickly.
b) I found the accents difficult.
c) There was a lot of information. I couldn't find the exact answers.
d) I didn't have time to write the answers to the questions.
e) There were words and phrases that I just couldn't understand.

1 How did you do the tasks?

a) I read the questions carefully first so I knew exactly what I had to listen for.
b) I looked quickly at the questions first but only read them carefully while I was listening.
c) I wrote as many answers as I could the first time I heard the text and checked them (or filled in gaps) the second time.
d) There were lots of things I couldn't understand and I panicked.

▸ *SF Listening (p. 134)* • *SF How to do well in a test (pp. 150–152)*

Writing

The fourth task in your test was a writing task. Work with a partner. Exchange the texts you've written and read your partner's text. Copy and fill in the assessment sheet[1] below. Remember: the idea is to help your partner with your feedback!

Assessment sheet	☹		😐		☺	
Name of partner ...	1	2	3	4	5	Comments
Did your partner ...						
1 ... write an interesting text/story?						
2 ... make grammar mistakes (with a tense, plural forms, etc.)?						
3 ... use interesting vocabulary or just easy words and phrases?						
4 ... write longer sentences with linking words or just short sentences?						
5 ... write a text that is clear and easy to understand?						

▸ *SF Writing Course (pp. 144–145)*

[1] assessment sheet *Beurteilungsbogen*

The road ahead

▸ Folie 5

Whiteboard Beamer ✓

1 Continue the road

L S R W

How do you think the road ahead might continue for the young people above? Choose two more pictures for each of them or draw/find pictures of your own. What would the young people say about the pictures or about their future? Write speech bubbles – the box on the right might help.

do something useful • famous • find the right boy/girl • get good A-level results • get qualifications • go on all the talk shows • graduate from university • have kids • help where help is really needed • inherit a fortune • look for work as ... • make a difference • open-air rock festivals • pass exams • scientist • skills • start a career • work hard

2 Which road?

L S R W

Which of these teenagers can you most identify with? In groups, explain your choice and why you finished their road the way you did.

3 Extra Your road

L S R W

Where are you heading in life? What might the 'road ahead' hold in store for you?
Research and collect suitable vocabulary and illustrations. Then produce a poster for yourself.

▸ **Text File 4** *(p. 107)* • *WB 1 (p. 18)*

PERSONALITY QUIZ
Where are you heading?

Want to know what sort of person you are and where that might lead you in life? Find out with this fun quiz!
(Check your score on page 100.)

1 The people you like best
- A walk around with their °heads in the clouds.
- B plan their lives and know where they're going.
- C are different from one day to the next.

2 You're invited to a party. Do you
- A go and °stick close to your friends?
- B go and talk to as many strangers as you can?
- C stay at home?

3 You have to stay home all weekend with no TV, phone, computer, game console or music. Which book do you choose to read?
- A Blue Eye – a beautiful love story
- B Red Eye – a magical fantasy novel
- C Neither: you read a computer mag instead.

Box: Voc., S.190

4 You're in charge of the bag of presents at the class Christmas party. Do you give
- A the nicest presents to your friends?
- B everyone the first present that comes out of the bag?
- C the best presents to the most popular kids?

5 In the middle of the night, how often do you feel so lonely you cannot sleep?
- A Sometimes. B Often. C No idea.

6 How often do you move the furniture around in your room at home?
- A Sometimes. B Never.
- C When your parents tell you to do it.

7 You're researching on the internet for a project at school. Do you
- A get sidetracked and surf from website to website for hours?
- B find the information you need quickly and get back to your project?
- C forget your project and chat with friends instead?

8 You're at home when the landline phone rings. Do you
- A hurry to answer it first?
- B hope someone else will answer it?
- C not even hear it because nobody ever phones you on the landline?

9 What sort of sports do you prefer?
- A Team sports.
- B Sports like tennis, where it's one against one.
- C No sports.

10 You're home and a soap starts on TV. Do you
- A get really involved with the story and characters?
- B watch it and talk to friends on the phone at the same time?
- C turn the TV off?

11 You have an appointment this afternoon. Will you
- A be late? B be on time?
- C cancel the appointment?

12 What do you spend most time thinking about?
- A The future of human civilization.
- B What you're going to do at the weekend.
- C The °boy/girl next door.

YOUR PERSONALITY

29–36 points

Your personal qualities:

You are a confident, energetic and flexible person.

You love an adventure. You are interested in art and you enjoy making things. You live life as it comes, but you get bored easily and you hate rules. You do not know how to sit quietly and listen, which others sometimes find annoying. You are good at starting things, but not very good at finishing them. Sometimes you try to do too many things at once and often do not have your feelings under control. You want life to be fun and exciting, don't like grey routines and would hate to give up your freedom.

20–28 points

Your personal qualities:

You are a calm, friendly, helpful, and polite person.

You are a great organizer, especially of free-time activities. You are more interested in people than things, but most interested in your dreams. You love meeting new people and can talk easily to anyone you meet. You're always keen to help people to understand their problems. But sometimes you only see the world the way you'd like it to be and not as it actually is. You're very close to your family and friends. You're good at working in a team and you want to change the world.

Box: Voc., S.190

12–19 points

Your personal qualities:

You are a reliable, organized, punctual and logical person.

You are interested in everything around you – plants, animals, technology – and you want to understand how things work. You love information and you spend a lot of time on the internet. You like people to give you clear instructions and you think rules are important. You are good at solving problems and will always come up with practical ideas. Actually, you are more interested in ideas than people and very serious about your work – perhaps too serious at times.

1 Your personality

L S R W

a) Do the quiz. Then, with a partner of your choice, take turns and guess which answers your partner has picked. Discuss the results.

– It says that I'm/you're ... but that's silly/...
– I (don't) think that's true at all.
– I think I'm/you're a ... person. You're ...
– ...

b) Did your results correspond 100 % with your real personality? Why do you think that is? Are magazine quizzes like this helpful? Or are they just for fun? Give reasons for your answers.

2 Your future

L S R W

Where are you heading?

You'll want to see the world before you settle down – but maybe you'll never settle down at all. But if you do, you'll travel a lot and have the wildest adventures first.

Where are you heading?

You won't let anyone force you along a particular path. You'll look inside yourself and follow your dreams, and won't mind if your family, friends and teachers disagree.

Box: Voc., S.191

Where are you heading?

If you don't know what you want to do with your life already, you soon will. And you'll take the necessary steps to make sure you reach your goals as quickly as you can.

a) Look at where the magazine thinks you are heading. Explain why you agree or disagree.

– Yes, I can imagine this road ahead for me because ...
– It says I'll ... but I already know ...
– They must be joking. I'm (not) going to ...

b) **Extra** *Suggest what would be a good job for your personality type. (Use a dictionary if you need to.) Explain your choice to a partner.*

▸ WB 2 (p. 19)

P1 WORDS Describing people

a) Look at the people in the pictures below. Pick one and write a profile of the person. What do you think they are like or their life is like? What are they going to do in the future? Try to use as many words and phrases from the boxes below as possible.

annoying • calm • confident • energetic • flexible • friendly • good at • head in the clouds • helpful • interested in • keen on • logical • organized • polite • practical • punctual • reliable • serious about • under control

follow his/her dreams • get qualifications (in) • get (good/bad) results (in) • get involved (in) • graduate (from) • enjoy/like/love/hate • keep to a routine • look for work • make a difference (to) • settle down • solve problems • spend time (on) • use his/her skills • work hard

b) Read your profiles to each other. What could you add to the profile your partner wrote?

c) **Extra** *Make notes on your own personal qualities, interests, future possibilities and write your profile. Remember what you did on page 35. You can put your profile in your DOSSIER.*

P2 MEDIATION Company profile

a) You are interested in web design, and you'd like to spend some time working with a British company. Read the company profile and make sure you understand everything. Guess or check the meaning of words you don't know.

Newstone Marketing

Newstone Marketing is based in London and was founded 25 years ago. Our experienced team has all the necessary skills for marketing products and services. We use all the latest technology and have experts in web design and video production. We help companies decide their aims, and we develop marketing methods to achieve success. We are a leader in the field and have worked with some of the world's largest companies.

b) How would you explain the situation to your friend in German? What kind of company are you applying to and how do you think it will give you the experience you want?

► WB 3 (p. 19)

P3 SPEAKING Could you tell me? (Asking for, confirming, giving information) 1.22–1.24

a) *Listen to the three conversations. In which one is Stella*
– asking for information? – giving information? – confirming information?

b) *Read through the phrases below and then put them under the correct heading. Some can perhaps go under more than one heading.*

ASKING FOR INFORMATION
GIVING INFORMATION
CONFIRMING INFORMATION

- Can I just confirm ...?
- Do you think you could ...?
- Excuse me, could you tell me ...?
- Have I got that right? Do I ... or do I ...?
- Hello, my name is ...
- I'm not quite sure about ... Is it/Are they/ ...?
- Is it right that ...?
- Now I'd just like to tell you ...
- OK, so let me put you in the picture. Now ...
- Sorry, I'd just like to know ...
- What else can I say? Well, I'm ...
- Would you mind telling me ...?

c) *Compare the two sentences. Which is more polite? What makes it more polite? Look for other phrases in your lists from b) which make sentences sound more polite.*

Tip
When talking English to someone you don't know, you should always try to be polite. English-speakers often find Germans too direct, which makes them sound impolite. Box: Voc., S.192

d) *Put this mixed-up conversation into the right order.*

B: Yes, of course. You go back out of this building, turn right, turn right again when you get to the path next to the statue, and that leads you straight to the °annex.
A: Oh, am I? I was told it was in the library. This is the library, isn't it?
A: Excuse me, could you tell me where the Newton Room is?
B: The Newton Room? Oh, I'm afraid you're in the wrong building.
A: Oh, I see. Would you mind telling me where that is?
B: Yes, this is the library, but the Newton Room is in the library annex.
B: Right. And the Newton Room is on the second floor.
A: Thanks very much.
A: OK, so I turn right out of this building and then take the path on the right next to the statue. Is that right?

e) *Check your results in a group until you all agree.*

f) ***Role play*** ***Partner A:*** *You have seen an advert for courses at a language school in the UK and phone for some more information.*
Partner B: *You work at the language school and try to answer your partner's questions when they phone you. Ask your teacher for your role cards. Study them and then act out the conversation together.*

▸ *SF Speaking Course (pp. 142–143)* • *WB 4–5 (pp. 20–21)*

A YEAR ABROAD

1 A CV

L S R W

Lukas Beyer wants to go to school in an English-speaking country for a year. His application to an exchange organization has to include a CV (British English) or résumé [1] (American English).

1 ['rezəmeɪ]

CURRICULUM VITAE [2]
Lukas Beyer

2 [kəˌrɪkjələm 'viːtaɪ]

Ohmstrasse 75B, 45143 Essen, Germany
Telephone: +49 (0) 201 000 8177 Mobile: +49 0178 000 4235
E-mail: lukbey30@gmx.de

Personal statement

I have always loved meeting new people and exploring new places. As English is my favourite subject at school, I am sure that spending a year at a British or American school will be a valuable experience.

I expect to improve my language skills and become a more independent person. I spent two weeks in Britain last year and now am really looking forward to getting to know the UK or the USA better and to telling people there about Germany.

Education

2004 to date	Secondary school: Alfred-Krupp-Schule, Essen
2000–2004	Primary/Elementary school: Bodelschwingh-Schule, Essen

Qualifications/Skills

Swimming	Gold youth swimming badge
IT skills	Good knowledge of MS Word, PowerPoint, Excel; basic knowledge of web design
Language skills	German native speaker; good written and spoken English; some French

Work experience

2008 to date	Regular job: delivering flyers by bike (1 hour per week)
May 2009	Placement: two weeks working at local IT company, organized by my school
2010 to date	Volunteer work: helping children with homework after school

Hobbies and interests

Member of school drama club; I play table tennis and basketball in after-school clubs; I enjoy reading, listening to and playing music and going to the theatre and cinema.

References

Available on request

a) *Imagine you are applying to go to school abroad. Read through Lukas's personal statement and think about it. Then write a personal statement of your own. Make notes first and look through Lukas's CV for useful phrases.*

b) Extra *Lukas has written his CV the way they do in the UK. Compare and contrast this CV with a German CV. Consider the headings, the style, what information is missing, …*

▸ SF Writing a CV (p. 148) • Text File 5 (p. 108)

2 Writing a CV

L S R W

a) Imagine you want to spend six months at a school abroad. Use these website tips and write your CV in English. Add your personal statement from page 38.

Job Searching | Find a Job | CVs / Letters | Getting a Job

How to write a good CV

NICE TOUCH

You want to apply for a place on an exchange programme? Or an interesting job? There will be many other candidates to choose from. So it is very important to produce a clear and effective CV.

CVs are very personal documents, different from applicant to applicant, and there is no particular 'correct' format. But these tips will help you write a good one.

1. Present your key skills, especially those the exchange organization or employer is looking for.
2. Keep it simple and do not make the pages too full. Two pages that are easy to read are better than one that is too crowded.
3. Most CVs should include:
   - Personal details: name, contact details and usually nationality. Your date of birth is not necessary.
   - Personal statement: explain what makes you suitable for the specific place or job, how it would help you develop and why you deserve to be successful in your application.
   - Education and qualifications: schools, subjects and exam results.
   - Work experience: list the jobs you have done, what you did and when, skills you used or learned there.
   - Achievements: list recent achievements (certificates, awards, etc.)
   - Extra-curricular activities: give brief information about your hobbies and interests, such as membership of and responsibilities in sport teams, clubs, organizations, etc.
   - General skills: driving licence, foreign languages and IT skills (give level, e.g. beginner, intermediate, advanced).
   - References: just write 'on request'. If employers need them they'll ask for them later.
4. Be positive. Use clear headings and language. Write short and °meaningful sentences. Check your language to avoid mistakes (spelling, grammar, etc.).
5. Format: use a clear and easy-to-read font, size 9 or 10 point. The use of bold or different sizes or colours can highlight important information.
6. Let someone else check your final CV before you send it.

b) *Sit in groups of four in a* ***correcting circle****. Pass your CV to the left. Read the CV you are given and make notes on what needs correcting (grammar, spelling, headings, layout, ...). Then pass the CV and your notes to the left. Do the same again with the other CVs until you receive your own again. Use the notes from your group to correct your CV. Put it in your DOSSIER.*

L S R W

3 A letter and some photos

Lukas needs to get in touch with his host family, and decides to send them a formal letter and some typical photos of his life.

Ohmstrasse 75B
45143 Essen
Germany

20 February 2011

Dear Host Family

I hope you don't mind me writing before we meet. I would like to introduce myself and to say thank you for the opportunity to stay with you while I go to school in your country.

Box: Voc., S.194

I am 15 years old and live in Essen, a large city in the west of Germany. I live with my parents and my younger sister, Julia. We have a nice flat with a big garden. My sister and I both go to the same school, which is near our flat. My parents both work. My father is an electrical engineer and my mother works in the city's housing dep…

Box: Voc., S.195

and I remember loving English from the very first lesson.

Before I arrive in your country, I would be very grateful if you could tell me a little about your family, the area you live in and the school I will go to.

I look forward to hearing from you soon and especially to meeting you.

Yours sincerely

Lukas Beyer

a) *What features of a formal letter can you see in Lukas's letter?*

b) *The exchange organization gives students tips about what to write to their future host families. Imagine you are applying to go to an English-speaking country for a year. Write your letter to your host family.*

- Give information about your personality, activities, interests, friends and goals.
- Describe what you like to do and what you have to do at home, at school, and in your community.
- Explain why you want to go to school abroad and live with a host family.
- Show your interest in *them* by asking about their activities and interests, their community and the school you will go to.
- Remember to say 'thank you' for the opportunity to live with them.

c) **Extra** *Use a* ***placemat*** *to note down the advantages and disadvantages of spending a year at a school abroad. Agree on the three most important advantages and disadvantages and write them in the middle.*
Explain your opinion in a class discussion.

► *WB 6–7 (pp. 21–22)*

P1 STUDY SKILLS Writing a formal letter

a) *Improve this covering letter for an application. What is missing at the beginning?*

Dear Ms Hall

I read with interest the ad on your website about spending six months at an American high school and I would like to get a place. Here is my CV. I am 17 years old and I've just done Year 10 at my German high school.

I am a friendly, helpful person and I enjoy my school work and what I do after school. I play sport (I'm in a volleyball club) and have flute lessons every week. I love music and I'd like to play in an orchestra one day. I have studied English for 6 years and my level is quite good.

I can't wait to hear from you.

Yours

Janine Neumann

Janine Neumann

b) *Replace the underlined parts with words and phrases from the box.*

advertisement • apply for • extra-curricular activities • I am a member of • I enclose • I have just completed • I look forward to hearing • I would like • six • Yours sincerely

STUDY SKILLS Writing formal letters

1. Formal letters start with your address and usually the address of the person/organization you are writing to. Do not forget the date.
2. If you start a formal letter with the words **Dear Sir/Madam** or **To whom it may concern** (AE), you usually end it with **Yours faithfully** or **Sincerely** (AE). If you start with **Dear Mr/Ms/Mrs/Miss + name**, you usually end with **Yours sincerely** or **Sincerely** (AE).
3. Avoid informal language and abbreviations such as 'ad'.

▸ *SF Writing formal letters (p. 146)*

c) **Extra** *Imagine you are a couple of years older and see this advert for a summer job in Britain. Write a formal letter and apply for the job.*

Ferienjob in Großbritannien?

Unsere Partnerstadt Bangor in Wales sucht deutschsprachige Aushilfen für die Touristeninformation in diesem Sommer.
Senden Sie Ihre **englischsprachigen Bewerbungsunterlagen** an:

Tourist Information Centre
°Town Hall
Ffordd Deiniol
Bangor LL57 2RE
Wales

P2 LISTENING Phoning about an interview 1.25–1.26

a) *Listen to the phone call. How would you complete the message?* (25)

Message for: *Mr White*
Message from: *Jon*
Caller's message:
Mr ... wanted to confirm – tomorrow at ...

Caller's contact details:
Phone No:

b) *Listen to the next call. How would you complete Jemma's notes?* (26)

Interview time: ...
Place: ... Street ...
big ... building
Ask for ... at the ... desk

▸ *WB 8–9 (pp. 22–23)*

P3 SPEAKING Job interview

a) *Partner B: Go to page 98.*
Partner A: You are having an interview for a summer job as a receptionist at a London hotel. The interviewer will probably ask you

- *about your experience of hotel work,*
- *how well you know London,*
- *the hours you would be available to work,*
- *your reason for applying.*

Think what you could say and make notes. Try to think of a couple of sentences for each answer. Then think of a question you could ask.

b) *Answer the interviewer's questions.*

c) *Find another partner who has already asked the questions and swap roles.*

P4 REVISION Things your parents tell you (Gerunds as subject and object)

a) *Use gerunds to complete the following sentences.*

1 ... can be dangerous.
Riding your bike at night can be dangerous.
2 I hate ...
3 ... is good for you.
4 ... is bad for you.
5 I try to avoid ...
6 I enjoy ...
7 ... can get you into trouble.
8 I don't mind ...
9 ... makes me angry.
10 ... always makes me cry.

▸ *GF 9.1: The gerund as subject and object (p. 174)*

b) *What else can be good for you, or dangerous? Add some fun sentences of your own.*
– Reading can be dangerous for your mind.
– Drinking too much water might change you into a fish!

Box: Voc., S.196

P5 REVISION The party committee (Gerunds after prepositions)

a) *Look at this information from a school notice board and complete it using prepositions from the box and the gerund of the verbs.*

at (2×) • in • of (2×) • on • to

- Are you tired ... (sit) alone at home?
- Are you interested ... (stay) at school after lessons?
- Are you good ... (organize)?
- Are you keen ... (get to know) new friends?
- Are you clever ... (solve) problems?
- Are you sick ... (go) to boring parties?
- Are you used ... (work) hard?

Then join the school party committee for our next end-of-year party!

b) **Extra** *Tell the °Head of the Committee why you could do a good job. Say what you are good at doing, disappointed about so far, what you look forward to, what you would like to °concentrate on, etc.*

▸ *GF 9.2: The gerund after prepositions (p. 175)*
• *WB 10–11 (p. 23)*

P6 STUDY SKILLS Using a grammar

Read this extract from a grammar. Then decide what the subjects of the gerunds in sentences 1–6 are.

1 John imagined living in Florida.
John stellte sich vor, in Florida zu leben.

2 John imagined his family living in Florida.
John stellte sich vor, dass seine Familie in Florida lebte.

3 John imagined them living in Florida.
John stellte sich vor, dass sie in Florida lebten.

A gerund construction can be **without its own subject** (example 1), or it can have **its own subject** (examples 2 and 3). The meaning of the sentence is different in each case.

In all three examples *John* is the subject of the whole sentence. In example 1 the gerund does not have its own subject. Therefore the subject of the whole sentence is understood as the subject of the gerund *living*. In examples 2 and 3 the gerund does have its own subject. This is the 'notional subject', **the person who carries out the action** of the gerund: *family/them*. *Living* relates to these subjects (and not to *John*). In this construction a personal pronoun has the object form (example 3: *them*).

1 I can't imagine going to Australia for a year.
2 I can't imagine my best friend going to Australia for a year.
3 Jill's mum is proud of Jill going to university.
4 Jill's mum is proud of going to university.
5 I'm worried about making a mistake.
6 I'm worried about you making a mistake.

STUDY SKILLS Using a grammar

A grammar can help you
– to correct or avoid mistakes,
– to revise for a test.
The table of contents and the index will help you to find the points you are looking for. But first you must know grammar words, like **tenses, clauses, adjectives, ...**

▸ *GF 9.3: The gerund with 'its own subject' (p. 175) • SF Using a grammar (p. 125)*

P7 MEDIATION School in New Zealand

a) *Partner B: Go to page 99.*
Partner A: You and your partner want to spend some time at a school in New Zealand. In German, tell your partner the most important information about Wellington High School.

Wellington High School is the only state co-educational secondary school in Wellington City. We believe that learning is central and that high expectations with effective teaching produce resilient, self-directed learners.

The school has an established reputation in visual and performing arts, supported by creative technologies. Students consistently win awards in journalism, drama, computer, creative writing, jazz, film-making and a range of sports.

WHS has accepted students from around the world since the 1950s. The 80 international students at the school live with home stay families, which usually costs NZ$210 per week, but students over 18 may choose to live in the hostel or a flat.

Sports, music, drama and art are all included in the programme and international students are expected to participate in at least one activity.

WHS has seven science laboratories, photography darkrooms, seven computer laboratories, two gymnasiums, technology workshops, music and drama rooms, a recording studio, a radio station and a modern library which supports the research-based learning across the school.

All the teachers are highly qualified and experienced. They are trained to teach students for whom English is not their first language.

b) *Listen to what your partner has to tell you about Onslow College.*

c) *In English, tell your partner which school you would prefer to go to and why.*

▸ *WB 12–13 (p. 24)*

THE BUSINESS: A REALITY TV SHOW

1 Interview tips

L S R W

Saturday **6.30 pm**

THE BUSINESS

Rita McQueen from fashion company RMQ is the 'big boss' on this week's show. How can candidates Lucy and Mani impress Rita in their interviews and win the prize, two weeks' placement as Rita's assistant? Life coach Simon Gubbins gave them some tips.

'Big boss' Rita McQueen. Who will she choose?

Which three tips do you think are the most important? Discuss your choice with a partner.

Relax. Before an interview listen to music, do yoga or breathe deeply.

Listen carefully to the questions.

Don't talk too quickly.

Smile in the interview.

Be punctual.

Research the company before the interview. Show your interest in it.

Prepare answers to typical interview questions like 'Can you tell us about yourself?' or 'What are your strengths and weaknesses?'.

Dress suitably for the job you are applying for. Be careful with bright colours and make-up.

Don't talk too much. But don't give one-word answers either.

2 VIEWING The interviews

V S R W

a) Watch the interviews. Make notes about Mani and Lucy on copies of this assessment sheet.

b) Did the candidates follow Simon's advice? Watch again. Discuss. Give examples.

c) Which candidate should win? Discuss in your group. Give reasons for your choice. Then vote in class.

Assessment Sheet	☹		☺		☺	
The candidate	**1**	**2**	**3**	**4**	**5**	**Comments**
1 was relaxed and friendly				✓		*smiled a lot*
2 dressed suitably						
3 listened carefully						
4 talked well (not too much/too little)						
5 gave good answers						
6 was well prepared						
7 Other comments:						

d) Watch the results. Discuss Rita's decision with the help of the assessment sheet.

3 Extra Internet forum 'TV talk'

L S R W

Here's what some people wrote after watching Lucy and Mani. Write a short comment of your own for this forum.

EJ (1 day ago) But he was just too °cheeky in the interview! Like when he said no when she asked him if he had any weaknesses. And he clearly didn't know much about Rita's business. She picked the wrong one if you ask me!

AliceW (1 day ago) Yeah! That °tie was crazy! The coach told them not to be shy – not a problem for Mani!

Max1234 (2 days ago) Did you see 'The Business' last night? I'm glad Mani won – he was cool.

Web-Code: EG21-A5-A-044

P1 STUDY SKILLS Visual aids in presentations

V S R W

a) Before they could become candidates for 'The Business', Mani and Lucy had to do a presentation on themselves for the programme's producers. Watch Mani and Lucy's presentations. Which did you think was better? Give reasons.

b) Read through the skills box. Then watch the presentations again. Which candidate used which visual aids? Rate how they used the visual aids from A (very good) to E (very poor).

Mani Wilson
Rita's next assistant

STUDY SKILLS Visual aids in presentations

Why visual aids?

1 Posters, transparencies and computer images show your audience the key points of your presentation. They also help you to stay organized during your presentation.

How to create visual aids

2 Keep your visual aids simple and well-structured and focus on the key points.
3 Make your pictures BIG, °bold and °brilliant. But keep them clear.
4 Use a large font size and dark colours so that everybody in the room can read your visual aid.

During your presentation

5 Don't talk to the visual aids, hide behind them or turn away from the audience.
6 Show your visual aids one by one – not all at once.

▸ *SF Visual aids in presentations (p. 131)*

Lucy Shaw

c) Discuss your ratings with a partner and try to agree on them.

d) Do the same again in a group.

e) Work out and practise a presentation on one of the following:

- a great free-time activity
- the best computer game
- the best pet
- the most exciting theme park
- a wonderful book to read
- a dream holiday
- an interesting museum
- yourselves

Create visual aids to illustrate your presentation. The skills box will help. Then give your presentation to the class.

L S R W

HOME NEWS MUSIC SPORT SCIENCE BUSINESS MORE ››

BUSINESS

How to be a teenage millionaire

Before you read the text, talk about these questions:
How do teenagers usually earn money?
Do you know anybody with their own business?

1 [kwɒlz, kwɔːlz]

She hasn't got a rich family. She hasn't won the °lottery. But at 17, Ashley Qualls [1], a °computer geek from Detroit, is a millionaire. She's a successful °businesswoman with her own company and she has bought a house for $250,000. But she's still too young to vote!

Ashley's idea was very simple. Her website, whateverlife.com, offers free designs that teenagers can use for their myspace.com pages.

Ashley, who is known as "AshBo" to her friends, has been working with websites since she was about nine years old. While other children were watching TV or having fun, she was teaching herself °HTML. She loved working with colours and designs for myspace.com layouts.

In 2004, she borrowed $8 from her mother to buy the whateverlife.com °domain name. She didn't want to set up a business. She just wanted a website to show her layouts to her friends.

More and more people started to visit the website and download Ashley's designs. Within a few weeks, she had 100 visitors. Then 5,000. Now her website has over 3,000 designs and gets over 7 million visitors a month. "I used to be excited when there were two people on the site and one was me!" says Ashley.

Advertisers started to get interested in advertising on her site and in September 2005 Ashley received her first °cheque from the big

Ashley with some of her friends

°advertising company, Value Click Media. It was for $2,700. "It was more than I made in a month," her mother says. That was just the start. The next cheque was for $5,000, the third was for $10,000.

When the first money arrived, her mother couldn't believe it. She wasn't sure if it was really possible to make money from a website. But Ashley was confident. She told her mother: "No, I really trust this. I think it's really °gonna happen."

Although she was an excellent student at her high school, Ashley found it difficult to go to school and run a company. In January 2006, six months before her 16th birthday, she left school. She decided to continue studying from home so that she would have more time for the business. It was a big decision, so how did people react? "Everybody was shocked," she says. "They asked, 'Are you sure you know what you're doing?' But I had this crazy opportunity to do something different."

Most websites for teenagers are designed by adults. When you go to Ashley's site, it is clearly something that has been made by a teenager. This gives Ashley a big advantage because she understands what teenagers want. "They look at me and think, 'She's my age, she must know what I like.'"

The business now °brings in as much as $70,000 a month. (The designs are still free. The money comes from advertising.) Ashley is learning how to be the 'big boss'. Her mother now works for her as a manager and she has a business adviser to help her too. She also pays some of her friends to work for her after school and at the weekend.

It's not easy to be a boss and a friend. Last year one of Ashley's friends was helping her, but Ashley thought she wasn't working hard enough. Ashley says that things were difficult between them for a while, but they are friends again now and get along well. Now she has a set of rules for everyone who works for her. "I tell them I need a minimum of 25 layouts a week to get paid," Ashley says. "It's just business."

Ashley had the right idea at the right time, and some people would say she was just lucky. But she clearly has a lot of ambition and determination and she works hard to make her business a success. "You have to have faith in yourself and believe in what you're doing," says Ashley. "These have been the best few years of my life, and also the most stressful … If people think running WhateverLife has always been easy, they are wrong," she points out. Box: Voc., S.198

Sometimes Ashley misses the normal life of a teenager. More than once she has gone back to her old school, Lincoln Park High School, just for the day. "I miss the fact that I won't be graduating with my friends. They're all getting excited and it's sad to know I won't be a part of that exact moment."

And the future? Ashley hasn't got any definite plans. She wants to go to college, and she's thinking of going to design school in New York, which she calls her "dream city".

Working with the text

L S R W

1 An outline

a) *Work with a partner. Complete this outline of the article in the best way you can.*

b) *Compare results in a group and try to improve your outline.*

► SF Outlining (p. 129)

Teenage millionaire: Ashley Qualls

I Why Ashley is unusual
II The basic idea
III Ashley's hobby
  A How it started
  B Domain ...
  C Number of ...
  D ...
IV Leaving school
  A Reasons ...
  B ...
V Ashley's site
...

L S R W

2 Talk show

a) *Ashley is appearing on a talk show. Write down her answers to these questions.*

1 Ashley, what's the basic idea behind your website?
2 When did you first become interested in this kind of thing?
3 And how did the website become a business?
4 What about school?
5 Do you run the business on your own?
6 Are there any problems with being the boss?
7 What do you think is the reason for your success?
8 Are there any disadvantages to the job?
9 And what about the future?

b) *Act out the conversation with a partner without looking at what you've written.*

L S R W

3 Extra Find out more

a) *What else would you like to find out about Ashley? Make a list of three or four questions.*

b) *Try to find the answers to your questions on the internet. Use what you find to write a few more paragraphs for the article.*

c) *Where would these new paragraphs best go?*

► SF Research (p. 128)

L S R W

4 Your opinion

a) *What do you think of Ashley's story? Would you like her life? Make some notes and tell a partner what you think. Give reasons.*
I'd like to ... / But I wouldn't want to..., because ...

study at home • earn lots of money • pay my friend/mum to work for me • be the boss • work so hard • have no time to relax • ...

b) *Write a comment about Ashley's story for this internet forum.*

Today at 13:49:17 Maria wrote:
I disagree with Chris. It wasn't luck. It was ambition, determination and hard work. The formula is: ambition + determination + ACTION = success. Remember! It is better to do one action than to think about 10 actions. Well done Ashley! She's a role model for me.

Today at 13:36:53 Chris wrote:
I don't agree. I don't think she's a role model. She's just a lucky person. We only read about her because she has lots of money. There are lots of young people who are much better role models. I'd prefer to read about young people who are trying to help other people.

Today at 13:32:38 Lea wrote:
Ashley's a role model for young people.

► WB 14 (p. 25)

P1 REVISION WhateverLife (Simple and progressive tenses)

Choose the correct verb form.

1 Ashley borrowed (borrowed/was borrowing) $8 from her mother.
2 Ashley's mother … (didn't believe/wasn't believing) her daughter would make any money.
3 But Ashley … (knows/is knowing) what young people want.

P2 Exploring language Activity verbs and state verbs

a) *Look at these examples.*

Ashley's friends are having fun.
(have = *erleben* – an activity, in progress ▸ progressive)
She has a business adviser.
(have = *haben, besitzen* – a state ▸ simple, not progressive)

Ashley was thinking of going to design school.
(think = *überlegen, darüber nachdenken* – an activity, in progress ▸ progressive)

She thought her friend wasn't working hard enough.
(think = *meinen, glauben* – a state ▸ simple, not progressive)

Some verbs can express either an activity or a state. With activities we can use either the simple or – if the activity is in progress – the progressive form. With states, only the simple form can be used.

▸ *GF 2: Aspect (pp. 159–160)*

b) *Translate these sentences into German.*

1 I'm looking at this job advert. 2 That looks interesting.

P3 Cashpoint story (Activity verbs and state verbs)

Complete the story with the correct form of the verbs.

Yesterday 17-year-old Matthew went to the cashpoint. He thought (thought/was thinking) that perhaps he … (had/was having) £20 in the bank. When he put his card in, he saw that the figure was £10 million. Matthew took out £1,000, went to the shops and bought lots of CDs and computer games, which all … (looked/were looking) cool. He … (had/was having) a great time, he told himself as he paid for everything. Of course it was a big mistake by the bank, and Matthew will have to pay back the money. 'I … (look/am looking) for a Saturday job,' he said. 'I … (think/am thinking) of asking my uncle if I can work in his sports shop.'

P4 WORDS Job interview (Phrasal verbs)

Phrasal verbs are 'two-word verbs' (verb + adverb). Put one of these phrasal verbs in each sentence.

find out • give up • keep on • look up • put on • show off • work out

1 Try to work out what you'd like to say in your job interview.
2 Before the interview, … the company on the internet.
3 … as much as possible about it.
4 … some nice clothes for the interview.
5 In the interview, just answer the interviewer's questions – don't try to …
6 If you don't get a job at first, don't … trying – you need to … applying.

▸ *WB 15–16 (p. 26)* • *Self-evaluation 1–2 WB (p. 27)* • **Skills Check 2** *WB (pp. 28–33)*

Unit 3 Stand up for your rights

Whiteboard Beamer

On 10 December 1948, the United Nations passed the °Universal Declaration of Human Rights. Among these rights are

- freedom from discrimination
- freedom of religion
- freedom of speech
- the right to choose your government
- the right to education

A

B

L S R W

1 Human rights

a) *Match each human right to the correct picture (A–E). Describe what each picture is about.* Box: Voc., S.198

Picture C shows different religious symbols. It's about freedom of religion.

b) **Extra** *What other rights do you think might be in the Universal Declaration of Human Rights? Come up with a few ideas.*

C

D

E

2 SONG Get up, stand up 1.27

L S R W

This song is sung by Jamaican singer Bob Marley (1945–1981), the most famous reggae musician in the world.

a) *Read the chorus of the song. What does Bob Marley want you to do/not to do in your life?*

b) *Listen to the song. Why do you think Marley repeats the chorus so often?*

L S R W

Lektüre
Speak

First Amendment *(adapted from the novel Speak by Laurie Halse Anderson)*

Not all the new words here are in the Dictionary at the back of the book. You can work out a lot of the meanings yourself.

In this chapter, Melinda, the narrator, is in her 8th grade History class.

Mr. Neck storms into class, a bull chasing thirty-three red flags. We °slide into our seats. I think for sure he's going to explode.

IMMIGRATION. He writes it on the board. I'm pretty sure he spelled it right.

Mr. Neck: "My family has been in this country for over two hundred years. We built this place, fought in every war from the first one to the last one, paid taxes, and voted."

A cartoon bubble forms over the heads of everyone in the class. ("WILL THIS BE ON THE TEST?")

Mr. Neck: "So tell me why my son can't get a job."

A few hands go up. Mr. Neck ignores them. It isn't a real question, it's one he asked so he could give the answer. I relax. This is like when my father complains about his boss. The best thing to do is to stay awake and look sympathetic.

His son wanted to be a firefighter, but didn't get the job. Mr. Neck is sure that this is some kind of °reverse discrimination. He says we should close our borders so that real Americans can get the jobs they deserve.

I concentrate on trying to draw a pine tree.

Mr. Neck writes on the board again: "DEBATE: America should have closed her borders in 1900." That gets a reaction. I can see kids counting backward on their fingers, trying to figure when their grandparents or great-grandparents were born, when they came to America, if they would have made the Neck Cut. When they figure out they would have been stuck in a country that hated them, or a place with no schools, or a place with no future, their hands shoot up. They do not share Mr. Neck's opinion.

I don't know where my family came from. Someplace cold, where they eat beans on Thursday and hang their wash on the line on Monday. I don't know how long we've been in America. We've been in this school district since I was in first grade; that must count for something. I start drawing an apple tree.

The arguments jump °back and forth across the room. A few °suck-ups quickly figure out which side Mr. Neck is on, so they fight to throw out the "foreigners". Anyone whose family immigrated in the last century has a story to tell about how hard their relatives have worked, what they do for the country, the taxes they pay. A member of the °Archery Club tries to say that we are all foreigners and we should give the country back to the Native Americans, but she's buried under disagreement. Mr. Neck enjoys the noise, until one kid challenges him directly.

Brave kid: "Maybe your son didn't get that job because he's not good enough. Or he's lazy. Or the other guy was better than him, no matter what his skin color. I think the white people who have been here for two hundred years are the ones pulling down the country. They don't know how to work – they've had it too easy."

The supporters of immigration clap and cheer.

Mr. Neck: "You watch your mouth, mister. You are talking about my son. I don't want to hear any more from you. That's enough debate – get your books out."

The Neck is back in control. Show time is over. I try to draw a °branch coming out of a tree °trunk for the 315th time. It looks terrible. I have no idea how to make it °come alive. I'm concentrating on the drawing, so I don't notice at first that David Petrakis my lab partner has stood up. The class stops talking. I put my pencil down.

Mr. Neck: "Mr. Petrakis, take your seat."

David Petrakis is never, ever in trouble. He is the kid who never misses a class, who helps the staff find °bugs in the computer files of report cards. What is he thinking? Has he finally gone crazy under the pressure of being smarter than everyone?

David: "If the class is debating, then each student has the right to say what's on his mind."

Mr. Neck: "I decide who talks in here."

David: "You opened a debate. You can't close it just because it is not going your way."

Mr. Neck: "Watch me. Take your seat, Mr. Petrakis."

David: "The Constitution does not recognize different classes of citizenship based on time spent living in the country. I am a citizen, with the same rights as your son, or you. As a citizen, and as a student, I am protesting the tone of this lesson as racist, intolerant, and xenophobic."

Mr. Neck: "Sit your °butt in that chair, Petrakis, and watch your mouth! I try to get a debate going in here and you people turn it into a race thing. Sit down or you're going to the principal."

David stares at Mr. Neck, looks at the flag for a minute, then picks up his books and walks out of the room. He says a million things without saying a word. I make a note to study David Petrakis. I have never heard a more °eloquent silence.

Fact File

The Constitution of the United States (1789) set up the country's system of government. Power was divided on the one hand between the states and the central government and on the other between the President, Congress and the courts. Many other democracies such as Germany have a basic law influenced by the US Constitution. Box: Voc., S.200–201

Since 1789, 27 amendments have been made to the Constitution. The first ten were made together in 1791 and are known as the °Bill of Rights. The First Amendment guarantees freedom of speech and the press, freedom of religion, freedom of assembly and the right to protest to the government.

Working with the text

1 Understanding the story
L S R W

After looking at the fact file, give reasons why this chapter of the novel is called 'First Amendment'.

2 The main characters
L S R W

a) *What kind of person is Mr Neck? How do you know? Find examples in the text.*

b) *Compare Mr Neck and David Petrakis. What are their views on immigration and human rights?*

c) *Imagine you are in Mr Neck's class. Write a diary entry about what happened in class, what David Petrakis did, and about free speech.*

3 The topic: freedom of speech
L S R W

a) *Write down some situations where you can express your own opinion.*

b) *Compare your answers with a partner. Then list reasons why freedom of speech is important.*

c) **Extra** *Do a **placemat** activity: what are the limits to freedom of speech? Are there things one should not be allowed to say?*

4 Extra Game
L S R W

*Do a °**freeze frame** for page 52, line 16: 'A few hands go up.' Imagine the scene. Act out where Mr Neck and the students are. Think of how they look and what they are thinking.*

L S R W

5 A book review

Read the following book review, which gives a brief summary and opinion about the novel Speak.

Review
***Speak* by Laurie Halse Anderson**

When Melinda Sordino starts high school, she is an °outcast, avoided by the other students. No one knows why she called the police and broke up the party that everyone was enjoying. Melinda becomes °withdrawn, refusing to speak to anyone. What is the secret she won't speak about?

Luckily Melinda is helped by her Art teacher Mr Freeman. Having recognized her talent, he encourages her to express her feelings through art. Her lab partner David Petrakis also earns her respect. We finally learn the reason for Melinda's silence. This is a well-written and heart-warming book, which is sad and funny at the same time.

a) *Does the review make you want to read the novel? Why or why not?*

b) **Extra** *Are there other books in English that you would like to read? Your teacher can help you with some suggestions for novels and stories that you might like. You should also recommend a novel or story to your classmates. Here is an example:*

I think *Speak* is a great novel. It's about a girl at high school who won't speak to anyone, but you don't find out the reason why until near the end of the book. I really enjoyed reading it. It's a bit scary and it's funny too.

V S R W

6 VIEWING 'That's enough debate'

Watch the film version of the classroom scene.

a) *What is different from the novel? What is the same?*

b) *Some of the students come from families that immigrated later than Mr Neck's family. Compare how this is shown in the novel and in the film.*

c) *Melinda is the narrator in the novel. How is this shown in the film? Why do you think it is done this way?*

Lektüre
Speak

P1 REVISION Freedom of religion (Active and passive)

Compare the active and passive sentences.
The Pilgrims held services at the Meeting House. (active)
Services were held at the Meeting House. (passive)
The active sentence tells us about the Pilgrims and what they did. The passive sentence tells us about the services and where they were held.

Complete the sentences about the Pilgrims, who went to the New World for religious reasons. Sometimes you need the active and sometimes the passive.

1 Pilgrims – found – Plymouth colony
The Pilgrims landed in America. They founded the Plymouth colony.
2 but – Native Americans – help – Pilgrims
There were lots of problems for the Pilgrims. But they were helped by the Native Americans.
3 first winter – kill – half of the Pilgrims
The first winter was terrible. It ...
4 everyone – celebrate – first harvest
The first harvest was a great event. It ...
5 Pilgrims – invite – Native Americans
We don't know exactly what the Pilgrims did. Maybe they ...
6 Americans – celebrate – Thanksgiving – every November
Thanksgiving is important. Even today it ...
7 Henry Hornblower – start – Plimoth Plantation museum – 1947
Have you heard of Henry Hornblower? He ...
8 lots of tourists – visit – Plimoth Plantation
Plimoth Plantation is a famous attraction. It ...

► *GF 3: The passive (pp. 161–163)*

P2 REVISION Ellis Island (Passive verb forms)

a) *Put each verb in brackets into the correct passive form. Be careful with the tenses.*
Over the last 400 years Ellis Island, in New York Harbor, has been used (use) for a number of different purposes. 200 years ago a fort ... (build) there by the US Army. From 1892 to 1954 it ... (use) as an °immigration station. At one time the island was much smaller. It ... (make) bigger by using earth that ... (take) away when tunnels ... (make) for the New York subway.

Around 1900, millions of immigrants came through Ellis Island after the journey from Europe. On the island they ... (see) by a doctor, and many of them were afraid they ... (might – send) back if they weren't healthy. But almost all of them ... (allow) to enter the country.

Today the station is an Immigration Museum. It ... (visit) by almost two million people every year. 40 per cent of US citizens have someone in their family's past who came through Ellis Island. Their history ... (can – find) on the museum's website.

► *GF 3: The passive (pp. 161–163)*

b) **Extra** *Using at least two passive sentences, write a paragraph about a famous place.*

P3 REVISION Human Rights Watch (Participle clauses instead of relative clauses)

a) *Read this paragraph.*

Human Rights Watch (HRW) is an organization that defends human rights. It publishes reports on situations where people do not have rights and it tries to make governments do something about the problem. It has told the world about people who have been made homeless in wars and those who live in camps, children who work in factories and children who sleep on the streets. By making what is happening public, HRW also tries to help people who have been sent to prison for protesting, journalists who have been arrested for asking questions and people who are discriminated against because of their religion.

b) *Use the information from a) to complete this flyer about HRW with participle clauses.*

HUMAN RIGHTS WATCH

Join us and help:

- people made homeless in wars
- people living ...
- children ...
- ...

► *GF 10.2: Participle clauses instead of relative clauses (p. 176)*

P4 Radio reporter (Verbs of perception + object + present participle)

a) *Look at these sentences with* ***see/hear + object + present participle****. How would you translate the sentences into German?*

I can **see a crowd of people waiting** to vote.
(= A crowd of people are waiting to vote. I can see them.)
I **heard a man** shouting slogans.
(= A man was shouting slogans. I heard him.)

b) *A radio reporter is describing riots in a city. What does she say for the pictures below?*

1 *I saw people breaking a shop window.*
2 *I saw them ...*
3 *I heard ...*

c) *Describe a situation to your partner, e.g.*
I can see lights flashing. And I can hear loud music playing.
Your partner has to say where you are:
You are probably at a concert.

people – break – shop window

they – steal – things

dogs – bark

police cars – speed – through – streets

police officer – say – something – through – °megaphone

helicopter – fly – over

► *GF 10.3: The present participle after certain verbs (pp. 176–177)*

P 5 Exploring language | Participle clauses

a) *Look at these sentences:*
Walking out of the room, David wins Melinda's respect.
Called on °911, the police were quickly on the scene.
Walking out of the room *and* ***Called on 911*** *are participle clauses. They are used instead of adverbial clauses with* ***because*** *or* ***when****:*
Because he walks out of the room, David wins Melinda's respect. When they were called on 911, the police were quickly on the scene.

b) *Here are some more sentences with participle clauses. Can you rewrite them? (Where would you use the conjunction* ***when****, and where would you use* ***because****? Where could you use* ***when OR because****?)*
1 Arriving in class, Mr Neck went to the board.
2 Feeling bored, Melinda started drawing.
3 Avoided by the other students, Melinda became an outcast.

c) *Can you rewrite the following sentences? (Think about which action happened first.)*
1 Having looked at the flag, David leaves the room.
2 Having recognized Melinda's talent, Mr Freeman encourages her to draw.

d) *Translate the sentences in b) and c) into German.*

e) *How could you translate the following sentences into German? Which linking words would you use – 'und' or 'indem' or 'wobei' or …?*
1 Melinda sat in the corner, refusing to speak to anyone.
2 Counting on their fingers, the students tried to figure out if they were 'real Americans'.

► *GF 10.4–10.5: Participle clauses (pp. 177–178)*

P 6 Screenplay (Participle clauses)

a) *The screenplay of a film contains dialogue and sometimes also describes the action. Read the descriptions of a scene in the film* Speak *and rewrite the sentences so that they are in informal English. There is sometimes more than one way of doing this.*

1 Having °waited in line, Melinda is given her lunch.
After she has waited in line, Melinda is given her lunch.
2 Taking her meal, she moves away from the counter.
She takes her meal …
3 Standing there with her meal, she looks for somewhere to sit.
4 Recognizing her, one boy throws some potato, which lands on her T-shirt.
5 Shocked by this, Melinda stands there for a moment.
6 Throwing her food down, she runs out.
7 Having run to the restroom, she cleans the potato off her T-shirt.

b) *Decide if you need a* ***present*** *or a* ***past*** *participle and shorten the following sentences.*
1 When she thought about what David said, Melinda was impressed.
2 After he left the room, David walked around for a while.
3 The other students sat quietly because they were surprised by what had happened.

P7 Film reviews (Compound participles)

a) *Fill in the gaps of these sentences from film reviews with words from the box on the right.*

1 The film has two famous and ... stars.
2 The ending is sad. Actually it's ...
3 The US is attacked by ... monsters.
4 The ... Brad Pitt plays the hero.
5 It's an exciting and ... movie.
6 The writing is good. The dialogue is ...

well-written • action-packed • Oscar-winning • heart-breaking • human-eating • good-looking

b) *Now use other compound adjectives to rewrite the sentences.*

1 She plays a teenager who loves animals.
2 It's a moment which stops your heart.
3 He has to make decisions that will change his life.

P8 High school (Participle clauses)

Rewrite the following sentences about a day at a high school. Use participle clauses.

1 The students were coming into school, and they were chatting to each other.
The students were coming into school chatting ...
2 The class did a test and they were watched by the teacher.
3 A few kids were still in the cafeteria where they had finished their lunch.
4 A lot of boys go to basketball practice because they hope to be on the school team.
5 One girl was sent home to change her clothes and she had to call her mum to fetch her.
6 Members of the school band stayed late at school because they were practising for a concert.

P9 Extra The Constitution (Participle clauses with conjunctions)

a) *Sometimes you need a conjunction in front of a participle clause to make clear exactly what you mean. Compare:*

1 Having lunch with friends, the President fell asleep.

2 After having lunch with friends, the President fell asleep.

b) *Rewrite the following sentences. Use participle clauses with conjunctions.*

1 After they had won the war against the British, the United States needed to set up a system of government.
2 Before it °became law, the Constitution was discussed in Philadelphia by people from the different states.
3 Although it was written in 1789, the US Constitution is still the basic law of the country today.
4 Amendments can be made to the Constitution if they are °approved by three quarters of the states.
5 While you are visiting Washington, why not take a tour of the White House Gardens?

P 10 The Stars and Stripes (Participle clauses)

Rewrite the information using participle clauses for the underlined parts.

The US flag is probably the most famous in the world. Because it is seen by many as a symbol of freedom and by others as a symbol of American power, it can create very different feelings in different people. In America the flag is everywhere. On most public buildings you can see it as it flies 24 hours a day. There's a flag in American classrooms. When they stand and look at the flag every morning, students promise to be loyal to their country.

It is not certain who designed the flag. The popular story is that the first one was made in 1776 by a woman who was called Betsy Ross. They say that George Washington himself, when he had drawn a flag, asked her to make it.

A law of Congress which was approved in 1777 said that the new country's flag should have 13 red and white stripes and, on a blue background, 13 white stars, which would represent the 13 states. The stripes have not changed, and they still represent the original states, but the number of stars has increased over the years, which has been caused by the increase in the number of states. However, the number has not changed now for over 50 years, after it had increased to 50 in 1959, when Hawaii became a state.

P 11 Extra School rules (Participle clauses)

a) *Below you can see some written rules about how to behave at a US high school. On the right an American student is explaining the rules to a new student. Complete the rules using participle clauses and complete the explanations using other structures.*

- Check that you have all your books and materials before leaving home.
- Clothes worn in school must be normal everyday clothes and not part of a fashion show.
- Students ... will be sent home.
- °Put your hand up before speaking in class.
- You must report to a teacher ...
- Do not interrupt other students trying to study.
- Wash your hands ...
- When planning to leave school early, you must bring a note from home.

You must check that you have all your books and materials before you leave home. And clothes ... have to be normal everyday clothes because it's not a fashion show. There's also a rule that students who bring alcohol into school will be sent home. What else? Oh, yes, you have to put your hand up ... And I hope you won't be bullied – you should report to a teacher if you're bullied by other students. And you're not allowed to interrupt other students ... There's a rule that says you have to wash your hands after you use the restroom, but I hope you know that already. Oh, and something important – ..., you must bring a note from home.

b) *Compare the written rules above with the way this student explains them. What differences can you see in the use of some types of participle clauses?*

Box: Voc., S.202

RUNNING FOR OFFICE

L S R W

One important human right is the right to vote. Another is the right to run for office. In the US you can't run for president until you're 35, but in most states you can run for mayor at 18, as you can in Germany. What would you think if your community had an 18-year-old mayor?

Eighteen-year-old mayor may be youngest in US

Roland, Iowa. Sam Juhl[1] [dʒu:l] wants to study history one day, so it seems right that he's °making history of his own first.

The 18-year-old Juhl was elected mayor of Roland in November. He ran his first City Council meeting Monday in front of about 35 people in the town's City Hall.

Mayor Sam Juhl (front row, center) and members of Roland City Council

He watched the clock as the °second hand came around. It was time.

"All right, it's seven," Juhl said. "First thing is °roll call."

And history was made.

Juhl, who was 18 on Nov. 3, is believed to be the youngest mayor in the United States. Two other 18-year-olds were elected mayor in November. But they are both more than a month older.

With two television stations filming everything, Juhl led the five-member council through the meeting in 40 minutes. That's shorter than his debate class at Roland-Story High School.

The town of about 1,300 is planning a new library, which took up much of the discussion.

Juhl slipped up only once. He read out a report about economic development, but he went to the next agenda item without hearing comments from the council.

"Oh," said Juhl, when the city °clerk pointed it out. "°Oops."

Juhl did his homework before Monday's meeting. He studied °parliamentary procedure.

"I got the °Idiot's Guide," Juhl said. "It made it a lot easier."

Two years ago, no one ran for the office of mayor in Roland. It was then that Juhl told his parents that if it happened again when he was 18, he'd run for office himself.

"We thought 'yeah, right'," his mother Judy said.

But when he won with 48 percent of the votes, it was official. Soon he'll be working with a partner to develop a budget proposal.

Hard work isn't a new idea for Juhl. He gets up daily at 4 a.m. to deliver newspapers. It's his main source of income.

"It's better paid than being mayor," said Juhl, who will make about $1,500 annually through his two-year term.

The people who know him best said he will do great things for Roland.

"He's a very positive person," said °Councilman Duane Canny. "He's got just a great view on life."

Juhl is looking forward to °getting down to business. That might mean less time playing video games. It might also mean less time cleaning his messy bedroom. "Mayor °comes first," Juhl said. ■

Adapted and abridged from an article in The Tribune, *Ames, Iowa, 2006*

Working with the text

1 Understanding the article
L S R W

a) *Explain why the election of the mayor of Roland was interesting news.*

b) *Write down five questions about the article, then ask your partner the questions.*

2 Looking for detail
L S R W

a) *Lines 1–63 are called the 'body' of the article. What are the other parts of the article?*

b) *Which paragraph gives you the most important information ('Who?', 'What?', 'Where?', 'When?')?*

c) *The report appeared on 10 January. Write down a few words about what happened at each of these times:*
- *about two years ago,*
- *about two months before,*
- *less than a week before.*

In what order do these events appear in the article? Explain why the writer chose this order.

3 Young or old?
L S R W

Would you vote for a young person as mayor or is this a job for someone older?
Think *about the pros and cons and write down one or two sentences.* ***Pair:*** *Discuss your ideas with a partner and add to what you have written. Then* ***share*** *your ideas with the rest of the class.*

4 Extra What would you do?
L S R W

a) *Think of two things you would like to change if you were mayor of your community. Make appointments with three partners. Compare your ideas.*

b) *Write some ideas on the board. Vote which idea is the most popular.*

c) *As a citizen of your community, is there any way you can take part in political decisions? Discuss.*

5 TV news
L S R W

a) *Imagine you work for a national TV company that is filming the council meeting in Roland, Iowa. Write a short summary about the election and the meeting to go with the film. It should last 20 seconds (not more than 50 words). Just give the basic facts.*

... -old Sam Juhl presided ...

b) Extra *Read your report to a partner in the style of a newsreader.*

STUDY SKILLS **Summarizing a non-fictional text**

1. Give the important information but leave out the details.
2. If a main point is illustrated with examples, you should mention the point but leave out the examples.
3. You can usually leave out quotations used to illustrate a point.
4. Give basic information in your first sentence (5 Ws).
5. Make sure you explain the topic clearly. If necessary you can change the order to make things more logical.
6. Your summary should °hang together as a text.

▸ SF Summary writing (p. 149) • **Text File 6** (p. 109)

P1 WORDS Politics

a) *Match each verb with the words on the right. Then write a sentence using the expression.*

1 elect	a speech
2 give	an argument
3 run	for office
4 preside	a mayor
5 read	over a meeting
6 have	through a report

1 *elect a mayor – The people of Roland elected a new mayor.*

b) *Put the words from the box below in the correct sentence. Make sure you can pronounce the words. Notice where the stress is.*

politics • political • politician •
nation • national • nationality •
democrat • democracy • democratic

1 *Democracy means that we can vote.*
2 The civil war divided the …
3 We were listening to a … speech.
4 What … are you – British or German?
5 I think you'd be a good …
6 I never vote – I'm not interested in …
7 There are local and … elections.
8 It's not very … for one person to decide everything.

c) **Extra** *Collect all the 'political' words and phrases you know and organize them in a way you find helpful, such as a table, a wheel or a mind map. Use a German–English dictionary to find other words that you can add, e.g. party, unemployment, demonstration, …*

P2 EVERYDAY ENGLISH SPEAKING Talking about politics

a) *Match 1–6 to A–C.*
1 What's their policy on … ?
2 I'm going to vote for …
3 (They say) they're going to …
4 What would they do about … ?
5 They plan to …
6 I support …

A sagen, welche Partei du unterstützt
B nach der Politik einer Partei fragen
C sagen, was eine Partei vorhat

b) *Partner B: Go to page 99.*
Partner A: Ask your partner which party they support. Then ask four questions about that party's policy on human rights, education, transport and the environment. Comment on at least one of the policies, e.g.
I (don't) think that's a good idea. I think …

c) *Use the information on the flyer below to answer your partner's questions about the party you support: the 'Freedom Party'.*

P3 MEDIATION What you can and can't do

a) You are going on an exchange to the US and want to know what you may or may not do there, such as drink alcohol. You've found this article on the internet. Make notes then tell your partner in German what the main points are. Your partner adds points you have forgotten.

US drinking laws

Of all the countries in the world in which alcohol is allowed, the United States has the highest age at which you are allowed to buy alcohol. Since the °National Minimum Drinking Age Act of 1984, it has been illegal in the US for people under 21 to buy or 'publicly possess' alcoholic drinks. This law is opposed by many people and by organizations such as the National Youth Rights Association, which wants an end to 'age discrimination' in laws on drinking.

The exact rules about alcohol depend on the individual states. The National Act does not actually ban all drinking of alcohol by under-21s. In some states it is legal to drink alcohol at home with the family, but in others it is not. Some states allow young people to use alcohol when learning to cook or for religious or medical reasons.

b) Your partner is a 16-year-old American exchange student who is visiting you and wants to know what the rules are in Germany about young people going to discos and drinking alcohol. Read the information and tell your partner their rights in English.

Discobesuche

Unter 16 darfst du nur in eine Disco, wenn ein Erziehungs- oder Sorgeberechtigter dabei ist. Ab 16 darfst du dich immerhin bis 24 Uhr in einer Disco aufhalten. Danach heißt es nach Hause gehen. Das gilt auch, wenn ein Freund oder Freundin von dir schon volljährig ist. Ausnahmen gibt es aber bei Veranstaltungen von einem „anerkannten Träger der Jugendhilfe", das sind z. B. Jugendtreffs von Gemeinden, Vereinen oder der Kirche. Dann ist allen unter 16 die Anwesenheit bis 22 Uhr gestattet.

Alkohol

Wenn ein Erziehungsberechtigter dabei ist, darfst du ab 14 Jahren eine kleine Menge Wein oder Bier trinken, ansonsten ist das für dich verboten, genauso wie der Konsum anderer alkoholischer Getränke. Ab 16 Jahren bist du berechtigt, in Gaststätten und auch in Geschäften alkoholische Getränke zu kaufen. Das gilt aber nicht für Getränke mit hohem Alkoholgehalt wie z. B. Cocktails, Whiskey, Wodka und auch nicht für die neuen Mix-Getränke, denen „harter" Alkohol beigemischt ist. Für diese Getränke gilt: erst ab 18 Jahren.

P4 LISTENING WTNX News Time 1.28

a) *Listen to the news from Haybrook, Illinois. Put these headlines into the correct order:*

1 **Court decision on English**
2 **Voting early**
3 **°Record population increase**
4 **Today's weather**
5 **Haybrook woman shot**

b) *Listen again more carefully. Each sentence on the right has one detail wrong. Correct the mistakes.*

- A judge has decided that Jewish students at a °Catholic school must speak English.
- Some people have already voted in November's local election.
- Brownville, north of Haybrook, is one of only five cities that have grown more than 50 per cent.
- Temperatures today and tonight will be between 62 and 80 degrees.
- A woman was shot in the stomach as she stood on the balcony of an apartment.

P5 WRITING Protesters and police

a) *Last Saturday afternoon some people were injured during a demonstration in the capital of a former British colony. Read the following statements by people who saw what happened.*

'There were about 250 of them, demonstrating for freedom of speech – as if they haven't got it already – marching to the parliament building, and haven't they got anything better to do? The police moved forward to stop them. Quite right in my opinion. They had to use their °batons because the protesters were in the way. Then I saw some of them fighting with the police, so it was all their own fault. Four or five police officers were injured and were taken to hospital. I hope the people who did it go to prison.'

'The °marchers came from People's Park, and they were going to the parliament building. It happened right in front of me. They wanted to turn into Victoria Street, but there was a group of police officers there and suddenly they ran forward and attacked the marchers with batons. I was shocked because there were 200 to 250 people protesting peacefully against this new law to limit freedom of speech. Some of them ran away, and some were hit on the head as they tried to fight back. I counted 15 protesters taken away in ambulances.'

'I was standing at the corner of the street. I'd say there were at least 200 people marching, coming into Victoria Street, and the police were waiting for them. Suddenly the police ran towards the marchers and started hitting them with batons, hitting people on the head. It was awful. Some of the protesters ran away, but some of them fought with the police. Soon there were about 20 people lying on the ground, five of them police officers. Then the ambulances came.'

b) *In groups, decide what are the facts and what are people's opinions. Then write a report, including the facts but not any opinions.*

P 6 °Rock the Vote (Giving an oral summary)

a) *Read the following information about 'Rock the Vote'.*

Rock the Vote is a political organization started in Los Angeles in 1990. Its aim is to persuade young people to get involved in politics and to vote. Rock the Vote is supported by many celebrities, and it has produced a series of °promotional videos where stars tell young people in the USA to register and vote.

Tip

How to give an oral summary

1. You give an oral summary when you tell someone about something you've read or a film or TV programme you've seen.
2. Mention the main ideas or events but leave out the details, whatever you're summarizing. Use the present tense.
3. For a written summary you have time to organize your thoughts. For an oral summary you need to think quickly.
4. Try not to give your personal opinion.
5. The way you speak can help to get across what you want to say, e.g. through your tone of voice and the words that you stress. You might also have to answer questions from the person you are speaking to.

b) *Watch the clip of singer-songwriter Brendan James trying to do a promo video for RTV.*

▸ SF Speaking Course (pp. 142–143)

c) *Read what three people tell their friends about the clip. Say which is the best summary and why.*

1 Brendan James isn't very good at doing a °promo video for Rock the Vote because he stops and then he has to do it again. I think he's going to do a concert, so maybe he isn't concentrating. He's telling people to register and vote.

2 Brendan James is doing a °promo for Rock the Vote. People are getting ready for a concert, and he's interrupted several times when people play music or make a noise in the background. But finally he succeeds in recording a short promo where he tells people to register to vote.

3 It's a funny clip, and Brendan James laughs a lot. He doesn't finish what he wants to say. He's talking to the camera and something happens. So he tells us four or five times all about Rock the Vote and how people should register and vote, and the °web address is rockthevote.com, and this is important information.

d) *Watch the clip again and then summarize it with a partner.*

e) *Take turns to throw a dice and find out which of the topics below is yours. Think about what you can say and then tell your partner about it in two or three sentences. Mention the main action or ideas and leave out the details.*

1 – a film you saw I saw a film/movie about … who/that …	**4 – a trip you took** I travelled to … by air/train/…
2 – a book or story you enjoyed I read a book/novel/story about … who/that …	**5 – a concert or show you went to** I went to … with … It was …
3 – something you saw on television I saw a drama/comedy/documentary about …	**6 – something funny that happened to you** A funny thing happened … I was … when …

FREE AND EQUAL?

L S R W

1 The British 1.29

The Universal Declaration of Human Rights says that 'all human beings are born free and equal'. Read or listen to the poem and then say which part of it expresses this idea.
Not all the new words are in the Dictionary at the back of the book. You can work out a lot of the meanings yourself.

The British *by Benjamin Zephaniah* [1)]

Serves 60 million

Take some Picts, Celts and Silures
And let them settle,
Then overrun them with Roman conquerors.

Remove the Romans after approximately 400 years
Add lots of Norman French to some
Angles, Saxons, Jutes and Vikings, then stir vigorously.

Mix some hot Chileans, cool Jamaicans, Dominicans,
Trinidadians and Bajans with some Ethiopians, Chinese,
Vietnamese and Sudanese.

Then take a blend of Somalians, Sri Lankans, Nigerians
And Pakistanis,
Combine with some Guyanese
And turn up the heat.

Sprinkle some fresh Indians, Malaysians, Bosnians,
Iraqis and Bangladeshis together with some
Afghans, Spanish, Turkish, Kurdish, Japanese
And Palestinians
Then add to the melting pot.

Leave the ingredients to simmer.

As they mix and blend, allow their languages to flourish
Binding them together with English.

Allow time to be cool.

Add some unity, understanding, and respect for the future,
Serve with justice
And enjoy.

Note:
All the ingredients are equally important.
Treating one ingredient better than another will leave
a bitter unpleasant taste.

Warning: Box: Voc., S.205
An unequal spread of justice will damage the people and
cause pain.
Give justice and equality to all.

1 [ˌzefəˈnaɪə]

Working with the text

a) *In what context would you normally find these words:* stir, mix, sprinkle, ingredients, simmer? *Find another five words or phrases in the poem from the same context. Why are these words used in the poem?*

b) *Who are the British? Answer in one or two sentences.*

c) *Starting at the third verse (l. 8), make a list of the people who have come to Britain: Chileans, Jamaicans etc. Look at an English-language world map and find the matching countries.*

d) **Extra** *Write a similar poem called 'The Germans'.*

L S R W

Extra Background File WHY ARE THE BRITISH SUCH A MIXTURE ?

1 Two thousand years ago the people living in Britain were called °Celts or °Britons. They had come from Central Europe about 700 years before. Other tribes included the °Picts in Scotland and the °Silures in Wales.

William the °Conqueror

In 43 AD the Romans °invaded Britain, and most of it became a colony of the Roman °Empire. The Romans built roads and towns. They stayed in Britain until about 400 AD.

In the 6th century the °Angles, °Saxons and °Jutes came from Denmark and northern Germany. They sailed to Britain and °conquered the country. The Britons °retreated into Wales and Scotland. The °Anglo-Saxons lived in villages and their country was called 'England'.

There were more °invaders. In the 9th century the Vikings came from Norway and Denmark and conquered part of England. Then in 1066 the Normans came from France and °defeated the Anglo-Saxons. William the Conqueror °ruled England. The English became a mixture of Britons, Romans, Anglo-Saxons, Vikings and Normans. But the English language survived.

2 From about 1600, the British founded colonies along the east coast of North America. Some of the colonies used African slaves, brought in British ships, to work on the °plantations. Slaves were also used in the Caribbean. Britain °grew rich from the slave trade, which caused terrible °suffering to millions of Africans.

The North American colonies grew rich too, and in 1776 the war began that °resulted in their °independence as the United States.

African slaves

3 Britain and France were °rivals in the °struggle for colonies. But victory in wars during the 18th century gave Britain control over Canada and India.

Queen Victoria

Britain's East India Company was set up in 1600 to °trade with India. India supplied °raw materials such as tea to Britain, and Britain used India as a market for °manufactured goods. In the 19th century the British government °took complete control of the country. India was a country with a rich civilization. The British regarded it as the '°jewel in the crown' of their Empire.

The British Empire grew in the time of Queen Victoria and reached its °height about a hundred years ago, when it °covered a quarter of the world. The Empire included India, Canada, Jamaica, Australia, New Zealand and large parts of Africa. Trade and industry had made Britain rich and °powerful, and English became the most °widely-used language in the world. Soldiers °from all corners of the Empire would fight for Britain in two °world wars.

►►

►►

4 The movement for Indian independence had been growing before the Second World War (1939–1945), and India finally became independent in 1947. Countries with mainly white populations, such as Canada and Australia, had been °running their own affairs for some time. In the 1960s many other British colonies became independent, such as Jamaica, Malaysia and many African countries. Most became members of the Commonwealth, a °voluntary °association of former colonies.

After the war Britain didn't have enough workers. So people were encouraged to come to Britain from Commonwealth countries such as Jamaica to be °nurses, °bus drivers and factory workers. But there was a lot of prejudice against black people.

Jamaican immigrants

As well as Jamaicans, there were immigrants from Pakistan and India. As Commonwealth citizens, they all had the right to settle in Britain, but soon the government began to limit the numbers of people allowed in. At the same time laws made °race discrimination illegal.
The situation of black people °improved slowly. Soon there were black newsreaders, black England footballers, black government ministers. But °race relations are still far from perfect, and °on the whole °blacks do not have the same life chances as °whites.

5 In 2004 ten more countries joined the European Union. Hundreds of thousands of Eastern Europeans, mainly from Poland, came to Britain, where they could earn higher °wages

Workers from Eastern Europe

than at home. Some went back home after a time, but others stayed. At the same time Britain also °accepted a number of °asylum seekers from countries such as Nigeria and Somalia.

Although it is a member of the EU, Britain has strong links to Commonwealth countries and it has been a friend to America. As a US politician once said, Britain has lost an empire and not yet found a role.

L S R W

a) *Write a heading for each of the five parts of the text.*

b) *Expand each picture caption into a sentence.*
1 *William the Conqueror defeated ... and ...*

c) *Work with a partner. Make a timeline using information from this Background File. Then do some research and add more information and dates.*

d) *400 years ago English was spoken only in England. Today it is spoken by a third of the world's population, mostly as a second language. Why is this, do you think? Discuss in groups.*
► **Text File 7** *(pp. 110–111)*

P1 WORDS Prepositions

Complete the sentences with one of these prepositions: ***as, against, in, for, from, over, until, with****. If you're not sure, find an example in the Background File.*

1 The Romans stayed in Britain ... 400 AD.
2 Britain grew rich ... the slave trade.
3 By defeating France, Britain won control ... Canada and India.
4 The war resulted ... independence for the American colonies.
5 India was a country ... a rich civilization.
6 The movement ... independence was growing.
7 There was a lot of prejudice ... blacks.
8 ... Commonwealth citizens, Jamaicans had the right to settle.

P2 STUDY SKILLS Reading a poem aloud 1.30–1.32

Whosland *by Benjamin Zephaniah*

At °dawn one °morn
After eight weeks of sailing,
The Europeans landed
On the gold, sandy beach.

After praying
They °made their way
°Inland,
With their flags in their hands
And an empire °on their minds.

Soon they °came across a small village,
All the people came out to see them,
The °villagers thought they had come with
great knowledge
And wisdom °from afar.
Having never seen Europeans before
This was new and exciting.

When the captain of the ship
Met the °elder of the village
He still had a flag in his hand
And an empire on his mind.

'What did you call this land before
we arrived?'
said the captain.

'Ours'
said the village elder,

'Ours.'

Tip

Before reading a poem aloud, prepare carefully. Make sure you understand the poem and know how to pronounce all the words. You should practise reading the poem aloud, but you don't need to °learn it by heart.
Read the poem so that it makes sense to you and to the audience. Your voice should sound natural.
Speak loudly and clearly and not too fast.
Stand straight and look at your audience.

a) *Follow the tips on reading a poem. Practise reading 'Whosland' aloud alone.*

b) *Read the poem aloud in your group. Then listen to others in your group reading the poem. Comment politely on each reading.*

That was excellent/very ...
Thank you. I enjoyed ...
You spoke very clearly/slowly/...
I think you pronounced ... wrong.
Wasn't it a bit too fast/quiet ...?

c) **Extra** *Listen to three people reading the poem. Which reading did you enjoy most? Why? How was it different from the readings from the others in your group?*

1 WORDS Free-time activities

What do you do in your free time? Are you sporty? Is your hobby running? Or do you like reading a good book?

a) *Work with a partner. How many free-time activities can you add to the list below?*

riding • drawing and painting • listening to music • playing a musical instrument • watching TV or DVDs • playing basketball • playing football • cycling • using a computer • reading books or magazines • relaxing • meeting friends • ...

b) *Look at your list and put the activities into groups.*

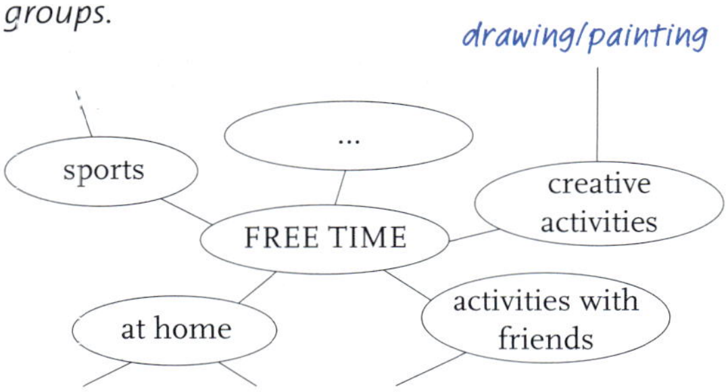

c) *Talk about all your free-time activities. Tell each other why you like/don't like doing them.*

A: I often go riding. I love horses and I think it's great to be with them every day.

B: Well, I don't agree. I think it's too much work. But I enjoy listening to music ...

2 WORDS Talking about films

You see this film review on a movie website. Find the missing words and phrases to complete the text. Put the verbs into their correct forms

(to) act • actor • award • (to) be based on • (to) be into • (to) come out • (to) end • main character • (to) tell the story

Take the Lead ● ● ● ● ○

'Ballroom dancing meets New York's gangs'

The film *Take the Lead* (1) tells the story of Pierre Dulaine, a ballroom dance teacher, who goes to work in one of New York's most difficult inner city schools full of problem kids. *Take the Lead* is actually (2) ... true events, and Pierre Dulaine is, in fact, a real person. He still works with American teenagers around the USA and has become quite famous since the film (3) ...

The star of the film is the Spanish American (4) ... Antonio Banderas. He plays the (5) ..., Pierre Dulaine. When Dulaine first arrives in the school, the kids all think he is crazy. They (6) ... hip hop, not classical dance. However, after Dulaine shows them a tango with another professional dancer, the kids start to get interested. The film (7) ... when they all take part in a national ballroom competition.

The kids are all 'normal' American teenagers and had never (8)... before. But they are all great natural acting talents and some of them are amazing hip hop dancers.

In 2006, *Take the Lead* won an (9) ... for 'Best Teen Movie'.

3 I'd love to be a movie star (Conditional sentences type 2)

Finish these sentences about being a famous movie star. All the sentences are conditional sentences type 2.

1 If a famous director *chose* (choose) me for one of his films, I*'d / would be* (be) famous too.
2 I ... (go) to Hollywood if I ... (become) a famous actor.
3 I ... (not live) here if I ... (be) rich.
4 If I ... (act) in a movie, all my friends ... (come) to see me.
5 If I ... (have) lots of money, I ... (buy) a yacht.
6 If I ... (play) a part in a movie, I ... (meet) famous actors every day on the film set.
7 But the problem is, if I ... (be) a movie star, I ... (not see) my family very often.
8 Perhaps I ... (not be) so happy if I ... (be) a film star!

► *GF 5: Conditional sentences (pp. 167–168)*

4 SPEAKING Having a conversation

Talk to your partner for about two minutes about something that interests you – films, magazines, music, what you did last weekend, the town where you live, ... The phrases below will help you.

starting a conversation	Hello. / Hi. / My name's ... / What's your name? / ...
likes and dislikes	I like / don't like ... / What about you? / And you? / ...
showing interest	Really? / Oh, that's interesting! / Sounds great! / Wow! / ...
agreeing and disagreeing	Yes, me too. / That's right! / Oh, I don't. / Sorry, I don't agree. / ...
asking questions	So when did you ...? / Why ...? / How long ...? / Where ...? / Sorry, can you say that again please? / ...
ending the conversation	See you soon. / Bye!

5 WORDS Tom and Kate (Words that describe feelings)

a) *Complete these sentences with words or phrases from the box on the right.*

angry • be afraid • be mad about sb./sth. • bored • confused • cool • different • excited • great • happy • independent • jealous • lonely • (to) look forward to sth. • nervous • proud • relaxed • responsible (for) • sad • safe • scared • silly • strange • surprised • terrible • tired • shy

1 Tom and Kate have been together for a month now and they ... still ... each other.
2 Kate was ... when Tom asked her if she'd like to date him. She thought he liked Laura.
3 Tom wasn't nervous on their first date. He is usually very ...
4 But last week, when Kate left his MP3 player on the bus, he was very ... with her.
5 Sometimes Kate is ... when Tom tries to be funny – his jokes are very strange!
6 First she didn't want to meet Tom's parents as she always feels a bit ... with new people.
7 When Kate met her old boyfriend Pete at a party, Tom was a bit ... – until he saw that she wasn't interested in Pete any more.
8 They're ... the summer holidays this year: they're going to Canada for three weeks!

b) *Write six sentences like these with words you haven't used in a).*

1 READING Dev Patel

Read the text from an online British movie magazine. Then tick the correct answer (A, B, C or D).

Meet Dev Patel, teenage movie star

***Slumdog Millionaire*, described as the 'feel-good film of the decade', won eight Oscars in 2009 and rocketed the young British actor Dev Patel to international stardom. The film tells the story of 17-year-old Jamal from the slums of Mumbai (he is a 'slumdog' in the local slang), who appears on the Indian TV show *Who wants to be a millionaire?* and wins the top prize – as well as finding the girl he loves.**

WHEN the then 17-year-old Dev Patel arrived in Mumbai to film *Slumdog Millionaire*, it was only his second visit to India. Indeed, learning the Mumbai accent was, he says, one of his hardest tasks. Nor was he a famous actor. He had enjoyed drama at school, and had played a small role in a British TV series, but he had no formal theatrical training and was certainly not well-known. So how did he end up getting the part of Jamal and how did he find the experience of suddenly becoming a superstar?

Dev was born the son of Indian immigrants near London in 1990. His dad is a computer technician, his mum a carer[1].

He attended a 'typical' English secondary school. Growing up, his early interests included martial arts, first karate then later tae-kwon-do, and he was good enough at both to represent England at the Youth Olympics. However, it was a part in a school play that led him to discover that his greatest love was to be acting. This was something that his parents wanted to encourage, and when Mrs Patel came across a small advertisement in a newspaper, she gave it to Dev. A British TV company was looking for fresh young people for a new series, called *Skins*, about a group of multicultural teenage friends. Dev got one of the parts. He was 14.

Three years later, the successful British film director Danny Boyle was planning *Slumdog Millionaire* and had a problem with the main character, Jamal. India has a booming film industry ('Bollywood') and there was no lack of actors. But none looked as if they had grown up in a slum – they were all too good-looking. It was Boyle's daughter, a long-time *Skins* fan, who suggested Dev. It took five auditions[2] before he was finally chosen. 'I was crying at the end because I didn't think I'd get the part,' he says.

For the young man from London, actually filming the movie was like a dream: working with a famous director, surrounded by famous Bollywood actors, playing opposite the beautiful young woman who is Jamal's girlfriend in the film. 'I grew up five years in those five months,' is how he sums it up.

Another amazing experience for Dev was to get to know the real slumdogs of Mumbai. It was above all their attitude to life that he noticed. 'Don't tell them we're poor,' they told him. 'Tell them we're happy. We aren't poor because we're happy.'

[1] carer ['keərə] *(Alten-)Pfleger/in* [2] audition [ɔː'dɪʃn] *Sprechprobe*

1 What role does Dev Patel play?
Someone who ...
A likes TV shows.
B moves to the Mumbai slums.
C wins a lot of money.
D wins an Oscar.

2 What was very difficult for Dev?
A Acting in a very poor environment.
B Dealing with his fame.
C Learning new pronunciation.
D Travelling to Mumbai.

3 What was Dev good at before he started acting at school?
A English
B Music
C Science
D Sports

4 What did his parents do when Dev found out that he liked acting?
They ...
A helped him find his first job.
B paid for acting lessons.
C printed an advert for him.
D wrote a letter to a TV company.

5 Why didn't the director Danny Boyle choose an Indian actor?
A Bollywood actors didn't want the role.
B Bollywood actors are too beautiful.
C Boyle's daughter didn't like Bollywood actors.
D There are very few good Bollywood actors.

6 How did Dev feel when he finally got the role?
A Anxious
B Funny
C Nervous
D Surprised

7 Why does Dev say that he grew up five years while filming?
Because ...
A filming was a lot of hard work.
B he fell in love with his partner.
C he worked with international stars.
D making the film took very long.

8 How does Dev feel about the people living in the Mumbai slums?
He ...
A admires them.
B avoids them.
C feels sorry for them.
D supports them.

1c 2c 3d 4a
5b 6d 7c 8a

2 READING Choosing a book

These American high school students are in their English literature class. They have to choose a book to read in order to present it to the class.

Look at the profiles of the five students and the seven book summaries below. Who will choose which book?

Answer: Student A – Book …

Student A : Conrad

Conrad doesn't really enjoy reading short stories or novels. He reads magazines, however, because he loves sport. He is also interested in music and skateboarding.

Student B : Brittany

Brittany has her own blog where she writes her thoughts. She is fascinated by young people, their loves and fears, their relationships, and their problems.

Student C : Jeanette

Jeanette loves reading stories. For her, a 'good book' is one where the characters have lots of real-life adventures. She doesn't like fantasy or horror stories.

Student D : John Paul

John Paul is interested in football but the thing he likes best is computer games. He particularly loves fantasy games where 'anything is possible'.

Student E : Ricki

Ricki's family came to the US from Puerto Rico. Now, as a teenager, he is interested in politics and wants to help people from ethnic minorities.

BOOK SUMMARIES

Fiction

1. **Dark Universe** Three teenage friends fall through a 'time hole' and find themselves in a parallel world where amazing and fantastic things happen. Can they survive – and will they ever return to their old lives?
2. **Something** Something is 'out there'. Waiting. Watching. Looking for you! VERY scary!
3. **Lola and the Detective Agency** When Lola and her friends find out about a crime, nobody believes them. They have to set up their own detective agency to catch the criminals. Lots of action right up to the last page!

Non-fiction

4. **Voices from the Fields** Fascinating interviews with migrant workers from Mexico who talk about their lives in the fields of California where they pick fruit.
5. **Strategies for Teens** Being a teenager is not always easy but this book is full of great advice about families, boy/girlfriends and many other aspects of teen life.
6. **The Journey West** The book uses diaries, letters and old photos to tell the fascinating story of the long journeys to the West in America's history.
7. **Babe** Babe Ruth was probably the greatest baseball player who has ever lived. This biography tells the true story of his life. Wonderful descriptions of exciting games!

3 MEDIATION A note to your friend

Your American friend is staying with you in Germany at the moment. Your friend would like to know about some interesting things to do. Read the brochure below and write a short note in English to your friend. Give the main points about the tours. Use the example on the right to help you.

Hi!
Hope you slept well. You wanted to know about some interesting things to do while I'm at school. I found out about some guided cycle tours that sound great. Here are the main points:
–
–

Erleben Sie die Stadt per Rad

Fahrrad-Stadtrundfahrten

Fahrrad-Rundfahrten durch die Stadt – für Gruppen von 10–15 Personen – begleitet von erfahrenen Stadtführern

Sehen Sie unsere Stadt und ihre Attraktionen vom Fahrrad aus. Wir machen Halt an interessanten Punkten. Dort werden Sie Informationen über die Geschichte der Stadt und touristische Highlights erhalten.

Dauer
Unsere abwechslungsreiche Tour führt durchs Stadtzentrum und verschiedene Stadtteile und dauert ca. 120 Minuten, in denen wir etwa 12 km zurücklegen.

Abfahrt
März–September
täglich 10:00 und 14:00 Uhr.

Treffpunkt ist vor dem Informationszentrum neben der Liebfrauenkirche im Stadtzentrum (bei schlechtem Wetter im Informationszentrum).

Preise
€ 29,– pro Person inkl. Fahrradmiete
(bei angemeldeten Gruppen mit mehr als 25 Teilnehmern € 22,50 pro Person)

4 SPEAKING Talking about a picture

a) *Look at the two photographs. Compare and contrast them.*
– What is similar?
– What is different?
– Which situation would you prefer and why?

b) *Talk about your sports activities (what, when, where, how often, why …)*

5 SPEAKING Planning a visit to the cinema

You and your friend want to go to the cinema together. Discuss what films are on and agree on which you want to see.

These ideas may help you:
– What kind of films are there?
– What may each film be about?
– Ticket price?
– Day/time?
– Personal preferences? Why? …

Mon -- Tue -- Thu
6 pm -- 8:30 pm
£ 7.50

Monday till Friday
6 pm -- 8:30 pm
£ 7.00

Tue -- Sat
6 pm -- 10:30 pm
£ 9.50

Tue -- Wed -- Fri
7 pm -- 9:30 pm
£ 7.50

Saturday and Sunday
3:30 pm -- 6 pm-- 8:45 pm **£ 6.50**

Self-evaluation

Check your answers to tasks 1 and 3 on page 263.

About the test

This second test gave you the chance again to try some of the kinds of tasks that you will do one day in your exam. This time, the tasks tested your reading, mediation and speaking skills. If you found some tasks difficult, don't worry. You've got lots of time to practise. Remember: 'Practice makes perfect!'

Reading

Task 1 and task 3 in the test were reading tasks. The following three questions will help you to think about how you did. Read the questions – which answer is right for you?

1 How hard or easy was each task?

	easy	OK	quite hard	very hard
Task 1				
Task 3				

1 What was difficult in the tasks?

a) The texts were quite long and complicated.
b) There were words and phrases that I just couldn't understand.
c) There was a lot of information. I couldn't find the exact answers.
d) The tasks weren't like the tasks that we do in class.

1 How did you do the tasks?

a) I always read the questions carefully so that I knew what to look for in the texts.
b) I tried to understand the main ideas of the text first. That helped me to guess words that I wasn't sure about.
c) If there was a question that I wasn't sure about, I left it out and came back to it later.
d) I scanned the text when I looked for a special piece of information.
e) I checked my answers at the end to make sure I hadn't made a 'silly'mistake.

Speaking

1 Copy and fill in the assessment sheet[1] below about your partner's presentation in the fourth task (Talking about a picture).

Assessment sheet	☹		☺︎		☺	
Name of partner ...	1	2	3	4	5	Comments
Did your partner ... 1 ... speak clearly and loudly enough?						
2 ... find enough to say?						
3 ... answer all the questions?						
4 ... have problems finding the right words?						
5 ... make grammar or vocabulary mistakes?						

2 Now look at the checklist on the right and talk about how well you did in the fifth task, the dialogue about your hobbies and interests.

– We listened to each other.
– We only gave short answers.
– We showed interest in each other.
– There was a good flow to our dialogue.[2]

► *SF Speaking Course (pp. 142–143)*

[1] assessment sheet *Beurteilungsbogen* [2] There was a good flow to our dialogue. *Unser Gespräch verlief flüssig.*

Unit 4 Teen world

Whiteboard Beamer

A

B

C

D

E

1 Teenagers 🎧 2.02–2.10

L S R W

a) *Look at the pictures for a few minutes. Then choose one for each of the topics in the list below. Note down your reasons for your choices.*

TEENAGERS HELP OUT
TEENAGERS IN LOVE
TEENAGERS IN TOUCH
TEENAGERS IN TROUBLE

b) *Discuss your choices in a group. Can you agree on the best picture for each topic? Which of the pictures could be from the area you live in?*

c) *Listen and match the extracts (1–9) to the pictures (A–I).*

2 Stories

L S R W

a) *Write a story of 50–100 words from the point of view of one of the people in the pictures. You might want to listen again before you begin. The story could take place before or after what you hear.*

b) **Extra** *Read your story to your group and listen to theirs. Can the listeners say which picture the story is linked with? You can put your story in your DOSSIER.*

▸ *WB 1 (p. 44)*

MOBILE LIFE AND LOVE

1 Mobile behaviour

Teen connection – the online mag that keeps teenagers in touch

Home | MOBILE LIFE | COMPETITION TIME | DOWNLOADS | CONTACT

Thanks to everyone who texted us their answers to our MOBILE LIFE questionnaire. Here are the results:

1. Is it OK to send a text message while you're talking to somebody?
   sure! 43 % no way! 51 % °dunno. 6 %
2. Is it OK to talk on a mobile in a café or restaurant?
   sure! 74 % no way! 19 % dunno. 7 %
3. Is it OK to send or receive text messages during lessons at school?
   sure! 50 % no way! 42 % dunno. 8 %
4. Would you secretly film someone or take a photo of them with your mobile?
   sure! 14 % no way! 71 % dunno. 15 %
5. Would you let your parents look at the texts and pictures on your mobile?
   sure! 20 % no way! 68 % dunno. 12 %
6. Is it a good idea to ask someone out on a date by text message?
   sure! 55 % no way! 32 % dunno. 13 %
7. Would you end a relationship by text message?
   sure! 42 % no way! 42 % dunno. 16 %
8. Do you feel unwanted if a whole day goes by and your mobile phone doesn't ring?
   sure! 34 % no way! 46 % dunno. 20 %

We had so many comments in our questionnaire forum on the role mobiles and °social networking sites play in relationships. Here are some highlights. Click here to see all the forum comments. (We're closing the forum next week, so send your comment soon!)

Facebook is a WEBSITE. It's NOT the REAL WORLD. Stop freaking out about it. Then one day you'll have a REAL relationship in REAL LIFE! *coolconcrete*

Sometimes I wish I didn't have a mobile. My boyfriend is always texting and phoning me. He's °like, 'Where are you? Who are you with?'. I never have any time for myself. That's °well out of order. *goodgirl*

My girlfriend has just chucked me. Did she tell me in person? Or phone me? Or even text me? No way! When I checked her Facebook status it said, 'Relationship: Single'. °That sucks! *jayjay95*

I have NEVER changed my Facebook status – it has always been single, even when I had a girlfriend. I think it's better this way, until you are VERY serious, because people talk and it can ruin your chances with other girls, °innit? *jonny-b-good*

My boyfriend cheated on me °big time. The other girl looked up his Facebook status. It said I was his 'official' Facebook girlfriend, and so she contacted me. We're going to °make his life hell. *cute_as_keira*

a) *Note down your own answers to the Teen Connection questionnaire on a piece of paper. At the top just write BOY or GIRL, not your name.*

b) *With a partner, compare all your answers.*

A: How did you answer question 1/2/...? I ...
B: Oh, I had the same answer as you. / My answer was different. I ...
A: I think it's OK to ... I've done it once/a few times/often. What about you?
B: I agree/don't agree. I've never ...

c) **Extra** *Do a survey on the class's answers. How does your class compare with the readers of* Teen Connection? *Is there a difference between boys and girls?*

d) *Read the forum comments and say who*

1 has contacted her boyfriend's other girlfriend,
2 has just found out his girlfriend has ended their relationship,
3 is worried her boyfriend is behaving like a spy,
4 thinks giving your relationship status on a social networking site is stupid,
5 wants to stay open for new relationships.

e) *Choose one of the forum comments and write your own reaction to it. Give your opinion on it: do you agree or disagree with it? Do you understand the writer? Do you feel sorry for them or angry about them?*

2 Teenage language

a) *There are some informal words and expressions used mainly by teenagers. In each sentence find an example of teenage language and give the adult version of the sentence.*

1 *This new computer game is just awesome.*
This new computer game is excellent.
2 You should chill out and not worry so much.
3 My girlfriend's always texting me, innit?
4 No, we didn't win – we lost big time.
5 I hate that movie – it sucks.
6 Just don't freak out – everything's OK.
7 My dad was like, 'Turn that music down!'

b) *Think of four teenage expressions in German. How would you explain them to an English-speaking teenager?*

3 Extra Text message love

HOME
MOBILE LIFE | COMPETITION TIME | DOWNLOADS | CONTACT

Where would our relationships and °friendships be without text messages? We use them for °arranging dates, keeping in touch, spreading the latest °gossip. But how about really showing how much you love someone? Send us your text message love poems and we'll publish the best ones. Like this one by *Julia Bird*.

14: a txt msg pom.
his is r bunsn brnr bl%,
his hair lyk fe filings
W/ac/dc going thru.
I sit by him in kemistry,
it splits my @oms
wen he :-)s @ me.

a) *List the ways the magazine says text messages play a role in relationships and friendships. In what other ways do text messages play a role in your social life? Add to the list.*

b) *Write your own text message poem.*

Translation:
14: a text message poem
his eyes are °bunsen burner blue,
his hair like °iron filings
with °ac/dc going through.
I sit °by him in chemistry,
it °splits my °atoms
when he smiles at me

► **Text File 8** *(pp. 112–113)* • *WB 2 (p. 44)*

Web-Code:
EG21-A5-A-081

P1 STUDY SKILLS Argumentative writing

a) Structuring your text

Imagine you have to discuss the topic 'Students should not be allowed to take mobiles to school' in a written English test. Brainstorm your ideas. Then use an outline to order your text.

"Yes, Jason, you may go to the °lavatory, but next time just °raise your hand."

Your outline should include
– arguments for and against,
– examples, support for the arguments, perhaps including statistics,
– your personal opinion.

► *SF Outlining (p. 129)*

STUDY SKILLS Argumentative writing

An outline can help you to structure your text before you start writing.

1 Introduction
2 First point of view
  2.1 First argument
  2.2 Second argument
  2.3 ...
3 Opposite point of view
  3.1 First argument
  3.2 ...
4 Conclusion
  4.1 Summing up
  4.2 Personal opinion

► *SF Argumentative writing (p. 147)*

b) Presenting the arguments

1 Introduction
First introduce the topic. Start with a personal experience or a general question.

2 The first point of view
Present one point of view. It's often better to start with the view you disagree with. Explain the arguments and give examples to support them.

3 The opposite point of view
Then present the arguments for the other point of view. Begin this part with a sentence that links it to the first point of view.

4 Conclusion
Sum up with your own point of view. Don't present new arguments.

Which other arguments and examples could you add? Where?

MOBILE PHONES AT SCHOOL

Nearly all students have mobiles. But should they be allowed to take them to school?

Some people say that students really need their mobiles at school. They might have to call their parents after school, for example when they miss the bus. Or parents might want to contact their children because ...

However, other people disagree. One common reason is because they think students might use them to get help from outside with a test. Another argument against mobiles is ...

After looking at both sides, I think there are more disadvantages than advantages for having mobiles at school. That's why they should not be allowed there. In my opinion, it's just unfair when some students use them to do better in a test. That has happened at my school. °Added to that ...

c) *Discuss the following in writing:*
'Students should rate their schools on the internet.'
Brainstorm arguments first, then outline your text. The phrases on the right and the text in b) might help.

► *WB 3 (p. 45)*

°Added to that • After looking at both sides • However • In my opinion • Other people disagree. • So ... • Some people say • That's why ... • To sum up, ...

P2 REVISION Is he cheating on me? (Indirect speech)

a) *Last week Keira and Zoe sent some text messages. What did they say? Use reporting verbs (ask, want to know, say, tell, reply, …) in the simple past, and remember the tense change.*

1. RU Luke's girlfriend? — *Zoe asked if Keira was Luke's girlfriend.*
2. Yes, I am. — *Keira said she …*
3. I'm Zoe. I went to a gig with Luke last weekend. Sorry, but I didn't know about U. — *Zoe told Keira she … to a gig …*
4. I can't stop him doing what he wants. Is he cheating on me?
5. He tried hard to get friendly with me.
6. How did U find out about me?
7. UR his girlfriend on Facebook.
8. I won't be much longer. I'm going to make his life hell.
9. Good idea. Hope I can help.

b) *Think of an interesting conversation you've had by text message recently, perhaps with a friend or someone in your family. Tell your partner what was said.*

► *GF 7: Indirect speech (pp. 170–171)*

P3 EVERYDAY ENGLISH Role play: Asking someone out

Partner B: Go to page 100.
Partner A: You want to ask Partner B out on a date. You'd like to go to the cinema and then to a party at a friend's house. You have never talked much to each other before and you are unsure about your partner's feelings. Try to persuade him/her to go out with you. Be as nice as you can. The words and phrases in the box will help you to get the conversation started and to say something nice.

Hey, <name>, I was wondering … • How about … • Have you seen … • I'd like to ask … • Have you got any plans for … • Guess what, … • Would you like to … • Let's go … • It's going to be a really fun party. • You'll love it. • There's a really good film on at … • Or we could go to … • It would be so cool if you … • I don't fancy going with anyone else … • I'll come and pick you up. • I'll take you home. • We'll °have a really great time, I promise.

► *WB 4–5 (pp. 45–46)*

TEENS IN TROUBLE

1 'ASBO has helped me'

L S R W

a) *Look at the photo below on the right and skim the article in 45 seconds. Explain to your partner what you think it is about. Do they agree?*

'°ASBO[1)] has helped me'

[1] ['æzbəʊ]

By Jeremy Armstrong

Shane Preston, from Darlington in the north-east of England, was a trouble-maker who kicked footballs against his neighbours' houses and cars, caused trouble at school, rode motorbikes on pavements and attacked other teenagers. Then the courts °hit him with a four-year anti-social behaviour order (ASBO).

Box: Voc., S.207

At just 14 he was banned from some areas of his hometown. He was not supposed to leave home between 9 pm and 7 am, and the police sent photos of him to hundreds of houses in the area.

It was tough – but the surprising thing is that it has worked. Now 17, Shane has volunteered with the YMCA and helped to build a children's °play area. He has also started training as a builder and hopes he can get a job when his training course finishes. 'I thought I'd better try to do something useful.'

Shane believes the ASBO has helped him to straighten up his life. 'If they hadn't given me an ASBO, soon I'd have found myself in even more trouble. I've had to change my behaviour. I've grown up, I think. It was embarrassing when pictures of me appeared around town. I used to hang out with other kids in front of the shops. But I've got different friends now. And in the end it's got nothing to do with others, it's up to me.'

Young Brits on their way to an ASBO?

ASBOs: What for?
ASBOs can be given to punish behaviour like
- spraying/writing graffiti
- using racist language
- making too much noise late at night
- being drunk in the streets
- smoking or drinking under age
- °dealing drugs
- violence
- vandalism

Every year thousands of people are given an ASBO. But many people think they don't work.

ASBOs: What happens?
Anti-social behaviour orders are given by courts. An ASBO tells you what you are not allowed to do, like
- go out at night
- go to particular places in your area
- go into particular shops, bars or cinemas
- carry particular things with you, like spray cans or alcohol
- meet more than one or two other people in public

If you break your ASBO, you can go to prison.

b) *Read the article again and say*
- *what Shane did wrong and how he was punished*
- *why Shane thinks the ASBO was good for him*
- *how his life has changed since he got the ASBO*
- *what Shane thought was the worst thing about the ASBO.*

► **Text File 9** *(pp. 114–119)* • **Text File 10** *(pp. 120–122)*

L S R W

2 Now you

a) *What kind of anti-social behaviour happens where you live? Look at the list under 'ASBOs: What for?' in the article for ideas.*

b) *What happens in your area/school to teenagers who cause trouble? Contrast this with the punishments listed in 'ASBOs: What happens?'.*

c) *Do you think ASBOs would be a good idea in your city/area? Why? Why not?*

3 Teenagers on the streets

L S R W

a) *Brainstorm arguments for and against:*
'15-year-olds should not be on the streets between 9 pm and 6 am.'
Note down your ideas on cards.

b) *Arrange your class for a* ***fishbowl discussion****. Four students sit on chairs in the middle and discuss the pros and cons of the statement. When other students want to take part, they stand behind the chair of a person they support and give their own opinion, agree, disagree, ask a question, etc.*

4 VIEWING High school boot camp

V S R W

High school boot camp is a film about the 'Eagle °Academy', a military-style school in Florida. Teenagers in trouble volunteer to go there for six months – no one makes them go. Here is what one of them, Dave Murray, said before he went to the camp:

> Right now I'm °screwing up, erm, °not listening to no one. What I expect to get out of this camp is to get bigger, stronger and straighten up my life.

a) *What do you think might happen at a boot camp? Collect ideas in a group.*

b) *Watch Part 1 of the DVD about the teenagers' first day at the camp. How do you feel about what happens there? Is it different from what you expected?*
– It's really shocking/funny/stupid/scary/...
– I think the boys were really scared/shocked/ ...
– The °drill instructors are loud/crazy/scary/...
– ...

c) *Watch Part 1 again. Take notes on as many things that happen as you can. Collect your notes in your group.*
Everyone chooses one thing from the notes and explains why they think it happens.

d) *Watch Part 2 of the DVD about the teenagers' last day at the camp. Do they feel good or bad about their time there? Give as many of their reasons as you can.*

e) *Look back at what Dave Murray said before he went to the boot camp. Do you think boot camps really help people like him to straighten up? Give reasons. Here are some key phrases to help:*

discipline doesn't ... • obey rules • forget later • get fit • learn discipline • think for yourself

f) **Extra** *Hang two poster-size pieces of paper on the classroom wall. At the top of one write:*
We NEED boot camps in Germany because ...
At the top of the other write:
We DON'T NEED boot camps in Germany because ...
Each student then adds an opinion to one of the posters.

▸ *WB 6 (p. 46)*

Lektüre
Holes

P1 SPEAKING Boot camps (Having a discussion) 2.11

a) Collect as many arguments for and against boot camps as you can. (Look back at your work from page 85.)

FOR	AGAINST
– boot camps help people to learn discipline	– kids soon forget about the boot camp and get in trouble again
– ...	– ...

b) Match the phrases in the box to the steps of a discussion that are shown on the right.

... because ... • Could you say that again? • First, .../Second, ... • For example ... • I agree (with you). • I don't think you can say ... • I see what you mean but ... • I think/I feel ... • In my opinion ... • No, that's not right. • Sorry, I don't agree with you. • Sorry, but I don't understand what you mean. • That's a good point. • That's why ... • Yes/Yeah, but ... • You're right.

Remember

Try to be polite in a discussion. Don't interrupt other speakers unless they will not let you speak. Then interrupt politely: 'Excuse me, but could I say something?' 'Could I just interrupt for a moment, please?'

c) Listen to a discussion about boot camps. Which of the phrases from b) can you hear?

d) **Extra** *Use your arguments from a) and the phrases from b) to continue the discussion you've just heard. Make sure at least one of you argues FOR and one AGAINST.*

e) In your group, choose one of the statements on the right as a topic for a discussion. Decide alone what your point of view is, think of arguments to support your point of view and note them down. Then have a short discussion on the topic.

Steps of a discussion

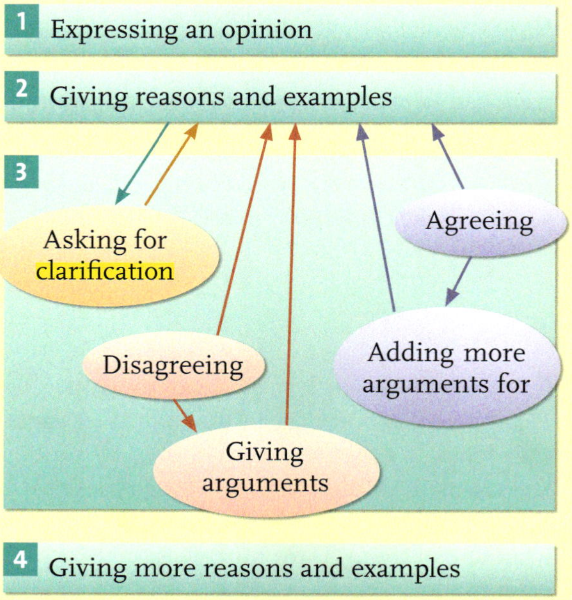

– 'We should ban violent computer games.'
– 'Teenagers should not be allowed to drive a car.'

► SF Speaking Course (pp. 142–143) • WB 7 (p. 47)

P2 REVISION ASBOs (Conditional sentences)

a) *Write the sentences on the left using long forms. Say which sentence on the right comes next.*

If you carry a knife, they'll arrest you.
If you carried a knife, they'd arrest you.
If you'd carried a knife, they'd have arrested you.

So I'm glad you didn't have one.
So please don't take it with you.
So I'm glad you haven't got one.

b) *Complete the following sentences with the correct form of the verb.*

1 If someone *sprays* (spray) graffiti, they can be given an ASBO.
2 Shane wouldn't have received an ASBO if he ... (not cause) trouble.
3 If he ... (break) his ASBO now, he would be in big trouble.
4 He ... (have) a better chance of getting a job if he gets a qualification.
5 If Shane had kept his old friends, he probably ... (not be) able to straighten up his life.
6 ... (there/be) less crime in Germany if there was a similar system?

► *GF 5: Conditional sentences (pp. 167–168)*

P3 REVISION Road signs (Modal verbs)

What do these British road signs mean? Complete the explanations. Use **can**, **be allowed to**, **have to**, **must**, **should** *and* **might**. *There may be more than one possible answer.*

1 You can't go at more than 50 mph. *2 You ... here.* *3 You ...* *4 ... less ...* *5 ... careful ...* *6 You ...*

1 Speed limit

2 Parking

3 No stopping

4 Minimum speed

5 Wild animals

6 Turn left

► *GF 4: Models and their substitutes (pp. 164–166)*

P4 °Curfew (should, had better and be supposed to)

The underlined words and phrases can all be translated by the German 'sollen':

You should work hard at school. (the right thing to do)
We'd (= we had) better call a doctor. (the best thing to do in a situation)
You're supposed to wait in the queue. (what you are expected to do, what the rule is)
This computer game is supposed to be good. (what people say)

a) *Complete the dialogue about a curfew (a time when people are not allowed to be on the streets). Put in* **should(n't)**, **had better (not)** *or* **be (not) supposed to**. *There may be more than one possible answer.*

Oliver What time should we meet tonight?
Kirsty Eight o'clock?
Oliver Don't forget there's a curfew. Teenagers ... be out after nine. We ... be late.
Kirsty Nine o'clock! That's crazy! We haven't done anything wrong, so we ... be punished.
Oliver The curfew ... keep us safe. That's what they say, anyway.
Kirsty They ... punish the people who cause the trouble.
Oliver Sure. But I don't want to get an ASBO for just walking along the street. We ... meet at seven and then come back early.

b) *Do you think such a curfew is a good idea? Is it fair? Discuss in groups.*

► *WB 8–9 (p. 48)*

GET INVOLVED

1 Club blogs

L S R W

Volunteer °Manatee

ABOUT US | PRODUCTS & SERVICES | PARTNERS | NEWS

PROGRAMS

ManaTEEN Projects

The ManaTEEN Club in Florida is one of the nation's largest teen volunteer programs with over 10,000 teen members. They do more than 1.7 million hours of volunteer work a year.

Springs °Clean-up

I recently went to the ManaTEEN °SOS project at Weeki Wachee Springs. What an experience it was!
Along with some of my ManaTEEN friends, I explored the °freshwater springs of Weeki Wachee. As we are trained divers, they let us °snorkel through the °crystal-clear water, collecting trash on our way. Although the water was clear, you had to swim along the bottom and look closely to find things like bottle caps, glass and plastic. I was shocked when I pulled up a huge piece of clear glass that was hard to see. °It could have easily cut someone's foot!
After a while, they made us have a break to get some rest and pizza. Then we all jumped back in the water to continue our search for trash. Afterwards it looked a lot cleaner down there. I also saw lots of fish and even happened to meet a turtle! This was by far my favorite ManaTEEN Club project! – *Patrick*

YOUTUBE | BLOG | GALLERY | SCHOLARSHIPS | CONTACT US

hickoryrecord.com

Powered by: Hickory Daily Record — FOR YOU. ABOUT YOU. EVERY DAY. 24 HOURS A DAY.

••• Hickory Soup Kitchen

This summer we haven't spent our time hanging out by the pool: we've been raising money for the Hickory Soup Kitchen, so others would have something to eat.

We both like helping and were hoping to get more involved. We announced what we were doing at our church and lots of people have donated. During vacation Bible school, all the kids had a competition to see who could bring in the most money, so a lot of coins and dollar bills have been donated. Box: Voc., S.209

Altogether we've raised $427 and collected 400 pounds of food for the hungry, which we gave to the soup kitchen as we received it. Then we went to the store today and bought 45 pounds of beef, 36 cans of green beans and 30 bottles of ketchup. We're having the food delivered to the soup kitchen tomorrow. – *Alex & Andrew*

a) *Describe what kind of community service the American students did.*
Find reasons they give for their volunteering. Why do they think it's a good idea?

b) *Can you name any organizations in your area that help to clean up the environment or give food to people in need?*

2 Community service, US-style

L S R W

Volunteering for community service is an important tradition in the US, where the state sometimes does not provide enough social services. Many young people get involved because they want to – but others do community service because their schools, churches or parents make them. They think it will be good for the young people, as this website shows:

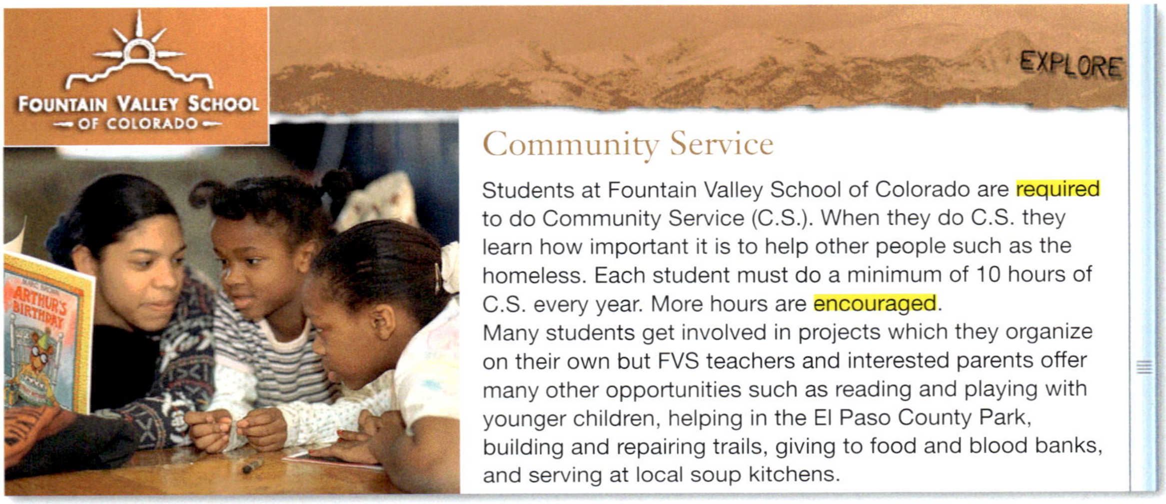
FOUNTAIN VALLEY SCHOOL OF COLORADO

EXPLORE

Community Service

Students at Fountain Valley School of Colorado are required to do Community Service (C.S.). When they do C.S. they learn how important it is to help other people such as the homeless. Each student must do a minimum of 10 hours of C.S. every year. More hours are encouraged.
Many students get involved in projects which they organize on their own but FVS teachers and interested parents offer many other opportunities such as reading and playing with younger children, helping in the El Paso County Park, building and repairing trails, giving to food and blood banks, and serving at local soup kitchens.

a) *Describe the system of community service at Fountain Valley School.*

b) *Students at FVS* have to *volunteer and do community service. Can it really be called volunteering if your school makes you do it?*

c) *Do you think it would be a good idea to have this system at your school? Why or why not?*

d) **Extra** *Who do you know who needs help from people doing community service? Say who helps them, how, and why.*

3 Now you

L S R W

a) *Have you ever volunteered for community service? What did you do and why? If you haven't volunteered, explain which sort of community service you would/wouldn't like doing.*

b) *What kind of service would help your town/area most? Use a* ***placemat*** *to find the best ideas in your group. Explain how you could help.*

P1 Look it up

a) *Look at these two sentences from the Hickory Soup Kitchen website.*

With the present state of the economy, the soup kitchen is serving 50 per cent more °clients than in the past. Donations are needed more now than ever; please consider helping out the soup kitchen while our budget is so stretched.

You want to check the meaning of the word donation. *Compare these entries from three types of dictionary and then answer the questions.*

English–English

do·na·tion [dəʊ'neɪʃn] *noun*

1 <C> goods or money given to someone or an organization who do charity work: *The company has promised to make a donation of €10 000 to the orphanage. – Our club received a handsome/substantial donation for renovating the grandstand.*

2 <C, U> **MED** giving blood or parts of the body to persons who need it: *a blood donation*

English–German

do·na·tion [dəʊ'neɪʃn] *Substantiv*

1 *von Geld usw.* Spende: ***He made a donation of €100.*** Er spendete 100 Euro.

2 MED *von Blut, Organen* Spende: **blood donation** Blutspende

°Thesaurus (dictionary of synonyms)

donation CLASS: GIVE, PRESENT – aid, alms, benefaction, charity, community service, endowment, gift aid, sponsoring

1. Which type of dictionary would you use to find out the meaning quickly?
2. Which type has a list of words with similar meanings?
3. Which shows other words that often go together with *donation*?
4. Which shows you what prepositions to use with *donation*?
5. Are there any advantages in reading a definition in English?

b) *Find out the information and say what type of dictionary you need.*

1. What does *economy* mean?
2. Look up *state* and find two phrases in the dictionary with *state of ...*
3. How would you translate *is serving*?
4. What verb + preposition could you use instead of *consider*?
5. Explain in English the meaning of *budget*.

STUDY SKILLS Online dictionaries

If you are working on your computer and do not have a printed dictionary at hand, you can use an online dictionary instead. However, printed dictionaries are usually more reliable.
There are both bilingual and monolingual online dictionaries. Don't forget to look carefully at the entries to make sure you get the right meaning.

► *SF Using a bilingual dictionary (p. 124)* •
SF Using an English–English dictionary (p. 125) •
SF Using a thesaurus (p. 125)

P 2 Charity work (the + adjective)

You can use ***the + adjective*** *to talk about whole groups of people:*
The old have more experience than the young.

But when you talk about one person or about a few people, you use ***woman, man, people****, etc.:*
The old man from upstairs is in hospital.
There was **an old woman** at the bus stop.
Some old people were sitting round a table.

Replace the underlined words with a phrase like ***the old, some old people, an old man/woman****.*
Use ***blind, disabled, homeless, hungry****.*

1 Some students are collecting money for people who have no home.
2 Outside the soup kitchen some people wanting a meal were already waiting.
3 Our class is helping to raise money for people who can't see very well.
4 We had a meeting with some people in wheelchairs to discuss their problems.
5 The money raised will go to feed people who don't have enough to eat.
6 Two people with nowhere to live were helped to find a place to go.
7 Some money was given to a man who cannot see who had been robbed.
8 We plan to make the building easier for people in wheelchairs to visit.

P 3 REVISION Beach °clean-up (Adverbs or adjectives after certain verbs)

Compare these sentences:
The beach looked **dirty**.
We looked **carefully** at our instructions.

Which is the adjective, which the adverb? Translate the two sentences into German. In which sentence does ***looked*** *express an activity, and where does it express a state?*

Choose the correct form:
Yesterday my friends and I did a beach clean-up. It doesn't sound very (exciting/-ly) *exciting*, I know, but it was fun doing it together. We wore gloves to pick up the trash. We moved (slow/-ly) along the beach putting it in our bags. You had to look (careful/-ly) because there were things hidden in the sand. I even found some pieces of glass that could (easy/-ily) have cut someone's foot. It's (crazy/-ily) to leave all this trash. People just don't behave (responsible/-bly). When we'd finished, my bag felt very (heavy/-ily). And the beach looked (clean/-ly) at last. We were getting (hungry/-ily) by then, so we went to have a hamburger.

P 4 Facebook (English verbs instead of German adverbs)

a) *Sometimes a verb is used in English where German has an adverb. Help a friend to translate these sentences for their Facebook page. Use an English verb to express the meaning of the underlined adverbs.*

1 Anscheinend sind alle meine Freunde bei Facebook.
All my friends seem to be on Facebook.
2 Englisch ist vermutlich die am meisten benutzte Sprache im Internet.
3 Unsere Familie hat früher auf dem Land gewohnt.
4 Zufällig wohnen wir jetzt in der Nähe eines Schwimmbads.
5 Hoffentlich schwimme ich eines Tages bei den Olympischen Spielen.
6 Ich fahre auch gern Rad, aber ich skate sehr ungern – ich falle immer wieder hin.

b) *Write sentences for your Facebook page.*
1 I like ... 2 I hate ... 3 I used to ... 4 I hope ...

► WB 10–12 (p. 49)

P 5 Jobs and privileges (let/make somebody do something)

The verbs *let* and *make* can be followed by an object + infinitive without to.
Compare:

They	let	us	have a break.	[jemandem erlauben, etwas zu tun]
	let +	object +	infinitive without to	
They	made	us	have a break.	[jemanden zwingen/veranlassen, etwas zu tun]
	make +	object +	infinitive without to	

a) *Teenagers have jobs and privileges at home. One of you is Jessica, the other Jacob. What can you tell each other about your home life? Use let or make + object + infinitive. Example:*
Clean the bathroom/twice a week. *My parents make me clean the bathroom twice a week.*

Jessica
- feed the cat / every day
- watch TV / two hours a day
- talk to my grandmother / once a month
- write Christmas cards / every year
- tidy up my room / every Saturday
- do a paper round to earn some money / every week
- talk to my friends on my mobile / every day

Jacob
- walk the dog / twice a day
- play computer games / one hour every day
- eat pizza / once a month
- watch the Champions League / whenever it's on
- ride my bike to school / every day
- study hard for school / every day
- look after my little brother / at the weekends

b) **Extra** *Who do you think has life easier at home – Jacob or Jessica? Discuss with a partner.*

c) *Tell your partner about your jobs and privileges at home.*

P 6 Why do it yourself? (have something done)

Have + object + past participle shows that someone is doing something for us and that we're not doing it ourselves. Compare:
We delivered the food to the soup kitchen. [We did it ourselves.]
We had the food delivered to the soup kitchen. [We arranged for someone else to do it for us.]

Look at the pictures. Did the people do it themselves or have it done?
The woman repaired her moped herself, but the man ...

▸ WB 13–14 (p. 50)

P7 READING Soup kitchen (Understanding adverts)

a) *Which advert attracts your attention more? Try to say why.*

b) *What are the adverts trying to make you do?*

c) *Describe one of the adverts to your partner and listen to their description of the other.*

d) *Describe the differences between the adverts. How do they get across their message? Explain how language, layout, colour, illustration, etc. play a part.*

P8 MEDIATION Volunteering in Germany

*You're thinking of doing community service for a year (*Freiwilliges Soziales Jahr*). You've found some information online. Explain in an e-mail to an American friend*

– what sort of jobs you can do,
– where you can do your community service,
– how it will help you in the future.

Ein Beitrag für sich und die Gesellschaft

Aus freien Stücken anderen helfen. Behinderte Menschen im Alltag unterstützen. Im Naturschutzpark Nistkästen anbringen und Fußwege sauberhalten. Im Jugendklub eine Disco organisieren oder einen Musik-Workshop vorbereiten. Mit alten Menschen mal einen Spaziergang unternehmen. In Russland in einem Kinderheim arbeiten. Im Sportverein Kids das Dribbeln beibringen. Sportspiele im Schulhort organisieren. Oder auf der Open-Air-Bühne mit Kindern Griffe auf der Rockgitarre üben – das und vieles mehr ist möglich im Freiwilligen Sozialen Jahr (FSJ) – oder im Freiwilligen Ökologischen Jahr (FÖJ). Dem freiwilligen Engagement sind keine Grenzen gesetzt und auch im Ausland gibt es zahlreiche Möglichkeiten.

Wer sich dafür entscheidet, zwischen Schule und Ausbildung einen Freiwilligendienst zu absolvieren, bekommt oft mehr als nur eine berufliche Orientierung. Erste Fachkenntnisse und die erworbenen sozialen Kompetenzen machen junge Menschen fit für den Berufseinstieg und erhöhen ihre Beschäftigungschancen. Zugleich tut es gut, sich für andere einzusetzen und Verantwortung zu übernehmen. Manch einer sammelt dabei die ersten Auslandserfahrungen. Von dem Engagement profitieren also beide Seiten: die jungen Freiwilligen und die Gesellschaft.

Quelle: Bundesministerium für Familie, Senioren, Frauen und Jugend

▸ WB 15 (p. 51)

The caller

by Robert D. San Souci (abridged and adapted) 2.12–2.18

What would happen if you lost your mobile phone? Or if it was stolen? Think about what would happen. Then look at the pictures in the following story. Who do you think 'the caller' in the story might be? Some new words are translated in the footnotes at the bottom of each page.

2.12 It was hot at Aunt Margaret's funeral. Lindsay Walters had to stand in the hot sun, sweating in her ugly[1], black dress, while the minister prayed.

Lindsay was angry because she should be at Missy's, helping her best friend get ready for a party.

A cell phone rang. Lindsay knew from the ringtone that it was her father's. He went red in the face. At least she knew enough to turn hers off at a funeral. Her father pulled his phone out and shut off the signal but looked quickly at the caller's number. He checked his watch.

At the end of the funeral, Lindsay went behind a tree, took out her own cell phone, and dialed Missy's number. It was busy. Probably her friend was making plans with Noelle or Candice for the party. She made a face at the phone, turned, and bumped into[2] her father, who was talking into his phone.

She went back to her mother, who introduced her to some boring old ladies[3]. She had to nod and look sad as they talked about her aunt. When her father returned, Lindsay asked, "Can we go now?"

"I just have to make one more call," her father said. He moved off again.

When the last old lady and the minister had gone, Lindsay said to her mother, "Please, please, please make Daddy get off the phone so we can go!"

"Stop whining[4]," her mother said. But she waved impatiently[5] at Lindsay's father. She ordered Lindsay and her brothers, Darren and David, to the car, then marched over to where Mr. Walters was still talking on the phone. She made him end his call. Now both of them were angry. Mr. Walters put his cell phone into his coat[6] pocket. "All right, let's get this show on the road[7]," he said.

2.13 Some people from the funeral had stopped by the house. Lindsay's sad-looking parents and their guests drank coffee and talked about how nice Aunt Margaret had been.

"As long as you didn't make her angry," said Mr. Walters with a laugh. "I remember as a kid she could be terrible if she thought someone had been rude or was lying[8] or cruel." Lindsay knew what he was talking about. Lindsay thought of her aunt in heaven, terrorizing the angels for not being holy[9] enough.

But the guests finally left. Lindsay ran to her room to change so that her father could drive her to Missy's party. When she was ready she took out Aunt Margaret's gold ring with real diamonds[10]. She had always loved it, and Aunt Margaret had promised it to her just before she died. Her mother told her to only wear the ring at special times. Well, showing off to Missy and Noelle and Candice and the others was special!

Her cell phone rang.

There was some strange static, then a lot of whispering, sounding like a crowd. Finally a tired, dry, old voice said, "Lindsay, darling[11], this is Aunt Margaret."

"Right! Nice try, Missy, guys – see you in a few minutes." Lindsay hung up and put her phone into her party bag. Putting her ring in her jeans pocket so her parents wouldn't see, she ran down the stairs two at a time.

"Where's Dad? He's supposed to drive me to Missy's."

"He's in the car looking for his cell phone," her mother said. "It fell out of his pocket."

Lindsay helped her father search[12] the car, but the phone was gone. He was in a bad mood[13]. She was glad she was spending the night at Missy's after the party.

2.14 At Missy's party, all the girls were jealous of the real diamonds on Lindsay's finger. She forgot about their phone joke.

---

[1] ugly ['ʌgli] *hässlich* [2] (to) bump into sb. *jn. anstoßen* [3] lady *Dame* [4] (to) whine [waɪn] *quengeln* [5] impatient [ɪm'peɪʃənt] *ungeduldig* [6] coat [kəʊt] (AE) *Jackett* [7] Let's get the show on the road. *(infml) Fangen wir an.* [8] (to) lie *lügen* [9] holy ['həʊli] *heilig* [10] diamond ['daɪəmənd] *Diamant* [11] darling ['dɑːlɪŋ] *Liebling* [12] (to) search sth. [sɜːtʃ] *etwas durchsuchen* [13] (to) be in a bad mood [muːd] *schlechte Laune haben*

"I hated to go to that smelly old folks' home," Lindsay told them. "I just pretended[14] I wanted to go, because I wanted this ring."

Her cell phone rang and she answered it.

Lots of static, more whispers, the same dry voice saying, "Lindsay, this is Aunt Margaret. I must talk to you."

Clearly it wasn't her friends trying to trick her. That meant it had to be Darren and David. She whispered to her friends, "It's my creepy[15] brothers pretending to be my aunt's ghost[16]." The others rolled their eyes.

"Is it *really* you, Aunt Margaret?" asked Lindsay, trying to sound little-girl scared.

"Yes. I just wanted to hear your voice again. You were my favorite. You loved me best."

Lindsay held up the ring as she talked. "Well, it was really your ring I loved. I hated going to that place where you stayed. And all that stuff you told me about when you were young was so boring. So thanks for the ring and goodbye, *Aunt Margaret!*" Lindsay ended the call.

She pushed *69 and saw that her brothers were calling from her father's cell phone.

"They're using my dad's phone that he lost. They must have found it in the car. They are going to get so *busted*[17] for this when I get home."

2.15 When the party ended and the other girls left after dinner, Missy's parents said they were going to visit neighbors. As soon as they were gone, the girls went upstairs to Missy's room to call their friends. Lying at opposite ends of Missy's bed, they chatted into their cell phones.

Lindsay was just going to dial her boyfriend of the week when her phone rang.

"Lindsay, I am very disappointed in you." The same voice. "I don't think you deserve my ring. I'm coming to get it back."

"Get real!" Lindsay ended the call. It had come from her father's cell phone. She dialed the number but the phone just rang and rang. She hung up and dialed her home. Her mother answered.

"Mom," she said, "Darren and David found Dad's phone. They've been using it to call and bug[18] me. They just did it again."

"That's not possible," said her mother. "They've been watching TV for the past hour. And your father is sure he dropped his phone at the funeral this afternoon." Now her mother sounded worried. "Perhaps it's a crank caller[19]."

"The calls are coming from Dad's cell phone," Lindsay explained. "But –"

2.16 There was some loud static. The phone went dead. Missy looked up as her phone went dead too. The lights in the house dimmed[20], then went out. "Blackout[21]," said Missy. All the other houses in the neighborhood were dark.

"I don't think that would shut off our phones," said Lindsay.

"Well, it did," said Missy. "Anyway[22], I was bored. This is cool. We can tell ghost stories."

"I don't want to," said Lindsay, wishing she were home and not in a house without lights.

"Chicken[23]!" her friend said.

There was a knock downstairs at the front door. Thump. Thump. Thump.

Missy got up to answer it.

"Don't!" cried Lindsay. She couldn't say why she was frightened, but she was.

"You are so stupid," said Missy. "My folks forgot their keys or something. Probably the doorbell doesn't work in the blackout."

"Please, don't go!"

---

[14] (to) pretend [prɪ'tend] *so tun, als ob* [15] creepy ['kri:pi] *nervig* [16] ghost [gəʊst] *Gespenst, Geist* [17] (to) bust sb. [bʌst] *(infml) etwa: jn. zur Schnecke machen* [18] (to) bug [bʌg] *nerven* [19] crank caller ['kræŋk ˌkɔ:lə] *jd., der andere anruft, um sie zu ärgern* [20] (to) dim [dɪm] *schwächer werden* [21] blackout ['blækaʊt] *Stromausfall* [22] Anyway, ... ['eniweɪ] *Aber egal, ... / Wie dem auch sei, ...* [23] chicken ['tʃɪkɪn] *(infml) Feigling*

"Stay here if you're so scared," said Missy, shaking her head. "What a wuss[24]!" She left.

2.17 Lindsay closed the bedroom door and locked it. She heard the front door open and close a moment later. She thought she heard a soft sound like something falling. Then quiet.

Her cell phone rang.

She grabbed it, hoping it was her mother.

"Lindsay, I've come for my ring, you unhappy child. I'm at the bottom of the stairs right now. Let's play that game I played when you were a little girl. The one your father told me not to play, because it frightened you so? But you loved it – you loved being scared. Don't you like being scared anymore?"

"Missy? Is this a trick? This isn't funny."

But Missy's phone was still on the bed where she had left it.

"One step, two – I'm coming for you," said the voice on the phone.

Thump, thump on the stairs.

"Three steps, four – better lock the door. Five steps, six – say your prayers quick."

2.18 If the phone was working, Lindsay thought, she could call for help. She hung up and dialed home. It was answered on the third ring.

"Seven steps, eight – not long to wait," said her mother's voice.

She hung up and dialed 911.

"Nine steps, ten – we're near the end," said a man's voice.

She hung up and threw the phone onto the bed beside Missy's.

"Eleven, twelve, and one step more – too late for you, I'm at the door!" It was Aunt Margaret's angry voice.

Someone knocked loudly.

THUMP! THUMP! THUMP!

"Go away! Leave me alone! I didn't mean what I said!" Lindsay started to cry.

"Gotcha[25]!" cried Missy through the door. "You're crying! This is better than telling ghost stories! Wait till Noelle and Candice hear I made you cry. You and that stupid ring you think is so cool."

Angry at how she'd been tricked, Lindsay wiped away her tears and opened the door.

"I never want to talk to you again!" she shouted.

But it wasn't Missy holding Lindsay's father's phone in a muddy[26] hand as the lights came on.

Working with the text

L S R W

1 The story

a) *When you have read the short story once, finish these sentences:*

1 Lindsay gets a diamond ring from ...
2 Before Lindsay goes to Missy's house, she ...
3 Lindsay doesn't believe that the caller ...
4 At Missy's house, Lindsay gets another call ...
5 While Lindsay is speaking to her mum ...
6 When everything is dark, ...
7 Missy wants to ... but Lindsay ...
8 When Lindsay opens the door, ...

b) *Whose 'muddy hand' do you think it is at the end of the story?*

---

24 wuss [wʊs] *Dummkopf* 25 Gotcha! [ˈgɒtʃə] (= I've got you!) *Hab dich! Reingelegt!* 26 muddy [ˈmʌdi] *schlammig, matschig*

2 An exciting story?

a) *Look for examples of how the author of "The caller" creates suspense and makes it rise and fall. For instance, look at lines 66–67:*
'Lindsay, darling, this is Aunt Margaret.'

b) *Where does the story reach a climax?*

c) **Extra** *Draw a line chart for the story to show how the suspense rises and falls. Put degrees of suspense on the vertical axis and line numbers on the horizontal axis.*

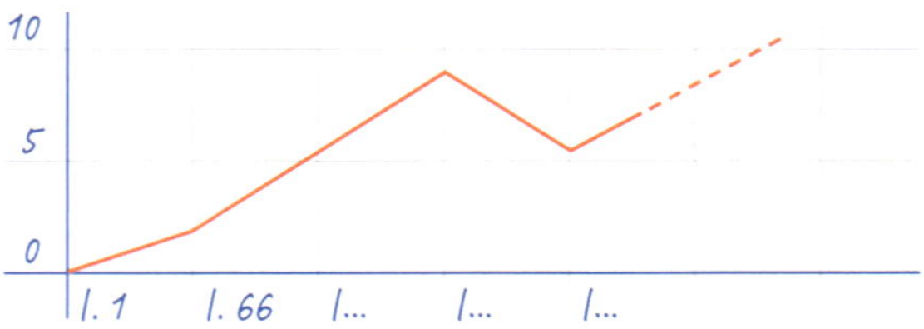

STUDY SKILLS Reading literature (4)

Suspense
Writers can make a story exciting by creating suspense. How? They can make something unexpected happen. They can end a story, or part of it, in the middle of an exciting event. They can offer explanations for events and then show why they can't be right. They might use noises, rhythm, repetition. They can leave the reader 'hanging over a cliff' at the climax of a story.

▸ *SF Reading literature (pp. 138–139)*

3 Lindsay's character

a) *Read lines 15–20, 60–62, 68–69 and 81–83 again. What do they tell you about Lindsay's character? Describe what is important to her in her relationship to Missy and the other girls.*

b) *How does Lindsay feel about her aunt? Find a quotation from the story that shows this well. Compare your idea with a partner's. Who has the better quotation?*

c) *Discuss a freeze frame for the following part of the story:*
'She had to nod and look sad as they talked about her aunt.' (ll. 23–25)
Try to imagine the scene. Where are the people standing/sitting? What might Lindsay be thinking/hoping/feeling at the moment? Does her appearance show what she is feeling? Then act the freeze frame for the class. Take a photo of your freeze frame for your DOSSIER.

d) **Extra** *Choose another part of the story and discuss and act a freeze frame for it. Can the other groups guess which part of the story it is?*

e) **Extra** *Does the story have a moral or a message? If you think it has, what is it? How is it connected to Lindsay's character?*

4 Extra °Beyond the story

a) *Do you like scary stories like "The caller", or scary films? Give reasons for your answers.*

b) *Write a script for a three-minute film based on this story.*

c) *The story ends with the door opening. But can you imagine how it might continue? Write two or three more paragraphs and end the story in your own words.*

▸ *WB 16–17 (pp. 51–52) • Self-evaluation 3–4 WB (p. 53)*

Unit 1 **Part B**

P 2 LISTENING Learning to surf

b) ***Role play***
Use the role card on the right and act out the telephone conversation.

Name: Matt
- You work at the surf school.
- You answer the phone.
- You have to find out
  - if the caller has gone surfing before.
  - if she can swim.
  - if she has her own equipment.
- You offer the EasySurf course.
- You can also offer the Surf Girl course, which is like EasySurf but only for girls. It costs 85 dollars for two hours.

Unit 1 **Part C**

P 2 REVISION On holiday in Australia (Question word + *to*-infinitive)

a) *Listen to Partner A and decide what to say. You can use phrases like 'Why don't you …?' or 'You should …'.*

1 A bottle of water, a hat and some sunscreen.
2 Be there by 5:30 am.
3 Just take the lift.
4 Meet in front of the hotel.
5 See the people at the tour desk.

b) *Partner B: You're on holiday in Australia and need some help. Tell your partner what your problems are. Start with 'I don't know/I'm not sure …', add a question word and an infinitive construction and finish with 'Can you help? / Any ideas? / Do you know?'.*

I don't know	who where when how what	ask about plane tickets check out of the hotel get from here to Sydney send a postcard to wear on the plane

A: I don't know how to get from here to Sydney.
B: I think you should go by plane.

Unit 2 **Part B**

P 3 SPEAKING Job interview

a) *Your role is to help your partner practise an interview for a job as a receptionist in a London hotel. You will need to ask:*
- *whether he/she has worked in a hotel before,*
- *why he/she is applying for the job,*
- *whether he/she could work at night or at weekends,*
- *how well he/she knows London.*

Think of one other question you could ask.

b) *Practise the interview. Thank your partner for coming and ask your questions. Then ask if he/she has any questions. Finish by saying that you will phone him/her tomorrow.*

c) *Find another partner who has already answered the questions and swap roles.*

Unit 2 **Part B**

P7 MEDIATION School in New Zealand

a) *Partner B: You and your partner want to spend some time at a school in New Zealand. Listen to what your partner has to tell you about Wellington High School.*

b) *In German, tell your partner the most important information about Onslow College (subjects that they teach, extra-curricular activities, accommodation and help for international students).*

Onslow

- Onslow College is a co-educational state school with about 1150 students and is situated 10 minutes north of central Wellington, the capital of New Zealand.
- It is driven by a sense of community rather than conformity. Our challenge is to enable students to develop their potential through high quality education in a cooperative, friendly, stimulating and well-disciplined environment.
- Onslow has a long tradition of welcoming international students and has run cultural exchanges for many years. Some international students live with their families who work for their country's embassy. Over 10% of all our students are from non-English-speaking backgrounds.
- Academic subjects available for international students include Computer Studies, Drama, Music, Art Design, Photography and Economics as well as Spanish, Japanese, German, Maori and Chinese.
- In their English course, international students are also taught the necessary study skills to function effectively in their classes including time management, exam preparation, note-taking, setting goals and vocabulary learning.
- Sports include skiing, basketball, tennis, badminton, rowing, rugby, table tennis and soccer. Students can learn clarinet, drums, flute, guitar, keyboards, recorder, saxophone, trombone, trumpet or voice. The school has bands, chamber ensembles, a jazz band, a choir and an orchestra.
- The school arranges accommodation with a host family ($220 per week) and provides training and support for the host parents, who are contacted and visited regularly.

c) *In English, tell your partner which school you would prefer to go to and why.*

Unit 3 **Part B**

P2 EVERYDAY ENGLISH SPEAKING Talking about politics

a) *Your partner will ask you four questions about the party you support, which is the 'Progressive Party'. Use the information on the flyer to answer his or her questions.*

b) *Ask your partner which party he or she supports. Then ask four questions about that party's policy on human rights, education, transport and the environment. Make a comment on at least one of the policies.*

Unit 4 **Part A**

P3 EVERYDAY ENGLISH Role play: Asking someone out

Partner B: Partner A wants to ask you out on a date. You aren't sure yet whether you like the idea or not. While you talk to your partner, you have to make a decision. Try to be nice and polite – you don't want to hurt your partner's feelings.
You must either agree to go out with your partner or explain that you don't think it's a good idea. The words and phrases in the two boxes will help you to say what you want and to be nice and polite about it.

That sounds like a great idea. • Sounds good. • Why not? • That will be so much fun. • Yeah, I'd like that. • I'm really looking forward to ... • Yes, thank you. • Cool, I'd love to. • I'm flattered.

I need some time to think about this. • I'm not sure. • I'll have to ask my parents. • I have to be home by ... • Sorry, I'm not allowed to. • You're a nice guy/girl, but ... • I'm sorry but ... • It's very sweet of you, but ... • I'm afraid I can't. • I'll give you a call, OK?

2 Part **A** B C D

PERSONALITY QUIZ RESULTS CHECKER

Score points as follows:

	A	B	C
1	2	1	3
2	1	2	3
3	3	2	1
4	3	2	1
5	2	1	3
6	2	1	3
7	2	1	3
8	1	2	3
9	2	3	1
10	1	2	3
11	2	1	3
12	1	2	3

TF 1–12		Inhalt	Seite	
Unit 1	TF 1	*Project:* The magic of Australia	102–103	
Unit 1	TF 2	*Bilingual module* Ecosystems in Australia	104–105	
Unit 1	TF 3	Australian signs	106	
Unit 2	TF 4	The right advice?	107	
Unit 2	TF 5	Going to school in England	108	
Unit 3	TF 6	Checks and balances	109	
Unit 3	TF 7	The monarchy and Parliament	110–111	
Unit 3	TF 8	Luuurve debate	112–113	
Unit 3	TF 9	Who's guilty?	114–119	
Unit 4	TF 10	*Bilingual module* A different kind of justice	120–122	

TF 1 Project: The magic of Australia

Australia is the world's smallest continent and the only continent occupied by just one country. A small continent, but a huge country. Doing a project about different aspects of the place may help you to understand more about the magic of Australia.

a) *Divide the class into groups. Each group works on one of the topics here or another topic of their choice. Some students might like to work alone.*

b) *Work on the project. Groups can give different tasks to different students.*

c) *Present your project to the class. Use appropriate visual aids (transparencies, handouts, computer presentation, ...).*

d) *Listen to or look at the other groups' presentations and evaluate them.*

▸ *SF Visual aids in presentations (p. 131)* • *SF Project skills (pp. 132–133)*

Topic 1 The geography Australia

Australia is a huge place and has lots of different landscapes, from desert to rainforest to coral reefs. You could do your project on one of these landscapes, on the island of Tasmania, or on an important city. Where are they located? Find out what these places are like, who or what lives there, how they survive, what the places are famous for, what visitors can do there. You might even like to plan a trip to Oz.

The Great Barrier Reef

A famous Sydney landmark

Topic 2 Culture and art in Australia

Australia is not just a place of natural wonders. Humans have lived there for at least 40,000 years and human culture always involves[1] the production of art, music, dance, literature. Find out about the culture and art of Australia: you could look at ancient Aboriginal rock art or modern Aboriginal painting, the Australian popular music scene, movies or the theatre. Or about great Australian literature from Dreamtime stories to modern novelists and poets. How about performing an Australian song, poem or dance?

An Aborigine dot painting

[1] (to) involve sth. [ɪnˈvɒlv] *mit etwas zu tun haben*

Topic 3 The animals of Australia

Everyone has heard of the kangaroo, and everybody loves koalas. But Australia has lots of other fascinating animals. You might want to research which ones can only be found in Australia. Which ones are dangerous? Are any of them threatened? Why are rabbits such a problem? Check out your local zoo for animals from Oz.

A platypus [1)] 1 ['plætɪpəs]

A Tasmanian Devil

A salt-water crocodile, or 'salty'

Topic 4 The first people of Australia

Perhaps you'd like to learn more about the Aboriginal people of Australia: How do they live in modern Australia – are their lives different from those of white Australians? What can you find out about their beliefs and legends or their art and music? Perhaps you can find a Dreamtime story and act it out.

People at an Aboriginal settlement in the Northern Territory

Topic 5 Dry Australia

Australia is the world's driest inhabited continent. Find out what that means for the environment and the people who live in it. How are Australians touched by drought[2] and bushfires? What effects will climate change have on the country? Find out about water restrictions in Sydney or Adelaide and try to live according to them for a day or so.

An Australian bushfire

[2] drought [draʊt] *Dürre*

TF 2 Ecosystems[1] in Australia

L S R W

1 Food chains[2]

Plants and animals need energy, which they get from food. Plants make their own food by photosynthesis, so they are called ***producers.*** *Animals must get their food by eating plants or other animals, so they are called* ***consumers****.*

Complete the food chain in Diagram A. Use the words in the box.

insects • crocodiles • plants • frogs

Diagram A: A food chain

Producer ⟶ Primary consumer ⟶ Secondary consumer ⟶ Tertiary consumer[3]

.... are eaten by .... are eaten by .... are eaten by ....

L S R W

2 Food webs

a) *A food web consists of many connected food chains, like those shown in the food web below. Find six food chains in the food web an write them down, e.g.* grass > kangaroo > dingo
How many different kinds of food do the different animals eat?

1 ['kʊkəbʌrə]

Diagram B: A food web

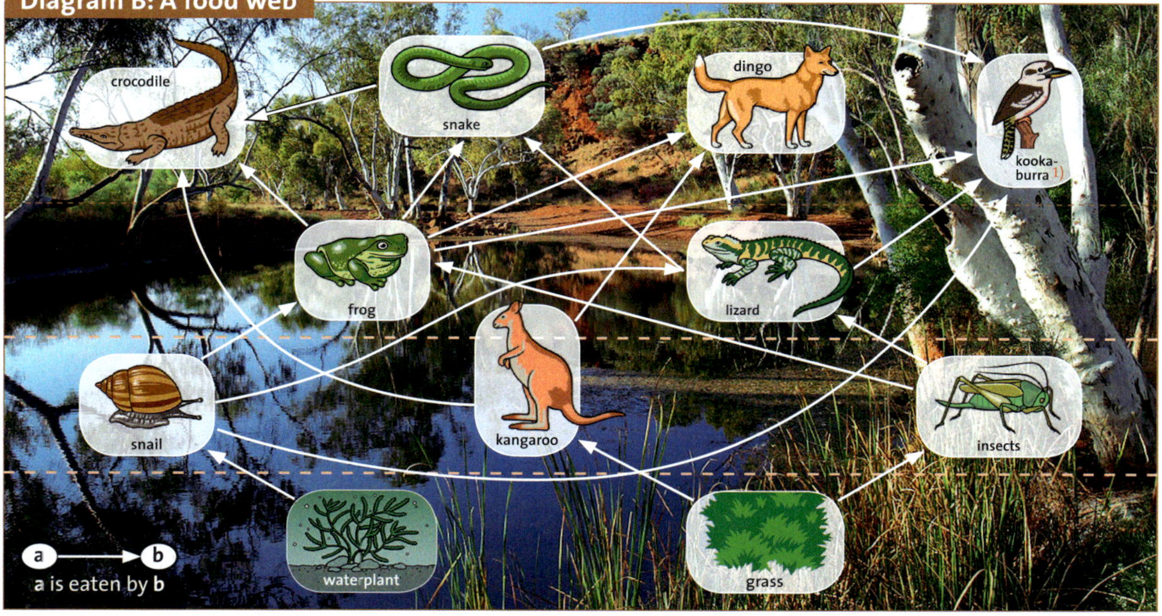

b) *What will happen if the population of one part of the food web in Diagram B increases or decreases?*

If the population of	snakes kangaroos ...	increases, decreases,	then the population of	frogs dingoes ...	will increase. decrease.

BIOLOGY SKILLS Talking about food webs

If the population of one part of a food web changes, the populations of other parts of the food web will also change. Some animals will eat more of another animal or plant. Some animals will not have enough food and they will die.

[1] ecosystem ['i:kəʊsɪstəm] *Ökosystem* [2] food chain ['fu:d tʃeɪn] *Nahrungskette* [3] primary/secondary/tertiary consumer ['praɪməri kən,sju:mə, 'sekəndri, 'tɜ:ʃəri] *Primär-/Sekundär-/Tertiärkonsument* [4] (to) increase [ɪn'kri:s] *anwachsen, zunehmen* [5] (to) decrease [dɪ'kri:s] *zurückgehen, abnehmen, sinken*

3 An ecosystem in disorder[1]

a) Look at the photos, the map and the fast facts box. Describe what they show.

TOADZILLA!

27 March 2007

A toad as big as a small dog was found in Australia this week. The cane toad was 20 cm long – twice as big as most cane toads.

In 1935, farmers in Queensland brought 102 cane toads to Australia because they had problems with insects in their fields. They wanted the cane toads to eat the insects.

Unfortunately that was a really bad idea! Today there are about 200 million cane toads and native Australian animals are in danger.

The government is now asking people to hunt cane toads and kill them.

So, why is the situation so bad for the native animals of Australia?

The main reason is the fact that cane toads are poisonous. Animals (like crocodiles, snakes, lizards and birds) that try to eat the cane toad, or its eggs, die from the poison.

Also cane toads eat anything that moves, including native snakes, frogs, lizards and birds.

Scientists are searching for a way to control the cane toad population in Australia ... before it's too late.

Fast facts: Cane toads

From: South America

Scientific name: Bufo marinus

Size: About 100 to 150 mm long

What do they eat? Almost anything, including cat and dog food, insects, lizards, frogs and small snakes

What are they eaten by? Snakes, lizards, crocodiles, birds

Reproduction: Cane toads have about 8,000 to 25,000 eggs twice a year. It is estimated that about 0.5% survive to become adult toads.

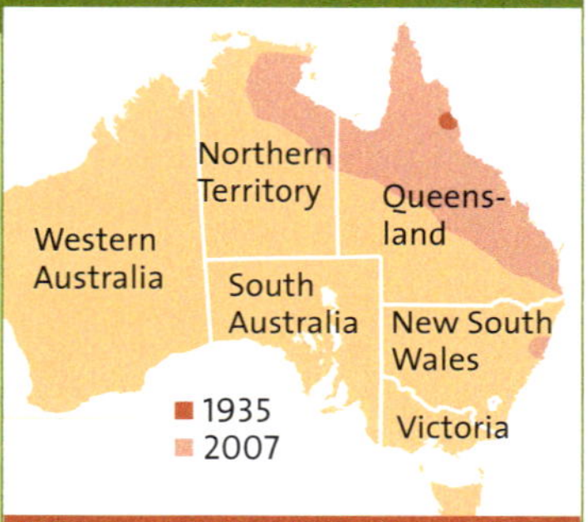

Where cane toads are found

b) Find out how cane toads came to Australia, why they are such a serious problem now, and what the Australian government wants people to do about them.

c) Look at Diagram B on page 104 again. What will happen if the cane toad arrives in this place?

d) The article says that scientists are looking for a way to control the cane toad population. Do you think that it would be a good idea to bring a new animal to Australia that could eat the cane toad? Why/Why not?

I think it might make the situation better/worse because ...

Activate your English

- The photo/map/fast facts box shows/gives information about ...
- It says that .../It shows ...
- This is a photo/map of ...
- In 1935 cane toads were found in ...
  In 2007 they were found in ...

4 Introduced species

Write about another introduced species and its effects, e.g. the rabbit in Australia, the raccoon in Germany, the kudzu vine in the USA or the red-eared terrapin in Britain. Say where the species came from and how/why it was introduced. Include a fast facts box, a map and/or a diagram.

[1] in disorder [dɪs'ɔːdə] *in Unordnung; (funktions)gestört* [2] toad [təʊd] *Kröte*

TF 3 Australian signs

L S R W

1 Signs talk

a) *Work in groups of five. Each person describes one of the signs 1–5. You might need to look up words you don't know in a dictionary.*

b) *Discuss where you would expect to find each of the signs, what they mean and what they tell you about Australia.*

2 Funny signs

L S R W

a) *What is the message of the sign below?*

b) *Draw a sign of your own – it can be serious or funny. Swap signs with a partner. Explain what you think your partner's sign is trying to say.*

TF 4 The right advice? 2.19–2.22

L S R W

a) The following four poems and a song all give advice on life in some way. Read them and choose the one which you feel is most relevant to your life. Write a few sentences that explain the 'message' of the poem.

b) Find a partner who has chosen the same poem. Compare your explanations of the message.

c) Now get together with a partner who has chosen a different poem. Explain the message of your poem to them and listen to their explanation. Tell them why you find your poem relevant.

From Breathe (2 AM) 2.19

Anna Nalick

'Cause you can't jump the track, we're like cars on a cable[1]
And life's like an hourglass[2], glued to the table
No one can find the rewind button, girl.
So cradle your head in your hands
And breathe ... just breathe,
Oh breathe, just breathe

Dreams 2.20

Langston Hughes

Hold fast to dreams
For if dreams die
Life is a broken-winged bird
That cannot fly

Hold fast to dreams
For when dreams go
Life is a barren[3] field
Frozen with snow.

Somewhere in the sky 2.21

Leo Aylen

Somewhere
In the sky,
There's a door painted blue,
With a big brass knocker seven feet high.
If you can find it,
Knock, and go through –
That is, if you dare.
You'll see behind it
The secrets of the universe piled on a chair
Like a tangle of wool[4].
A voice will declare
'You have seven centuries in which to unwind[5] it.
But whatever
You do,
You must never,
Ever,
Lose your temper and pull.'

I meant to do my work today 2.22

Richard LeGallienne

I meant to do[6] my work today –
But a brown bird sang in the apple tree,
And a butterfly flitted across the field,
And all the leaves were calling me.

And the wind went sighing over the land
Tossing[7] the grasses to and fro[8],
And a rainbow held out its shining hand –
So what could I do but laugh and go?

[1] car on a cable ['keɪbl] *(gezogene) Straßenbahn* [2] hourglass ['aʊəglɑːs] *Stundenglas, Sanduhr* [3] barren ['bærən] *unfruchtbar, öde*
[4] wool [wʊl] *Wolle* [5] (to) unwind [ˌʌn'waɪnd] *(etwas Verheddertes) mühsam aufdrehen* [6] (to) mean to do sth. [miːn] *vorhaben, etwas zu tun*
[7] (to) toss [tɒs] *werfen* [8] to and fro [frəʊ] *hin und her*

TF 5 Going to school in England

L S R W

Just imagine you've gone back in time and you're growing up and going to school again, but this time in England. How will your life be different?

1 Your years of fun and play at nursery school[1] won't be as easy and they'll come to an end more quickly in England. You have to start primary school in the term after your fifth birthday – there are three school terms in England: from September to Christmas, from January to Easter, after Easter to July. Some parents send their children to primary school earlier, so perhaps you'll only be four when you start your six years there!

2 In this new life, you'll move to secondary school from Year 7. If your parents are wealthy, they might send you to an independent school. These are private schools and you have to pay to go there. Seven per cent of school students in England go to independent schools. The most traditional ones are called public schools. Some independent schools are also boarding schools[2], so you might have to live and sleep there during term. But unless you're a wizard[3], you won't go to Hogwarts.

3 So your mum and dad aren't rich? You'll end up in an ordinary state comprehensive school[4]. They offer a general education to students of all abilities. What will you learn there? Well, all students have to do the subjects on the National Curriculum[5]. Many subjects are similar[6] to those in Germany, but there is Citizenship[7] in Years 7–11, Design & Technology in Years 7–9 and Work-related Learning in Years 10–11.

4 How will you find out how you're doing? Your teachers will assess you and there are exams in Year 9 and national GCSE exams in Year 11 (you might do GCSEs in some subjects in Year 10).

5 At the end of Year 11 you could leave school. Or go to a College of Further Education. But if you stay at school for years 12 & 13, known as the Sixth Form, or go to a Sixth Form College, you'll study four or five subjects and take AS exams in year 12 and then do A2 exams in three subjects in Year 13. AS and A2 together make up A-levels. With good A-level results, you might be able to get a place at a university.

Describe the main similarities and differences between the German and the English school systems. You might like to draw a diagram to help you.

[1] nursery school ['nɜːsəri] *(BE) Kindergarten* [2] boarding school ['bɔːdɪŋ] *Internat* [3] wizard ['wɪzəd] *Zauberer, Zauberin*
[4] comprehensive school [ˌkɒmprɪ'hensɪv] *Gesamtschule* [5] curriculum [kə'rɪkjələm] *Lehrplan* [6] similar ['sɪmələ] *ähnlich*
[7] Citizenship ['sɪtɪzənʃɪp] *Staatsbürgerkunde*

TF 6 Checks and balances[1]

1 What do you know?

Say what you already know about politics in the USA. Can you name any US Presidents, past and present? What is the Constitution?

2 LISTENING The US system of government

2.23

a) *Look at the chart and listen.*

b) *Then try to complete a copy of the chart with the information you have heard. Listen again and add any missing information.*

c) *Compare your chart with that of a partner. Then ask each other questions to see if you have understood everything.*

d) *Do some research on the President and members of Congress. How are they elected and for how long? Add the information to your chart.*

3 A government puzzle

Make five statements about the US system of government and write them down. For each statement you will need three of these pieces.

- are there for life
- The nine judges
- the basic law
- is to pass laws for the whole country
- that the President has
- The most important job
- that Congress has
- who sit on the Supreme Court
- The veto is
- The Supreme Court is
- that all other laws have to agree with
- the branch of government
- that interprets the laws
- a power
- The Constitution is

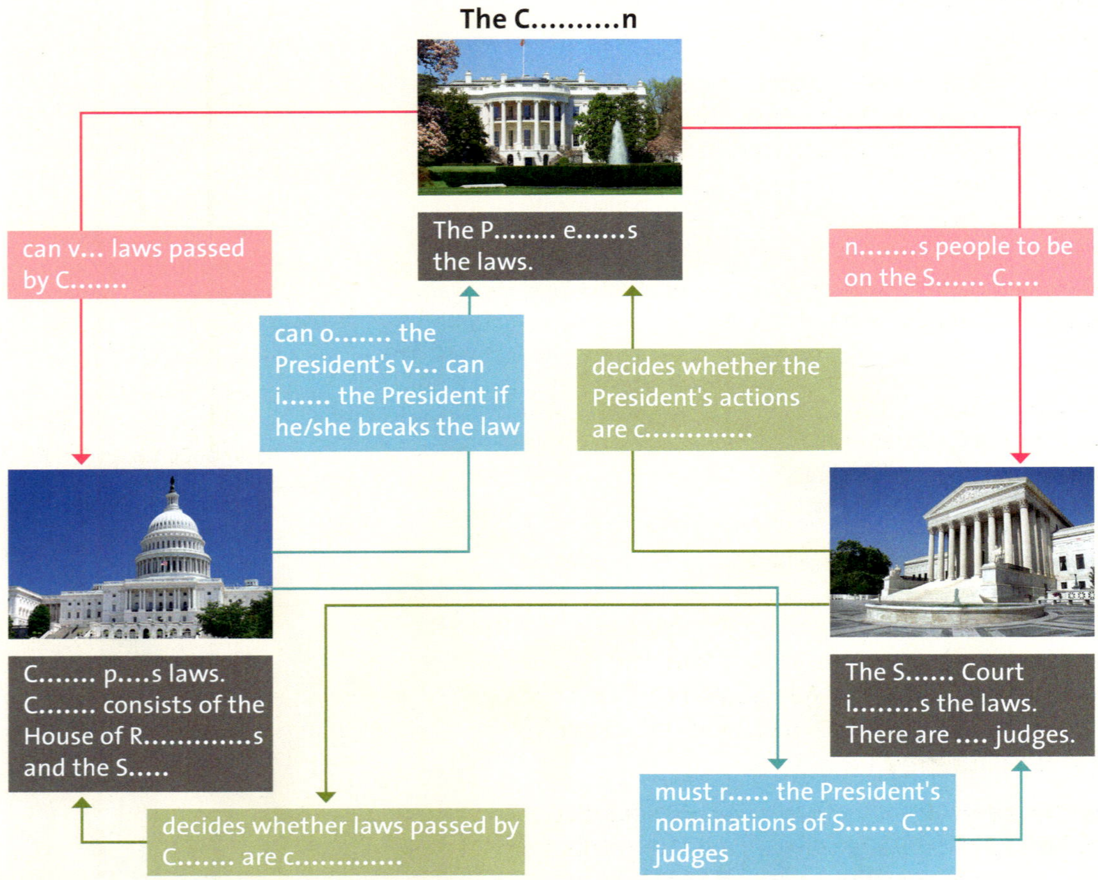

[1] checks and balances ['bælənsɪz] *gegenseitige Kontrolle (checks) und Machtgleichgewicht (balances) der Regierungsgewalten*

TF 7 The monarchy and Parliament

The Queen opening Parliament

L S R W

1 The royal family

a) *What do you know about the Queen and other members of the royal family? Why are people so interested in them?*

b) *Do you think the following statements are true or false? Check your answers when you have finished 3 on the next page.*

The British monarch ...
... chooses the Prime Minister.
... writes a speech telling the government what to do.
... is head of the Church of England.
... is elected by Members of Parliament.

L S R W

2 From absolute monarchy to parliamentary democracy

a) *Read the six texts A–F carefully and work out what the correct order is. Then you can complete the texts with these dates: 1215 • 1534 • 1649 • 1689 • 1832 • 1918 • 1969.*

b) *Match these six titles to the texts: More men get the vote • An early Parliament • A new kind of monarchy • Death of a king • Britain no longer Catholic • Votes for all*

A William and Mary arrived with an army, and James fled[1]. In ___, a year after this 'Glorious[2] Revolution', William and Mary signed the Bill[3] of Rights. This guaranteed Parliament's rights. Britain had become a constitutional monarchy. The Bill of Rights also said that a Catholic could never be monarch, and this is still the law today.

B Two hundred years ago only rich men (and no women) could vote. Several reform bills went through Parliament (the first, called the Reform Act[4], in ___) and gave democratic rights to more and more people. But by the end of the 19th century women still did not have the vote.

C Up to the early 13th century, people had few rights. However, in ___ a group of barons made King John sign the Magna Carta. The King agreed to consult[5] a council of barons before taking certain decisions. This council became a place for talking (French: parler) and discussing laws: a parliament.

D Three centuries later, King Henry VIII (the man who was married six times) wanted a divorce[6] from his first wife. The Pope[7] said no. So in ___ King Henry broke with the Church of Rome and, with Parliament's agreement, founded the Church of England and made himself its head, a position still held by the monarch today.

E It was thanks to women like Emmeline Pankhurst and the suffragette[8] movement that women over 30 got the vote in ___, and full voting equality followed ten years later. In ___ the voting age was reduced to what it is today – 18.

F About a hundred years after Henry VIII, another king, Charles I, tried to rule without Parliament. This led to a civil war, which Parliament won. Charles was executed[9] in ___, and for a few years England was a republic. But 40 years later the Catholic King James II again tried to rule without Parliament. So some of its members secretly invited James's daughter Mary and her Protestant husband William of Orange to become King and Queen.

Emmeline Pankhurst being arrested outside Buckingham Palace

[1] (to) flee – fled – fled *fliehen* [2] glorious ['glɔːriəs] *ruhmreich* [3] bill *Gesetzentwurf* [4] act *Gesetz* [5] (to) consult [kən'sʌlt] *zurate ziehen* [6] divorce *Scheidung* [7] Pope *Papst* [8] suffragette [ˌsʌfrə'dʒet] *Frauenrechtler/in* [9] (to) execute *hinrichten*

3 Britain's political system today

KING/QUEEN
the official head of state

GOVERNMENT

PRIME MINISTER
the leader of the biggest party in the House of Commons

CABINET[10] MINISTERS
for defence, education, health, etc.

PARLIAMENT

HOUSE OF LORDS
about 730 members (unelected peers[11])

HOUSE OF COMMONS
about 650 Members of Parliament (MPs) elected for a maximum of five years

EUROPEAN PARLIAMENT
Members of the European Parliament (MEPs) elected for five years

OTHER PARLIAMENTS OR ASSEMBLIES
the Scottish Parliament, the Welsh Assembly and the Northern Ireland Assembly

VOTERS
Every Briton over 18 may vote in a general election (for the House of Commons), in the European elections, for other Parliaments or assemblies (in certain areas) and in local elections.

→ elects → chooses → officially appoints[12] → can usually control

a) Study the diagram and decide who or what statements 1–8 below refer to.

1 He/She is the most powerful British politician and has the same sort of job as the German *Bundeskanzler/in*.
2 He/She has no real power. The speech he/she gives at the opening of Parliament is written by the government.
3 Its role is to make the laws.
4 It can delay bills and suggest amendments, but it has little power.
5 It helps to make European laws.
6 They make important decisions. Each is head of a government department.
7 Almost all of them belong to a party such as Labour or the Conservatives.
8 They were created to give more independence to parts of the United Kingdom other than England.

b) *Choose one of these three group tasks:*

1 Compare the history of voting rights in Britain and Germany. Make a chart with two columns: one for Britain, one for Germany.
2 Prepare a presentation on Emmeline Pankhurst and the suffragettes. Use information from history books, the internet, etc.
3 How do you think the British system could be made more democratic? Exchange your ideas and then write one or two paragraphs for a political leaflet suggesting a programme of changes.

---

[10] cabinet ['kæbɪnət] *Kabinett* [11] peer [pɪə] *Adlige(r)* [12] (to) appoint [ə'pɔɪnt] *ernennen*

TF 8 Luuurve debate (adapted from *Don't call me Ishmael* by Michael Gerard Bauer) 2.24–2.27

L S R W

Ishmael, Orazio ('the Razz') and Scobie are in the debating team of their school. They go to a workshop to learn more about debating. But is Ishmael's mind on the talk?

2.24 The day of the debating workshop at Moorfield High School was the day I first saw Kelly Faulkner. Not that she noticed me, of course. I was just one of the thirty or so students taking the workshop. But I noticed her, and Orazio Zorzotto also noticed me noticing her.

"Hey, Leseur, stick your tongue back in – you're starting to dribble."

It was the lunch break. Orazio and I were waiting outside a classroom for Scobie, the captain of our team. He was still talking to one of the workshop presenters inside.

"What?"

"Come on, you can't fool the Razz. You've been perving at[1] that weird chick in the red T-shirt all day," he said and nodded at a group of girls sitting under a tree.

"What? I wasn't perving at anyone."

"If you say so."

"And she's not weird," I added, perhaps a little too quickly.

"Woo ... Sorry, I didn't mean to say anything bad about your girlfriend."

"Girlfriend! What are you talking about?"

"Look, don't get me wrong. I don't blame you. She is *kinda* cute in a ... weird sort of way. It's just, she's not my type, you know?"

I didn't really know, but I guessed Razza's type would be someone like Britney Spears or Paris Hilton. You know, the sex-goddess-next-door type.

"You should go and chat her up."

2.25 Oh yes, that'll happen. What a terrific idea. I could just go over and say, "Excuse me. My name is Ishmael Leseur ... Yes, I agree, it is an interesting name ... Anyway, I thought you might be dying to leave all your friends and join a complete stranger in a conversation. Or, on the other hand, you and your friends might prefer just to stare at me, like I'm a three-headed zombie, before you laugh and point at me and call me things like 'complete loser,' and 'absolute dork'."

"Look, Razza, I don't know what you're talking about. I haven't been *looking* at anyone, I don't want to *talk* to anyone, and I'm not *interested* in anyone, okay?"

"Really? Then how about telling me the four steps of good debating."

"What?"

"The four steps of good debating. Go on – we just had a talk on them."

"What's that got to do with anything?"

"Well, it's just that the speaker-dude in there told us those steps about a zillion times *and* put them up on the overhead projector. So unless your mind was on some babe in a red T-shirt during the whole talk, you'd have to remember them, wouldn't you? So, come on, lover-boy, I'm waiting."

"This is stupid. I don't have to do this!"

"*Can't* do it, you mean. Look, I'll make it easy for you: just give us a couple of the steps – they don't even have to be in the right order. How about one, then? Oh my god. Don't tell me you can't even remember one? This is worse than I thought! Quick, help me get this arrow from your heart before it's too late!"

2.26 Suddenly Razza had both hands on my chest and was pulling at my shirt. "Arrrgh! Curse you, Cupid!"

"Back off!" I said. "I bet you can't even remember them yourself."

Razza froze immediately and then told me the steps, like a robot. "First: say what the other team said. Second: say why they are wrong. Third: say what your team says. Fourth: say why you are right."

"So I wasn't listening. So what?" I said quietly. "What does that prove[2]?"

"It proves to *me*, Ishmael, my man, that when you should have been learning about good debating, you were in fact" – and here he leaned close to my ear and whispered – "logged on to the website of luuurve!"

---

[1] (to) perve at sb./sth. [pɜːv] *jn./etwas anglotzen* [2] (to) prove [pruːv] *beweisen*

"You're mad," I said and pushed him away. "You realize that, don't you? They shouldn't let people like you into the community with normal people."

Razza stuck out his jaw and spoke to an empty bench[3] in front of him. "Ladies and gentlemen, *chair*[4], I give to you the four steps of good debating. One: my love-struck colleague, Ishmael, said that I was mad. Two: my lover-boy friend is wrong, because he is not a doctor and so cannot make such a diagnosis. Three: I say my teammate is accusing me of being mad to cover the fact that he is totally in love with a certain red T-shirt-wearing girl but doesn't want to admit it. And four: I am right, because if anyone can make such a diagnosis, it is I, because I am the Razzman, and the Razzman is the doctor of luuurve!"

I looked at the smiling face before me. I wanted to kill him ... slowly.

"I pretty much think that's game, set and match[5] to me, Ishmael, old pal. And just in time. Here comes our leader."

2.27 Finally some sense.

"Herr Scobie, I am sorry to report that I no longer think Comrade Leseur here can be a member of our team. He hasn't taken any notes and I have discovered to my horror that he doesn't even know the four steps of good debating. I'm sorry, but his mind is just not on the job. What on earth do you think is wrong with him, Herr Scobmeister?"

Scobie looked at me, then turned to Razza. At last, he was going to put Razza in his place.

"He was probably staring at that girl in the red T-shirt all morning?"

Razza put both arms into the air and threw his head back. "Whoo, hooo! Yes! The Scobster slam-dunks it! You da man, Scobie baby. You–da–*man*!"

Orazio Zorzotto danced around me, pushed me in the back, messed up my hair. When I look back, I realize that I should have killed him then, while I had the chance. When the jury[6] heard all the evidence, they would probably have only given me a few hours' community service.

1 The main point

Read the extract, take notes and then write a summary of it together. Partner A starts and writes a sentence, then Partner B adds a second sentence, and so on. Write no more than eight sentences.

2 The characters

Which of the following characters would you most like to meet? And which would you not like to meet? Explain why.

Ishmael – Orazio – Scobie – Kelly

3 What's so funny?

What is the funniest part of the extract for you? Can you explain why?

4 The language

a) *The story has many examples of the sort of informal language young people often use. Look at the following. How could you say them in more formal/normal English? You might need to use a dictionary.*

1. ll. 14–15: You've been perving at that weird chick ...
2. l. 26: She is kinda cute ...
3. l. 32: You should go and chat her up.
4. ll. 36–37: I thought you might be dying to leave all your friends ...
5. l. 43: ... absolute dork.
6. l. 54: ... the speaker-dude ...
7. l. 55: ... a zillion times ...
8. l. 85: ... logged on to the website of luuurve!
9. ll. 124–125: The Scobster slam-dunks it!
10. l. 125: You da man, Scobie baby.

b) *What effect does this use of informal language have on the reader?*

[3] bench [bentʃ] *Bank (zum Sitzen)* • [4] chair *Herr Vorsitzender, Frau Vorsitzende* • [5] game, set and match *(im Tennis) Spiel, Satz und Sieg* • [6] the jury ['dʒʊəri] *die Geschworenen*

TF 9 Who's guilty[1]? (abridged and adapted from *Just* by Ali Smith)

Cast

Dead body ___ Townsperson 1
Victoria ___ Townsperson 2
Albert ___ Mrs Wright

A body is lying on the ground in the middle of the stage. It's dead. It has an umbrella sticking out of its back. Stage left is a big green pot plant. Stage right is a bus stop with a bench next to it. Victoria enters and stands at the bus stop for a minute. She looks at the pot plant, frowns. She gets out a map book and looks at it, like she's not sure where she is. She looks at the bench and thinks about sitting on it, decides not to. Then she senses[2] something behind her, turns around and sees the body.

Victoria ___ Oh my – oh my God.

She goes over to take a look. She stands over the body and looks all around for what can have happened. She shakes her head. She looks at the body from head to feet without touching it. She looks disgusted[3], but then looks at the handle of the umbrella. She looks around, as if to check that no one can see, then leans forward as if she is going to touch the handle. Just as she leans forward, Albert enters from the back. He's dressed as a policeman. As Victoria gets closer with her arm, juts about to touch, Albert comes forward.

Albert ___ Oh my God! Oh my God, what have you done?

Victoria ___ No, it wasn't me. I was just –

Albert ___ What have you done here?

Victoria ___ But that's just what I'm trying to tell you. I didn't – I was just standing at the bus stop.

Albert ___ What happened?

Victoria ___ Like I say, just standing at the bus stop, thinking about, well it sounds a bit strange maybe, but I was thinking about apples. And I got this creepy[4] feeling at the back of my neck, and I turned, and I saw this, him, just, well, lying here, like that, and I said 'Oh my God,' exactly like you just did, and I came over.

Albert ___ Did you have a big argument?

Victoria ___ Who with?

Albert ___ *(points at the body)* Was it, like, a lover's tiff[5]?

Jack ___ No, no, I just told you, I don't know him –

Albert ___ You *don't know* him?

---

[1] guilty ['gɪlti] *schuldig* [2] (to) sense sb./sth. *etwas/jn. spüren* [3] disgusted *angewidert* [4] creepy (infml) *unheimlich* [5] tiff *Streit*

Victoria No.

Albert Oh my God. You didn't even know him. I mean, I could have understood it if you'd argued. A crime of fashion, that's OK.

Victoria A crime of what?

Albert People get very upset when there's fashion. And rightly so.

Victoria Eh, I think you might not mean –

Albert I'm the type of person who can forgive things done in the name of fashion.

Victoria You mean passion[6].

Albert That's what I said.

Victoria You said fashion.

Albert No I didn't. You're twisting my words.

Victoria No I'm not.

Albert And you killed this man in old blood.

Victoria In what?

Albert I saw you.

Victoria But you didn't. You didn't see what you think you saw. Like you didn't say what you think you said.

Albert Yes I did. I *instinctly* saw you.

Victoria You keep saying things wrong.

Albert No I don't.

Victoria You don't mean instinctly. You mean distinctly[7].

Albert That's what I said.

Victoria No it isn't.

Albert Don't argue with me. It was one of the most distinctly things I've ever seen in my life. You stabbed that man with that umbrella.

Victoria Well, if that's what you saw you must be totally blindly as a fuckingly batly[8].

Albert It makes me shiver to be anywhere near someone so old-blooded.

Victoria It's cold-blooded. Cold-blooded.

Albert It's quite exciting. You're under arrest.

Victoria Look. I can explain. I was just reaching forward. In that way you do. Like for *Excalibur*.

Albert The film?

Victoria No, I mean, yes, it is, but I mean it's like Excalibur the sword.

Albert There's a sword as well as a film?

Victoria looks at him like she can't believe he doesn't know the story.

Albert I just didn't know there was both a film and a sword called Exc... that word. And that's not my fault, is it? Not as if I had the chance to know and turned it down and said no, I simply don't *want* to know that it's a sword and a film. Not as if someone said to me, Albert, do you want to know all the things that ... that word ... can mean, and I said, no thank you, I do not wish to know.

Victoria What are you talking about?

Albert The film. And the sword. Both with that name. See, I know there's a sword now too. I'm a quick learner.

Victoria So.

Albert So.

Victoria Where were we again?

Albert Uh, you know. The sword.

Victoria Yes. Right. Sword in the stone.

Albert In the what?

Victoria You know. Excalibur. For fuck sake.

Albert Oh, so there's a stone now as well called it, is there?

Victoria Called what?

Albert Ex... cammimur.

Victoria What?

Albert You know. That word.

Enter the two Townspeople from stage left at the front, walking across the stage. They speak their lines in chorus. Victoria and Albert turn and watch them.

Townspeople
Here's the lovely pot plant.
Ooh, it's looking very clean!
Someone's done its leaves again.
D'you think with Mr Sheen[9]?
Ooh they're very shiny.
Mr Sheen brings out the green.

---

[6] passion [ˈpæʃn] *Leidenschaft* [7] distinct *deutlich* [8] blind as a bat *„blind wie ein Maulwurf"* [9] Mr Sheen *Markenname eines Reinigungsmittels*

D'you think a real Mr Sheen
exists?
I often wonder.
D'you think the rain'll hold off?
Weather said thunder.
Ooh, here's the bus stop.
Let's wait for the bus.
Ooh, we're first in the queue.
Great!
No one here but us.

Townspeople stand at the bus stop and wait.

Victoria — Am I imagining it, or are they speaking in rhyme??

Albert — Don't try and change the subject.

Victoria — Not very good rhyme either.

Townspeople hear this and are angry. They turn to look at Victoria.

Townspeople —
Ooh! Look! A body!
Ooh, I say[10]!
That's not something you expect to
See every day.
Ooh! He's been stabbed!
Ooh! It's *The Bill*!
Ooh, look at her.
She looks really evil!

Victoria — I do not!

Townspeople —
Ooh! Look at the murder weapon!
You'd think she might have hid it.
You'd think she might have tried.
Look at her. Evil. She definitely did
it.

Victoria — I did not.

Townspeople —
Ooh, that's that policeman
That gets his words wrong.
I knew his mother.

They nod darkly at this to each other. Townsperson 1 taps his or her head twice.

Townsperson 1 —
Do you recognise that evil-looking
one?

Townspeople —
She's not from round here, is she?
No.
Do you recognise that fella?
No. Me neither. Well, if it rains
We can always borrow his
umbrella.

They laugh really loudly then stop and look at their watches.

Townspeople —
Ooh, look at the time!
I think we've missed the bus.
Ooh well, let's walk home.
A walk'll be good for us.

Townspeople go off, stage right. Victoria and Albert watch them go, then go back to their argument.

Victoria — Where were we, again?

Albert — I was arresting you for murder.

Victoria — Yes. See, I thought for a minute that this, all this, this sticking up in the air like this, was like a kind of grotesque Excalibur.

Albert — I know. It's a sword, and a film and a stone.

Victoria — Well, it's not a stone, it's *in* the stone.

Albert — I know! I know!

He clearly doesn't.

Victoria — So you know the story of Excalibur, then?

Albert — Oh, so it's not just a sword and a stone and a film, now it's a story too, is it?

Victoria — Well, yes.

Albert — Are you deliberately trying to infuse me?

Victoria — *(takes a deep breath)* The story of Excalibur, *you* know.

Albert — I know, I know – I know it really well, actually, don't go thinking I don't ... just remind me of the beginning of it again.

Victoria — You know, first it's stuck in the stone and only the rightful[11] king can take it out, and all the strong people try and pull it out and they can't, then, a little weak guy comes along and because he's the rightful king it just slides out of the stone in his hand and he's King Arthur.

---

[10] I say! (BE infml, old-fashioned) *Meine Güte!* [11] rightful *rechtmäßig*

As if the sword is waiting for him and him alone!

Albert — *(nodding, echoing her just after she's spoken, as if he knows, though he doesn't)* Him and him alone ...

Victoria — And then the lake, and the hand coming out of it, and someone throws it into the lake, I can't remember who, and an arm comes out of the lake and catches it, the Lady of the Lake, and it disappears for ever under the water till the rightful king comes to claim it again.

Albert — Anyway, you're still under arrest.

Victoria — No, listen, because I was reaching forward when you saw me, because I just wondered, for a moment, just a moment, what it would be like to ... unlikely, I know. But the point is, I never actually held it. I never actually touched it. When you look for fingerprints on it, they won't be my fingerprints.

Albert — That's 'cause I saw you wiping them off.

Victoria — You did *not*!

Albert — I know what I saw.

Victoria — But you don't. You so clearly don't.

Albert — Don't you tell me what I know and what I don't know.

Victoria — Yeah, I know. You saw me 'instinctly'.

Albert — Are you making fun of me?

Victoria — Show me exactly what you think you saw. You came round the corner, there, and you *distinctly* saw me do *what* exactly?

Enter Mrs Wright at the back. She carries a handbag and is blindfolded.

Albert — *(miming what he saw)* I *distinctally* saw you let go of the handle of the murder weapon, and you letting go of the handle was distinctally immediately after you'd distinctally run at the victim even though he was a total stranger to you, who you didn't even know enough to have had an argument of fashion with. And then you stabbed him in the back with it. And then you carefully wiped your fingerprints off the handle of the murder weapon.

Victoria — But I *didn't*.

Mrs Wright — *(coming blindly forward)* Oh my God. What have you people done?

Albert — Begging your pardon, ma'am, but as usual it wasn't me.

Victoria — It wasn't me either. And what do you mean, as usual?

Mrs Wright — I saw it. I saw all of you.

Victoria — But you're blindfolded.

Mrs Wright — I am blindfolded to prevent me from being biased[12] about what I see. And I heard you *(to Victoria)* with your hand raised in that violent way. I heard you with your hand on the – the murder weapon. And *(to Albert)* I heard you watching like an accomplice.

Victoria — No. I was just waiting for a bus. I was thinking about apples. I'm an apple-farmer – well, I used to be.

Mrs Wright — Objection[13]. Irrelevant.

Victoria — Up to last year I had my own apple-farm. Orange Pippin. Ashmead's Kernel. Discovery. Worcester. Charles Ross. Russett. Gascoyne's Scarlet. And apples from all over the world. Ida Red. Jonathan. McIntosh. Northern Spy. And those are just a few. Over the last year or so my life has changed completely. Anyway, enough about me. The point is – I was at the bus stop and I happened to see the body, and I came over to have a look because I couldn't believe my eyes, and then, weirdly, the handle of it looked a bit like it might be Excalibur –

Albert — *(to himself)* Excabilur.

---

[12] biased ['baɪəst] *voreingenommen* [13] objection *Einspruch*

Victoria — so I just put my hand out – like this, and then out of nowhere this person here accused *me* of *murder*.

Albert — because I know the truth.

Victoria — I know the truth too!

Mrs Wright — Neither of you knows the truth. Only I know the true truth. You are both guilty. My mind's eye sees everything. You *(pointing wildly, blindly, at nobody)* are Ida the Red. And you *(pointing wildly in the opposite direction)* are Jonathan McIntosh. You are both northern spies.

Enter Townspeople again, same as before, stage left, crossing the stage, speaking, as before. Mrs Wright lifts her blindfold a little, to see them and nod hello, and to check for herself who Albert is.

Townspeople —
Here's the lovely pot plant.
Ooh, see how much bigger it's got!
Look! Someone's written graffiti on a leaf.
Disgusting! Whoever did it should be shot.
Protesters are worse than hooligans.
Off with their heads!
Ooh, look at him with the umbrella stuck in him.
Still there. Still dead!
Ooh, look. It's Mrs Wright. It's be all right now.
And there's that policeman who gets his words wrong.
And there's that evil cow.

At this, Victoria stares them down. They look away.

Mrs Wright — Now, where were we? Oh, I know. Guilty! Guilty! Guilty!

1 Twenty questions

Before you perform the play, discuss the following questions in your group.

1 Where is the action taking place?
2 Who are the characters?
3 Why are they here?
4 Who is the dead person?
5 Who is the murderer?
6 What problem does the policeman have with words?
7 What things does he say he saw, things that never really happened?
8 How does Victoria react to this?
9 Why do King Arthur and Excalibur come up?
10 Who are the Townspeople and why don't they have a name?
11 Why do they speak together? Why do they speak in rhyme?
12 Why do the townspeople know the policeman and Mrs Wright?
13 Why is Mrs Wright blindfolded?
14 Why does she lift her blindfold once?
15 Why does Mrs Wright call Victoria Ida the Red? And the policeman Jonathan McIntosh?
16 Is anyone really waiting for the bus?
17 What is the purpose of the pot plant?
18 What is going to happen next?
19 Would you call the play realistic or absurd? Funny or exciting?
20 Who's guilty?

2 The wrong words

Look for all the examples of where the policeman uses the wrong word. Make sure you understand what the wrong and right words mean. Use a dictionary if necessary.

3 Putting on the play

a) *Divide the class into groups of students who would like to …*

- *act (12 students – two for each character),*
- *find props, make costumes and think of make-up (4–6),*
- *choose the music and do the lighting (2–4),*
- *design a programme (2–4).*

b) Work in your groups as follows:

Actors

First go through the play and divide it into scenes (they should end/start where people exit or enter). Practise reading a couple of scenes. You might like to change/add to the stage directions. Discuss how characters walk, move and speak.

Tip

Stage directions

The stage directions sometimes tell you about the scenery, props and the actors, e.g. what they should do, how they should do it, or how they speak or feel.
The stage directions in this play are quite detailed. Check them carefully – you can change them if you need to.

Props, costume and make-up artists

Go through the play and decide what props you need and when.

- We need an umbrella for the dead man's back.
- Yes, and a bench ... Perhaps we can use ...
- Then there's a ...

Make a list of the characters and decide on what clothes they should wear and if make-up is necessary.

- Victoria is an apple farmer, so she should ...
- Albert has to look like a policeman. How can we do that?
- I think Mrs Wright should ...

Music and lighting

Choose music and lighting that match the atmosphere in each part of the play.

- This is obviously all happening outside, so the light needs to be ...
- Perhaps there should be some music every time somebody enters or exits. But what sort?

Programme designers

Design a programme for the audience. Think of an illustration for the cover that will show people something about the play and make them want to see it. Include a cast list and the names of the actors. Write a short summary of the play (but don't give away too much). Don't forget the time and place of the performance.

- We have to design a poster too because the cover of the programme should be the same as the poster.

TF 10

A different kind of justice[1]

L S R W

1 Crime in England and Wales: some facts and figures

a) *Look at the chart and describe what it shows.*

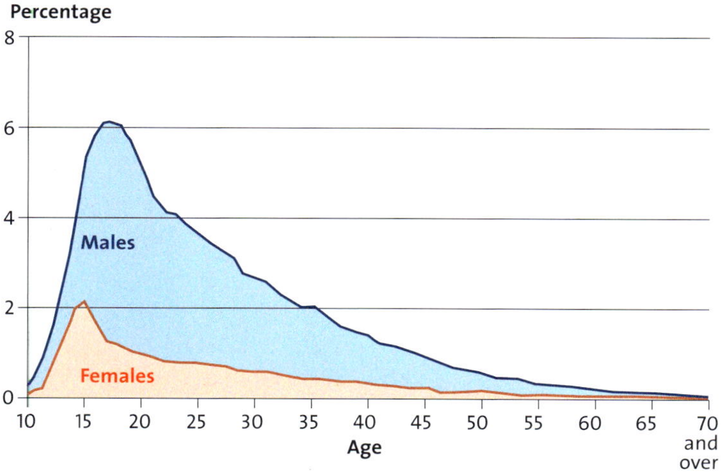

Offenders[2] as a percentage of the population: by age, 2006, England and Wales

Activate your English

– The chart shows us ...
– From the chart we can see that ...
– It gives us the figures/ percentages/numbers/... for ...
– With the facts and figures we can compare ...
– They show that more/fewer ... than ...
– The percentage of ... is/rises/ drops ... between (the age of) ... and ...

b) *Discuss the other facts and figures with your partner.*

- In **2006**, **1.42** million offenders were found guilty[3] of crimes or were warned in England and Wales.
- **80 per cent** of these offenders were male.
- **7** per cent were aged under 18.
- In June **2006** there were **10,230** young offenders aged **15–20** in prison.
- **Four** out of every **10** young offenders commit another crime in their first year after leaving prison.

L S R W

2 Bus attack (Part 1)

Now read this case study of two young offenders in England.

Over a period of time two boys had been throwing stones at the Number 67 bus as it went past Gateway School. The bus wasn't hit but some passengers were frightened[4].

One day a stone came through the bus window next to the seat of 71-year-old Margaret Wilson. Mrs Wilson was shocked and had a mild heart attack.

The bus driver, Phil Saunders, stopped the bus and called an ambulance. Mrs Wilson was taken to hospital.

Mr Saunders had never experienced anything like this in his fifteen years as a bus driver and was shaken up by the attack. His bus company contacted the police.

[1] justice ['dʒʌstɪs] *Gerechtigkeit* [2] offender [ə'fendə] *Straftäter/in* [3] (to) find sb. guilty ['gɪlti] *jn. schuldig sprechen, für schuldig befinden*
[4] frightened ['fraɪtənd] *verängstigt*

Sergeant Brian Yates, a police officer who works with schools, went to Gateway School. He held an assembly[1] in which he told the students about the attack and asked them to put a note in a box if they knew who the stone-throwers were.

The notes in the box named two 15 year-old boys, Luke and Reece. After Sergeant Yates spoke to them, Luke and Reece admitted[2] that they were guilty.

a) *Match the sentence halves correctly.*

1 Two boys sometimes threw stones
2 One day a stone
3 It shocked
4 She had
5 She was taken
6 A police officer held
7 He asked students to write notes
8 Two boys, Luke H and Reece B,

a a mild heart attack.
b an assembly at Gateway School.
c an old lady.
d at the Number 67 bus.
e if they knew who the stone-throwers were.
f to hospital.
g went through the bus window.
h were named.

b) *Why do you think Luke and Reece threw stones at the bus? Collect ideas in class.*
fed up with school, to look big[3], …

c) *What do you think will happen next?*

Luke and Reece will	go to court get an ASBO …

d) **Extra** *What would happen to them if they were students at your school? Discuss.*
see the head teacher, have to apologize, …

"Here's my report Dad.
I got an A, an S, a B and an O."

3 Bus attack (Part 2)

Sergeant Yates didn't want Luke and Reece to be prosecuted[4] and get a criminal record[5]. He said the boys were still young and they had never been in trouble with the police before. So he suggested a restorative justice conference[6] where the two boys would meet the people they had harmed[7] face to face.

Next, Yates visited the boys' families. Luke lived with his grandparents. They were terribly upset by the case, especially by what had happened to the victim, Margaret Wilson.

At first Luke and Reece were not sorry about what they had done – only about

[1] assembly [ə'sembli] *Versammlung* [2] (to) admit [əd'mɪt] *zugeben* [3] (to) look big *groß tun, sich wichtig machen* [4] prosecuted ['prɒsɪkju:tɪd] *strafrechtich verfolgt* [5] criminal record [ˌkrɪmɪnl 'rekɔ:d] *Vorstrafe* [6] restorative justice conference [rɪˌstɔ:rətɪv 'dʒʌstɪs ˌkɒnfərəns] *ein außergerichtliches Treffen von Täter/in, Opfer und Vermittler/in mit dem Ziel des Täter-Opfer-Ausgleichs* [7] (to) harm [hɑ:m] *schaden, schädigen*

getting caught. So Brian Yates and some teachers at the school spent a lot of time with them before the conference. They wanted to help them understand what harm they had done.

At the conference, Luke and Reece sat face to face with people from the police and the bus company. And with the bus driver and Mrs Wilson's daughter.

The conference had a very big effect on Luke and Reece.

'I'm sure Mum would be sad to see how upset the boys are,' Mrs Wilson's daughter told the conference. 'And she'll be happy to hear that they've promised to make up for[1] what they've done.'

In the end, the agreement was that Luke and Reece would go to the bus company every Saturday for six months to clean the buses. And they did. Their families reported that it had changed their behaviour.

But Luke and Reece still didn't understand why other students had 'grassed'[2] on them. So Sergeant Yates arranged another assembly at school. Here, a number of children explained why they had named Luke and Reece. They said it had given Gateway School a bad reputation[3] and that someone could have been badly hurt.

Luke and Reece were respected more at school for cleaning the buses. The other students thought it showed they were sorry. The two boys felt they had made up for what they had done and this made a big difference to them.

a) *Were you surprised by what happened in the case after the boys had thrown stones at the bus? Why (not)?*

b) *Give a short summary of the case.*

Activate your English
- This is a case study of a crime in ...
- The crime was committed by ...
- They admitted they were ...
- The victim of the crime was ...
- The boys were not prosecuted ...
- They went to a restorative justice conference.
- They made up for their crime by ...

4 Discussing the case

Discuss the case in your group. The following questions might help you. Present your ideas to the class.
- Should the bus company or the victim have prosecuted Luke and Reece? Why/Why not?
- Was the restorative justice conference a good idea in their case? Give reasons.
- Do you think the agreement at the conference was fair? Or would some time in prison or an ASBO have been better? Explain your opinion.
- Was it right of other students to 'grass on' Luke and Reece? Give reasons.

► *SF Having a discussion (p. 143)*

SOCIAL STUDY SKILLS Case study

You usually look at a case from the outside. Then think about:
- **the people**: who was involved in the case and what did they do?
- **the people**: what happened exactly?
- the possible **solutions** and the **consequences** (e.g. for the offenders)
- what you can **learn from** the case.

You can also try to look at the case from the **inside**. Consider:
- how the people who were involved might have felt.
- what you would have done in their position.

[1] (to) make up for sth. *etwas wieder gutmachen* [2] (to) grass on sb. [grɑːs] *(infml) jn. verpfeifen* [3] a bad reputation [ˌrepjuˈteɪʃn] *ein schlechter Ruf, ein schlechtes Ansehen*

Skills File – Inhalt

Seite

STUDY AND LANGUAGE SKILLS

REVISION Using a bilingual dictionary 124
REVISION Using an English–English dictionary 125
Using a grammar 125
Using a thesaurus 125
REVISION Learning words 126
REVISION Describing pictures 126
Talking about statistics 127
REVISION Research 128
REVISION Outlining 129
REVISION Giving a presentation 130
REVISION Handouts 130
Visual aids in presentations 131
Project skills 132–133

LISTENING AND READING SKILLS

REVISION Listening 134
REVISION Taking notes 135
REVISION Marking up a text 135
REVISION READING COURSE 136–137
Working out the meaning of words 136
Skimming and scanning 136
Finding the main ideas of a text 136
Careful reading 137
Text types: fiction and non-fiction 137
Reading literature 138–139

MEDIATION SKILLS

REVISION Mediation 140

SPEAKING AND WRITING SKILLS

REVISION Paraphrasing 141
REVISION Brainstorming 141
SPEAKING COURSE Zusammenfassung 142–143
Having a conversation 142
Asking for, confirming, giving information 142
Giving an oral summary 143
Having a discussion 143
REVISION WRITING COURSE 144–145
Writing better sentences 144
Using paragraphs 144
Linking paragraphs 145
Correcting your text 145

Seite

Writing different types of text 146–149
REVISION Writing a report 146
REVISION Writing a letter to a magazine 146
Writing formal letters 146
Argumentative writing 147
Writing a CV 148
REVISION Summary writing 149

EXAM SKILLS

REVISION How to do well in a test 150–152

Im **Skills File** findest du Hinweise zu Arbeits- und Lerntechniken. Was du in den Skills-Kästen der Units gelernt hast, wird hier näher erläutert.

Was du bereits aus Band 4 von English G 21 kennst, ist mit **REVISION** gekennzeichnet, z. B.

– **REVISION Describing pictures**, Seite 126
– **REVISION Giving a presentation**, Seite 130.

Viele neue Hinweise helfen dir bei der Arbeit mit Hör- und Lesetexten, beim Sprechen, beim Schreiben von eigenen Texten und beim Lernen von Methoden.

STUDY AND LANGUAGE SKILLS

SF REVISION Using a bilingual dictionary

Wann brauche ich ein zweisprachiges Wörterbuch?

Du verstehst einen Text nicht, weil er zu viele Wörter enthält, die dir unbekannt sind, und die Worterschließungstechniken (► *Working out the meaning of words, p. 136*) helfen dir nicht weiter?
Du sollst einen Text auf Englisch schreiben, und dir fehlt das eine oder andere Wort, um deine Ideen auszudrücken? Du willst z. B. über die Ankunft eines Einwanderers in einem neuen Land schreiben und kennst das Wort für „Grenze" nicht? Dann hilft dir ein zweisprachiges Wörterbuch.

Wie benutze ich ein zweisprachiges Wörterbuch?

- Die **Leitwörter** *(running heads)* oben auf der Seite helfen dir, schneller zu finden, was du suchst. Auf der linken Seite steht das erste Stichwort, auf der rechten Seite das letzte Stichwort der Doppelseite.
- **drehen** ist das **Stichwort** *(headword)*. Stichwörter sind alphabetisch geordnet: **d** vor **e**, **da** vor **de** und **dre** vor **dri** usw.
- Die ***kursiv* gedruckten** Hinweise helfen dir, die für deinen Text passende Bedeutung zu finden.
- Die **Ziffern** 1, 2 usw. zeigen, dass ein Stichwort mehrere ganz verschiedene Bedeutungen hat.
- **Beispielsätze** und **Redewendungen** sind dem Stichwort zugeordnet. In den Beispielsätzen und Redewendungen ersetzt eine **Tilde** (~) das Stichwort.
- Im englisch-deutschen Teil der meisten Wörterbücher findest du außerdem Hinweise auf **unregelmäßige Verbformen**, auf die **Steigerungsformen der Adjektive** und Ähnliches.
- Die **Lautschrift** gibt Auskunft darüber, wie das Wort ausgesprochen und betont wird.
- Bei kniffligen Wörtern gibt es in vielen Wörterbüchern **Info-Boxes**, in denen dir mehr Hilfen und Hinweise gegeben werden.

Dr.

Dr. (*Abk. für* ***Doktor***) Dr., Doctor
Drache dragon
Drachen *Papierdrachen* kite; *Fluggerät* hang glider

Drehbuch screenplay, script
drehen **1** *Verb mit Obj* turn; *Film* shoot*; *Zigarette* roll **2**: ***sich*** **~** turn; *schnell* spin*; ***sich*** **~ *um*** *übertragen* be* about
Drehkreuz turnstile; **Drehorgel** barrel organ ['ɔːgən]; **Drehort** location; **Drehstuhl** swivel chair; **Drehtür** revolving door
Drehung turn; *um eine Achse* rotation
Drehzahl (number of) revolutions *Pl od.* revs *Pl*
Drehzahlmesser rev counter
drei three
Drei three; *Note etwa* C; ***ich habe eine* ~ *geschrieben*** I got a C
dreidimensional **1** *Adj* three-dimensional **2** *Adv*: ***etwas* ~ *darstellen*** depict sth. three-dimensionally; **Dreieck** triangle ['traɪæŋgl]; **dreieckig** triangular [traɪ'æŋgjʊlə]

bringen

bring (**herbringen; mitbringen**) wird nur verwendet, wenn jemand oder etwas zum Ort des Sprechers oder Hörers gebracht wird:

Schön, dass du zu meiner Party	I'm glad you can come to my party. Can

take (**weg-, hinbringen; mitnehmen**) wird verwendet, wenn jemand oder etwas woanders hingebracht oder mitgenommen wird:

Kannst du morgen deinen Bruder zur Schule bringen?	Can you take your brother to school tomorrow?

Also: Lies immer erst den **gesamten Wörterbucheintrag**, bevor du dich für eine bestimmte Übersetzung entscheidest. Nimm nicht einfach die erste Übersetzung, die dir angeboten wird.
Wenn du unsicher bist, ob du die richtige Übersetzung gefunden hast, schau dir den Eintrag zu dieser Übersetzung an. Wenn du z. B. überprüfen willst, ob „spin" im zweiten Satz unten die richtige Übersetzung für „drehen" ist, such einen Eintrag unter „spin" und lies ihn dir durch.

„drehen"=?

She's a good dancer, she loves to ... round and round as fast as she can.

Lots of Hollywood stars come to Berlin to ... their films here.

SF REVISION Using an English–English dictionary

Wenn du englische Texte liest oder selbst einen englischen Text schreibst, kannst du ein einsprachiges englisches Wörterbuch zur Hilfe nehmen. Hier findest du mehr über ein englisches Wort heraus als in einem zweisprachigen Wörterbuch:

- Das einsprachige Wörterbuch erklärt die **Bedeutung** eines englischen Wortes **auf Englisch**. Manche Wörter haben mehrere Bedeutungen. Lies alle Einträge und Beispielsätze genau und vergleiche sie mit deinem englischen Text, um die richtige Bedeutung herauszufinden.
- –Das Wörterbuch hilft dir auch, die passende **Verbindung mit anderen Wörtern** zu finden, z.B. zu Verben, Präpositionen oder in bestimmten Wendungen. Das ist besonders nützlich, wenn du selbst einen englischen Text schreiben willst und nach den richtigen Wörtern suchst.

deadly ['dedli] *adj*
1 *able or likely to kill people* {= lethal}: This is no longer a deadly disease.
deadly to The HSN virus is deadly to chickens.
a deadly weapon The new generation of biological weapons is more deadly than ever.
2 (*only before noun*) {= complete}: ***deadly silence*** There was deadly silence after his speech.
a deadly secret Don't tell anyone – this is a deadly secret.
in deadly earnest *completely serious:* Don't you laugh – I am in deadly earnest!
3 (*informal*) *very boring*: Many TV programmes are pretty deadly!
4 *always able to achieve something*: The new Chelsea striker is said to be a deadly

SF Using a grammar

▸ Unit 2 (p. 43)

Vielleicht hast du beim Korrigieren deiner Klassenarbeiten schon einmal bemerkt, dass du immer die gleichen Fehler machst. Um diese zu vermeiden, kannst du ein Grammatikbuch zu Hilfe nehmen, dass dir bei der Verwendung bestimmter grammatischer Strukturen helfen kann. In einem zweiten Schritt kannst du mit einer Grammatik auch an der Verbesserung deines Stils arbeiten, wenn es z.B. um die Verwendung von Partizipien in formalen Texten geht.

Schritt 1: Lege eine individuelle Fehlerstatistik an, d.h. notiere dir aus den Korrekturen deiner Klassenarbeiten die Fehlersorten Wortschatz, Grammatik, Satzbau, Stil, ...

Schritt 2: Suche dir aus dem Bereich, in dem am häufigsten Fehler auftreten, einen Schwerpunkt heraus, z.B. tenses.

Schritt 3: Suche im Inhaltsverzeichnis deiner Grammatik die betreffenden Kapitel heraus und lies sie dir nochmals gründlich durch. Vergleiche sie mit den Fehlern, die du in deinen Klassenarbeiten machst.

Schritt 4: Schreib dir einige wenige Mustersätze und Merkregeln zu diesen grammatischen Strukturen auf einen Merkzettel. Vor der nächsten Klassenarbeit solltest du ihn dir nochmals anschauen.

Inversion ....
Question tags ....
Imperatives/Commands ....
Exclamations ....
Main clauses and subordinate clauses ....
Clause elements ....

The verb

Summary ....
Modal auxiliaries ....
Be, *have* and *do* ....
The short forms of the auxiliaries ....
Full verbs ....
Summary: the tenses of the full verbs ....
The tenses of the full verbs ....
Simple present ....
Present pro...
Simple pres... co...
Present per...
Present per...
Present per... per...
Since and f...
Simple pas...
Present perfect and simple past in contrast .
Past progressive ....
Simple past and past progressive in contrast
Past perfect ....
Past perfect progressive ....
Ways of expressing future time ....
Will-future ....
Going to-future ....
Present progressive ....
Simple present ....
Future progressive ....

He goes to school every day.
he, she it, ein -s muss mit!!!

SF Using a thesaurus

▸ Unit 4 (p. 90)

Ein Thesaurus ist ein Synonymwörterbuch. Ein Synonym ist ein Wort mit (annähernd) der gleichen Bedeutung wie ein anderes Wort.
Wenn du englische Texte schreibst, verwendest du manchmal zu oft die gleichen „einfachen" Wörter, wie z.B. *big*, *good* oder *run*. Ein Thesaurus kann dir helfen, deine Texte präziser, abwechslungsreicher, manchmal auch spannender zu machen. Er hilft dir, dich interessanter auszudrücken und Wiederholungen zu vermeiden. Auch die richtige Stilebene triffst du mit dem Thesaurus leichter. Ein Thesaurus verzeichnet oft auch Antonyme, also Wörter mit entgegengesetzter Bedeutung – achte auf die Bezeichnungen und Symbole.

sad (adj)
Definition: unhappy, depressed
Synonyms: bereaved, bitter, blue*, cheerless, dejected, despairing, despondent, disconsolate, dismal, distressed, doleful, down, down in dumps, down in mouth, downcast, forlorn, gloomy, glum, grief-stricken, grieved, heartbroken, heartsick, heavyhearted, hurting, in doldrums, in grief, in the dumps, languishing, low, low-spirited, lugubrious, melancholy, morbid, morose, mournful, out of sorts*, pensive,

SF REVISION Learning words

Worauf solltest du beim Lernen und Wiederholen von Vokabeln achten?

- Lerne neue und wiederhole alte Vokabeln regelmäßig – am besten jeden Tag 5–10 Minuten. Lerne immer 7–10 Vokabeln auf einmal.
- Lerne mit jemandem zusammen. Fragt euch gegenseitig ab.
- Schreib die neuen Wörter auch auf und überprüfe die Schreibweise mithilfe des *Dictionary* oder *Vocabulary*.

Wie kannst du Wörter besser behalten?

- Sammle **Gegensatzpaare**, z. B. alive – dead, majority – minority, find – lose.
- Sammle Wörter mit **gleicher Bedeutung**, z. B. (to) train – (to) practise.
- Sammle Wörter in **Wortfamilien**, z. B. (to) dance, dance, dancer, dancing lessons, shop, shopper, shopping, shopping list, shop assistant, ...
- Sammle und ordne Wörter in **Wortnetzen** *(networks)*.

SF REVISION Describing pictures

Wie kann ich Bilder beschreiben?

Wo?

- Um zu sagen, wo genau auf dem Bild etwas Bestimmtes dargestellt ist, verwende
  at the top/bottom • in the foreground/background • in the middle • on the left/right • behind • between • in front of • next to • under
- Um zu beschreiben, was die Personen auf dem Bild tun, verwende das **present progressive**.
  The girl is riding her horse.

Wie kann ich beschreiben, was die abgebildeten Personen fühlen?

Oft sollst du dich in eine Person auf einem Foto hineinversetzen und beschreiben, was sie fühlt oder denkt. Schau dir das Foto genau an und nimm dir Zeit, dir die Situation vorzustellen. Beim Formulieren helfen dir *phrases* wie:
Maybe the woman/man in the photo feels ... / is thinking about ... •
I think he/she might want to ...

SF Talking about statistics ▸ *Unit 1 (p. 10)*

Welche Arten von Diagrammen gibt es?

Diagramme bilden statistische Vergleiche zwischen mindestens zwei Sachverhalten grafisch ab. Die **Überschrift** des Diagramms ist sehr wichtig, denn sie gibt bereits genaue Informationen darüber, worum es bei der betreffenden Abbildung geht. Die **Darstellungsform** richtet sich häufig danach, ob man Zahlen oder Prozentsätze miteinander vergleichen will:

- ***Bar chart* (Säulendiagramm)**: Anzahl oder Größe von zwei oder mehr Dingen
- ***Pie chart* (Kreis-/Tortendiagramm)**: prozentuale Verteilung
- ***Table* (Tabelle)**: Vergleich unterschiedlicher Daten anhand von Zahlen und Prozentsätzen
- ***Line graph* (Kurvendiagramm)**: Entwicklung im Verhältnis unterschiedlicher Größen

Australia's population in millions

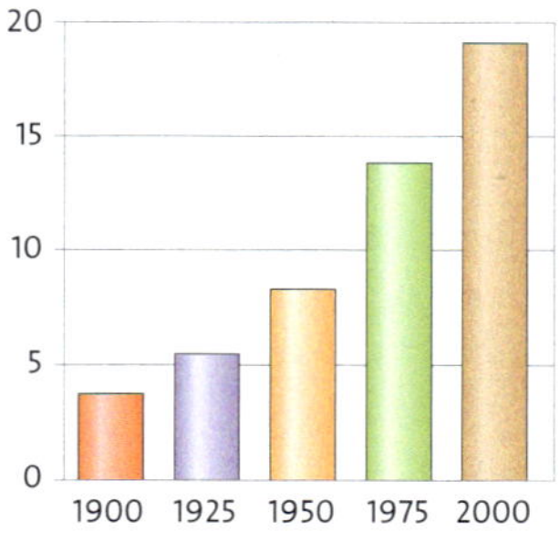

Wie beschreibe ich ein Diagramm?

Um ein Diagramm zu beschreiben, solltest du folgende Fragen beantworten:

- What is the graph/chart about?
  The bar/pie chart is about ... / It deals with ... / It is taken from ...
- What does the graph/chart/table refer to/compare?
  The pie chart compares the size/number of ... / It shows the different ... in ... / It is divided into ... slices which show ... / The graph/chart/table shows the relation between ... and ... / The table compares the population in terms of / with regard to ...
- What does the chart tell you? What information does it give you?
  ... has the largest/second largest/... / ... is twice/three times/... as big as ... / A huge majority/small minority is ... / ... per cent are ... / There are more than/ nearly twice as many ... as there are ...

Australia: origin of immigrants 2006

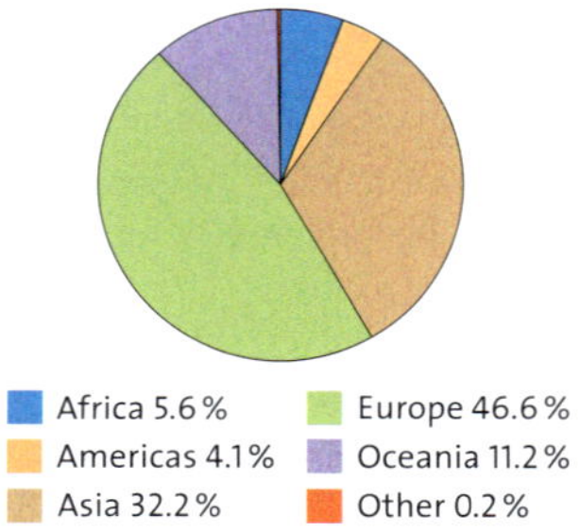

Manchmal kann es hilfreich sein, wenn du auch noch Aussagen über den Zeitraum der Statistik und/oder die Form der Darstellung machst:
It covers a period of ... months/years. / It shows a development of three months/ years from 2002 to 2005. / The vertical / horizontal line shows / represents... / The figures are expressed as a percentage of the total population / total number of ...

Country	Population (2008)
USA	304,721,000
Germany	82,400,996
UK	60,776,238
Australia	21,373,760

Achte bei der Beschreibung von Diagrammen auf die **Zeitformen** des Englischen:

- Benutze das *simple past*, wenn du dich auf einen Zeitpunkt in der Vergangenheit beziehst: **The rainfall was 2207 mm in Cairns in 2008**.
- Das *simple present* verwendest du bei allgemeingültigen Aussagen (**The average rainfall in Cairns is 1992 mm per year**) oder wenn du deine Schlussfolgerungen wiedergibst.
- Benutze das *present perfect*, wenn du dich auf einen Zeitraum beziehst, der von der Vergangenheit bis heute reicht: **Three millions Asians have come to Australia since 2000**.

Shark attacks in Australia 2000–2009

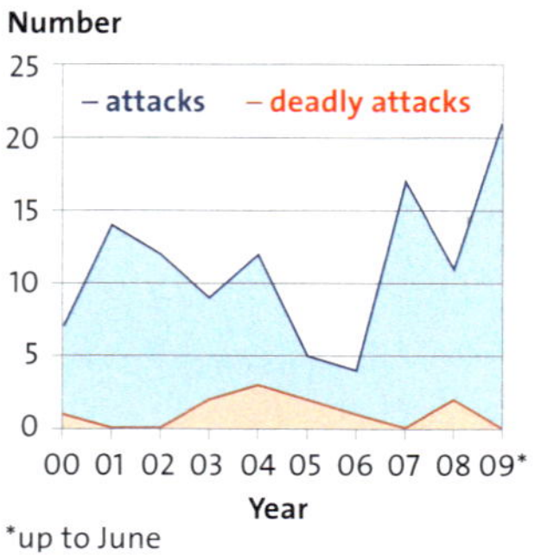

Wenn du dich auf die Zahlen bzw. Größen eines Diagramms beziehst, dann verwende **amount** für nicht zählbare Nomen: **A large amount of meat/rain/ food/...** Für zählbare Nomen benutzt du das englische Wort **number**: **The number of immigrants/Asians/people/...**

SF REVISION Research

Material sammeln (recherchieren)

Wenn du über ein Thema etwas schreiben oder einen Vortrag halten sollst, suchst du zuerst Informationen in Büchern oder in Zeitschriften, im Internet und in anderen Quellen. Verwende möglichst englischsprachige Quellen.

Damit du die Übersicht behältst, solltest du das Gefundene in einem Ordner sammeln und von vornherein sortieren. Orientiere dich dafür an der Gliederung bzw. *outline*, die du für deinen Text oder deine Präsentation vorbereitet hast (► *Outlining, p. 129*). Du kannst deine Materialien auch danach ordnen, ob es sich um sachliche Informationen, also Tatsachen, oder um persönliche Meinungen handelt.

Wichtiges herausschreiben (exzerpieren)

Sichte das Material und entscheide, welche Informationen du tatsächlich verwenden möchtest. Du kannst die betreffenden Passagen markieren (► *Marking up a text, p. 135*), herausschreiben oder auch ausschneiden und in fortlaufender Reihenfolge auf DIN-A4-Blätter kleben. Vergiss die Quellenangabe nicht. Deine eigenen Gedanken fügst du in Stichpunkten an den entsprechenden Stellen hinzu. Wenn du eine Präsentation vorbereitest, kannst du am Rand notieren, welche Medien du jeweils einsetzen möchtest.

Aus Materialien, die du im Internet gefunden und in elektronischen Ordnern gesammelt hast, überträgst du die wichtigen Informationen mit „Ausschneiden“ und „Kopieren“ in ein neues Dokument, wo du sie dann bearbeiten (also kürzen, ergänzen, umschreiben usw.) kannst.

Zitieren, umschreiben, Quellen angeben

Formuliere deinen Text oder deine Präsentation mit deinen eigenen Worten – schreibe nicht einfach aus deinen Quellen ab. Wenn du deine Argumentation einmal mit einer Expertenaussage unterstützen oder deinen Text mit einem Auszug aus einem Buch, einem Interview o.Ä. interessanter und abwechslungsreicher gestalten möchtest, markiere solche Zitate durch Anführungszeichen und gib Autor und Quelle einschließlich Seitenzahl an (bei Internetquellen die Webadresse und das Datum des Aufrufs). Das gilt auch dann, wenn du eine fremde Aussage mit eigenen Worten umschreibst. Gib auch bei einer Abbildung den Fundort an.

Kündige in deiner mündlichen Präsentation deine Zitate an und erkläre schwierige Wörter. Schaffe logische Übergänge zu deinen eigenen Argumenten.

Aber denk daran: Lange Zitate können deine Leser oder Zuhörer auch ermüden und erwecken leicht den Eindruck, dass du selbst nur wenig zu sagen hast. In der Kürze liegt die Würze!

http://www.shootingjozi.net/assets/images/gallery/142.jpg (17 April, 2010)

SF REVISION Outlining

Wenn du zu einem komplexen Thema einen Text schreiben oder eine Präsentation vorbereiten sollst, sammelst du zunächst Informationen und Unterlagen (▸ *Research, p. 128*). Eine zuvor erstellte Gliederung (*outline*) hilft dir dabei, denn so weißt du von vornherein genau, was du suchst. Und auch beim Ordnen deines Materials solltest du dich gleich an einer *outline* orientieren.

Outlines werden in Stichpunkten oder kurzen Sätzen verfasst. Schreibe dir zunächst deine Hauptpunkte auf. Bestimme dann Unterthemen und überlege dir, mit welchen Beispielen und Erläuterungen du deine Gedanken dazu unterstützen möchtest. Wenn du eine Mindmap erstellt hast, kannst du sie für deine Gliederung verwenden.

Achte auf eine logische Reihenfolge deiner Gedanken. Sie sollen sich in deiner *outline* widerspiegeln. Beim Gliedern kannst du verschiedene Möglichkeiten der Aufzählung (Zahlen, Groß- und Kleinbuchstaben, ...) nutzen. Mach dir einen Vermerk, z. B. am Rand des Blattes, welche Zitate, Statistiken, Bilder, Medienbeiträge usw. du an welcher Stelle einsetzen möchtest.

Die *outline* dient dir als Vorlage für deinen Text bzw. als Ausgangspunkt für deine Präsentation. Darüber hinaus kannst du sie dazu verwenden, deinen Lesern oder Zuhörern einen Überblick über dein Thema zu geben, indem du sie deinem Text oder deiner Präsentation voranstellst, z. B. bei einem mündlichen Vortrag auf einer Folie.

Building Golden Gate Bridge

OUTLINE

I. Location
- A. where it is
- B. how you got north of the city before
  - 1. by road
  - 2. by ferry → map of SF

II. History
- A. 1921: Joseph Strauss has idea for bridge
  - 1. how people liked it
  - 2. time for a new design
- B. 1933: Team design
  - 1. GGB statistics → table
  - 2. the colour

Merke dir also:
- Eine Gliederung (*outline*) hilft dir beim Recherchieren und beim Ordnen deines Materials.
- Bestimme zuerst die Hauptpunkte, dann die Unterthemen.

SF REVISION Giving a presentation

Wie mache ich eine gute Präsentation?

Vorbereitung

- Ordne deine Gedanken und notiere sie, z. B. auf nummerierten Karteikarten oder als Mindmap.
- Bereite ein Poster, eine Folie oder ein Handout (▸ *Handouts, siehe unten*) vor. Schreib groß und für alle gut lesbar.
- Übe deine Präsentation zu Hause vor einem Spiegel. Sprich laut, deutlich und langsam, mach Pausen. Reicht die Zeit?

Durchführung

- Bevor du beginnst, bereite deine Medien vor und sortiere deine Vortragskarten.
- Warte, bis es ruhig ist. Schau die Zuhörer an.
- Erkläre zu Anfang, worüber du sprechen wirst.
- Lies nicht von deinen Karten ab, sondern sprich frei.
- Schreibe die Gliederung sowie unbekannten Wortschatz und Eigennamen an die Tafel.

My presentation is about ... First, I'd like to talk about ... Second, ...

This picture/photo/ ... shows ...

Schluss

- Sag, dass du fertig bist.
- Frag die Zuhörer, ob sie Fragen haben.
- Bedanke dich fürs Zuhören.

That's the end of my presentation. Thank you for listening. Have you got any questions?

SF REVISION Handouts

Ein Handout enthält die wichtigsten Informationen einer Präsentation. Manchmal bietet es auch zusätzliche Informationen an, z. B. in Form von Statistiken, Quellenangaben oder Illustrationen.
Ein Handout kannst du vor, während oder nach deiner Präsentation austeilen:

- vor oder während der Präsentation, damit die Zuhörer die Gliederung deines Vortrags verstehen und ihm besser folgen können;
- nach der Präsentation, damit die Zuhörer später noch einmal nachlesen und sich besser an die Präsentation erinnern können.

Strukturiere dein Handout klar und übersichtlich, z. B. durch eine Überschrift, deinen Namen, das Datum, durch Teilüberschriften, Beispiele, tabellarische oder grafische Übersichten.

Du kannst in ganzen Sätzen schreiben, z. B. bei einer Zusammenfassung, oder in Stichpunkten.

Wenn du Abbildungen verwendest, gib ihnen eine Bildunterschrift und vergiss nicht die Quellenangabe. Mit Symbolen kannst du dein Handout übersichtlicher gestalten und die wesentlichen Informationen hervorheben.

Lass ausreichend Platz für die Notizen der Zuhörer, z. B. durch einen breiten Rand an der Seite oder im unteren Teil des Blattes.

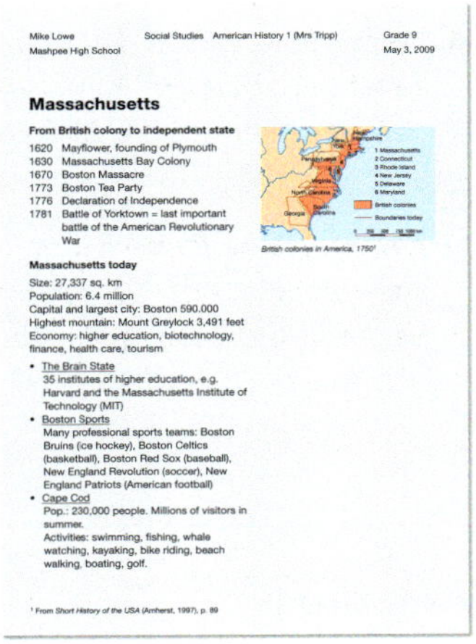

Mike Lowe | Social Studies American History 1 (Mrs Tripp) | Grade 9
Mashpee High School | May 3, 2009

Massachusetts

From British colony to independent state

1620 Mayflower, founding of Plymouth
1630 Massachusetts Bay Colony
1670 Boston Massacre
1773 Boston Tea Party
1776 Declaration of Independence
1781 Battle of Yorktown = last important battle of the American Revolutionary War

British colonies in America, 1750[1]

Massachusetts today

Size: 27,337 sq. km
Population: 6.4 million
Capital and largest city: Boston 590.000
Highest mountain: Mount Greylock 3,491 feet
Economy: higher education, biotechnology, finance, health care, tourism

- The Brain State
  35 institutes of higher education, e.g. Harvard and the Massachusetts Institute of Technology (MIT)
- Boston Sports
  Many professional sports teams: Boston Bruins (ice hockey), Boston Celtics (basketball), Boston Red Sox (baseball), New England Revolution (soccer), New England Patriots (American football)
- Cape Cod
  Pop.: 230,000 people. Millions of visitors in summer.
  Activities: swimming, fishing, whale watching, kayaking, bike riding, beach walking, boating, golf.

[1] From *Short History of the USA* (Amherst, 1997), p. 89

SF Visual aids in presentations ▸ Unit 2 (p. 45)

Um die Ergebnisse deiner Arbeit besser anschaulich zu machen, kannst du verschiedene Präsentationsmedien verwenden. Sie helfen dir außerdem, deine Präsentation gut strukturiert vorzutragen, und erleichtern deinen Zuhörern das Verständnis.

Es gibt sehr **unterschiedliche visuelle Präsentationsformen**. Poster, Overhead-Folien und Computerpräsentationen sind die am häufigsten verwendeten, aber auch eine Zeichnung an der Tafel kann sehr anschaulich sein.

Bei visuellen Hilfsmitteln musst du einige wesentliche Aspekte beachten, damit sie erfolgreich eingesetzt werden können:

1. Verwende je nach Form des Hilfsmittels eine **Schriftgröße**, die von allen überall im Klassenraum gelesen werden kann. Was man nicht lesen kann, hilft nicht! Überprüfe vor deiner Präsentation die Lesbarkeit von verschiedenen Stellen im Klassenzimmer aus.
2. Deine Folien, Poster usw. sollten eine **klare Struktur** haben. Benutze Fettdruck oder Großbuchstaben, um besonders wichtige Dinge hervorzuheben. Auch Symbole wie zum Beispiel Pfeile und Aufzählungszeichen helfen dabei.
3. **Vermeide zu viele Informationen auf einmal.** Eine Idee pro Folie reicht bei einer elektronischen Präsentation vollkommen. Vermeide, wenn möglich, längere zusammenhängende Texte. Halte nur die Hauptaspekte deines Vortrags fest.
4. **Bilder, Illustrationen und Grafiken** unterstützen das Gesagte und die Anschaulichkeit deines Vortrags. Auch hier gilt: auf die Größe achten!
5. Die einzelnen Visualisierungen brauchen einen **klaren Ablaufplan**, d.h. sie sollen deinen Vortrag begleiten. Verwende sie deshalb nacheinander und gib deinen Zuhörern die Möglichkeit, sie parallel zu deinem Vortrag lange genug wahrzunehmen.
6. Vermeide es, während der Präsentation selbst auf deine visuellen Hilfsmittel zu schauen bzw. dich hinter einem Poster oder einem Handout zu verstecken. Halte zu jeder Zeit den **Blickkontakt** mit deinen Zuhörern aufrecht.
7. Dein Körper ist ein wichtiger Teil der Visualisierung. Achte auf deine **Körpersprache**. Bleibe deinem Publikum zugewandt, halte Augenkontakt, stehe sicher vor der Gruppe und halte deine Hände oberhalb der Gürtellinie. Verstecke dich nicht hinter einem Skript. Auch ein Lächeln kann sehr überzeugend sein!

SF Project skills ▸ *Unit 1 (p. 7)*

Organisation ist (fast) alles

Bei einer Projektarbeit, die du mit anderen gemeinsam durchführst, kommt es darauf an, dass du dich und deine Arbeit sehr gut organisierst und die einzelnen Phasen eines Projektes berücksichtigst. Meistens findet die Bearbeitung eines Projektauftrags innerhalb einer gewissen Zeitspanne statt, während parallel dazu der Unterricht weitergeht. Oft findet also ein Großteil der Arbeit außerhalb des Unterrichts statt – ein guter Grund, um nochmals auf die einzelne Schritte einer Projektarbeit zu schauen, die dir helfen sollen, zur verabredeten *deadline* dein fertiges Produkt abgeben zu können.

Projektarbeit Schritt für Schritt

Schritt 1: Entscheide dich für dein Thema
Zuerst musst du dir darüber klar werden, welches Thema dich interessieren könnte. Zu welchem Thema weißt du vielleicht schon etwas, sodass du auf diesem Wissen aufbauen kannst?

Schritt 2: Finde deine Projektpartner
Nun musst du Mitschülerinnen und Mitschüler finden, die dein Thema ebenfalls interessant finden. Bei einer Projektarbeit kommt es auch darauf an, dass sich Menschen mit unterschiedlichen Talenten in einer Gruppe finden: Wer kennt sich gut mit dem Internet aus, wer kann zeichnen, wer schreiben, ...?

Schritt 3: Tauscht eure Ideen aus
Was weiß eure Gruppe schon über das gewählte Thema? Wie soll eure Arbeit aussehen? Sammelt alle Ideen und Anregungen – vielleicht in Form einer *placemat* oder Mindmap? Vergesst nicht, euch auch auf die Form eures Handlungsproduktes, dem Ergebnis eurer Projektarbeit, zu einigen. Das kann zum Beispiel ein Poster, ein Text, ein Booklet oder eine Präsentation sein.

Schritt 4: Plant eure Arbeit
Wer übernimmt welche Aufgabe? Setzt euch einen realistischen Zeitrahmen und überprüft regelmäßig euren Arbeitsstand.

Schritt 5: Recherchiert Material
Für euer Produkt braucht ihr Informationen, Material, Bilder und vieles mehr. Stellt sicher, dass jeder etwas beiträgt.
▸ *Research, p. 128*

Schritt 6: Seid effizient
Haltet euch nicht zu lange an Materialien und Ideen auf, die euch nicht zum Ziel führen. Bei der Auswahl helfen euch unter anderem die Lesetechniken *skimming* und *scanning*.
▸ *Skimming and scanning, p. 136*

Schritt 7: Schreibt eine Outline
Wenn ihr ausreichend Material zusammengetragen habt, dann ordnet es anhand einer Outline an.
▸ *Outlining, p. 129*

Schritt 8: Beginnt mit der Herstellung eures Produktes
Beginnt recht zügig, die einzelnen Teile eures Produktes zusammenzufügen. Text, Bilder, aber auch Poster oder elektronische Präsentationen brauchen viel Zeit. Zeigt euch regelmäßig den Stand eurer Arbeiten, um mögliche Fehler frühzeitig zu bemerken.

Schritt 9: Kontrolliert gemeinsam das Produkt
Bevor ihr fertig seid, müsst ihr einen letzten Durchgang der Fehlersuche und -korrektur durchführen. Auch an Stil und Layout kann man jetzt noch Verbesserungen vornehmen.

Schritt 10: Präsentiert eure Ergebnisse
Wenn ihr eure Ergebnisse in einer Präsentation vorstellen wollt, müsst ihr diese gut vorbereiten. Denkt an eine aussagekräftige Visualisierung und ein Handout.

- ▸ *Giving a presentation, p. 130*
- ▸ *Handouts, p. 130*
- ▸ *Visual aids in presentations, p. 131*

Schritt 11 (fakultativ): Beurteile deine eigene Arbeit
Denke zum Schluss an dein nächstes Projekt und beurteile daraufhin nochmals das gerade durchgeführte. Was ist euch gut gelungen? Worauf müsst ihr das nächste Mal stärker achten?

Schritt 12: Genießt die Ergebnisse
Ihr habt ganz selbstständig eine Aufgabe gemeistert und seid sicherlich zu tollen Ergebnissen gekommen. Genießt die Produkte der anderen Gruppen, lasst euch Zeit beim Anschauen und lobt eure Mitschülerinnen und Mitschüler für die Dinge, die ihnen besonders gut gelungen sind!

LISTENING AND READING SKILLS

SF REVISION Listening

Vor dem Hören

- Frag dich, was du schon über das Thema weißt.
- Nutze Überschriften oder Bilder um zu erahnen, was dich z. B. bei einer Geschichte erwarten könnte.
- Lies dir die Aufgaben auf deinem Aufgabenblatt genau durch und überlege, auf welche Informationen du dich konzentrieren musst.
- Bereite dich darauf vor, Notizen zu machen. Leg z. B. eine Tabelle oder Liste an.

Während des Hörens

Listening for gist:
Konzentriere dich beim ersten Hören auf allgemeine Informationen, z. B. die Personen (unterschiedliche Stimmen), das Thema, die Umgebung (Geräusche), die Atmosphäre (die Sprechweise der Leute).

Listening for detail:
- Mach dir noch einmal bewusst, worauf du genau achten willst (Hörauftrag), besonders bei Durchsagen (*announcements*), die du vielleicht nur einmal hören kannst.
- Gerate nicht in Panik, wenn du meinst, du hättest gerade etwas Wichtiges verpasst. Konzentriere dich auf die nächste wichtige Information.
- Lass dich nicht von anderen Einzelheiten oder Geräuschen ablenken.
- Mach nur kurze Notizen, z. B. Anfangsbuchstaben, Symbole oder Stichworte.
- Manche Signalwörter machen es dir leichter, den Hörtext zu verstehen.
  Aufzählung: **and**, **another**, **too**
  Gegensatz: **although**, **but**
  Grund, Folge: **because**, **so**, **so that**
  Vergleich: **larger/older/... than**, **as ... as**, **more**, **most**
  Reihenfolge: **before**, **after**, **then**, **next**, **later**, **when**, **at last**, **at the same time**
- Auch andere Details wie z.B. die Stimme, der Akzent oder der Tonfall des Sprechers oder der Sprecherin können dir helfen, Informationen über seine oder ihre Gefühle, Herkunft usw. zu bekommen.
- Unterteile Telefonnummern beim Aufschreiben: 0171 572 42 589.

Nach dem Hören

- Vervollständige deine Notizen sofort.
- Wenn du den Text ein zweites Mal hören kannst, konzentriere dich auf das, was du beim ersten Mal nicht genau verstanden hast.
- Schau dir noch einmal die Aufgabenstellung an. Sollst du die gehörten Informationen nutzen, um einen neuen Text zu schreiben? Dann achte auf die richtige Textform: Bericht, Beschreibung, ...

SF REVISION Taking notes

Worum geht es beim Notizen machen?

Wenn du beim Lesen oder Zuhören Notizen machst, kannst du dich später besser daran erinnern, wenn du etwas vortragen, nacherzählen oder einen Bericht schreiben sollst.

Wie mache ich Notizen?

In Texten oder Gesprächen gibt es immer wichtige und unwichtige Wörter. Die wichtigen Wörter werden **Schlüsselwörter *(key words)*** genannt und nur die solltest du notieren. Meist sind das Substantive und Verben, manchmal auch Adjektive oder Zahlen.

Deine Notizen sollten knapp sein:

- Verwende Ziffern (z. B. „7“ statt „seven“).
- Verwende Symbole und Abkürzungen, z. B. ✔ (für Ja) und + (für und) oder GB für Great Britain, K für Katrina.
  Du kannst auch eigene Symbole erfinden.
- Verwende not oder ✗ statt „doesn't“ oder „don't“.

SF REVISION Marking up a text

Wann sollte ich einen Text markieren?

Du hast einen Text mit vielen Fakten vor dir liegen und sollst später über bestimmte Dinge berichten. Dann wird es dir helfen, die für dich wichtigen Informationen im Text zu markieren.

Wie gehe ich am besten vor?

Lies den Text und markiere nur die für dein Thema wichtigen Informationen. Nicht jeder Satz enthält Informationen, die für deine Aufgabe wichtig sind, und oft reicht es aus, nur ein oder zwei Wörter in einem Satz zu markieren.

- Du kannst wichtige Wörter einkreisen.
- Du kannst sie unterstreichen.
- Du kannst sie mit einem Textmarker hervorheben.

ABER:
Markiere nur auf Fotokopien von Texten oder in deinen eigenen Büchern.

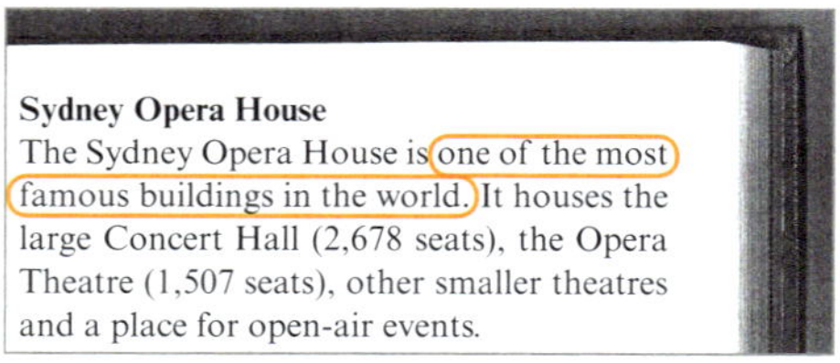

Sydney Opera House
The Sydney Opera House is one of the most famous buildings in the world. It houses the large Concert Hall (2,678 seats), the Opera Theatre (1,507 seats), other smaller theatres and a place for open-air events.

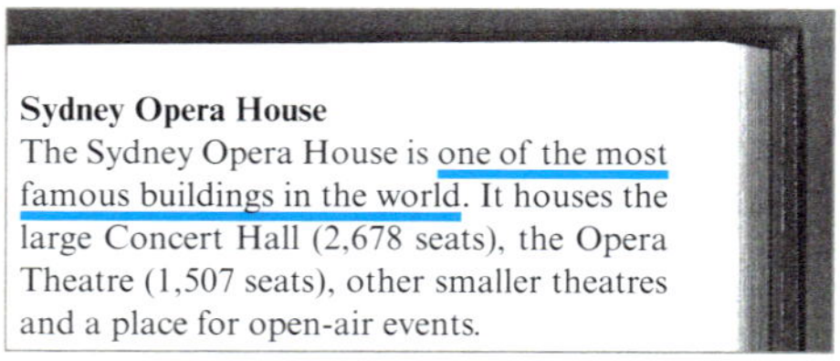

Sydney Opera House
The Sydney Opera House is one of the most famous buildings in the world. It houses the large Concert Hall (2,678 seats), the Opera Theatre (1,507 seats), other smaller theatres and a place for open-air events.

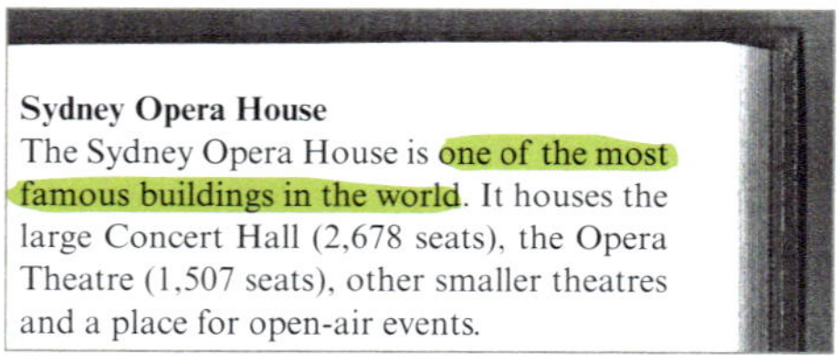

Sydney Opera House
The Sydney Opera House is one of the most famous buildings in the world. It houses the large Concert Hall (2,678 seats), the Opera Theatre (1,507 seats), other smaller theatres and a place for open-air events.

REVISION Reading course – Zusammenfassung

Working out the meaning of words

Das Nachschlagen unbekannter Wörter im Wörterbuch kostet Zeit und nimmt auf Dauer den Spaß am Lesen. Oft geht es auch ohne Wörterbuch:

1. Bilder und Zeichen erklären und ergänzen oft Dinge aus dem Text. Schau sie dir deshalb vor und nach dem Lesen genau an.
2. Manche Wörter erklären sich aus dem Textzusammenhang, z.B. *When we **reached** the station, Judy bought our tickets.*
3. Zu manchen englischen Wörtern fallen dir vielleicht deutsche, französische oder lateinische Wörter ein, die ähnlich geschrieben oder ausgesprochen werden, z. B. **excellent**, **millionaire**, **nation**, **reality**.
4. Es gibt neue Wörter, in denen du bekannte Teile entdeckst, z. B. **friendliness**, **helpless**, **understandable**, **gardener**, **tea bag**, **waiting room**.

Skimming and scanning

Beim **Skimming** überfliegst du einen Text schnell, um dir einen **Überblick** zu verschaffen. Du willst dabei herausfinden, worum es in dem Text geht. Achte dabei auf
- die **Überschrift**,
- die **Zwischenüberschriften** und hervorgehobene Wörter oder Sätze,
- die **Bilder** und **Bildunterschriften**,
- den **ersten Satz** und den **letzten Satz** jedes Absatzes,
- **Grafiken**, **Statistiken** und die **Quelle** des Textes.

Beim **Scanning** suchst du nach **bestimmten Informationen**. Dazu suchst du den Text nach Schlüsselwörtern (*key words*) ab und liest nur dort genauer, wo du sie findest. Geh dabei so vor:

Schritt 1: Denk an die Schlüsselwörter und geh mit deinen Augen oder dem Finger schnell durch den Text, in breiten Schlingen wie bei einem „S“ oder „Z“ oder von oben nach unten wie bei einem „U“. Die gesuchten Wörter werden dir sofort „ins Auge springen“.

Schritt 2: Wenn das gesuchte Wort nicht im Text vorkommt, überlege dir andere, themenverwandte Wörter (z. B. **lesson** → **school**, **subject**) und suche nach diesen.

Finding the main ideas of a text

Zeitungsartikel, Berichte oder Kommentare verstehst du besser, wenn du ihre wesentlichen Aussagen erkennst und dir klar machst, wie sie zusammenhängen. Die wichtigsten Aussagen findest du so:

1. Jeder Text hat ein Thema mit mindestens einer Hauptaussage, z. B.: *Drinking soda is one of the worst things you can do to your health.*
   Diese Hauptaussage findest du oft im **ersten Absatz**.

2. Die Hauptaussage wird in der Regel durch weitere Aussagen bzw. Gedanken unterstützt, z. B.: *Experts agree that sugary soft drinks and fast food are the main reasons why so many American teenagers are fat.*

3. Diese weiteren Aussagen bzw. Gedanken werden oft durch Beispiele und Begründungen ergänzt, z. B.: *About 7% of the calories that they take in come from soft drinks alone.*

Careful reading

Schwierige Texte musst du besonders sorgfältig und konzentriert lesen, damit du alle darin enthaltenen Informationen und Gedanken verstehst.

1. Lies den Text genau. Welches sind seine wesentlichen Aussagen? (► *Finding the main ideas of a text, pp. 136–137*)

2. Manchmal musst du dir die Antwort auf eine Frage aus einzelnen Informationen erschließen, die du an verschiedenen Stellen im Text findest. Nimm zum Beispiel den Text auf S. 17: Warum ist in der Überschrift von einem „racist ideal" die Rede? Für die Antwort musst du mehrere Aussagen aus dem Text zusammentragen:

FACTS: • *Zita Wallace and thousands of other mixed-race children with fair skin were taken from their Aboriginal families.* • *The government wanted them to forget their Aboriginal traditions and grow up like white children.* • *The children were hit if they spoke their own language.* • *They had to work all the time and didn't get any real education.*

CONCLUSION: The government thought that Aboriginal culture had no value. The mixed-race children were forced to grow up among white people, but at the same time they were discriminated against.

Text types: fiction and non-fiction

Wenn du einen Text liest, ist es sinnvoll sich klar zu machen, ob er von einer vom Autor erdachten Welt handelt (*fictional text*, deutsch: Dichtung) oder sich mit der Wirklichkeit auseinandersetzt (*non-fictional text*, deutsch: Sachtext).

Fiktionale Texte sind z. B. Kurzgeschichten und Romane. Der Autor wählt Figuren (*characters*) aus und erzählt von ihren Gefühlen und Handlungen, von deren Motiven und Hintergründen. Die Handlungen finden in einem oder mehreren Handlungsrahmen statt, z. B. an einem Ort, zu einer bestimmten Zeit und unter bestimmten Umständen (*setting*). Die Ereignisse können aus verschiedenen Perspektiven erzählt werden (*point of view*). Oft verwendet der Autor für seine Geschichte eine anschauliche Sprache, z. B. ausschmückende Adjektive, Metaphern, Vergleiche, direkte Rede oder er lässt den Leser an den Gedanken seiner Figuren oder des Erzählers teilhaben.

Nicht-fiktionale Texte sind z. B. Berichte in Zeitungen, wissenschaftliche Artikel, Aufsätze oder Kommentare. Hier informiert der Autor über ein Thema der realen Welt oder nimmt Stellung dazu.

Es gibt auch Texte, die ein **Mischform** aus beiden Textarten sind.

SF Reading literature ▸ *Unit 1 (pp. 24–25), Unit 4 (p. 97)*

Sachtexte und literarische Texte

Wenn du englische Texte liest, können dies Sachtexte oder literarische Texte sein. **Sachtexte** – z.B. Zeitungsberichte oder Reden – wollen vorwiegend informieren oder zu etwas auffordern. **Literarische Texte**, die oft in einer besonderen Form oder Sprache verfasst sind, zeigen eine Welt oder Umgebung, die der Autor oder die Autorin erdacht hat. Im Englischen nennt man diese Texte auch *fiction*, weil sie von einer erdachten oder erfundenen (englisch: *fictional*) Welt handeln, im Gegensatz zu *non-fiction*, die sich mit der wirklichen Welt auseinandersetzt.

Alles, was du bereits über das Lesen von Texten im Allgemeinen gelernt hast (▸ *Reading course, pp. 136–137*), wird dir auch beim Lesen von Literatur helfen. Markiere deshalb, wenn es dir möglich ist, auch in einem literarischen Text Dinge, die dir auffallen und die du wichtig findest.

Literarische Gattungen und ihre Merkmale

Grundsätzlich unterscheidet man drei **Arten von literarischen Texten** bzw. literarischen Gattungen (*genre*): Gedichte (Lyrik = *poetry*), Erzähltexte (Epik = *fiction*; damit wird der Begriff *fiction* im Englischen auch in einem etwas anderen, engeren Sinne gebraucht) und Dramen (Dramatik = *drama*).

Du erkennst sie meist schon an ihrer äußeren Form. In der Regel
- bestehen Gedichte aus gebundener Sprache, d.h. aus Verszeilen und Strophen,
- haben Erzähltexte fortlaufenden Text,
- ist ein Drama in Monologen und Dialogen als direkte Rede gesetzt.

Du kannst Literatur natürlich einfach zum Vergnügen lesen, zum Beispiel, weil dir die Geschichte, ein bestimmtes Thema oder die dargestellten Personen interessant, spannend oder unterhaltend erscheinen. Zum besseren Verständnis kann es aber beitragen, wenn du etwas über formale, stilistische oder technische Besonderheiten des Textes weißt. Bemerkst du diese beim Lesen, kannst du dir überlegen, warum der Autor oder die Autorin wohl ausgerechnet diese Mittel einsetzt und welcher Eindruck oder welches Gefühl bei dir dadurch während des Lesens entsteht.

Solche Besonderheiten sind beispielsweise
- in einem Erzähltext die Entwicklung der Handlung (*plot*), die Beschreibung der Figuren (*characters*) und des Schauplatzes (*setting*) und die dadurch geschaffene Atmosphäre (*atmosphere*) oder der Aufbau von Spannung (*suspense*),
- bei einem Gedicht die äußere Aufteilung in Strophen (*stanzas*), die Verwendung von Reim (*rhyme*) und Rhythmus (*rhythm*) oder eine auffällig bildhafte Sprache (*images*, z.B. *metaphors*)
- und bei einem Drama die Art und Weise, wie die Handlung in Dialogen (*dialogues*) und Monologen (*monologues*) sichtbar gemacht wird.

Es kommt auch vor, dass du Texte – vor allem literarische Texte – nicht nur verstehen, sondern umsetzen musst, indem du sie darstellst oder sprichst, eigene kleine Formen von Literatur verfasst, sie um- oder weiterschreibst. Gerade dann ist es wichtig, dass du dir über die Besonderheiten des zugrundeliegenden Textes im Klaren bist.

Dreams
Hold fast to dreams
For if dreams **die**
Life is a broken-winged bird
That cannot **fly**
Hold fast to dreams
For when dreams **go**
Life is a barren field
Frozen with **snow**.

Langston Hughes

Gedichte können Reime und Metaphern enthalten.

It was as **slow and hot** travelling along the Dog Fence. The more they drove inland, the hotter the air became until Colm felt **he was breathing fire**. He and Rusty tried sticking their heads out of the window, but it was worse than the burning heat inside the car.

From A Prayer for Blue Delaney *by Kirsty Murray*

In Erzähltexten wird der Schauplatz (*setting*) häufig durch bildhafte Adjektive und Metaphern beschrieben.

Über literarische Texte sprechen

Wenn du über Texte schreiben oder sprechen musst, sind folgende Formulierungen hilfreich:

The story/novel/play/poem/song is about …
The story is set in …
The text tells the story of …
The author uses a …

The main character/hero/heroine is …
He/she comes across as a strong/weak/aggressive/brave/… person.
You can see this in line …

I liked it/didn't like it when …
I found the ending/story/characters interesting/funny/confusing …
The words and expressions in the text create an exciting/thrilling/… atmosphere.
The text made me feel happy/sad/angry/…

The poem consists of … verses/stanzas, each with … lines.
The lines of the poem (don't) rhyme.
Every other line rhymes.
I think the … is a metaphor/symbol for …
With it the author wants to express …

In the dialogue between … and … there is a lot of emotion/tension/anger …
The action takes place during …
The stage directions are (not) very detailled.

Victoria ____ Show me exactly what you think you saw. You came round the corner, there, and you *distinctly* saw me do *what* exactly?

Enter Mrs Wright at the back. She carries a handbag and is blindfolded.

Albert ____ *(miming what he saw)* I *distinctally* saw you let go of the handle of the murder weapon, and you letting go of the handle was distinctally immediately after you'd distinctally run at the victim even though he was a total stranger to you, who you didn't even know enough to have had an argument of fashion with. And then you stabbed him in the back with it. And then you carefully wiped your fingerprints off the handle of the murder weapon.

Victoria ____ But *I didn't*.

Mrs Wright ____ *(coming blindly forward)* Oh my God. What have you people done?

From Just *by Ali Smith*

In einem Drama ergeben sich sowohl aus den Dialogen als auch als den Bühnenanweisungen (*stage directions*) Handlungsanweisungen für die Darsteller.

MEDIATION SKILLS

SF REVISION Mediation

REVISION Wann muss ich zwischen zwei Sprachen vermitteln?

Manchmal musst du zwischen zwei Sprachen vermitteln. Das nennt man **mediation**.

1. Du gibst englische Informationen auf Deutsch weiter:
   Du fährst z.B. mit deiner Familie in die USA und deine Eltern oder Geschwister wollen wissen, was jemand in einem Café gesagt hat oder was an einer Informationstafel steht.
2. Du gibst deutsche Informationen auf Englisch weiter:
   Vielleicht ist bei dir zu Hause eine Austauschschülerin aus den USA oder Dänemark zu Gast, die kein Deutsch spricht und Hilfe braucht.
3. In schriftlichen Prüfungen musst du manchmal in einem englischen Text gezielt nach Informationen suchen und diese auf Deutsch wiedergeben. Oder du sollst Informationen aus einem deutschen Text auf Englisch wiedergeben.

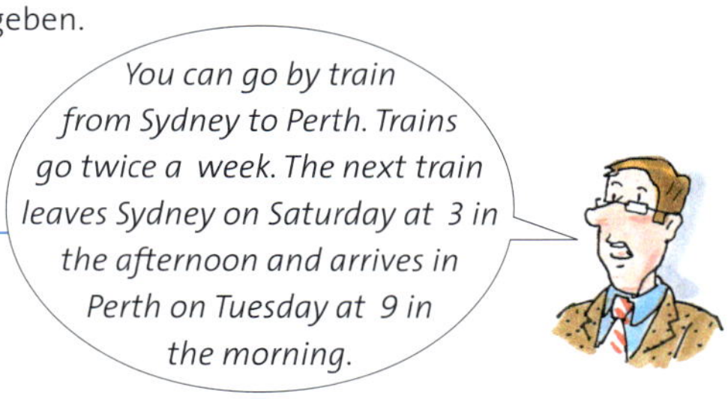

Worauf muss ich bei *mediation* achten?

- Übersetze nicht alles wörtlich, sondern gib den Sinn wieder.
- Gib nur das Wesentliche weiter, lass Unwichtiges weg.
- Verwende kurze und einfache Sätze.
- Wenn du ein Wort nicht kennst, umschreibe es oder ersetze es durch ein anderes Wort.

Was kann ich tun, wenn ich ein wichtiges Wort nicht kenne?

Vielleicht findest du es manchmal schwer, mündliche Aussagen oder schriftliche Textvorlagen in die andere Sprache zu übertragen, z.B. weil
- dein Wortschatz nicht ausreicht,
- dir bekannte Wörter „im Stress" nicht einfallen,
- spezielle Fachbegriffe auftauchen.

Manche Wörter kannst du umschreiben, z.B. mithilfe von Relativsätzen wie:
It's somebody/a person who ...
It's something that you use to ...
It's an animal that ...
It's a place that/where ...

▸ *Paraphrasing, p. 141*

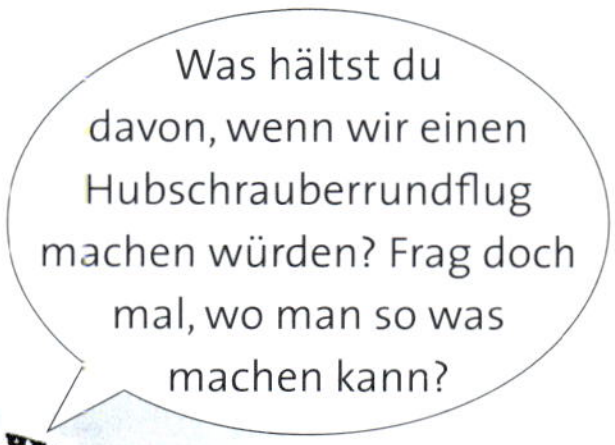

SPEAKING AND WRITING SKILLS

SF REVISION Paraphrasing

Worum geht es beim Paraphrasing?

„Paraphrasing“ bedeutet, etwas mit anderen Worten zu erklären. Das ist hilfreich, wenn dir ein bestimmtes Wort nicht einfällt oder wenn dein Gegenüber dich nicht verstanden hat. Paraphrasing ist auch besonders nützlich für **mediation** (► *Mediation, p. 140*).

Wie gehe ich beim Paraphrasing vor?

- Man kann mit einem Ausdruck umschreiben, der dieselbe Bedeutung hat:
  'To wonder' is the same as 'to ask yourself'.
  Oder man sagt das Gegenteil:
  'Alive' is the opposite of 'dead'.
- Manchmal braucht man mehrere Wörter, z. B. wenn man etwas beschreibt oder erklären will, wie man etwas verwendet. Dabei verwendet man ein allgemeines Wort (**general word**) und nennt weitere Eigenschaften:
  A skyscraper is a very tall building.
- Oder du umschreibst das Wort mit **... is/are like ...**
  A lodge is like a small house or cabin. You find it in the country.
- Du kannst auch einen Relativsatz (**relative clause**) verwenden:
  She looks after small children. – Ah, she's a nanny!
  A ticket office is a shop where you can buy tickets for shows and concerts.

SF REVISION Brainstorming

Was ist Brainstorming und wofür ist es gut?

Bei vielen Aufgaben ist es nützlich, wenn du im ersten Schritt möglichst viele Ideen zum Thema sammelst. Beim Sammeln und beim Auswerten der Ideen helfen dir die folgenden Techniken.

Drei verschiedene Brainstorming-Techniken

Technik 1: Making a list
Schreib die Ideen so auf, wie sie dir einfallen, und zwar für jede Idee eine neue Zeile. Lies im zweiten Schritt alle deine Ideen durch. Überlege, welche Ideen davon für dein Thema sinnvoll sind und nummeriere sie nach Nützlichkeit.

6. watch DVDs
3. swimming pool
   no jobs for parents
   parents not at home
1. sleep late – every morning
   ~~hang out~~
2. no homework
5. disco/party with friends
   watch TV
4. see friends cinema

Technik 2: Making a mind map
Leg eine Mindmap an. Überlege dafür, welche Oberbegriffe zu deinem Thema passen. Verwende unterschiedliche Farben für jeden Oberbegriff. Ergänze jede Idee, die zu einem Oberbegriff passt, auf einem Nebenast. Nimm dafür nur wichtige Schlüsselwörter. Du kannst statt Wörtern auch Symbole verwenden und Bilder ergänzen.

Technik 3: The 5 Ws
Schreib die Fragewörter **Who? What? When? Where? Why?** in eine Tabelle. Die Ideen, die dir zu der jeweiligen Frage kommen, werden darunter geschrieben.

SPEAKING COURSE – Zusammenfassung

Having a conversation ▸ *Unit 1 (p. 14)*

Ein Gespräch beginnen

Ein Gespräch auf Englisch zu beginnen ist einfacher, als du vielleicht denkst. Es gibt immer mehrere Möglichkeiten:

- **Wenn du etwas erfragen willst** (z.B. den Weg oder die Uhrzeit) **oder um Hilfe bitten möchtest:**
  Excuse me, do you know ... • Excuse me, can you tell me ... • Excuse me, do you know where... • Could you help me, please?
- **Wenn du jemanden begrüßen möchtest oder kennen lernst:**
  Hi! • Hello! • Good morning. • (bei Erwachsenen) Good afternoon.
  Oft kann man das Gespräch dann mit einer allgemeinen Bemerkung weiterführen: Great day today! • Nice concert, isn't it? • ...
  Oft hört man zur Begrüßung auch How are you? oder How do you do? Das sind einfache Begrüßungsformeln, auf die keine ausführliche Antwort erwartet wird. Am besten sagst du einfach Fine, thanks. How about you?
- **Wenn du jemanden wiedertriffst:**
  Hi, ..., how are things? • Hi, how is it going? • How are you? • Hi, good to see/meet you.

Ein Gespräch führen

Für den weiteren Verlauf des Gesprächs sind diese Wendungen nützlich:

- **Sich vorstellen:** By the way, my name's ... • I'm ...
- **Sich kennen lernen:** Have you ... before? • Have you ever ...? • What about you?
- **Sich bedanken/auf Dank reagieren:** Thanks! • Thanks for your help. • You're welcome.
- **Sich verabschieden:** See you tomorrow/next week. • Bye!

Und wenn du einmal etwas nicht verstanden hast, kannst du nachfragen:
Sorry, I didn't get that. • Sorry, can you say that again, please?

Asking for, confirming, giving information ▸ *Unit 2 (p. 37)*

Ein Gespräch ist mehr als nur der Austausch von Informationen; es kommt auch auf einen höflichen und angenehmen Ton an. Das gilt natürlich auch für Gespräche auf Englisch. Diese Wendungen können hilfreich sein:

- **Asking for information:** Oft beginnt man eine Anfrage oder Auskunft mit Excuse me... • Excuse me, could you tell me, ... • Would you mind telling me ... • Sorry, I'd just like to know ... • I'm not quite sure about ... • Is it/Are they ...? • Is it right that ...? • Can I just ask ... • Excuse me, I've just got a question ... • Excuse me, do you think you could ...?
- **Confirming information:** Wenn du nachfragen oder sicher gehen möchtest, dass du etwas richtig verstanden hast, kannst du das z.B. so tun: Can I just confirm ...? • Is it right that ...? • Have I got that right ...? • ..., (is that) right? • Could you just say that again, please? Auch question tags drücken den Wunsch nach Bestätigung aus: This is the library, isn't it?

Denke auch daran, dich für die erhaltenen Informationen freundlich zu bedanken.

- **Giving information:** Auch wenn du selbst eine Auskunft erteilst, versuche freundlich und höflich zu sein, z.B. mit einer kurzen Einleitung:
  Sure. • **Of course, no problem.** • **Well, just a second.** • **Give me a minute to think about it.**
  Wenn du nicht weiter helfen kannst, drückst du dein Bedauern aus:
  Oh, I'm sorry, I don't know. • **Sorry, I'm afraid I can't help you.**

Giving an oral summary ► *Unit 3 (p. 65)*

Wenn du etwas, was du gehört, gesehen oder gelesen hast, für jemanden anderen zusammenfassen willst, tust du dies oft spontan. Du hast also nicht lange Zeit zum Überlegen und solltest auch nicht zu lange reden.

- Gib **nur das Wesentliche** des Inhalts wieder. Du brauchst dich nicht unbedingt an die chronologische Reihenfolge der Handlung zu halten:
  I watched that film ... last night. • **Yesterday I read that web article about ...** • **I've recently come across that ad/article about ...** • **I've just read that story about ...**
- Verwende das **Präsens** zum Nacherzählen:
  There's this kid ... In this one scene he's running away from ... then it starts raining ... and he's trying ... so she has to get out of the car ...
- **Halte deine Meinung** zu dem betreffenden Film, Buch usw. **zurück**. Natürlich kannst du durch die Art und Weise, wie du erzählst, indirekt deinen Eindruck wiedergeben, z.B. durch den Ton deiner Stimme, deine Körpersprache und deine Wortwahl.

Having a discussion ► *Unit 4 (p. 86)*

Seine Meinung sagen und erklären

- **Expressing an opinion:** In einer Diskussion ist es gut, wenn du möglichst klar und deutlich sagst, was du zu einer bestimmten Frage denkst:
  I think ... • **I feel ...** • **In my opinion ...**
- **Giving reasons and examples**: Es ist aber noch wichtiger, dass du Beispiele und Argumente nennst, die deine Meinung unterstützen – schließlich willst du deine Gesprächspartner ja überzeugen: **because ...** • **First ... / Second ...** • **For example ...** • **Let me explain ...** • **That's why ...**

Auf andere reagieren

- **Asking for clarification:** Manchmal ist es notwendig nachzuhaken:
  Could you say that again? • **Sorry, but I don't understand what you mean.**
- **Agreeing with someone:** Die Meinung eines anderen unterstützt du mit
  I agree (with you/...). • **That's a good point.** • **You're right.**
- **Disagreeing with someone:** Oft widerspricht man nicht direkt, sondern leitet seine Reaktion z.B. mit **Sorry, ...** ein. Zeig immer Respekt für die Meinung anderer.
  I don't think you can say ... • **I see what you mean but ...** • **No, that's not right.** • **Sorry, I don't agree with you.** • **Yes, but ...,** • • **Well, I don't think you can say that ...** • **Ah, come on, ...**

► *Classroom English (pp. 242–243)*

REVISION Writing course – Zusammenfassung

The steps of writing

1. Brainstorming – Ideen sammeln und ordnen (▸ *Brainstorming, p. 141*)
2. Schreiben. Dabei achte darauf,
   – deine Sätze zu verbinden und auszubauen (*Writing better sentences*),
   – deinen Text gut zu strukturieren (*Using paragraphs*),
   – bei einem Bericht die 5 Ws abzudecken (▸ *Writing a report, p. 146*),
   – bei einem Leserbrief an eine Zeitschrift eine höfliche Anrede und Schlussformel zu verwenden (▸ *Writing a letter to a magazine, p. 146*).
3. Deinen Text inhaltlich und sprachlich überprüfen (*Correcting your text*)

Writing better sentences

Linking words verbinden Sätze und machen sie interessanter. Verwende z. B.
– **Time phrases** wie **at 7 o'clock**, **every morning**, **in the afternoons**, **a few minutes later**, **suddenly**, **then**, **next ...**,
– **Konjunktionen** wie **although**, **and**, **because**, **but**, **so ... that**, **that**, **when**, **while**,
– **Relativpronomen** wie **who**, **which** und **that**.

Auch mit **Adjektiven** und **Adverbien** kannst du deine Sätze verbessern.
– **Adjektive** bestimmen Personen, Orte, Gegenstände oder Erlebnisse genauer und machen sie ebenfalls interessanter:
The man looked into the room. → **The young man looked into the empty room.**
– Mit **Adverbien** kannst du beschreiben, wie jemand etwas macht:
The young man looked nervously into the empty room.

Using paragraphs

Structuring a text

Einen Text versteht man viel besser, wenn er in Absätze gegliedert ist:
– eine Einleitung (**beginning**) – hier schreibst du, worum es geht;
– einen Hauptteil (**middle**) – hier schreibst du mehr über dein Thema,
– einen Schluss (**end**) – hier bringst du den Text zu einem interessanten Ende.

Am Anfang eines Absatzes sind kurze, einleitende Sätze (**topic sentences**) gut, die den Lesern sofort sagen, worum es geht, z. B.
– Orte: **My trip to ... was fantastic. / ... is famous for ... / ... is a great place.**
– Personen: **... is great/funny/interesting/clever/...**
– Aktivitäten: **... is great fun. / Lots of people ... every day.**

Wie kann ich meine Absätze interessant gestalten?

– Beginne mit einem interessanten Einstiegssatz:
Guess what happened to me today! / Did I tell you that ...?
– Fang für jeden neuen Aspekt einen neuen Absatz an.
– Beende deinen Text mit einer Zusammenfassung oder etwas Persönlichem.

Linking ideas

Damit sich dein Text flüssig liest und beim Leser Interesse weckt, solltest du auf gute Übergange von einem Absatz zum nächsten achten. Die folgenden Formulierungen kannst du verwenden

- um zu zeigen, wie dein Text aufgebaut ist:
  In the article, the writer describes how … Firstly, he states that … Secondly, … Then he goes on to say that … Another point he makes is that … Finally, …
- um etwas zu begründen:
  Because of / As a result of the growing population, …
  … had been in trouble with the police, so …
- um zwei oder mehr Gedanken einander gegenüberzustellen:
  Although one could say that …, I believe …
  While most people would …, the Prime Minister has said …
  Serious scientists all say that … However/But some politicians …
- um Beispiele zu geben:
  This is true in a number of cases, for example / for instance / e.g. …
- um Ergebnisse und Folgen zu erklären:
  As a consequence, / All in all, one can say that …
  To sum up, I would like to say …

Correcting your text

Lies jeden Text, den du geschrieben hast, mehrmals durch

- um zu sehen, ob er vollständig und gut verständlich ist,
- um ihn auf Fehler zu überprüfen, z. B. **Rechtschreibfehler** ***(spelling mistakes)*** und **Grammatikfehler** ***(grammar mistakes)***.

Spelling mistakes

Beachte folgende Regeln:

- Manche Wörter haben Buchstaben, die man nicht spricht, aber schreibt, z. B. **talk**, **climb**.
- Manchmal ändert sich die Schreibweise, wenn ein Wort eine Endung erhält, z. B. **take** → **taking**, **terrible** → **terribly**, **lucky** → **luckily**, **try** → **tries** (aber **stay** → **stays**), **run** → **running**, **drop** → **dropped**.
- Beim Plural tritt manchmal noch ein *-e* zum *-s*, z. B. **church** → **churches**.

Grammar mistakes

Diese Tipps helfen dir, typische Fehler zu vermeiden:

- Im **simple present** wird in der 3. Person Singular **-s** angehängt: **she knows**
- **Unregelmäßige Verben**: Manche Verben bilden die Formen des *simple past* und des Partizip Perfekt *(past participle)* unregelmäßig. Die unregelmäßigen Formen musst du lernen. Die Liste steht auf S. 256–257.
  go – went – gone; **buy – bought – bought**
- **Verneinung**: Im *simple present* werden Vollverben mit **don't/doesn't** verneint, im *simple past* mit **didn't**.
- **Satzstellung**: Im Englischen gilt immer (auch im Nebensatz):

a) subject – verb – object (SVO): **… when I saw my brother.**
… als ich meinen Bruder sah.

b) Orts- vor Zeitangabe: **I bought a nice book in the city yesterday.**

Writing different types of text

SF REVISION Writing a report – organizing ideas

Hierauf kommt es bei einem Bericht an:
- Gib dem Leser eine **schnelle Orientierung**, was passiert ist.
- Beginne mit **wichtigen Informationen** und gib erst dann Detailinformationen.
- Gib Antwort auf die **5 Ws**: **Who? What? When? Where? Why?** und manchmal auch auf **How?**.
- Verwende das *simple past*.

SF REVISION Writing a letter to a magazine

Wenn du auf einen Zeitschriftenartikel reagieren und einen Leserbrief schreiben möchtest,
- beginne deinen Brief mit **Dear + (Name der Zeitschrift/des Autors des Artikels)**,
- lege deine Meinung dar und begründe sie (**I would like to comment on ..., I agree/disagree with ..., I think ..., That is why ..., For example, ...**),
- beende deinen Brief mit **Yours sincerely** oder **Yours**.

SF Writing formal letters ▸ *Unit 2 (p. 41)*

Bei Briefen unterscheidet man zwischen privaten Briefen (*informal letters*) und Geschäftsbriefen (*formal letters*). Da du mit Geschäftsbriefen ein Anliegen bei einer Behörde, einer Firma oder einer Organisation verfolgst, sollten sie knapp, präzise, objektiv, aber trotzdem höflich formuliert sein (*KISS rule: Keep it short and simple*).

(1) Schreibe deine Adresse (ohne Namen) und das Datum in die rechte obere Ecke. Verwende keine typisch deutschen Buchstaben wie z.B. ß, ä, ö oder ü.

(2) Die Anschrift steht links.

(3) Die Anrede lautet *Dear Sir or Madam*. Wenn du den Namen des Adressaten kennst, beginne deinen Brief mit *Dear Mr/Mrs/Ms ...*

(4) Verwende Langformen (*I am, I would like* statt *I'm, I'd like* usw.), vermeide unnötige Abkürzungen.

(5) Nenne zu Beginn den Grund deines Briefes.

(6) Bedanke dich bei Bitten und Anfragen im Voraus (*I look forward to hearing from you. Thank you.*).

(7) Beende den Brief mit *Yours faithfully*, wenn du den Adressaten nicht kennst. Hast du den Adressaten am Anfang des Briefes mit Namen angeredet, dann schreibe *Yours sincerely*. (Im amerikanischen Englisch heißt es dagegen in beiden Fällen *Sincerely*.)

(8) Unterschreibe den Brief und tippe zusätzlich deinen Namen.

(1) Schillerstr. 17
37067 Goettingen
Germany

(2) Jane Hall
Meadows Home Farm Shop
Harston
Cambridge CB22 4BE
Great Britain

4 May 2010

(3) Dear Ms Hall

(5) I (4) am writing to you about the advertisement from April 21st in the Cambridge Weekly News. I would love to (4) work for you at Meadows Home Farm this summer.

I am 16 years old and I have a good level of English but would like to improve my speaking skills. I am hard-working, friendly and a fast learner. At home I look after two horses so farm work is not new to me. I have also worked in a sports shop so I have experience in serving people and working in a team. My hobbies are horse riding, playing volley ball and hiking. Please find my CV with this letter.

Thank you for your time. I look forward to hearing from (6) you.

(7) Yours sincerely

(8) *Tamara Wille*
Tamara Wille

SF Argumentative writing ► *Unit 4 (p. 82)*

„Schriftliche Diskussion“

Argumentative writing ist ähnlich der deutschen Erörterung die **schriftliche Diskussion eines Gedankens oder eines Themas**. Dabei müssen Argumente, Beispiele und Belege zu einer logisch aufgebauten Struktur zusammengefügt werden.

Oft verlangt die Aufgabenstellung von dir, dass du **Argumente für und gegen etwas** findest (z.B. *“Students should wear school uniforms.” Discuss.*). Manchmal musst du auch eine Problemstellung oder eine Frage mit Argumenten belegen (häufig als W-Frage formuliert, z.B. *What should young people do in their free time?*). In beiden Fällen sollst du – in der Regel am Ende deines Textes – auch deine **eigene Meinung** äußern. Bemühe dich aber dennoch um einen **objektiven Stil**. Formulierungen wie *That’s total nonsense* oder *I think it’s very stupid* sind völlig fehl am Platz!

Wie gehe ich vor?

Vorbereitung:
- Lies die Aufgabenstellung sorgfältig, achte besonders auf die Arbeitsanweisungen oder „Operatoren“ (► *How to do well in a test: Aufgabenstellungen verstehen, p. 151*) und entscheide, um welche Art von *argumentative writing* es sich handelt.
- Werde dir über deine eigene Meinung zum Thema klar.
- Sammle Ideen, Argumente, Belege und Beispiele (► *Brainstorming, p. 141*) und ordne sie, z.B. in einer Mindmap.
- Fertige eine Gliederung (► *Outlining, p. 129*).

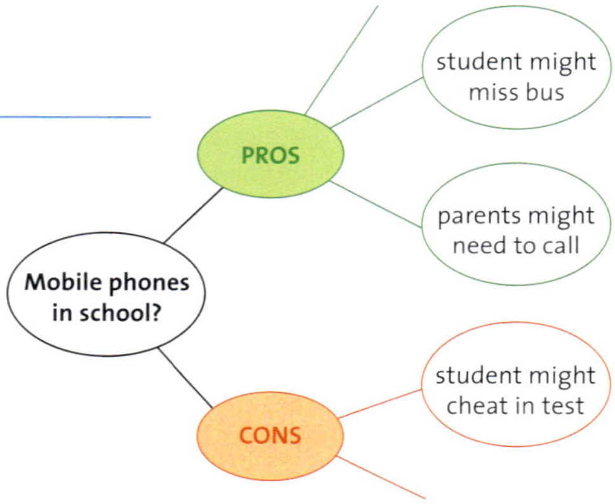

Verfassen des Textes:
- Wie fast jeder Text ist auch das Ergebnis deines *argumentative writing* grundsätzlich in drei Hauptabschnitte gegliedert: Mit der Einleitung führst du zum Thema hin und weckst das Interesse deiner Leser, im Hauptteil entwickelst du deine Argumente (dies kann auch in mehreren Absätzen geschehen), mit dem Schluss fasst du zusammen und präsentierst deine Meinung oder auch einen Kompromiss.
- Verbinde die einzelnen Teile gut miteinander (z.B. mit **on the one hand, on the other hand, first/second/third, however, additionally, moreover, contrary to that**) und belege und begründe die jeweiligen Argumente (**that’s why, because, a reason for it is**).
- Im Schlussteil (**all in all, to come to a conclusion, I would like to finish by saying**) solltest du keine neuen Argumente mehr anführen.

Introduction	Most students have mobiles. Should they be allowed in school?
Main body	Pros: student might miss bus parents might need to call … Cons: student might cheat in test …
Conclusion	More disadvantages than advantages → Should not be allowed

Überprüfen des Geschriebenen:
- Wie immer beim schriftlichen Arbeiten solltest du deinen Text am Ende überprüfen und korrigieren (► *Correcting your text, p. 145*). In Zweifelsfällen hilft dir ein Wörterbuch (► *Using a bilingual dictionary, p. 124, Using an English–English dictionary, p. 125*).

SF Writing a CV ▸ *Unit 2 (p. 38)*

Das Leben auf einen Blick

Dein Lebenslauf ist eine **klar gegliederte Zusammenfassung** deiner persönlichen Daten, Fähigkeiten und Erfahrungen und gibt Auskunft über die wichtigen Stationen deines Lebens. Da der Adressat sich schnell informieren will, ist es wichtig, dass der Lebenslauf fehlerfrei und übersichtlich, d.h. in der Regel in tabellarischer Form, erstellt worden ist.

Wie sollte ein Lebenslauf aussehen?

Weil Lebensläufe ganz persönliche, individuelle Dokumente sind, unterscheiden sie sich inhaltlich natürlich stark voneinander. Dennoch gelten bestimmte **inhaltliche und formale Regeln** – für englische Lebensläufe manchmal andere als für deutsche:

- Der Lebenslauf muss Namen, Kontaktdaten (Adresse, Telefonnummer, ggf. E-Mail-Adresse) und Nationalität enthalten. Das Geburtsdatum oder Auskünfte zur Familie sind nicht unbedingt notwendig.
- Die Lebensstationen sollten zeitlich lückenlos dargestellt werden. Sie können chronologisch (also beginnend mit den frühesten Daten) oder umgekehrt chronologisch (beginnend mit der Gegenwart) angeordnet sein.
- Die Daten und Informationen werden nach unterschiedlichen Aspekten gegliedert, z.B. *Education* (welche Schulen hast du wann besucht?), *Qualification/Skills* (welche besonderen Fähigkeiten hast du?), *Work experience* (wo hast du schon gearbeitet?), *Achievements* (hast du vielleicht eine Auszeichnung erhalten, einen Preis gewonnen oder etwas Besonderes erreicht?), *Hobbies and interests, References* (schriftliche Beurteilungen, Empfehlungsschreiben).
- Empfehlungsschreiben musst du, außer wenn es ausdrücklich verlangt wird, nicht sofort zur Verfügung stellen, sondern kannst sie auf Nachfrage zusenden.
- Im Englischen kann der Lebenslauf z.B. zusätzlich zu den nüchternen Daten und Fakten auch einige persönliche Ausführungen enthalten. In einem solchen *personal statement* kannst du einige deiner persönlichen Vorzüge hervorheben und erläutern, warum du die betreffende Position oder diesen bestimmten Arbeitsplatz anstrebst. Übertreibe es aber nicht – also nicht: *I am a very clever and intelligent person*, sondern etwas bescheidener (und leichter zu belegen): *I have always been quite successful at school.*
- In der Regel musst du einem englischen Lebenslauf kein Bild beifügen. Auch unterschreiben musst du ihn nicht.

SF REVISION Summary writing

Wenn du einen Lese- oder Hörtext oder einen Filmausschnitt zusammenfassen möchtest, schreibst du eine *summary*. Dabei gehst du folgendermaßen vor:

1. Lies dir den Text noch mindestens einmal genau durch (bzw. hör ihn dir ein weiteres Mal an oder sieh dir den Filmausschnitt noch einmal an). Bei einem Lesetext markierst du wichtige Passagen oder machst am Rand des Textes kurze Anmerkungen. Auch bei Hörtexten und Filmausschnitten machst du dir Notizen (▸ *Listening, p. 134*).
2. Wenn es sich um einen geschriebenen Text handelt, lies ihn jetzt ein weiteres Mal, Satz für Satz. Wenn du mit einer Kopie arbeitest, unterstreiche die Passagen im Text, die dir Antwort auf die **5 Ws** geben:
   Who? Who does ... / Who is the ... about?
   What? What happens? / What does he/she do?
   When? When does it take place?
   Where? Where does it happen?
   Why? Why does he/she act in this way?

   Zusätzlich zum Unterstreichen kannst du alle Sätze, Satzteile und Wortgruppen einklammern, die *nicht* zu den wesentlichen Gedanken des Autors gehören. Dazu gehören auch Beispiele, Vergleiche, symbolhafte Ausdrücke, Zitate, direkte Rede, ausschmückende Adjektive und andere Textteile, die der Beschreibung dienen.
3. Notiere dir alles, was du nicht eingeklammert hast, in Stichpunkten auf einem separaten Blatt Papier. Überprüfe noch einmal, ob du wirklich alle unnötigen Textstellen weggelassen hast.
4. Alternativ kannst du deine Notizen auch so anfertigen: Teile ein Blatt Papier in zwei Spalten ein. Notiere die Hauptaussagen des Textes auf der linken Seite. Suche dann zu diesen Aussagen Beispiele, Erläuterungen, Zitate, Zahlenund Fakten. Entscheide, welche du für besonders wichtig hälst, und notiere sie auf der rechten Seite deines Arbeitsblatts, neben den Hauptaussagen.
5. Nun schreibe mit deinen eigenen Worten einen neuen Text im *simple present* (auch wenn du eine Geschichte zusammenfasst, die in der Vergangenheit spielt). Bringe die Informationen in eine logische Reihenfolge. So kannst du anfangen:
   The story is about ... • The text describes ... • The article shows ... • In the story we get to know ...
   Im Hauptteil solltest du die wichtigsten Ereignisse einer Geschichte oder die Hauptpunkte eines Artikels wiedergeben. Verwende dafür deine Notizen zu den 5 Ws. Schreib den Text nicht ab, sondern verwende deine eigenen Worte.
6. Überprüfe deinen Entwurf noch einmal. Enthält dein Text wirklich die wichtigsten Gedanken, Ereignisse, Ideen aus dem Original? Achte auch auf sprachliche Fehler, besonders auf
   - die Rechtschreibung,
   - die Verwendung des *simple present*,
   - die Wortstellung,
   - logische Übergänge zwischen den Sätzen durch *linking words* (*and, therefore, that's why, but, because* ...).
7. Bringe den korrigierten Entwurf in eine Reinschrift.

EXAM SKILLS

SF REVISION How to do well in a test

▸ *Getting ready for a test (pp. 26–31, 70–77)*

Countdown zum Testerfolg

Ein Test ist angekündigt? Kein Grund zur Panik. Wichtig ist, dass du weißt, worauf du dich vorbereiten musst. Im Zweifelsfall frag deine Lehrerin oder deinen Lehrer. Der Countdown kann beginnen!

Eine Woche vor dem Test

1. Lies noch einmal die **Texte** der zuletzt durchgenommenen Unit (A-Section und Text, eventuell auch das Background File). Fasse mündlich oder schriftlich zusammen, worum es ging.

2. Wiederhole den **Wortschatz** der Unit mit Hilfe des *Vocabulary* oder des *Wordmaster*. Schreibe dir die Wörter und Wortverbindungen, die du immer wieder vergisst, auf ein Blatt Papier. Eine Mindmap oder ein Wortfeld helfen beim Behalten.

3. Geh auch noch mal die neue **Grammatik** durch. Aufgaben zur Selbstüberprüfung und zum Üben findest du im *Practice*-Teil, auf der Seite „How am I doing?", im *Grammar File* (S. 153–166), in deinem *Workbook* und im *e-Workbook*.

Zwei Tage vor dem Test

1. Wiederhole den **Wortschatz**. Manche Wörter sitzen noch nicht? Schreibe einen kurzen Text, in dem du sie verwendest.

2. Lies die **Texte** ein weiteres Mal.

3. Erkläre einem Freund oder einer Freundin die neue **Grammatik**. Das klappt nicht richtig? Dann lies nochmal im *Grammar File* nach.

Am Abend vor dem Test

1. Entspanne dich. Du kannst lesen, dich in die Badewanne legen, Musik hören, fernsehen, ...

2. Geh zur gewohnten Zeit ins Bett.

Am Morgen des Tests

1. Steh rechtzeitig auf, damit du nicht hetzen musst.

2. Lies irgendetwas „zum Aufwärmen", aber schau nicht mehr in dein Schülerbuch.

Während des Tests

1. Denk daran: Du hast dich gut vorbereitet. Es gibt keinen Grund, nervös zu sein.

2. Konzentriere dich auf den Test, lass dich nicht ablenken.

3. Lies dir die Aufgaben genau durch. Dann löse zuerst die Aufgaben, die dir einfach scheinen. Wende dich erst danach den schwereren Aufgaben zu.

4. Aufgaben, die du bearbeitet hast, hakst du ab. So siehst du, wie du vorankommst, und behältst den Überblick.

5. Schau ab und zu auf die Uhr. Du solltest dir für den Schluss noch etwas Zeit einplanen, um deine Antworten noch einmal durchzulesen und wenn nötig zu korrigieren.

Aufgabenstellungen verstehen

Bevor du anfängst, die Aufgaben zu bearbeiten, vergewissere dich, dass du genau weißt, was du tun sollst. Lies die Aufgabe Wort für Wort langsam und gründlich und von Anfang bis Ende durch. Du kannst besonders wichtige Teile der Aufgabenstellung unterstreichen und die Aufgabe, wenn nötig, für dich in einzelne Schritte unterteilen.

Den folgenden Arbeitsanweisungen begegnest du häufig:

Add Verbinde eine Information oder einen Sachverhalt mit einer/einem anderen auf die geforderte Art und Weise.

Choose Wähle zwischen verschiedenen Möglichkeiten die passende Information aus.

Comment Kommentiere einen Sachverhalt durch die Darstellung deiner eigenen Meinung dazu. Begründe und erläutere sie möglichst genau.

Compare Vergleiche Dinge, Wörter oder Sachverhalte, indem du prüfst, ob und auf welche Weise sie gleiche oder verschiedene Eigenschaften, Aussehen, Bedeutungen oder Funktionen haben.

Complete Ergänze eine Information, indem du sie an dem dafür vorgesehenen Platz einträgst und damit z. B. einen Satz sinnvoll beendest.

Describe Beschreibe ein Objekt oder eine Person, d.h. stelle dar, wie sie aussehen, wie das Objekt funktioniert oder die Personen handeln. Vermeide eigene Wertungen wie z. B. „beautiful", „useful" oder „great".

Discuss Diskutiere ein Thema, eine Behauptung oder eine Aussage. Untersuche möglichst viele Seiten davon, z. B. Vor- und Nachteile, und stelle diese geordnet dar.

Explain Erkläre einen Sachverhalt, d. h. gib wesentliche Fakten über ihn und erläutere, wie sie logisch zusammenhängen.

Fill in Trage die geforderten Informationen in den dafür vorgesehenen Platz ein, z. B. in eine Lücke oder eine Tabelle.

List Schreibe einzelne oder mehrere Informationen übersichtlich und geordnet auf, z. B. in einer Reihe, Tabelle oder einem anderen Verzeichnis.

Listen Höre dir einen Text, einzelne Informationen oder Sachverhalte an.

Match Ordne die angegebenen Informationen einander zu, wie es die Aufgabe erfordert. Finde z. B. Satzanfänge und passende Satzenden und füge sie zusammen.

Use Verwende eine Tatsache, ein Wort usw. so, wie es in der Aufgabe gefordert wird.

Write a ... Schreibe etwas in einem geforderten Textformat auf, z. B. deinen Kommentar zu etwas oder eine Geschichte.

Ein besonderer Aufgabentyp sind **Multipe-choice-Fragen**. Tipps für den Umgang mit solchen Aufgaben findest du im folgenden Abschnitt.

►►

Worauf sollte ich bei Multiple-choice-Aufgaben achten?

- Lies die Frage oder den Satz sehr genau durch.
- Bevor du dir die Lösungsangebote anschaust, deck sie mit Papier ab. Überleg dir, was die richtige Antwort sein könnte. Wenn das dann auch als eine Lösungsmöglichkeit angeboten wird, ist es meistens richtig.
- Lies immer alle vorgegebenen Lösungen, bevor du dich entscheidest.
- Achte darauf, dass du nur eine der Antworten ankreuzt – es sei denn, dass in der Aufgabenstellung ausdrücklich gesagt wird, dass mehrere Antworten richtig sein können.
- Mach erst alle Aufgaben so gut du kannst. Lass keine Aufgabe aus, aber geh zum Schluss zu den Fragen zurück, bei denen du unsicher bist.
- Wenn das alles nichts hilft, such nicht mehr nach der richtigen Antwort, sondern nach den falschen Antworten. Weil drei Antwortmöglichkeiten falsch sein müssen, kannst du erschließen, dass die vierte Antwort richtig ist. Hier ist ein Beispiel. Stell dir vor, du hörst folgenden Dialog:

  Boy *Wow, that was great, Dad. Thanks. Can we do it again next weekend?*
  Dad *Sure, Greg – if the weather's nice. But let's find an easier tour then – I'm a bit tired.*

  Dazu wird dir diese Multiple-choice-Aufgabe gestellt:

1. Greg and his dad have just
- A been swimming.
- B been to a fitness club.
- C seen a movie.
- D been on a bike ride.

Greg und sein Vater müssen etwas im Freien gemacht haben, denn Gregs Dad spricht über das Wetter. Also sind die Antworten B und C falsch. Man schwimmt keine Touren, also ist A auch falsch. Daher muss D die richtige Antwort sein.

Grammar File – Inhalt

		Seite
GF 1	**The tenses** Die Zeitformen	154
	1.1 **Tense and time** Grammatische Zeitform und wirkliche Zeit	154
	1.2 **Talking about the present** Über die Gegenwart sprechen	154
	1.3 **Talking about the past** Über die Vergangenheit sprechen	155
	1.4 **Talking about the past and the present** Über die Vergangenheit und die Gegenwart sprechen	156
	1.5 **Talking about the future** Über die Zukunft sprechen	157
GF 2	**Aspect: the simple form and the progressive form** Aspekt: die einfache Form und die Verlaufsform	159
	2.1 **Simple and progressive form in contrast** Einfache Form und Verlaufsform im Vergleich	159
	2.2 **Activity verbs** Tätigkeitsverben	160
	2.3 **State verbs** Zustandsverben	160
GF 3	**REVISION The passive** Das Passiv	161
	3.1 **Active and passive** Aktiv und Passiv	161
	3.2 **Use** Gebrauch	161
	3.3 **Form** Form	162
	3.4 **Passive sentences with *by* ...** Passivsätze mit *by* ...	162
	3.5 **The passive of verbs with two objects** Das Passiv von Verben mit zwei Objekten	162
GF 4	**REVISION Modals and their substitutes** Modale Hilfsverben und ihre Ersatzverben	164
	4.1 **Modal auxiliaries** Modale Hilfsverben	164
	4.2 **Substitutes** Ersatzverben	164
	4.3 **Modal auxiliaries: speech functions** Modale Hilfsverben: Sprechabsichten	165
GF 5	**REVISION Conditional sentences** Bedingungssätze	167
GF 6	**REVISION Relative clauses** Relativsätze	168
	6.1 **Defining relative clauses** Bestimmende Relativsätze	168
	6.2 **Contact clauses** Relativsätze ohne Relativpronomen	168
	6.3 **Relative clauses with *which* to refer to a whole clause** Satzbezogene Relativsätze mit *which*	169
	6.4 **Non-defining relative clauses** Nicht bestimmende Relativsätze	169
GF 7	**REVISION Indirect speech** Indirekte Rede	170
	7.1 **Statements** Aussagesätze	170
	7.2 **Questions** Fragen	170
	7.3 **Commands and requests** Aufforderungen und Bitten	171
GF 8	**The *to*-infinitive** Der Infinitiv mit *to*	172
	8.1 **REVISION Verb + object + *to*-infinitive** Verb + Objekt + *to*-Infinitiv	172
	8.2 **REVISION Question word + *to*-infinitive** Fragewort + *to*-Infinitiv	172
	8.3 **The *to*-infinitive instead of a relative clause** Der *to*-Infinitiv anstelle eines Relativsatzes	172
GF 9	**The gerund** Das Gerundium	174
	9.1 **REVISION The gerund as subject and object** Das Gerundium als Subjekt und als Objekt	174
	9.2 **REVISION The gerund after prepositions** Das Gerundium nach Präpositionen	175
	9.3 **The gerund with 'its own subject'** Das Gerundium mit „eigenem Subjekt"	175
GF 10	**Participles** Partizipien	176
	10.1 **REVISION Participle forms** Formen des Partizips	176
	10.2 **REVISION Participle clauses instead of relative clauses** Partizipialsätze anstelle von Relativsätzen	176
	10.3 **The present participle after certain verbs** Das Partizip Präsens nach bestimmten Verben	176
	10.4 **Participle clauses instead of adverbial clauses** Partizipialsätze anstelle von adverbialen Nebensätzen	177
	10.5 **Participle clauses giving additional information** Partizipialsätze zur Angabe von Zusatzinformationen	178
Grammatical terms (Grammatische Fachbegriffe)		179

GF 1 The tenses Die Zeitformen

1.1 Tense and time

Grammatische Zeitform und wirkliche Zeit

Wenn man von **„Zeit"** spricht, muss man zwischen **Zeitform** *(tense)* und **wirklicher Zeit** *(time)* unterscheiden.

1a Emily is visiting her aunt in Bath right now.
1b Next week she's visiting her uncle in Bristol.

2a I bought a new computer last week.
2b If Dad bought a new computer, he would give my sister his old one.

◄ Die **Zeitform** ist ein grammatischer Begriff.
Die grammatischen Zeitformen können sich auf verschiedene Zeiten in der Wirklichkeit beziehen:
In Satz **1a** bezieht sich das *present progressive* auf die Gegenwart, in Satz **1b** auf die Zukunft.
In Satz **2a** bezieht sich das *simple past* auf die Vergangenheit, in Satz **2b** auf die Zukunft.

I've been in the team since 2007.	**Present perfect**
Ich bin seit 2007 in der Mannschaft.	**Präsens**
I'll take the fish, please.	***will*-future**
Ich nehme den Fisch, bitte.	**Präsens**

◄ Außerdem werden im Englischen und im Deutschen in vergleichbaren Situationen oft unterschiedliche Zeitformen verwendet.

▸ *The simple form and the progressive form: pp. 159–160*

1.2 Talking about the present

Über die Gegenwart sprechen

The simple present

Das ***simple present*** wird verwendet,

Dave Wilson **usually** gets the bus to school.
On Mondays his mother takes him in the car.
He **never** cycles to school because it's too far.

◄ um über Handlungen und Ereignisse zu sprechen, die **wiederholt, regelmäßig, immer** oder **nie** geschehen (oft mit Zeitangaben wie *always, usually, sometimes, often, every week, on Mondays, never* usw.).

Dave and his family live in Manchester.
His mum is Italian, so he speaks two languages.
He plays hockey and collects models of old cars.
His dad works for a computer company.

◄ um über **Dauerzustände** sowie über **Hobbys** und **Berufe** zu sprechen.

The present progressive

Das ***present progressive*** wird verwendet,

What's Dave doing? –
Just now he's cleaning his bike.

◄ um über Handlungen und Ereignisse zu sprechen, die **jetzt gerade** im Gange sind (oft mit Angaben wie *at the moment, now, just*).

Dave (on the phone) I'm busy, Jack. I'm cleaning my bike.

! Die Handlung, um die es geht, kann für einen Augenblick unterbrochen sein, z.B. durch ein Telefonat. Wichtig ist, dass sie noch nicht abgeschlossen ist.

This week Dave's grandma is staying at the Wilsons' because Dave's mum is ill.

◄ um über **vorübergehende Zustände** zu sprechen (begrenzter Zeitraum: *this week*).

In English: Talking about the present

Simple present:	when something happens regularly, often, always or never
	when we talk about something permanent, for example hobbies, jobs, abilities
Present progressive:	when an action or event is in progress and not yet complete

1.3 Talking about the past

Über die Vergangenheit sprechen

The simple past

Last Friday Katie's family flew to Spain.
Two years ago they went to Italy.
Letzten Freitag ist Katies Familie nach Spanien geflogen / flog Katies Familie nach Spanien. ...

Yesterday Katie went to town with a friend. **First** they looked round the shops and Katie bought a CD. **Then** they tried on shoes in four shops, but they didn't buy any. **After that** they had an ice cream.

Das ***simple past*** wird verwendet,

- um über abgeschlossene Handlungen und Ereignisse zu sprechen, die **zu einem bestimmten Zeitpunkt in der Vergangenheit** stattfanden (oft mit genauen Zeitangaben wie *last Friday, two years ago, yesterday, in 2006, ...*).
- wenn man über vergangene Ereignisse berichtet oder eine Geschichte erzählt (oft mit *first ..., then ..., after that ...*).

! Im Deutschen steht oft das Perfekt, wo im Englischen das *simple past* stehen muss.

„Früher ...": *used to* + infinitive / *would* + infinitive

We used to live in Manchester.
Wir wohnten früher in Manchester.
Manchester United used to be my favourite team.
Früher war Manchester United meine Lieblingsmannschaft.
I used to spend lots of money on sports magazines.
Ich habe früher immer viel Geld für Sportzeitschriften ausgegeben.

Wenn man beschreiben will, was **früher der Fall war**, aber heute nicht mehr, dann kann man die Konstruktion ***used to* + Infinitiv** verwenden.

Grandpa would visit us every Sunday after church.
Opa besuchte uns jeden Sonntag nach der Kirche. /
Opa pflegte uns jeden Sonntag nach der Kirche zu besuchen.
We would often go for long walks in the woods.
Wir haben oft lange Spaziergänge im Wald gemacht. /
Wir pflegten lange Spaziergänge im Wald zu machen.

Zum Ausdruck von **früher gewohnheitsmäßig wiederholten Handlungen** wird auch ***would* + Infinitiv** verwendet.

The past progressive

Yesterday at 3.30 Angela was walking home from school. It was raining, so lots of people were hurrying to the bus stop.

Angela was just crossing the road when she saw her boyfriend.

Das ***past progressive*** wird verwendet,

- um über Handlungen und Ereignisse zu sprechen, die **zu einem bestimmten Zeitpunkt in der Vergangenheit** noch im Gange, also noch nicht abgeschlossen waren.
- wenn man beschreiben will, was gerade vor sich ging *(she was just crossing the road)*, als etwas anderes passierte *(she saw her boyfriend)*.

The past perfect (simple)

When Emma arrived home, her parents had already eaten.
Als Emma zu Hause eintraf, hatten ihre Eltern bereits gegessen.

I couldn't buy a bus ticket because I had forgotten my money.
Ich konnte keine Busfahrkarte kaufen, weil ich mein Geld vergessen hatte.

Das ***past perfect*** (Plusquamperfekt, Vorvergangenheit) wird verwendet, um auszudrücken, dass etwas **vor etwas anderem in der Vergangenheit** stattgefunden hatte.

▸▸▸

The past perfect progressive

Emma was very tired when she arrived home because she had been studying for a test all day.
... denn sie hatte den ganzen Tag für einen Test gelernt.

We had been playing tennis for half an hour when it started to rain.
Wir hatten eine halbe Stunde Tennis gespielt, ...

Das ***past perfect progressive*** wird verwendet, um auszudrücken, dass eine Handlung **vor einem Zeitpunkt in der Vergangenheit** begonnen hatte und bis (oder fast bis) zu jenem Zeitpunkt andauerte.

In English: Talking about the past

Simple past:	when we want to say or ask when something happened when we talk about things in the past or tell a story
Past progressive:	when an action or event was in progress at a particular time in the past
Past perfect:	when an action or event had already happened before a time in the past
Past perfect progressive:	when an action or event had already begun before a time in the past and had continued up to (or almost up to) that time

1.4 Talking about the past and the present

Über die Vergangenheit und die Gegenwart sprechen

Present perfect und ***present perfect progressive*** haben mit der **Vergangenheit und** mit der **Gegenwart** zu tun.

The present perfect (simple)

Das ***present perfect*** wird verwendet,

1 Will Smith is great. I've seen all his films.
2 My sister loves books about horses. She's read hundreds of them.
3 Mel has lost her mobile. Now she can't phone her friends and her mum is angry.
4 I've bought some new jeans, look. They'll look good with my red top.
5 Luke has **already** done his Maths homework, but he has**n't** started his French **yet**.
6 I've **never** been to Paris. Have you **ever** been there?
– No, I haven't. But I've **always** wanted to go.

◀ um über Handlungen und Ereignisse zu sprechen, die **irgendwann in der Vergangenheit** geschehen sind. Oft hat das Geschehen **Auswirkungen auf die Gegenwart oder die Zukunft (3, 4)**.
Ein genauer Zeitpunkt wird nicht genannt. Häufig werden jedoch Adverbien der unbestimmten Zeit wie *already, always, just, not ... yet, often, never* in *present perfect*-Sätzen verwendet **(5, 6)**.

We've had our new car **since April**. Wir haben unser neues Auto seit April.	We've had our new car **for three months**. Wir haben unser neues Auto seit drei Monaten.
***since* + Zeitpunkt**	***for* + Zeitraum**

◀ um über **Zustände** zu sprechen, die in der Vergangenheit begonnen haben und jetzt noch andauern (oft mit ***since*** bzw. ***for*** = deutsch „seit").
Zustandsverben, die oft mit der einfachen Form des *present perfect* verwendet werden, sind z.B. *be, have, know, like, hate.*
▸ *Zustandsverben: 2.3 (p.160)*

How long have you lived in Manchester?
Wie lange wohnt ihr in Manchester?

– **Since last August.** – Seit letztem August.	– **For two years.** – Seit zwei Jahren.

Mit ***How long ...?*** + *present perfect* kann man fragen, seit wann oder wie lange ein Zustand schon andauert.

! Im **Deutschen** benutzt man meist das **Präsens**, aber im **Englischen** muss das ***present perfect*** stehen:
Ich kenne ihn seit ... *I've known him since/for ...*

The present perfect progressive

1 I've been writing e-mails all day.
Ich schreibe (schon) den ganzen Tag E-Mails.

2 Anna has been playing in the hockey team since May.
Anna spielt seit Mai in der Hockeymannschaft.

3 We've been learning French for four years.
Wir lernen seit vier Jahren Französisch.

Das ***present perfect progressive*** wird verwendet, um auszudrücken, dass eine Handlung **in der Vergangenheit** begonnen hat und jetzt noch andauert (auch wenn die Handlung nicht ununterbrochen im Gange war wie etwa in den Sätzen 2 und 3).

! Auch in diesen Fällen benutzt man im **Deutschen** meist das **Präsens**. Im **Englischen** steht das ***present perfect progressive***:
Wir spielen seit ... *We've been playing since/for ...*

In English: Talking about the past and the present

Present perfect: when we want to say that something has happened (not when it happened)
when we want to say since when or how long a state has already lasted
Present perfect progressive: when an action or event began in the past and has continued up to (or almost up to) the present

1.5 Talking about the future

Über die Zukunft sprechen

The *will*-future

Das **Futur mit *will*** wird verwendet,

I'll be 15 next October.
It will be cold and windy, and we will get some rain in the afternoon.

◄ um **Vorhersagen** über die Zukunft zu äußern. Oft geht es dabei um Dinge, die man nicht beeinflussen kann, z.B. das Alter oder das Wetter.

I suppose Ella will be late again as usual.
Ich nehme an, Ella kommt wie üblich wieder zu spät.

◄ um eine **Vermutung** auszudrücken (oft eingeleitet mit *I suppose, I think, I'm sure, I expect, maybe*).

Just a moment. I'll open the door for you.
Moment. Ich mache Ihnen die Tür auf.
I won't tell anyone what's happened. I promise.
Ich sage niemandem, was passiert ist. ...

◄ wenn man sich **spontan** – also ohne es im Voraus geplant zu haben – zu etwas **entschließt**. Oft geht es dabei um **Hilfsangebote** oder **Versprechen**.

The *going to*-future

Das **Futur mit *going to*** wird verwendet,

After school I'm going to study IT – I hope.
Nach der Schule werde ich IT studieren / habe ich vor, IT zu studieren ...
My boyfriend says he's going to be an engineer.
Mein Freund sagt, er will Ingenieur werden.

◄ um über **Vorhaben** und **Pläne** für die Zukunft zu sprechen.

Look at those clouds. There's going to be a storm.
... Es wird ein Gewitter geben.

◄ um auszudrücken, dass etwas **wahrscheinlich gleich geschehen wird** – es gibt bereits deutliche **Anzeichen** dafür.

The present progressive (future meaning)

We're driving to Scotland next weekend to visit my grandparents.
I'm meeting a friend in town tomorrow at 12.
All my friends are coming to my birthday party on Friday.

Auch das ***present progressive*** kann futurische Bedeutung haben. Es wird verwendet, wenn etwas **für die Zukunft fest geplant** oder **fest verabredet** ist (manchmal spricht man vom *diary future*). Durch eine Zeitangabe *(next weekend; tomorrow)* oder aus dem Zusammenhang muss klar sein, dass es um etwas Zukünftiges geht.

►►►

The simple present (future meaning)

The next train to Bath goes in ten minutes.
Our cookery classes start on 2 September.

Auch das ***simple present*** kann futurische Bedeutung haben. Es wird verwendet, wenn ein **zukünftiges Geschehen** durch einen **Fahrplan**, ein **Programm** oder Ähnliches festgelegt ist (manchmal spricht man vom *timetable future*). Verben wie *arrive, leave, go, open, close, start, stop* werden häufig so verwendet.

The future progressive

This time next week my sister will be flying to Spain – and I'll be doing my Maths exam.
Nächste Woche um diese Zeit wird meine Schwester (gerade) nach Spanien fliegen – und ich werde dabei sein, meine Mathe-Prüfung zu machen.

Das ***future progressive*** wird verwendet, um über Handlungen und Ereignisse zu sprechen, die **zu einem zukünftigen Zeitpunkt im Gange** sein werden (noch nicht abgeschlossen sein werden).
Typische Zeitangaben sind *a week today* („heute in einer Woche"), *this time next week* oder Ähnliches.

The future perfect

On Friday we will have finished all our exams.
Am Freitag werden wir alle unsere Prüfungen geschafft haben.

And **by the end of next week** we'll have received our results.
Und bis Ende nächster Woche werden wir unsere Ergebnisse erhalten haben.

Das ***future perfect*** wird verwendet um auszudrücken, dass etwas **zu einem bestimmten Zeitpunkt in der Zukunft geschehen oder getan sein wird**. (Meist wird dieser Zeitpunkt auch genannt – hier: *on Friday; by the end of next week.*)

In English: Talking about the future

***will*-future:**	for predictions or assumptions about the future for spontaneous decisions (e.g. offers and promises)
***going to*-future:**	for intentions and plans for the future when something will very probably happen (there are already signs of it happening)
Present progressive:	when something is definitely planned or arranged for the future
Simple present:	for future events that are a fixed part of a timetable, programme, schedule, etc.
Future progressive:	when an action or event will be in progress at a point of time in the future
Future perfect:	when an action or event will be complete at a point of time in the future

GF 2 Aspect: the simple form and the progressive form
Aspekt: die einfache Form und die Verlaufsform

2.1 Simple and progressive form in contrast

Tense	Simple form	Progressive form
present tense	sing(s)	am/are/is singing
present perfect	have/has sung	have/has been singing
past tense	sang	was/were singing
past perfect	had sung	had been singing
***will*-future**	will sing	will be singing

Einfache Form und Verlaufsform im Vergleich

Anders als im Deutschen gibt es im Englischen eine **einfache Form *(simple form)*** und eine **Verlaufsform *(progressive form)*** des Verbs. Mit diesen Formen bringt man im Englischen zum Ausdruck,
- ob eine Handlung regelmäßig oder wiederholt stattfindet oder ob sie sich gerade im Verlauf befindet,
- ob eine Handlung abgeschlossen ist oder ob sie noch andauert.

Vergleiche die folgenden Beispiele.

The simple form

1a Tom works at a garage on Saturdays.
(regelmäßig, jeden Samstag)
2a Mr Jones goes to work by bike.
(immer, jeden Tag)
3a Olivia has written two letters this morning.
(sie ist fertig und kann die Briefe jetzt abschicken)

◄ Die ***simple form*** wird verwendet
- für regelmäßig oder wiederholt stattfindende Handlungen (**1a**)
- für Dauerzustände (wenn etwas immer so ist) (**2a**)
- für abgeschlossene Handlungen (**3a**).

The progressive form

1b Tom is working at the garage right now.
(er ist gerade dabei, die Arbeit ist im Gange)
2b This week Mr Jones is going to work by bus.
(nur diese Woche, denn sein Rad ist kaputt)
3b Olivia has been writing letters all morning. *(sie ist noch dabei)*

◄ Die ***progressive form*** wird verwendet
- für Handlungen, die gerade im Verlauf sind (**1b**)
- für vorübergehende Zustände (wenn etwas nur vorübergehend der Fall ist) (**2b**)
- für Handlungen, die noch nicht abgeschlossen sind (**3b**).

He was doing the dishes when he heard a funny noise.
Er war gerade beim Abwaschen, ...

! Im Deutschen gibt es keine Verlaufsform. Aber manchmal sagt und hört man Sätze wie „Ich bin gerade dabei, meine Hausaufgaben zu machen" oder „Er war (gerade) beim Abwaschen", um zum Ausdruck zu bringen, dass etwas im Gange und noch nicht abgeschlossen ist bzw. war.

! **Beachte:** Nur **Tätigkeitsverben *(activity verbs)*** wie *do, drink, go, sit, write* können in der *progressive form* verwendet werden.

► *Tätigkeits- und Zustandsverben: 2.2–2.3 (p. 160)*

2.2 Activity verbs

(in a shop window) This shop repairs bikes!
(on the phone) Jack is repairing his bike. Can he call you back?

It gets dark very early here in winter.
At 6 o'clock it was already getting dark.

Tätigkeitsverben

Tätigkeitsverben bezeichnen **Tätigkeiten** *(do, go, read, repair, ...)* oder **Vorgänge** *(become, get, rain, ...)*.
Sie können sowohl in der *simple form* als auch in der *progressive form* verwendet werden.

2.3 State verbs

The price doesn't include breakfast.
Emily seems really happy at her new school.
Jake's uncle owns a nice house in the country.

Do you believe their story?
I don't know the answer to question 5.
Anna didn't understand what Julie meant.

Lucy doesn't like people who talk a lot.
I don't mind waiting for you here.
We prefer brown bread to white. It's healthier.

Zustandsverben

Zustandsverben *(state verbs)* bezeichnen keine Tätigkeiten oder Vorgänge, sondern **Zustände**. Sie werden in der Regel **nur in der *simple form*** verwendet.

Zu den **Zustandsverben** gehören

- Verben, die **Eigenschaften**, **Besitz** oder **Zugehörigkeit** ausdrücken: *be, include, seem, sound, mean* („bedeuten"), *need, own, belong, ...*
- Verben des **Meinens** und des **Wissens**: *believe, know, mean* („meinen"), *remember, suppose, understand, ...*
- Verben des **Mögens** und **Wollens**: *like, love, hate, mind, prefer, want, ...*

States and activities

Julie has dark hair.	**state:**	*haben*
Julie is having a shower.	**activity:**	*duschen*
We were having fun/a great time.	**activity:**	*Spaß/eine tolle Zeit haben, erleben*
Do I look silly with my hair like this?	**state:**	*aussehen*
I didn't see the man. I wasn't looking.	**activity:**	*(hin)schauen, gucken*
The flowers smell wonderful.	**state:**	*riechen*
Sophie is smelling the roses.	**activity:**	*riechen (an etwas)*
The pasta tastes good.	**state:**	*schmecken*
I'm tasting the soup now.	**activity:**	*kosten, probieren*
I think that's a great idea.	**state:**	*denken, meinen*
He was thinking of moving to Paris.	**activity:**	*überlegen, nachdenken*

Einige wenige englische Verben können als **Tätigkeits- oder als Zustandsverb** verwendet werden (mit jeweils unterschiedlichen deutschen Entsprechungen).

Als **Zustandsverb** stehen diese Verben immer in der *simple form*.

Als **Tätigkeitsverb** kommen sie in beiden Formen vor.

Vergleiche die Beispiele links.

In English: Activity verbs and state verbs

1 **Activity verbs** *(do, read, watch, work, ...)* can be used in the simple form and in the progressive form:
*Tom **does** his homework every evening. Look, Tom **is doing** his homework now.*

2 **State verbs** *(seem, belong, believe, know, like, need, ...)* are not used in the progressive form:
*I **believe** you. (not: ~~I'm believing~~ you.)*

3 A few verbs are used as state verbs and as activity verbs – with different meanings:
*The soup **tastes** good. Look, Grandpa **is tasting** the soup now.*

GF 3 REVISION The passive Das Passiv

3.1 Active and passive

Aktiv und Passiv

Active: **Alexander Fleming** discovered penicillin in 1928.
Alexander Fleming entdeckte 1928 das Penicillin.

Passive: **Penicillin** was discovered in 1928.
Penicillin wurde 1928 entdeckt.

◄ Beide Sätze beschreiben denselben Sachverhalt, betrachten ihn aber aus unterschiedlichen Blickwinkeln:

Der **Aktivsatz** handelt von Fleming und informiert uns über eine Entdeckung, die er 1928 machte.

Der **Passivsatz** handelt von Penicillin und informiert uns über den Zeitpunkt seiner Entdeckung.

Active: The manager asked **Mel** to help out.
Passive: **Mel** was asked to help out.
Mel wurde gebeten auszuhelfen.

Active: The manager paid **her** £6 an hour.
Passive: **She** was paid £6 an hour.
Ihr wurden £6 die Stunde bezahlt. /
Sie erhielt £6 die Stunde.

◄ Das Passiv lässt sich im Englischen von allen Verben bilden, die im Aktivsatz ein Objekt haben.

3.2 Use

Gebrauch

1 A new sports centre has been opened in Paddington. ... ist eröffnet worden ...

2 The first goal was scored in the seventh minute. ... wurde erzielt ...

3 Breakfast is served from 7 to 10.30 am. ... wird serviert ...

4 The two bank robbers have been sentenced to ten years. ... sind verurteilt worden ...

... müssen vor dem 15. Juli zurückgegeben werden.

Mit einem **Passivsatz** kann man Handlungen beschreiben, ohne zu sagen, wer die Handlung ausführt.

Oft ist nicht bekannt oder dem Sprecher nicht wichtig, wer die Handlung ausführt (Sätze 1 und 2), manchmal ist es auch offensichtlich und daher nicht erwähnenswert (Sätze 3 und 4).

Das Passiv findet man oft in Nachrichten, in Zeitungsartikeln (z.B. über Unfälle, Sportereignisse, Verbrechen), in offiziellen Texten, in technischen Beschreibungen und auf Schildern.

The woman was taken to hospital.
Man brachte die Frau ins Krankenhaus.

Their CDs can be ordered online now.
Man kann ihre CDs jetzt online bestellen.

Das Passiv wird im Englischen häufiger verwendet als im Deutschen. Einem englischen Passivsatz entspricht oft ein deutscher Aktivsatz mit „man“.

3.3 Form

Form

The passive

Simple present	I am often invited to parties.
Present progressive	Some new shops are being built in Carlton Street.
Simple past	The bridge was completed in 1952.
Past progressive	I couldn't mail you. My computer was being repaired.
Present perfect (simple)	All the sandwiches have been eaten.
Past perfect (simple)	Ed didn't go to the party because he hadn't been invited.
***will*-future and modal auxiliaries**	The last match of the season will be played next Friday. Mobile phones must be turned off during lessons. Concert tickets can be bought online.
***going to*-future**	Look, the lions are going to be fed soon.
Future perfect	I hope my bike will have been repaired by Saturday.

Das Passiv bildet man mit einer **Form von *be*** und der 3. Form des Verbs (Partizip Perfekt, *past participle*).

Bei den *progressive forms* wird das Passiv mit *being* gebildet: *are being built; was being repaired.*

3.4 Passive sentences with *by* ...

Passivsätze mit *by* ...

The ***Times*** **is read** by almost 2 million people every day.
... wird jeden Tag von 2 Millionen Menschen gelesen.

This picture **was painted** by a 12-year old girl.
... wurde von einem 12-jährigen Mädchen gemalt.

Part of this building **was destroyed** by fire.
... wurde durch ein Feuer zerstört.

Wenn man in einem Passivsatz den „Täter" oder „Verursacher" der Handlung nennen möchte, verwendet man die Präposition ***by*** („von", „durch").

3.5 The passive of verbs with two objects

Das Passiv von Verben mit zwei Objekten

Active	Indirect object	Direct object
The manager offered	her	**a part-time job.**

Der Geschäftsführer bot ihr eine Teilzeitstelle an.

Manche Verben haben zwei Objekte nach sich:
- ein **indirektes Objekt** (meist eine Person, daher auch: **Personenobjekt**)
- ein **direktes Objekt** (meist eine Sache, daher auch: **Sachobjekt**).

Passive (English)

Subject	
She	was offered **a part-time job.**

◄ Im Englischen wird meist das **indirekte Objekt** (das **Personenobjekt**) zum **Subjekt des Passivsatzes.** *
Diese Art des Passivs nennt man *personal passive* (deutsch: „persönliches Passiv").

Passive (German)

Dativobjekt		Subjekt	
Ihr	wurde	eine Teilzeitstelle	angeboten.

◄ Im Deutschen kann nur das **direkte Objekt** (das **Sachobjekt**) zum **Subjekt des Passivsatzes** werden.
Die Dativform des Personenobjekts bleibt im deutschen Passivsatz erhalten: *Ihr wurde ... angeboten.*

* Manchmal wird auch im Englischen das Sachobjekt zum Subjekt des Passivsatzes. In diesem Fall wird das Personenobjekt mit *to* angehängt: A part-time job was offered to her.

Weitere Beispiele für das *personal passive* findest du auf der nächsten Seite.

We were given the necessary information.
Man hat uns die nötigen Informationen gegeben.

I've been promised a new computer if I pass my exams.
Mir ist ein neuer Computer versprochen worden, wenn ich meine Prüfungen bestehe.

The students were shown the film of the book.
Den Studenten wurde die Verfilmung des Buches gezeigt.

We were told the true story about the first Thanksgiving.
Uns wurde die wahre Geschichte über ... erzählt. / Man erzählte uns die wahre Geschichte über ...

◄ Häufig vorkommende Verben mit zwei Objekten sind *give, offer, pay, promise, send, show, tell.*

Vergleiche die englischen Passivsätze mit ihren deutschen Übersetzungen – im Deutschen verwendet man oft einen Aktivsatz.

In English: The passive

1 The **passive** is used more in English than in German. In German an active sentence with 'man' is often preferred.

2 We find the passive mainly in news reports, official texts, signs, etc. when the 'doer' of the action is not named (because the 'doer' is not known or not important or because it's clear who does the action):
The thief was arrested.
(it's clear who did it: the police)

3 If you want to name the 'doer', you use ***by*** (German 'von', 'durch'):
Penicillin was discovered in 1928 ***by*** *A. Fleming.*
Our car was damaged ***by*** *falling stones.*

4 In English, the indirect object of an active sentence (the 'person object') can be the subject of a passive sentence ('personal passive'):
Active: *They've offered* ***him*** *a place at Bristol University.*
Passive: ***He*** *has been offered a place at Bristol University.*

GF 4 REVISION Modals and their substitutes
Modale Hilfsverben und ihre Ersatzverben

4.1 Modal auxiliaries

1 Can you play the piano?
2 – Yes, I can. / No, I can't.

3 Sue is good at drawing. She should study art.

4 Could you do the exercise? I couldn't.

5 Can we help you in the kitchen, Mum?
6 We can play tennis on Saturday if you like.

Modale Hilfsverben

Modale Hilfsverben wie ***can, may, must, should*** drücken aus, was jemand tun **kann, darf, muss, soll** usw.
Sie werden zusammen mit dem **Infinitiv eines Vollverbs** verwendet (1).
Nur in Kurzantworten können sie allein stehen (2).

Weitere Merkmale modaler Hilfsverben:

- Sie haben nur eine Form, es gibt also keine Endungen auf *-s*, *-ing* oder *-ed* (3).
- Frage und Verneinung werden ohne *do/does/did* gebildet (4).
- Sie beziehen sich in der Regel auf die Gegenwart oder die Zukunft (5, 6).

4.2 Substitutes

1 I'd love to be able to speak Spanish.
2 Being able to speak Spanish must be great.
3 We weren't allowed to use a dictionary.

Ersatzverben

Modale Hilfsverben können **nicht alle Zeitformen** bilden. Daher gibt es zu bestimmten modalen Hilfsverben **Ersatzverben** mit ähnlicher Bedeutung, von denen man den Infinitiv (1), die *-ing*-Form (2) und alle Zeitformen (3, *simple past*) bilden kann.

„können": *can – (to) be able to*

My little brother can / is able to swim.	***present:***	*can* und *am/is/are able to*
Tim could / was able to read when he was four. I could smell fire, but I couldn't see any smoke.	***past:***	*could* und *was/were able to* *could* steht vor allem in verneinten Sätzen und Fragen sowie mit Verben der Wahrnehmung *(smell, see, hear, ...)*.
Jacob hasn't been able to finish his essay.	***present perfect:***	*have/has been able to*
I'm taking driving lessons, so next year I'll be able to drive.	***will-future:***	*will/won't be able to*

„dürfen": *can, may – (to) be allowed to*

Can / May I have a sleepover on Friday, Mum? We aren't allowed to stay up late in the week.	***present:***	*can, may* und *am/is/are allowed to*
When I was a kid I could / was allowed to watch TV for an hour a day.	***past:***	*could* und *was/were allowed to*
I've always been allowed to have pets.	***present perfect:***	*have/has been allowed to*
Will you be allowed to go to the party on Friday?	***will-future:***	*will/won't be allowed to*

Jeans must not be worn at this school.
At my school we're not allowed to wear jeans.

! Für ausdrückliche **Verbote** wird *must not (mustn't)* oder *be not allowed to* verwendet.

„müssen“: *must – (to) have to*

Teacher You must work harder, Noah. His teacher says Noah has to work harder. I needn't get up at 6 tomorrow. / I don't have to get up at 6 tomorrow.	***present:***	*must* und *have/has to* (*have/has to* ist häufiger als *must*) ! **Verneinung:** *needn't* oder *don't/doesn't have to*
I had to rewrite my essay. We didn't have to wait long.	***past:***	*had to* ! **Verneinung:** *didn't have to*
Lauren has had to go to the dentist's.	***present perfect:***	*have/has had to*
You will have to go to the dentist's too if you eat so many sweets.	***will-future:***	*will/won't have to*

4.3 Modal auxiliaries: speech functions

Modale Hilfsverben: Sprechabsichten

can

I can speak French and a little German.	**Fähigkeit**
Can I borrow this CD? / Can you be quiet, please?	**Bitte/Aufforderung**
You can use my pen. / You can't take photos in the museum.	**Erlaubnis/Verbot**
Can/Can't we go on a bike trip on Saturday?	**Vorschlag**
I think that's Luke. – No, it can't be him. He's in Scotland.	**Möglichkeit**

could

My sister could read when she was only four.	**Fähigkeit** *(konnte)*
I could stay up late on Saturdays when I was ten.	**Erlaubnis** *(konnte/durfte)*
But I couldn't watch late night films.	**Verbot** *(konnte/durfte nicht)*
Could you show me how to start the DVD?	**Bitte/Aufforderung** *(könntest)*
Could/Couldn't we go to the cinema tonight?	**Vorschlag** *(könnten)*
Where's Mum? – She could be at Grandma's.	**Möglichkeit** *(könnte)*

may

May I use your phone, please?	**Erlaubnis**
Students may not use mobile phones during lessons.	**Verbot**
May I help you with your bags?	**Angebot**
Sarah may still be at her friend's.	**Möglichkeit** *(könnte)*

might

John might come today if he's in town.	**Möglichkeit** *(könnte vielleicht)*

must

You've got a temperature. You must stay at home.	**Notwendigkeit, Zwang**
You haven't eaten since breakfast. You must be hungry.	**Wahrscheinlichkeit**

mustn't

You mustn't tell Mel about the concert. It's a surprise.	**Verbot** *(darfst nicht)*

▶▶▶

needn't

You needn't tell Mel about the concert. She already knows.	**Fehlen einer Notwendigkeit/ eines Zwangs** *(brauchst nicht/ musst nicht)*

shall

Shall we eat now and go shopping later?	**Vorschlag** *(sollen/wollen)*
Shall I help you with the dishes?	**Angebot** *(soll)*

should

You should talk to the teacher about your problem.	**Ratschlag**
Dogs should be left outside.	**Verpflichtung**
It should be a sunny day tomorrow. The weather report is good.	**Wahrscheinlichkeit**

will

I suppose there will be a lot of people at Al's party, as always.	**Vorhersage, Vermutung**
There's somebody at the door. It will be Janet.	**Wahrscheinlichkeit**

would

Would you help me to tidy these papers, please?	**Bitte/Aufforderung**
Would you like to stay for dinner?	**Angebot**
When we were kids we would play in the woods for hours. ... spielten wir immer stundenlang im Wald.	**frühere Gewohnheit**

In English: Modals and their substitutes

1 Modal auxiliaries (or **modals**) like *can, could, may, might, must*, etc.

- have only one form: *Tom may come tomorrow.*
- form negatives and questions without *do/does/did*: *They can't hear you.*
- are followed by an infinitive without *to*: *You should relax more.*
- usually refer to the present or future: *Could I have a glass of water, please? Can you call me back tomorrow?*
- can express more than one speech function:
  can *I can play tennis.* (ability)
  Can I borrow your ruler? (request)
  You can borrow my pen. (permission)
  That can't be Joe. Joe's in Spain. (possibility)
- cannot form all tenses.

2 Substitutes are used to form other tenses:

- *can* („können") – *(to) be able to:*
  I'll be able to drive next year.
- *can, may* („dürfen") – *(to) be allowed to:*
  Were you allowed to use a dictionary in the test?
- *must* („müssen") – *(to) have to:*
  I had to do extra homework yesterday.

*umbrella [ʌm'brelə] *Regenschirm*

GF 5 REVISION Conditional sentences Bedingungssätze

Subordinate clause	Main clause
If you give me your number,	I'll call you.
Wenn du mir deine Nummer gibst,	rufe ich dich an.

Main clause	Subordinate clause
I'll call you	if you give me your number.
Ich rufe dich an,	wenn du mir deine Nummer gibst.

Bedingungssätze („Wenn ..., dann ...“-Sätze) bestehen aus einem **Hauptsatz** *(main clause)* und einem **Nebensatz** *(subordinate clause)*.
Der Nebensatz wird in der Regel durch die Konjunktion ***if*** („wenn/falls“) eingeleitet und nennt eine Bedingung. Der *if*-Satz kann vor dem Hauptsatz stehen (er wird dann mit einem Komma abgetrennt) oder auf den Hauptsatz folgen (ohne Komma).

Es gibt **drei Grundtypen** von Bedingungssätzen:

if + present	*will*-future

If I miss the bus, I'll take a taxi.
Wenn ich den Bus verpasse, nehme ich ein Taxi.

If Dan misses the bus, he can/should/must take a taxi.
If you miss the bus, take a taxi.

◄ **Typ 1 („Was ist, wenn ...“-Sätze)**
Diese Bedingungssätze beziehen sich auf die **Gegenwart** oder die **Zukunft**. Sie drücken aus, was unter bestimmten Bedingungen **geschieht/geschehen wird** oder **nicht geschieht/nicht geschehen wird**.
Statt des Futurs mit *will* können im Hauptsatz auch die modalen Hilfsverben *can, should, must* usw. oder ein Imperativ stehen.

if + past	*would* + infinitive

If I missed the bus, I would take a taxi.
Wenn ich den Bus verpasste/verpassen würde, würde ich ein Taxi nehmen.

If Dan missed the bus, he could/might take a taxi.

◄ **Typ 2 („Was wäre, wenn ...“-Sätze)**
Diese Bedingungssätze beziehen sich auch auf die **Gegenwart** oder die **Zukunft**. Sie drücken aus, was unter bestimmten Bedingungen **geschehen** oder **nicht geschehen würde**.
Statt *would* können im Hauptsatz auch *could* oder *might* stehen.

if + past perfect	*would have* + past participle

If I had missed the bus, I would have taken a taxi.
Wenn ich den Bus verpasst hätte, hätte ich ein Taxi genommen.

If Dan had missed the bus, he could/might have taken a taxi.

◄ **Typ 3 („Was wäre gewesen, wenn ...“-Sätze)**
Diese Bedingungssätze beziehen sich auf die **Vergangenheit**. Sie drücken aus, was unter bestimmten Bedingungen **geschehen** oder **nicht geschehen wäre**.
Der *if*-Satz nennt eine Bedingung, die nicht eingetreten ist *(Ich habe **nicht** den Bus verpasst)*. Der Sprecher stellt sich nur vor, was geschehen wäre, aber in Wirklichkeit nicht geschehen ist *(Ich hätte ein Taxi genommen)*.
Statt *would have* können im Hauptsatz auch *could have* oder *might have* stehen.

Additional information *

If I **knew** the answer, I **would have told** you.
If I **had had** his chances in life, I**'d be** rich now.
If she **could have told** you the reason,
she **would have done**.

◄ Wie im Deutschen sind **je nach Situation auch Mischformen** möglich, besonders bei Typ 2 und Typ 3.
Es kommen also auch andere Kombinationen von Zeitformen vor als die oben beschriebenen.

* Abschnitte mit der Überschrift **Additional information** enthalten Grammatik, die du verstehen solltest, aber nicht selbst anwenden musst.

►►►

In English: Conditional sentences

Type 1:			
	present	***will*-future** or **modal auxiliary + infinitive**	! No present tense in the main clause.
	If you give me your number,	*I will/can call you.*	
Type 2:			
	past	***would/could/might* + infinitive**	! No *would* in the *if*-clause.
	If you gave me your number,	*I would/could/might call you.*	
Type 3:			
	past perfect	***would have/could have/might have* + past participle**	
	If you had given me your number,	*I would have/could have/might have called you.*	

GF 6 REVISION Relative clauses Relativsätze

6.1 Defining relative clauses

1 Do you know **the girl** who/that works at the Oxfam shop?
... das Mädchen, das im Oxfam-Shop arbeitet?

2 That's **the shop** which/that sells cheap books and CDs.
... der Laden, der billige Bücher und CDs verkauft.

Bestimmende Relativsätze

Bestimmende Relativsätze werden mit den Relativpronomen ***who*** oder ***that*** für **Personen (1)** und ***which*** oder ***that*** für **Dinge (2)** eingeleitet.

Ein bestimmender Relativsatz gibt Informationen über ein Nomen, die **zum Verständnis des Satzes notwendig** sind. Ohne die Relativsätze
– ... *the girl who/that works at the Oxfam shop* bzw.
– ... *the shop which/that sells cheap books and CDs*
würde man nicht wissen, welches Mädchen bzw. welcher Laden gemeint ist.

! Beachte, dass ein bestimmender Relativsatz nicht durch Kommas abgetrennt wird.

6.2 Contact clauses

1 Lilly is **the girl** who I met at the library.
or Lilly is **the girl** I met at the library.
... das Mädchen, das ich ... kennengelernt habe.

2 These are **the photos** that Dad took.
or These are **the photos** Dad took.
... die Fotos, die Dad gemacht hat.

3 Jake is **the boy** [who invited] us to the party.
... der Junge, der uns auf die Party eingeladen hat.

Relativsätze ohne Relativpronomen

Wenn das Relativpronomen **Objekt der Relativsatzes** ist, wird es oft **weggelassen (1, 2)**.
Relativsätze ohne Relativpronomen werden *contact clauses* genannt.

! Wenn das **Relativpronomen direkt vor dem Verb** steht, ist es **Subjekt** und darf **nicht** weggelassen werden **(3)**.
Vergleiche:
– ... *the boy who invited us to the party*
(„... der Junge, der uns ... eingeladen hat“)
– ... *the boy who we invited to the party* oder
... *the boy we invited to the party*
(„... der Junge, den wir ... eingeladen haben“)

6.3 Relative clauses with *which* to refer to a whole clause

We're moving to Leeds in the summer, which means I'll have to change school.
..., was bedeutet, dass ich die Schule wechseln muss.

My sister thinks I should do a language course in France in the holidays, which is a good idea.
..., was ich für eine gute Idee halte.

Satzbezogene Relativsätze mit *which*

Relativsätze mit *which* können sich auch auf einen ganzen Satz beziehen. Sie kommentieren die Aussage im vorausgehenden Hauptsatz.

Im Deutschen werden solche Relativsätze mit „was" eingeleitet.

! Beachte das Komma vor satzbezogenen Relativsätzen.

Additional information

6.4 Non-defining relative clauses

Agatha Christie, **who died in 1976**, wrote about 70 detective novels and 17 plays.

At 11.35 we landed at Atlanta International, **which is one of the world's busiest airports.**

Nicht bestimmende Relativsätze

Nicht bestimmende Relativsätze kommen hauptsächlich in geschriebenem Englisch vor. Sie geben **zusätzliche Informationen**, die zum Verständnis des Satzes nicht notwendig sind.

! – In nicht bestimmenden Relativsätzen können *who, which* und *whose* verwendet werden, aber nicht *that*!
– Nicht bestimmende Relativsätze werden durch Kommas abgetrennt.

In English: Relative clauses

1 A **defining relative clause** gives **necessary** information about the noun that it refers to:
*That's the boy **who sold Jack the cheap DVDs**.*
We can only leave out the relative pronoun when it is the **object** of the relative clause:
*That's the boy **who Jack asked about cheap DVDs**.* or
*That's the boy **Jack asked about cheap DVDs**.* (contact clause)

2 Relative clauses with ***which*** can **refer to the whole main clause**:
*I got an 'A' in my Maths test**, which was a big surprise**.*

3 A **non-defining relative clause** gives **extra** information about the noun that it refers to:
*My friend Michael**, whose parents are German,** is bilingual.*

GF 7 REVISION Indirect speech — Die indirekte Rede

7.1 Statements — Aussagesätze

Kate	I **love** basketball. I'**m training** hard for our next match.	
Direct speech	Kate says, 'I **love** basketball. I'**m training** hard for our next match.'	◄ In der **direkten Rede** wird **wörtlich** wiedergegeben, was jemand sagt, schreibt oder denkt.
Indirect speech (reporting verb: simple present)	Kate says that she loves basketball. She says she's training hard for their next match.	◄ In der **indirekten Rede** (*indirect* oder *reported speech*) wird berichtet, was jemand sagt, schreibt oder denkt. Einleitende Verben sind *say, tell sb., answer, add, explain, think*.
Indirect speech (reporting verb: simple past)	Kate said that she loved basketball. She told me she was training hard for their next match.	◄ Steht das **einleitende Verb im *simple past*** (*said, told sb., answered* usw.), werden die Zeitformen der direkten Rede meist um eine Zeitstufe in die Vergangenheit „zurückverschoben" *(backshift of tenses)*.

! Im Englischen steht vor der indirekten Rede **kein Komma** und das Wort *that* wird oft weggelassen.

Backshift of tenses after a reporting verb in the past

present	► **past**	***will*-future**	► ***would* + infinitive**
past	► **past perfect**	***going to*-future**	► ***was/were going to* + infinitive**
present perfect	► **past perfect**	***can, may***	► ***could, might***

! Verben im *past perfect* bleiben unverändert, da man sie nicht weiter „zurückverschieben" kann. In der Umgangssprache bleiben *past*-Formen der direkten Rede oft unverändert, werden also nicht ins *past perfect* „zurückverschoben":

Gina I didn't go out last Friday. ► Gina said she didn't go out last Friday.

7.2 Questions — Fragen

Wenn das einleitende Verb im *simple past* steht *(asked, wanted to know)*, erfolgt auch bei **Fragen** in der indirekten Rede die Rückverschiebung der Zeiten.

Direct question (yes/no question)	'Do you train every day, Kate?'	◄ Handelt es sich bei der direkten Frage um eine **Frage ohne Fragewort** *(yes/no question)*, dann wird die indirekte Frage mit ***if*** oder ***whether*** („ob") eingeleitet.
Indirect question	Alex asked Kate **if/whether** she trained every day.	
Direct question (with question word)	'**When** did you join the team?'	◄ Wenn die direkte **Frage mit einem Fragewort** beginnt (*why, how, what, when, where* usw.), dann wird das Fragewort in der indirekten Frage beibehalten.
Indirect question	Alex wanted to know **when** Kate had joined the team. ..., wann Kate sich der Mannschaft angeschlossen hat.	

! Die Wortstellung in indirekten Fragen ist wie in Aussagesätzen: **S – V – ...**
Es gibt keine Umschreibung mit *do/does/did*.

7.3 Commands and requests

Aufforderungen und Bitten

Indirect command

Kate told Alex to go to their next match.
She told him not to miss it.
Kate sagte Alex, er solle zu ihrem nächsten Spiel gehen. ...

◄ **Aufforderungen** werden in der indirekten Rede meist mit ***tell sb. to do sth.*** (bzw. ***tell sb. not to do sth.***) wiedergegeben.

Indirect request

Alex asked Kate to get him some tickets.
Alex bat Kate, ihm Eintrittskarten zu besorgen.

◄ **Bitten** werden meist mit ***ask sb. to do sth.*** (bzw. ***ask sb. not to do sth.***) wiedergegeben.

In English: Indirect speech

1. If the reporting verb is in the past *(said, told sb., asked, ...)*, there is usually a 'backshift' of tenses (present ▸ past, present perfect ▸ past perfect etc.).
   *Kate: 'I've hurt my knee.' ▸ Kate **said** that she **had hurt** her knee.*
2. In indirect questions the word order is the same as in statements: **subject – verb** – ...
   *Alex wanted to know when **Kate had joined the team**.*
3. In indirect commands and requests the *to*-infinitive is used after *tell sb.* and *ask sb.*
   *Kate **told Alex not to miss** the next match.*

GF 8 The *to*-infinitive — Der Infinitiv mit *to*

8.1 REVISION Verb + object + *to*-infinitive

Kim **helped** me to write my French essay.
Kim half mir, meinen französischen Aufsatz zu schreiben.

Sharon **asked** me not to use her photo.
Sharon bat mich, ihr Foto nicht zu verwenden.

Grandma **expects** us to save our pocket money.
Oma erwartet, dass wir unser Taschengeld sparen.

Ed **would like** me to go to town with him.
Ed möchte, dass ich mit ihm in die Stadt fahre.

We **want** you to help us to clean up the beach.
Wir wollen, dass du uns hilfst, den Strand zu säubern.

Verb + Objekt + *to*-Infinitiv

Nach bestimmten Verben kann ein **Objekt + *to*-Infinitiv** stehen, z.B. ***ask/help/invite/teach sb. (not) to do sth***.

Nach den entsprechenden deutschen Verben steht meist ein Infinitiv mit „zu":
jn. bitten/jm. helfen/..., etwas (nicht) zu tun.

◄ Auch nach den Verben ***cause, expect, tell, want, would like, would love*** kann ein **Objekt + *to*-Infinitiv** stehen.

! Nach den entsprechenden deutschen Verben steht ein Nebensatz mit „dass". Auf die englischen Verben darf jedoch kein *that*-Satz folgen:
*Wir **wollen**, dass du uns hilfst. We **want** you to help us.*
Nicht: *We want ~~that you help~~ us.*

8.2 REVISION Question word + *to*-infinitive

We **don't know** what to do.
(... what we should/could do)
Wir wissen nicht, was wir tun sollen/könnten.

Let's **ask** someone how to get to the bus station.
..., wie wir zum Busbahnhof kommen (können).

Can you **tell** us which direction to take?
..., welche Richtung wir nehmen müssen?

They **wondered** whether to go or to stay.
..., ob sie gehen oder bleiben sollten.

Fragewort + *to*-Infinitiv

Der *to*-Infinitiv steht oft nach einem **Fragewort** (*what, who, when, where, how* usw.) sowie nach *whether* („ob"). Er entspricht meist einem Nebensatz mit modalem Hilfsverb *(can, could, might, must, should)*.

Die Kombination aus Fragewort und *to*-Infinitiv steht oft nach den Verben *ask, explain, find out, know, show, tell, wonder*.

8.3 The *to*-infinitive instead of a relative clause

1 I expect **the last (person)** to arrive will be Jo.
(... the last person who arrives ...)
Tim was **the first (one)** to tell me the news.
(... the first one who told me ...)
We're **the only shop** to offer this service.
(... the only shop that offers this service)
Sophie was **the only person/the only one** to say what she thought.
(... the only person/one who said ...)

2 Who was **the youngest (girl or boy)** to take part in the competition?
(... the youngest girl or boy who took part ...)

Der *to*-Infinitiv anstelle eines Relativsatzes

Der *to*-Infinitiv kann **anstelle eines Relativsatzes** stehen:

1 nach *the first, the last, the next, the only*

! Nach *the only* muss ein Nomen oder *one/ones* stehen.

2 nach einem Superlativ.

Der *to*-Infinitiv kann **anstelle eines Relativsatzes mit modalem Hilfsverb** stehen:

1 nach einem **Nomen** (häufig nach *person, place, way*)

1 There are **clothes** to wash and **meals** to cook.
(... clothes that I/we must wash ...)
James is **the person** to ask about computers.
(... the person who you should ask)
Luigi's is the **place** to go for a good pizza.
(... the place that you must/should go to)
Look, this is **the way** to do it.
(... the way that you should do it)

2 nach den Zusammensetzungen mit ***some-, any-*** und ***no-*** (*someone, something, somewhere, anything, nowhere* usw.).

2 I'm looking for **someone** to share a flat with.
(... someone who I can share a flat with)
Lucy doesn't know **anybody** to play with.
(... anybody who she can/could play with)
There's **nothing** to do and **nowhere** to go.
(... nothing that I can do and nowhere that I can go)

In English: The *to*-infinitive

The *to*-infinitive is used

– after *ask, cause, expect, help, tell, want, would like,* ... + object	*Dad **would like you to help** him.*
– after a question word, instead of a subordinate clause	*I don't know **who to ask**.*
– after *the first (person), the last (one),* etc., instead of a relative clause	*Sue is always **the first to arrive**.*
	*Tom was **the oldest to join** us.*
– after nouns and *someone, anything, nowhere,* etc., instead of a relative clause	*I've got **some letters to write**.*
	*Is there **anybody to ask**?*

*(to) disturb [dɪˈstɜːb] *stören*

GF 9 The gerund Das Gerundium

9.1 REVISION The gerund as subject and object

Das Gerundium als Subjekt und als Objekt

Subject	Object
Cycling is fun.	I love cycling.
Radfahren macht Spaß.	Ich liebe das Radfahren. / Ich fahre sehr gern Rad.

I like riding **motorbikes.**
Ich fahre gern Motorrad.
Cycling **in the rain** can be fun too.
Radfahren im Regen kann auch Spaß machen. / Im Regen Rad zu fahren kann auch Spaß machen.

Wenn die *-ing*-Form eines Verbs die Funktion eines **Nomens** hat, wird sie **Gerundium** *(gerund)* genannt. Das Gerundium kann **Subjekt** oder **Objekt** eines Satzes sein.

Wie ein Verb kann das Gerundium erweitert werden, z.B. durch ein Objekt (hier: *motorbikes*) oder eine Orts- oder Zeitangabe (hier: *in the rain*).

! Beachte:

1 Nobody **enjoys** going to the dentist's.
Niemand geht gern zum Zahnarzt.
Imagine living in California!
Stell dir vor, in Kalifornien zu leben!
Tom **suggested** going for an ice cream.
Tom schlug vor, ein Eis essen zu gehen.

◄ **1** Nach einigen Verben – z.B. ***dislike, enjoy, finish, imagine, miss, practise, suggest*** – muss ein weiteres Verb als Gerundium stehen:
*I **enjoy** going ...; He **suggested** going ...*
Anders als im Deutschen darf nach diesen Verben **kein Infinitiv** stehen!
Also nicht: *I ~~enjoy to go~~ ...; He ~~suggested to go~~ ...*

2 When it **started** raining / to rain we all went home.
Als es anfing zu regnen, gingen wir alle nach Haus.
Will **loves** doing / to do crazy things.
Will liebt es, verrückte Sachen zu machen.

◄ **2** Nach ***begin/start, continue, hate, like, love, prefer*** kann jedoch – bei gleicher Bedeutung – entweder ein Gerundium oder ein *to*-Infinitiv stehen.

3 I'll never **forget** talking to Robbie Williams.
Ich werde nie vergessen, wie ich mit Robbie Williams gesprochen habe.
I **forgot** to phone Grandpa. I'm sorry.
Ich habe vergessen, Opa anzurufen. Es tut mir leid.

I **remember** posting the letter last Friday.
Ich erinnere mich daran, letzten Freitag den Brief eingeworfen zu haben.
I must **remember** to post this card tomorrow.
Ich muss daran denken *(= ich darf nicht vergessen)*, morgen diese Karte einzuwerfen.

I've **stopped** talking to Rob. We had a fight.
Ich habe aufgehört, mit Rob zu reden. / Ich rede nicht mehr mit Rob. ...
I **stopped** to talk to Jo. We chatted for a while.
Ich hielt an, um mit Jo zu reden.

I can't open the door. – **Try** kicking it.
... Probier mal, dagegen zu treten.
I **tried** to kick the door open and hurt myself.
Ich versuchte/bemühte mich, die Tür aufzutreten ...

◄ **3** Nach ***forget, remember, stop, try*** kann entweder ein Gerundium oder ein *to*-Infinitiv stehen, aber mit unterschiedlicher Bedeutung:

– ***forget doing** sth.*	vergessen, dass/wie man etwas *(in der Vergangenheit)* getan hat
***forget to do** sth.*	vergessen, etwas zu tun
– ***remember doing** sth.*	sich daran erinnern, dass man etwas *(in der Vergangenheit)* getan hat
***remember to do** sth.*	daran denken, etwas zu tun
– ***stop doing** sth.*	aufhören, etwas zu tun
***stop to do** sth.*	anhalten, um etwas *(anderes)* zu tun
– ***try doing** sth.*	etwas (aus)probieren
***try to do** sth.*	versuchen/sich bemühen, etwas zu tun

9.2 REVISION The gerund after prepositions

Das Gerundium nach Präpositionen

Boots are made **for walking**. So let's go!
... zum Wandern ...
In future, don't use my mobile **without asking**.
... ohne zu fragen
You can save petrol **by driving** more slowly.
... indem man langsamer fährt

Nach einer Präposition *(by, for, of, without, ...)* muss ein Verb als Gerundium stehen.

Adjektiv/Nomen/Verb + Präposition + Gerundium:

My little brother is **afraid of sleeping** in the dark.
... hat Angst davor, im Dunkeln zu schlafen.
I'm very **keen on playing** rugby.
Ich spiele leidenschaftlich gern Rugby.

–	*(to) be*	***afraid of*** ***good/bad at*** ***interested in*** ***keen on*** ***sick/tired of***	***doing** sth.*	**Adjektiv + Präposition**

Is there any **hope of winning** the final match?
Besteht Hoffnung, das Endspiel zu gewinnen?
What are his **reasons for leaving** school?
Was sind die Gründe dafür, dass er die Schule verlässt?

–	*the*	***advantage of*** ***chance of*** ***hope of*** ***reason for***	***doing** sth.*	**Nomen + Präposition**

Sue **is talking about moving** to London.
Sue redet davon, nach London zu ziehen.
I don't **feel like going** out tonight. Do you?
Ich habe keine Lust, heute Abend auszugehen. Und du?

–	*(to)*	***dream of*** ***feel like*** ***talk about*** ***think of***	***doing** sth.*	**Verb + Präposition**

Additional information

9.3 The gerund with 'its own subject'

Das Gerundium mit „eigenem Subjekt"

1a Ella can't **imagine moving** to Africa.
Ella kann sich nicht vorstellen, nach Afrika zu ziehen.
1b Ella can't **imagine** **her family** **moving** to Africa.
Ella kann sich nicht vorstellen, dass ihre Familie nach Afrika zieht.

◄ In Satz **1b** hat das Gerundium ein „eigenes Subjekt": *moving* bezieht sich auf *her family* (und nicht auf *Ella*, das Subjekt des ganzen Satzes).

2a His parents talked **about** **him** **going** to Paris.
2b His parents talked **about** **his** **going** to Paris.
Seine Eltern redeten davon, dass er nach Paris fährt.

◄ Wenn wie in Satz **2a** das Subjekt des Gerundiums ein Personalpronomen ist, dann steht es in der Objektform: ***him*** (nicht: *he*). In sehr formellem Englisch wird wie in Satz **2b** oft ein Possessivpronomen bevorzugt: ***his** going ...*

In English: The gerund

1. A **gerund** is an *-ing* form used as a noun. It can be the subject or the object of a sentence. — ***Singing** is fun. I like **singing**.*
2. After some verbs *(enjoy, imagine, suggest, ...)* we use a gerund, not an infinitive. — *Lucy suggested **asking** the head teacher.*
3. Verbs which follow a preposition take the form of a gerund. — *Don't cross the road without **looking**.*
4. Gerunds can have their own subject. — *Is there any chance of Pete/him **winning**?*

GF 10 Participles Partizipien

10.1 REVISION Participle forms

Formen des Partizips

Present participle *(-ing)*:

work	→ **working**	try	→ **trying**
dance	→ **dancing**	plan	→ **planning**

◂ Das **Partizip Präsens** *(present participle)* bildet man durch Anhängen von ***-ing*** an den Infinitiv. Beachte die Besonderheiten bei der Schreibung.

Past participle, regular verbs *(-ed)*:

work	→ **worked**	try	→ **tried**
dance	→ **danced**	plan	→ **planned**

◂ Das **Partizip Perfekt** *(past participle)* eines regelmäßigen Verbs wird durch Anhängen von ***-ed*** an den Infinitiv gebildet. Beachte auch hier die Besonderheiten bei der Schreibung.

Past participle, irregular verbs:

build	→ **built**	grow	→ **grown**
make	→ **made**	see	→ **seen**
teach	→ **taught**	write	→ **written**

Unregelmäßige Verben haben eigene *past participle*-Formen, die man einzeln lernen muss.

▸ *Unregelmäßige Verben (pp. 256-257)*

10.2 REVISION Participle clauses instead of relative clauses

Partizipialsätze anstelle von Relativsätzen

Partizipialsätze können Relativsätze verkürzen und werden daher oft anstelle von Relativsätzen verwendet.

The girl talking **to Leo** is my sister.
(The girl who is talking to Leo ...)
The man driving **the red car** didn't stop.
(The man who was driving the red car ...)

◂ Das ***present participle*** entspricht einem Relativpronomen + Verb im **Aktiv**: *is talking; was driving.*

We often buy strawberries grown **in California**.
(... strawberries which were grown ...)
The girls chosen **for the team** were only 15.
(The girls who were chosen for the team ...)

◂ Das ***past participle*** entspricht einem Relativpronomen + Verb im **Passiv**: *were grown; were chosen.*

10.3 The present participle after certain verbs

Das Partizip Präsens nach bestimmten Verben

Verb of perception + object + present participle

	Verb	Object	Present participle	
1 I	heard	people	shouting.	
2 Rob	saw	two men	running	out of the bank.
3 Sue	noticed	some men	getting	into a blue car.
4 We	watched	the car	driving	down the street.

Mit einem **Verb der Wahrnehmung + Objekt + Partizip Präsens** sagt man, dass man etwas wahrnimmt, das gerade im Verlauf ist.

Verben der Wahrnehmung sind *feel, hear, listen to, notice, see, smell, watch.*

1. Ich hörte Leute schreien.
2. Rob sah zwei Männer aus der Bank laufen.
3. Sue bemerkte, wie/dass einige Männer in ein blaues Auto stiegen.
4. Wir beobachteten, wie das Auto die Straße hinunterfuhr.

Im Deutschen verwendet man einen Infinitiv (1, 2) oder einen Nebensatz mit „wie" oder „dass" (3, 4).

Additional information

1 Rob **watched the car** stop at the corner.
2 He **saw a man** get out.
3 Rob **heard him** shout something to the others.
4 Then he **watched the car** disappear round the corner.

1 Rob beobachtete, wie das Auto an der Ecke anhielt.
2 Er sah einen Mann aussteigen.
3 Rob hörte, wie er den anderen etwas zurief.
4 Dann beobachtete er, wie/dass das Auto um die Ecke verschwand.

Nach **Verben der Wahrnehmung + Objekt** kann auch ein **Infinitiv** stehen (ohne *to*). Damit drückt man aus, dass das Geschehen **vollständig – von Anfang bis Ende –** wahrgenommen wird. Oft handelt es sich um kurze Handlungen. Vergleiche:

– *I saw a man **cross** the street.*
(Er überquerte die Straße.)
– *I saw a man **crossing** the street when a car hit him.*
(Er war dabei, die Straße zu überqueren, wurde aber angefahren, bevor er die andere Straßenseite erreichte.)

Additional information

We **stood** watching the street artists.
Wir standen da und sahen den Straßenkünstlern zu.

We **sat** chatting in a café.
Wir saßen in einem Café und unterhielten uns.

The dog **came** running towards me.
Der Hund kam auf mich zugerannt.

Das Partizip Präsens kann nach **Verben der Ruhe** *(stand, sit, stay, lie)* und nach **Verben der Bewegung** *(come, go)* stehen.

10.4 Participle clauses instead of adverbial clauses

Partizipialsätze anstelle von adverbialen Nebensätzen

Time

Seeing **Ellis Island for the first time,** Ava was very excited.
(When Ava saw Ellis Island for the first time, ...)
Als Ava zum ersten Mal Ellis Island sah, ...

Arriving **at the station,** we went straight to the platform.
Als wir am Bahnhof ankamen, ...

Asked **to turn down his MP3 player,** the boy started to shout at the bus driver. (When he was asked to turn down ...)
Als er gebeten wurde, seinen MP3-Spieler leiser zu stellen, ...

Reason

Feeling **tired,** Emily took the bus home.
(Because/Since she felt tired, ...)
Weil/Da sie sich müde fühlte, ...

Being **a doctor,** Marie knew exactly what to do.
Weil/Da sie Ärztin ist, ...

Warned **by his wife,** the man was able to escape.
(Because he was warned by his wife, ...)
Von seiner Frau gewarnt, ... / Weil er ... gewarnt wurde, ...

Partizipialsätze können **Nebensätze der Zeit** oder **des Grundes** verkürzen.

Solche Partizipialsätze gehen oft dem Hauptsatz voran. Sie sind **typisch für das geschriebene Englisch**.

In gesprochenem Englisch werden meist adverbiale Nebensätze bevorzugt.

►►►

Having + past participle

1 Having passed **his exams,** Mike applied for a job.
(After he had passed his exams, ...)
Nachdem Mike seine Prüfungen bestanden hatte, ...

2 Having been **to Italy twice,** we decided to go to Spain.
(Because/Since we had been to Italy twice, ...)
Da wir schon zweimal in Italien gewesen waren, ...

Not having seen **the film,** I bought the DVD.
(Because/Since I hadn't seen the film, ...)
Da ich den Film nicht gesehen hatte, ...

Partizipialsätze mit ***having* + Partizip Perfekt** drücken immer **Vorzeitigkeit** aus.

Partizipialsätze mit ***having* + Partizip Perfekt** entsprechen

1 einem adverbialen Nebensatz der **Zeit**, meist mit *after* eingeleitet

2 einem adverbialen Nebensatz des **Grundes**.

Additional information

1a **Reading** a really boring book, I fell asleep.
Als/Weil ich ein wirklich langweiliges Buch las, ...

1b **When/While reading** a really boring book, I fell asleep. *or* I fell asleep **when/while reading** a really boring book.

◄ Nicht immer ist eindeutig zu erkennen, ob ein Partizipialsatz einem Nebensatz der Zeit oder einem Nebensatz des Grundes entspricht (Satz **1a**).

Durch Voranstellen der **Konjunktion *when*** oder ***while*** macht man deutlich, dass der Satz **zeitlich** zu verstehen ist (Satz **1b**).

2a I saw a huge black dog **when/while walking** down the street.
(= I was walking down the street)
Ich habe einen riesigen schwarzen Hund gesehen, als/während ich die Straße hinunterging.

2b I saw a huge black dog **walking** down the street.
(= the dog was walking down the street)
Ich habe gesehen, wie ein riesiger schwarzer Hund die Straße hinunterging.

◄ Wenn der Hauptsatz ein Objekt enthält (hier: *a huge black dog*), gibt es oft große Bedeutungsunterschiede, je nachdem, ob der Partizipialsatz mit Konjunktion (Satz **2a**) oder ohne Konjunktion (Satz **2b**) verwendet wird.

3 **Although asked** to stop by the police, the man drove on.
He will have to wait outside **until asked** to enter.
If posted before 12 o'clock, the letter should arrive tomorrow.

◄ Partizipialsätze können auch durch andere Konjunktionen eingeleitet werden, z.B. ***although, until, if, after, before*** (Sätze **3**).

10.5 Participle clauses giving additional information

'I'll be back at 6,' he shouted, banging **the door** behind him.
... rief er und knallte die Tür hinter sich zu.

Using **a knife,** he was able to open the door.
Indem er ein Messer benutzte, ...

Lynn ran down the stairs, losing **a shoe.**
..., wobei sie einen Schuh verlor.

Partizipialsätze zur Angabe von Zusatzinformationen

Partizipialsätze werden oft verwendet, um Zusatzinformationen zu geben oder die Begleitumstände einer Handlung zu beschreiben. (Meist handelt es sich um zeitgleich oder fast zeitgleich stattfindende Handlungen oder Vorgänge.)

Im Deutschen steht meist ein Hauptsatz mit „und" oder ein Nebensatz mit „indem" oder „wobei".

In English: Participles

Participle clauses can be used

– instead of relative clauses	*The girl **talking to Jack** … / Wine **produced in Australia** …*
– after verbs of perception + object (when the action is not yet completed)	*I can **see somebody running** down the street.*
– instead of adverbial clauses of time or reason	***Travelling** by train, you meet some interesting people.*
	***Not having** much money, we stayed at a small B&B.*
– to give additional information	*Maggie ran down the road, **singing** her favourite song.*

Grammatical terms (Grammatische Fachbegriffe)

active ['æktɪv]	Aktiv	*Beckham **scored** the final goal.*
activity verb [æk'tɪvəti vɜːb]	Tätigkeitsverb	*do, go, make, read, repair*
adjective ['ædʒɪktɪv]	Adjektiv	*good, red, new, boring*
adverb ['ædvɜːb]	Adverb	*always, badly, here, really, today*
adverb of frequency ['friːkwənsi]	Häufigkeitsadverb	*always, often, never*
adverb of indefinite time [ɪnˌdefɪnət 'taɪm]	Adverb der unbestimmten Zeit	*already, ever, just, never*
adverb of manner ['mænə]	Adverb der Art und Weise	*badly, happily, quietly, well*
adverbial clause [ædˌvɜːbiəl 'klɔːz]	adverbialer Nebensatz	*I went to bed **because I was tired**.*
article ['ɑːtɪkl]	Artikel	*the, a/an*
aspect ['æspekt]	Aspekt	
auxiliary [ɔːg'zɪliəri]	Hilfsverb	*be, have, do; will, can, must*
backshift of tenses ['bækʃɪft]	Verschiebung der Zeitformen *(bei der indirekten Rede)*	*'I'**m** sorry.' ► Sam said he **was** sorry.*
command [kə'mɑːnd]	Befehl, Aufforderungssatz	*Open your books. Don't talk.*
comparison [kəm'pærɪsn]	Steigerung	*old – older – oldest*
conditional sentence [kənˌdɪʃənl 'sentəns]	Bedingungssatz	*I'd call him if I knew his number.*
conjunction [kən'dʒʌŋkʃn]	Konjunktion	*and, or, but; because, before*
contact clause ['kɒntækt klɔːz]	Relativsatz ohne Relativpronomen	*She's the girl **I love**.*
countable noun ['kaʊntəbl]	zählbares Nomen	*girl – girls, pound – pounds*
defining relative clause [dɪ'faɪnɪŋ]	bestimmender Relativsatz	*There's the girl **who helped me**.*
definite article ['defɪnət]	bestimmter Artikel	*the*
direct speech [ˌdaɪrekt 'spiːtʃ]	direkte Rede, wörtliche Rede	***'I'm sorry**.'*
future perfect [ˌfjuːtʃə 'pɜːfɪkt]	vollendete Zukunft, Futur II	*On Friday we will have finished our exams.*
future progressive [ˌfjuːtʃə prə'gresɪv]	Verlaufsform des *will-future*	*A week today I will be lying on the beach.*
gerund ['dʒerənd]	Gerundium	*I like **dancing**. **Dancing** is fun.*
***going to*-future**	Futur mit *going to*	*I'**m going to watch** TV tonight.*
***if*-clause** ['ɪf klɔːz]	*if*-Satz, Nebensatz mit *if*	***If I see Jack**, I'll tell him.*
imperative [ɪm'perətɪv]	Imperativ (Befehlsform)	*Open your books. Don't talk.*
indirect speech [ˌɪndərekt 'spiːtʃ]	indirekte Rede	*Sam said **(that) he was sorry**.*
infinitive [ɪn'fɪnətɪv]	Infinitiv (Grundform des Verbs)	*(to) open, (to) see, (to) read*
irregular verb [ɪˌregjələ 'vɜːb]	unregelmäßiges Verb	*(to) go – went – gone*
main clause	Hauptsatz	***I like Scruffy** because I like dogs.*
modal, modal auxiliary [ˌməʊdl‿ɔːg'zɪliəri]	modales Hilfsverb, Modalverb	*can, could, may, must*
negative statement [ˌnegətɪv 'steɪtmənt]	verneinter Aussagesatz	*I don't like bananas.*
non-defining relative clause [dɪ'faɪnɪŋ]	nicht bestimmender Relativsatz	*Madison, **who lives in Atlanta,** goes to M. L. King High School.*
noun [naʊn]	Nomen, Substantiv	*Sophie, girl, brother, time*

object ['ɒbdʒɪkt]	Objekt	*My sister is writing **a letter**.*
object form ['ɒbdʒɪkt fɔːm]	Objektform (der Personalpronomen)	*me, you, him, her, it, us, them*
participle ['pɑːtɪsɪpl]	Partizip	*planning, taking; planned, taken*
participle clause [ˌpɑːtɪsɪpl 'klɔːz]	Partizipialsatz	*I saw a boy **playing in the street**.*
passive ['pæsɪv]	Passiv	*The goal **was scored** by Beckham.*
past participle [ˌpɑːst 'pɑːtɪsɪpl]	Partizip Perfekt	*cleaned, planned, gone, taken*
past perfect [ˌpɑːst 'pɜːfɪkt]	Plusquamperfekt, Vorvergangenheit	*He cried – he **had hurt** his knee.*
past perfect progressive [ˌpɑːst ˌpɜːfɪkt prə'gresɪv]	Verlaufsform des *past perfect*	*She **had been working** in the garden since 12 o'clock.*
past progressive [ˌpɑːst prə'gresɪv]	Verlaufsform der Vergangenheit	*At 7.30 I **was having** dinner.*
personal passive [ˌpɜːsənl 'pæsɪv]	persönliches Passiv	*I was offered a job.*
personal pronoun [ˌpɜːsənl 'prəʊnaʊn]	Personalpronomen (persönliches Fürwort)	*I, you, he, she, it, we, they; me, you, him, her, it, us, them*
plural ['plʊərəl]	Plural, Mehrzahl	
positive statement [ˌpɒzətɪv 'steɪtmənt]	bejahter Aussagesatz	*I like oranges.*
possessive determiner [pəˌzesɪv dɪ'tɜːmɪnə]	Possessivbegleiter (besitzanzeigender Begleiter)	*my, your, his, her, its, our, their*
possessive form [pəˌzesɪv fɔːm]	s-Genitiv	*Jo's brother; my sister's room*
possessive pronoun [pəˌzesɪv 'prəʊnaʊn]	Possessivpronomen	*mine, yours, his, hers, ours, theirs*
preposition [ˌprepə'zɪʃn]	Präposition	*after, at, in, next to, under*
present participle [ˌpreznt 'pɑːtɪsɪpl]	Partizip Präsens	*cleaning, planning, going, taking*
present perfect [ˌpreznt 'pɜːfɪkt]	*present perfect*	*We**'ve made** a cake for you.*
present perfect progressive [ˌpreznt ˌpɜːfɪkt prə'gresɪv]	Verlaufsform des *present perfect*	*We**'ve been waiting** for an hour.*
present progressive [ˌpreznt prə'gresɪv]	Verlaufsform der Gegenwart	*The Hansons **are having** lunch.*
pronoun ['prəʊnaʊn]	Pronomen, Fürwort	
quantifier ['kwɒntɪfaɪə]	Mengenangabe	*some, a lot of, many, much*
question tag ['kwestʃən tæg]	Frageanhängsel	*This place is great, **isn't it?***
question word ['kwestʃən wɜːd]	Fragewort	*what?, when?, where?, how?*
reflexive pronoun [rɪˌfleksɪv 'prəʊnaʊn]	Reflexivpronomen	*myself, yourself, themselves*
regular verb [ˌregjələ 'vɜːb]	regelmäßiges Verb	*(to) help – helped – helped*
relative clause [ˌrelətɪv 'klɔːz]	Relativsatz	*There's the girl **who helped me**.*
relative pronoun [ˌrelətɪv 'prəʊnaʊn]	Relativpronomen	*who, that, which, whose*
reported speech [rɪˌpɔːtɪd 'spiːtʃ]	indirekte Rede	*Sam said **(that) he was sorry**.*
request [rɪ'kwest]	Bitte	*Can you help me with this?*
short answer [ˌʃɔːt_'ɑːnsə]	Kurzantwort	*Yes, I am. / No, I don't.*
simple past [ˌsɪmpl 'pɑːst]	einfache Form der Vergangenheit	*Jo **wrote** two letters yesterday.*
simple present [ˌsɪmpl 'preznt]	einfache Form der Gegenwart	*I always **go** to school by bike.*
singular ['sɪŋgjələ]	Singular, Einzahl	
state verb ['steɪt vɜːb]	Zustandsverb	*be, know, like, own, sound, want*
statement ['steɪtmənt]	Aussagesatz	
subject ['sʌbdʒɪkt]	Subjekt	***My sister** is writing a letter.*
subject form ['sʌbdʒɪkt fɔːm]	Subjektform (der Personalpronomen)	*I, you, he, she, it, we, they*
subordinate clause [səˌbɔːdɪnət 'klɔːz]	Nebensatz	*I like Scruffy **because I like dogs**.*
substitute ['sʌbstɪtjuːt]	Ersatzverb (eines modalen Hilfverbs)	*be able to, be allowed to, have to*
tense [tens]	Zeitform	
uncountable noun [ʌn'kaʊntəbl]	nicht zählbares Nomen	*bread, milk, money, news, work*
verb [vɜːb]	Verb	*hear, open, help, go*
verb of perception [pə'sepʃn]	Verb der Wahrnehmung	*feel, hear, listen to, see, smell*
***will*-future**	Futur mit *will*	*I think it **will be** cold tonight.*
word order ['wɜːd_ˌɔːdə]	Wortstellung	
yes/no question	Entscheidungsfrage	*Are you 13? Do you like comics?*

Diese Wörterverzeichnisse findest du in deinem Englischbuch:

- Das **Vocabulary** (S. 181–210) enthält alle neuen Wörter und Wendungen aus Band 5, die du lernen musst. Sie stehen in der Reihenfolge, in der sie in den Units vorkommen.
- Das **Dictionary** (S. 211–252) enthält den Wortschatz der Bände 1 bis 5 in alphabetischer Reihenfolge. Dort kannst du nachschlagen, was ein Wort bedeutet, wie man es ausspricht oder wie es genau geschrieben wird.

So ist das Vocabulary aufgebaut:

- Hier siehst du, wo die Wörter vorkommen.
  p. 10 = Seite 10
  p. 11/P 3 = Seite 11, Übung 3
- Die Lautschrift zeigt dir, wie ein Wort ausgesprochen und betont wird.
- Eingerückte Wörter lernst du am besten zusammen mit dem vorausgehenden Wort, weil die beiden zusammengehören.
- Die blauen Kästen solltest du dir besonders gut ansehen.

Tipps zum Wörterlernen findest du im Skills File auf Seite 126.

p. 10 **useful** ['ju:sfl] — nützlich

p. 11/P 3 **rainfall** ['reɪnfɔ:l] — Niederschlag *(Regen)*; Regenfälle

honest ['ɒnɪst] — ehrlich — ! silent letter **h:** **honest** ['ɒn
Be ~. Say what you really
I **~ly** think ... = Ich glaube.
Ⓕ honnête Ⓛ honest

a **dirt bike**

dirt bike ['dɜ:t baɪk] — Geländemotorrad

dirt [dɜ:t] — Schmutz, Dreck

adjective: **dirty** – nou

Neither. ['naɪðə, 'ni:ðə] — Weder noch.

neither

Which of your two sisters can speak French? – **Neither.**	Welche deiner Schwes – Keine der beiden.
Neither of my two sisters can speak French.	Keine meiner zwei Sch
Neither Jane **nor** Sophie can speak French.	Weder Jane noch S
Jane can't speak French, and **neither** can Sophie.	... und Sophi
Jane can't speak French, and Sophie **can't either**	

Abkürzungen:

n	= *noun*	*v*	= *verb*
adj	= *adjective*	*adv*	= *adverb*
prep	= *preposition*	*conj*	= *conjunction*
pl	= *plural*	*no pl*	= *no plural*
p.	= page	pp.	= pages
sb.	= somebody	sth.	= something
jn.	= jemanden	jm.	= jemandem
AE	= *American English*	*infml*	= *informal*
BE	= *British English*	*fml*	= *formal*

Symbole:

! Hier stehen Hinweise auf Besonderheiten, bei denen man leicht Fehler machen kann.

◄► ist das „Gegenteil"-Zeichen: **alive** ◄► **dead** (**alive** ist das Gegenteil von **dead**)

~ Die **Tilde** in den Beispielsätzen steht für das neue Wort.

Ⓕ verwandtes Wort im Französischen
Ⓛ verwandtes Wort im Lateinischen

Unit 1 – Australia

p. 6 (to) **subscribe to** sth. [səb'skraɪb]	etwas abonnieren; etwas abonniert haben	We **~ to** the *Times*, but my dad sometimes buys another newspaper on the way to work.
complete [kəm'pli:t]	komplett, vollständig	My Beatles collection is **~**: I have all their CDs!
(to) **complete** [kəm'pli:t]	vervollständigen; abschließen, beenden	The gallery was started in 1999 and **~d** in 2003. I began my education in 1995 and **~d** it in 2015.
profile ['prəʊfaɪl]	Profil; Beschreibung, Porträt	! stress and pronunciation: **profile** ['prəʊfaɪl]

barbecue ['bɑːbɪkjuː]	Grillfest, Grillparty	
(to) **be catching** ['kætʃɪŋ]	ansteckend sein	Some diseases **are ~**: they are passed from one person to another.

... used to be/do ...

With **used to ...** you can talk about something that was the case in the past but is not the case today:

I **used to do** a lot of sport, but I haven't got the time now.	Ich habe früher (immer) viel Sport getrieben, ...
Dad **used to smoke**, but he gave up when I was born.	Dad hat (früher) geraucht, ...
We **used to live** in London, but now we live in Berlin.	Früher haben wir in London gewohnt, ...

! Pronunciation: I **used to** ... [juːst tə]
I **use** ... („ich benutze") [juːz]

! Questions and negative statements are formed with **did** and **didn't**:

Did you **use** [juːs] **to cry** a lot when you were little?	Hast du viel geweint, als du klein warst?
He **didn't use** [juːs] **to be** so rude. What happened?	Er war früher nicht so unhöflich ...

(to) **carry** ['kæri]	tragen	**!** • He's **carrying** a suitcase. (Er trägt einen Koffer.) • He's **wearing** jeans and a red shirt. (Er trägt Jeans und ein rotes Hemd.) 
instructor [ɪn'strʌktə]	Lehrer/in, Ausbilder/in	= a person whose job it is to teach sb. a skill or sport **driving ~**, **flying ~**, **skiing ~**, **swimming ~** (Fahr- Flug-, Ski-, Schwimmlehrer/in)
serious ['sɪəriəs]	ernst(haft)	She's very funny but always has a ~ face. John has had a ~ accident and is in hospital. (F) sérieux, se (L) serius
seriously ['sɪəriəsli]	ernsthaft; *(infml)* sehr	Stop laughing and work ~ now. I love Lucy's jokes: she's a ~ funny girl.
gorgeous ['gɔːdʒəs] *(infml)*	äußerst schön und attraktiv	Her whole face is pretty, and her eyes are ~.
the bush [bʊʃ]	der Busch *(unerschlossenes, „wildes" Land in Australien, Afrika)*	
bush [bʊʃ]	Busch, Strauch	
(to) **freak out** [ˌfriːk_'aʊt]	ausflippen	
magical ['mædʒɪkl]	zauberhaft, wundervoll	(F) magique (L) magicus
No worries! [ˌnəʊ 'wʌriːz] *(bes. australisches Englisch)*	Kein Problem!	Thanks very much for helping me. – **No worries!**

debate [dɪ'beɪt]	Debatte	After a long ~, parliament voted for the new law. (F) le débat
mate [meɪt] *(infml)*	Freund/in, Kumpel	= a good friend
forever [fər'evə] *(adv)*	endlos; ewig	That skyscraper is so tall! It seems to go up ~. Will you love me when I'm old? – I'll love you ~!
mainly ['meɪnli]	vorwiegend, hauptsächlich	The hotel was full of tourists, ~ from Germany.
dirt road ['dɜːt rəʊd]	unbefestigte Straße	
the outback ['aʊtbæk]	das Hinterland Australiens	
shock [ʃɒk]	Schock, Schreck	Germany got a ~ when England beat them 5–1.

PART A BACKGROUND FILE Australia

p. 8 **flag** [flæg]	Fahne, Flagge	The German ~ is black, red and gold.
(to) **create** [kri'eɪt]	(er)schaffen, kreieren	(F) créer (L) creare
shell [ʃel]	Muschel(schale)	 shells
goods *(pl)* [gʊdz]	Waren, Güter	
Aborigine [ˌæbə'rɪdʒəni]	*Ureinwohner/in Australiens*	noun: **Aborigine** – adjective: **Aboriginal** [ˌæbə'rɪdʒənl]
(to) **develop (from … into …)** [dɪ'veləp]	entwickeln; sich entwickeln (aus … zu …)	The company **~s** and sells software. The village **~ed into** a town in only ten years.
landscape ['lændskeɪp]	Landschaft	
figure ['fɪgə]	Zahl, Ziffer	The **~s** aren't 100 per cent correct. Please check them again. ! stress: **figure** ['--]
despite [dɪ'spaɪt]	trotz	~ the bad news = **although** the news was bad
convict ['kɒnvɪkt]	Sträfling, Strafgefangene(r)	= a prisoner *(nach dem Schuldspruch)*
former ['fɔːmə]	ehemalige(r, s), frühere(r, s)	Australia is a ~ British colony.
independent [ˌɪndɪ'pendənt]	unabhängig	Australia became ~ from Britain in 1901. (F) indépendant/e
either … or … ['aɪðə, 'iːðə]	entweder … oder …	
close [kləʊs]	eng	Australia kept its ~ links to Britain after 1901. We've been ~ friends since kindergarten.
(to) **do business (with)** ['bɪznəs]	Handel treiben (mit); Geschäfte machen (mit)	Germany **does** a lot of ~ **with** Russia and China. Does your company **do** much ~ **with** Britain?
business ['bɪznəs]	Geschäfte; Unternehmen	Mike started his own ~ when he was 17.
p. 9 **rate** [reɪt]	Rate	If a country's **death** ~ is higher than its **birth** ~, the population usually gets smaller.
cancer ['kænsə]	Krebs *(Krankheit)*	About 25 % of all Germans die from ~. (F) le cancer (L) cancer
origin ['ɒrɪdʒɪn]	Herkunft; Ursprung	44 million Americans are **of** German ~. The word 'kangaroo' is **of** Aboriginal ~. (F) l'origine *(f)* (L) origo *(gen.* originis*)*

fair [feə]	hell *(Haut; Haare)*	
dark [dɑːk]	dunkelhaarig	

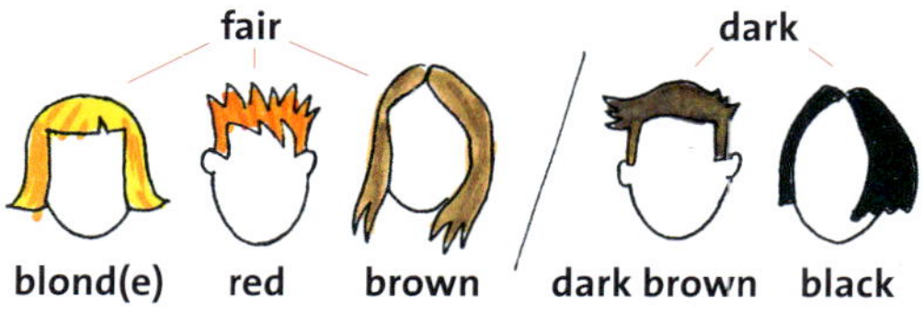

equator [ɪ'kweɪtə]	Äquator	
climate ['klaɪmət]	Klima	! pronunciation: **climate** ['--] Ⓕ le climat
suntan ['sʌntæn]	Sonnenbräune	Despite the dangers to the skin, most people still think they look good with a ~.
ozone hole ['əʊzəʊn həʊl]	Ozonloch	
ultraviolet rays *(pl)* [ˌʌltrəˌvaɪələt 'reɪz]	ultraviolette Strahlen	
earth [ɜːθ]	Erde	! on **earth** = auf der Erde Erde = **1.** *(Erdreich)* **soil**; **2.** *(Planet)* **earth**
atmosphere ['ætməsfɪə]	Atmosphäre; Stimmung	! stress: **atmosphere** ['---] The earth's ~ is 78.1 % N_2 and 20.1 % O_2. There was an unfriendly ~ in the room.
protective [prə'tektɪv]	Schutz-, schützend	This work is dangerous, so wear ~ gloves.
sunscreen ['sʌnskriːn]	Sonnenschutzmittel	Remember to put on ~ before you go out in the sun.
(to) **seek** [siːk], **sought, sought** [sɔːt] *(fml)*	suchen	Police are still **~ing** the convicts who escaped. = (to) **look for**
shade [ʃeɪd]	Schatten	

unique [ju'niːk]	einzigartig, einmalig	Everybody's eyes are ~: all eyes are different. James has a ~ collection of Frank Zappa CDs. Ⓕ unique Ⓛ unicus
emu ['iːmjuː]	Emu	an **emu**

reef [riːf]	Riff	= rocks or a sandbank under the water
naked ['neɪkɪd]	nackt	with the **naked** eye = mit dem bloßen Auge ! two syllables: **naked** ['--]
species ['spiːʃiːz], *pl* **species**	Art *(biologisch)*, Spezies	The grey wolf belongs to the ~ *Canis lupus*.
dolphin ['dɒlfɪn]	Delfin	
whale [weɪl]	Wal	

	sadly ['sædli]	leider; traurig	**Sadly**, my parents are getting divorced. He shook his head ~ and said no.
	by two degrees/ten per cent	um zwei Grad/zehn Prozent	My pocket money has gone up ~ £1 to £8.
p. 10	**statistics** *(pl)* [stə'tɪstɪks]	Statistik	Government ~ show that the UK's population will be bigger than Germany's by 2050.
	table ['teɪbl]	Tabelle	! **table** = **1.** Tisch; **2.** Tabelle
	detailed ['di:teɪld]	ausführlich, detailliert	He drew a very ~ map of the way to his house.
	bar chart ['bɑ: tʃɑ:t]	Balkendiagramm	
	pie chart ['paɪ tʃɑ:t]	Tortendiagramm	

a **bar chart** a **pie chart**

	(to) **make** sth. **up**	etwas bilden	Immigrants ~ **up** 2.8 % of Saxony's population. This book **is made up of** four units. (= besteht aus)
	percentage [pə'sentɪdʒ]	Prozentsatz, prozentualer Anteil	What ~ of your pocket money do you spend on sweets? (F) le pourcentage
	(to) **contrast** A **and/with** B [kən'trɑ:st]	A mit B kontrastieren *(= die Unterschiede aufzeigen)*	! stress: **contrast** *(verb)* [-'-] If you ~ the town **and/with** the country, you'll find lots of differences.
	contrast (to/with sth., **between** two things**)** ['kɒntrɑ:st]	Gegensatz (zu)	! stress: **contrast** *(noun)* ['--] **In** ~ **to** you, I'm not very clever.
	(to) **connect** A **with/to** B [kə'nekt]	A mit B verbinden	We've **~ed** our four computers in a network. = (to) link (L) connectere
	connection [kə'nekʃn]	Verbindung	Is there a direct ~ from Berlin to New York? = link (L) connexio
	useful ['ju:sfl]	nützlich	
	(to) **conclude** (sth. **from** sth.) [kən'klu:d]	(etwas aus etwas) schließen	The meeting **~d** with a speech by our boss. **From** his accent, she **~d** that he was German. **To** ~, ... = Zum Schluss ... (F) conclure (L) concludere
	conclusion [kən'klu:ʒn]	Schluss(folgerung)	We can **draw the** ~ that ... = Wir kommen zu dem Schluss, dass ... (F) le conclusion (L) conclusio
p. 11/P 3	**rainfall** ['reɪnfɔ:l]	Niederschlag *(Regen)*; Regenfälle	

PART B Two Australian teenagers

p. 12	**nowhere** ['nəʊweə]	nirgendwo(hin)	It's the only hotel. There's ~ else to stay. Jeannie lives miles away from the nearest town in **the middle of** ~. *(etwa: ...* am Ende der Welt*)*
	honest ['ɒnɪst]	ehrlich	! silent letter **h: honest** ['ɒnɪst] Be ~. Say what you really think. I **~ly** think ... = Ich glaube, ehrlich gesagt, dass ... (F) honnête (L) honestus

	racing ['reɪsɪŋ]	Rennsport	car/motor/Formula 1/boat/motorbike ~ ! *If the word stands alone, it means* **horse racing**.
	(to) **race** (sb./sth.) [reɪs]	(mit jm./etwas) um die Wette laufen/schwimmen/fahren/...	Let's ~ to that tree to see who's fastest.
	race [reɪs]	Rennen, (Wett-)Lauf	= a competition to see who is fastest
	dirt bike ['dɜːt baɪk]	Geländemotorrad	a **dirt bike** 
	dirt [dɜːt]	Schmutz, Dreck	adjective: **dirty** – noun: **dirt**
	(to) **attach (to)** [ə'tætʃ]	anhängen, anheften (an) *(an Brief, Mail)*	You can ~ the photos and mail them to me. I'm ~ing some photos of Ashley's party. Ⓕ attacher (à)
p.14/P 1	(to) **react (to/against sth.)** [ri'ækt]	reagieren (auf etwas)	noun: **reaction** – verb: (to) **react**
	(to) **be on** *(in the cinema, theatre, etc.)* [ɒn]	laufen *(im Kino, Theater usw.)*	What'**s** ~ at the cinema this week?
p.15/P 2	**wetsuit** ['wetsuːt]	Nassanzug *(Tauch- oder Surfanzug)*	
	private ['praɪvət]	privat	! stress and pronunciation: **private** ['praɪvət] **private** ◄► **public**
p.15/P 3	**tricky** ['trɪki]	verzwickt, heikel	a **tricky** situation/problem/question
p.15/P 4	**jealous (of)** ['dʒeləs]	neidisch (auf); eifersüchtig (auf)	You get so much pocket money! I'm really ~. Sarah is really ~ **of** her baby brother. She thinks her parents love him more. Ⓕ jaloux, se

PART C The Aboriginal people of Australia

p.16	(to) **exist** [ɪɡ'zɪst]	existieren	Some people believe that life ~**s** on Mars. Ⓕ exister
	lizard ['lɪzəd]	Eidechse	a **lizard** 
	track [træk]	Spur, Fährte; Pfad, Weg	The police followed the convict's ~ in the snow. I went along a ~ through the fields (= **path**).
	(to) **make love**	miteinander schlafen, sich lieben	(to) **make love** = (to) **have sex**
	(to) **sink** [sɪŋk], **sank** [sæŋk], **sunk** [sʌŋk]	sinken	The ship **is sinking**. 
	cave [keɪv]	Höhle	Ⓕ la caverne Ⓛ cavus
	culture ['kʌltʃə]	Kultur	
	(to) **respect** sb./sth. **(for sth.)** [rɪ'spekt]	jn./etwas (wegen einer Sache) achten, respektieren	You are always honest, and I ~ you **for** that. Ⓕ respecter
	respect (for) [rɪ'spekt]	Achtung, Respekt (vor)	**With** ~ *(= Bei allem Respekt)*, you're wrong.

p.17	**generation** [ˌdʒenəˈreɪʃn]	Generation	**!** stress: **generation** [ˌ--ˈ--] Ⓕ la génération
	racist [ˈreɪsɪst]	rassistisch; Rassist/in	Ⓕ raciste; le/la raciste
	race [reɪs]	Rasse	Ⓕ la race
	ideal [aɪˈdiːəl]	Ideal, Idealvorstellung	**!** stress and pronunciation: **ideal** [aɪˈdiːəl] Ⓕ l'idéal *(m)*
	orphan [ˈɔːfən]	Waise, Waisenkind	= a child without living parents Ⓕ l'orphelin,e Ⓛ orbus, orba
	(to) **run** sth. [rʌn], **ran** [ræn], **run**	etwas leiten *(Hotel, Firma usw.)*	My aunt **~s** an old people's home *(= Altenheim)*.
	nun [nʌn]	Nonne	
	monk [mʌŋk]	Mönch	
	(to) **trick** sb. **into** doing sth. [trɪk]	jn. mit einer List / einem Trick dazu bringen, etwas zu tun	The thief **~ed** the girl **into** opening the door.
	(to) **trick** sb.	jn. austricksen, reinlegen	I saw he had **~ed** me and I felt embarrassed.
	truck [trʌk]	Lastwagen, LKW	a **truck** 
	mattress [ˈmætrəs]	Matratze	**!** stress: **mattress** [ˈ--] 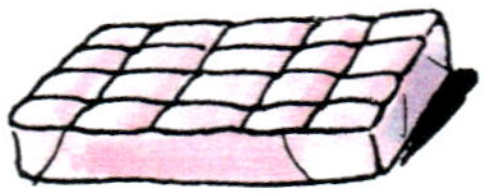
	blanket [ˈblæŋkɪt]	Decke *(zum Zudecken)*	
	(to) **apologize (to** sb. **for** sth.**)** [əˈpɒlədʒaɪz]	sich (bei jm. für etwas) entschuldigen	= (to) say sorry He **~d for** not writing sooner.
	rabbit-proof [ˈræbɪt pruːf]	kaninchen-sicher, kaninchen-fest	Words with **-proof**: a **weatherproof/windproof/rainproof** jacket; a **waterproof** watch; a **fireproof** door; a **childproof** bottle

PART D In the outback

p.20	**lonely** [ˈləʊnli]	einsam	
	heat [hiːt]	Hitze	adjective: **hot** – noun: **heat**
	(to) **break down** [ˌbreɪk ˈdaʊn]	eine Panne haben; zusammenbrechen	We were late because our car **broke ~**. When she saw the accident, she **broke ~** and cried.
	(to) **crash (into** sth.**)** [kræʃ]	gegen etwas fahren/laufen; abstürzen	The car **~ed into** a wall. The plane **~ed into** a hill and 50 people died. My computer **~ed** and I lost lots of work.
p.21	**fly** [flaɪ]	Fliege	a **fly** 

	(to) **fall asleep** [ə'sli:p]	einschlafen	The lesson was so boring that I almost **fell** ~.
	frightening ['fraɪtnɪŋ]	schrecklich, erschreckend	His face was so ~ that I went white with fear. The rate of skin cancer in Australia is ~.
	(to) **frighten** ['fraɪtn]	verängstigen, erschrecken	Don't look at me like that: it **~s** me. I was **~ed** by a noise in the middle of the night.
	tin [tɪn]	Dose	 You **eat** food that was in a **tin**: tuna, meat, vegetables, soup, beans, etc.
	can [kæn]	Dose	You **drink** drinks that were in a **can**. 
	(to) **kneel (down)** [ni:l], **knelt, knelt** [nelt]	sich hinknien	She went into the church, **knelt** ~ and prayed.
	beside [bɪ'saɪd]	neben	There's a shop ~ our house, on the right. = next to
			a **poisonous** snake 
p.22	**poison** ['pɔɪzn]	Gift	(F) le poison
	poisonous ['pɔɪzənəs]	giftig	Be careful! That snake could be ~. If you eat ~ plants, you might die.
	salt [sɔ:lt]	Salz	Too much ~ on your food is unhealthy. 
	pepper ['pepə]	Pfeffer	Not enough ~ on your food is boring.
p.23	**nearby** [ˌnɪə'baɪ]	*(adj)* nahegelegen; *(adv)* in der Nähe	If you visit Berlin, you should also go to the ~ city of Potsdam. Our house is in a good location: there are parks, a school and lots of shops ~. ! (*not:* ~~in the near~~)
	apart from [ə'pɑ:t]	außer	Everybody had finished ~ **from** me: I was last. = except
	strength [streŋθ]	Kraft, Stärke	adjective: **strong** – noun: **strength**
	conscious (of sth.**)** ['kɒnʃəs]	(sich einer Sache) bewusst; bei Bewusstsein	We are ~ **of** the problem and will solve it soon. Help, Jo's fallen from a tree. – Is he ~? ! **conscious** ◄► **unconscious** (= *bewusstlos*) (L) conscius
p.24	**literature** ['lɪtrətʃə]	Literatur	! stress: **literature** ['---]
	plot [plɒt]	Handlung	= the story in a play, book, film, etc.
	flashback ['flæʃbæk]	Rückblende	Many events in this film are not in order, but **~s**.
p.25	**setting** ['setɪŋ]	Schauplatz	The ~ of the play is 11th-century Scotland.
	(to) **be set in** [set]	spielen in	*Marienhof* **is ~ in** Cologne but filmed in Munich.

imagery ['ɪmɪdʒəri]	Metaphorik	= language that creates pictures in your head and helps you to imagine things
image ['ɪmɪdʒ]	Bild, Vorstellung	 Whenever I hear a bell, I have an ~ of food in my head. (F) l'image *(f)* (L) imago
simile ['sɪməli]	Vergleich	'Skin as white as snow' is a ~. (L) simile
metaphor ['metəfə, 'metəfɔ:]	Metapher	! stress: **me̲taphor** ['---]
author ['ɔ:θə]	Autor/in	The narrator of *A prayer for Blue Delaney* is called Colm, but the ~ is Kirsty Murray.
easy-going [ˌi:zi 'gəʊɪŋ]	gelassen, unbeschwert	She never gets angry but is always very ~-~.
stupid ['stju:pɪd]	blöd, dämlich	**stupid ◄► clever** (F) stupide (L) stupidus

Unit 2 – The road ahead

p.32 **ahead (of** sb./sth.**)** [ə'hed]	(jm./etwas) voraus	Darwin's ideas were ~ **of** his time.
the road ahead	die Straße vor uns	
A-level exams, A-levels *(pl)* ['eɪ ˌlevl]	*die höchsten Abschlussprüfungen des Schulsystems in England, Wales und Nordirland*	After he had passed his **A-levels** *(oder* **A-level exams***)*, he worked abroad for a year, then went to university. **A** = **advanced** [əd'vɑ:nst] (fortgeschritten)
level ['levl]	(Lern-)Stand, Niveau	What ~ is this course? – It's for beginners. The crime ~ in this city is very high.
exam [ɪg'zæm]	Prüfung	She got good results in her ~**s**.
qualification [ˌkwɒlɪfɪ'keɪʃn]	Abschluss, Qualifikation	! stress: **qualifica̲tion** [ˌ---'--] mostly plural: What ~**s** do you need for this job? (F) la qualification
university [ˌju:nɪ'vɜ:səti]	Universität, Hochschule	The oldest **universities** in the UK are Oxford (1167) and Cambridge (1209).
(to) **inherit** sth. **(from** sb.**)** [ɪn'herɪt]	etwas (von jm.) erben	When his grandmother died, Peter ~**ed** £2,000,000 and a large house **from** her.
fortune ['fɔ:tʃu:n]	Vermögen; Glück	He made his ~ in the cotton industry. The king sent the prince away to seek his ~.
(to) **pass** [pɑ:s]	bestehen *(Test, Prüfung usw.)*	Did you ~ the test? – Yes, I got a B.
scientist ['saɪəntɪst]	Naturwissenschaftler/in	= someone who studies or has studied science a **scientist**  (F) le/la scientifique (L) sciens

PART A Personality quiz: Where are you heading?

p.34	**personality** [ˌpɜːsəˈnæləti]	Persönlichkeit	(F) la personnalité
	(to) **head for/to/towards** sth. [ˈhed]	auf etwas zugehen, -fahren, -steuern	I was **~ing towards** the bus when I realized I had forgotten my homework. Be careful with that old car: you're **~ing for** an accident!
	stranger [ˈstreɪndʒə]	Unbekannte(r), Fremde(r)	Young children shouldn't speak to **~s**. (F) l'étranger, -ère
	strange [streɪndʒ]	fremd	It's easy to get lost in a ~ city. ! **strange** = **1.** seltsam; **2.** fremd
	Neither. [ˈnaɪðə, ˈniːðə]	Weder noch.	

neither – neither ... nor – not either

Which of your two sisters can speak French? – **Neither**.	Welche deiner Schwestern kann Französisch? – Keine der beiden.
Neither of my two sisters can speak French.	Keine meiner zwei Schwestern kann Französisch.
Neither Jane **nor** Sophie can speak French.	Weder Jane noch Sophie ...
Jane can't speak French, and **neither** can Sophie.	... und Sophie auch nicht.
Jane can't speak French, and Sophie **can't either**.	... und Sophie auch nicht.

	(to) **be in charge of** sth./sb. [tʃɑːdʒ]	für etwas/jn. verantwortlich sein; etwas leiten	When Mum's away, I'm **in ~ of** my little sisters. Who is **in ~ of** this project?
	Christmas [ˈkrɪsməs]	Weihnachten	We always stay at home **at ~**. = an/zu Weihnachten What presents did you get **for ~?** = zu Weihnachten  a **Christmas** tree
	(to) **get sidetracked** [ˈsaɪdtrækt]	abgelenkt werden	Our teacher stopped talking because he **got ~** for a moment by a bird at the window.
	landline [ˈlændlaɪn]	Festnetzleitung	**landline** phone ◄► **mobile** phone
	(to) **cancel** sth. *(BE:* **-ll-***)* [ˈkænsəl]	etwas absagen	The concert was **~led** because of the rain. ! jm. absagen = (to) tell sb. you can't come
	civilization [ˌsɪvəlaɪˈzeɪʃn]	Zivilisation	! stress: **civilization** [ˌ---ˈ--]
p.35	**confident** [ˈkɒnfɪdənt]	selbstbewusst, (selbst)sicher	I felt ~ before the test because I'd revised well. My dad isn't ~ when he drives in strange cities. (F) confident,e (L) confidens
	energetic [ˌenəˈdʒetɪk]	dynamisch, tatkräftig, energisch	He's an active and ~ person who loves sport. (F) énergique
	flexible [ˈfleksəbl]	flexibel, anpassungsfähig	I'll come whenever you want: I'm very ~.
	annoying [əˈnɔɪɪŋ]	ärgerlich, lästig	I find people who know everything very ~.
	(to) **annoy** [əˈnɔɪ]	ärgern, verärgern	It **~s** me when people don't say hello.
	(to) **be/get annoyed (with** sb., **about** sth.)	sich (über jn./etwas) ärgern	I **was ~ with** my friend because he was so late. My dad often **gets ~ about** the government.

at once [ət 'wʌns]	gleichzeitig, zugleich, auf einmal	Some women say men can't do two things **at ~**.
(to) **give** (sth.) **up** [ˌɡɪv‿'ʌp]	(etwas) aufgeben	Don't **~ up** yet, try again!
freedom ['friːdəm]	Freiheit	= liberty **!** *If we talk about a specific case, we usually use the word* **freedom** *and not* **liberty**: **freedom of speech, ~ of thought, ~ of expression, ~ of religion, ~ of information**.
calm [kɑːm]	ruhig, still	Don't panic in an emergency: just **keep ~**. (F) calme
anyone ['eniwʌn]	jede(r) (beliebige)	

any, anyone, etc.

The words **any**, **anyone**, etc. are

in questions:	Do you know **anybody** here? Would you like **anything** else to eat?	
in negative statements:	We're **not** going **anywhere** this summer: we're staying at home.	
They can also be used in positive statements:	You're wrong. **Anybody** can see that. I've finished my work. Now I can do **anything** I want. If I had enough money, I could go **anywhere**.	*Jeder Beliebige* *alles, egal was* *überall hin*
They are often used in *if*-clauses:	If I could choose **any** job, I'd be a fireman.	*irgendeinen*

(to) **be keen to do** sth., **on doing** sth. [kiːn]	wild darauf sein, etwas zu tun	I'm not very **~ on going / ~ to go** to the concert because there's a party on at the weekend.
punctual ['pʌŋktʃuəl]	pünktlich	You're late again. You must try to be more ~.
logical ['lɒdʒɪkl]	logisch	a ~ person *(ein logisch denkender Mensch)* (F) logique
technology [tek'nɒlədʒi]	Technologie	**!** stress: **technology** [-'---]
practical ['præktɪkl]	praktisch	
(to) **settle down** [ˌsetl 'daʊn]	zur Ruhe kommen, sesshaft werden	OK, everybody, be quiet now and **~ down**! After a wild youth, he is **settling ~** now.
particular [pə'tɪkjələ]	bestimmte(r, s), spezielle(r, s)	= specific Is there a ~ style of music you like? (F) particulier, -ière
(to) **mind** sth. [maɪnd]	etwas dagegen haben	

(to) mind

You **won't mind** if they disagree.	Es wird dir nichts ausmachen, ...
I **don't mind helping** in our shop, but I hate having to get up so early.	Es macht mir nichts aus, ...
I'd like to ask you a few questions, **if you don't mind**.	..., wenn Sie nichts dagegen haben.
Do you mind if I open the window?	Stört es dich, ...
Would you mind waiting outside, please?	Würden Sie bitte draußen warten?

HA für 23.11.

	necessary ['nesəsri]	notwendig, nötig	Water is ~ for life. You can phone me on my mobile if ~. (F) nécessaire (L) necessarius
	goal [gəʊl]	Ziel	= aim ! **goal** = **1.** Tor *(im Sport)*; **2.** Ziel
p. 37/P 3	(to) **confirm** [kən'fɜːm]	bestätigen	Please ~ that you have received this e-mail. (F) confirmer (L) confirmare
	impolite [ˌɪmpə'laɪt]	unhöflich	= rude (F) impoli,e

Negative prefixes

A negative prefix in front of an adjective or participle changes the meaning to 'not ~' or 'the opposite of ~'.
Most adjectives (mostly of German or French origin) use the prefix 'un-':

un- **unable, unafraid, unavailable, uncomfortable, unequal, unfair, unfriendly, unhappy, unimportant, unlucky, unpopular, unreal, unrealistic, unreliable, unsafe**
and adjectives formed from participles, e.g. **uninteresting** or **unanswered**.

Others (mostly of Latin origin) use 'in-': **inaccurate, incorrect, indirect, inexact, inexpensive**

! 'in-' changes to:

- il- in front of the letter **l**: **illegal**
- im- in front of the letter **p**: **impossible, imperfect, impersonal, impolite**
- ir- in front of the letter **r**: **irregular**

! The stress is never on the prefix but stays on the same syllable as in the original adjective:
safe, unsafe; able, unable; possible, impossible. This is different from German.

PART B A year abroad

p. 38	**CV** [ˌsiː 'viː] **(curriculum vitae** [kəˌrɪkjələm 'viːtaɪ]**)** *(BE)*	Lebenslauf	= the history of your life that you send when you apply for a job
	résumé ['rezəmeɪ] *(AE)*	Lebenslauf	
	application [ˌæplɪ'keɪʃn]	Bewerbung	**letter of ~** = Bewerbungsschreiben
	applicant ['æplɪkənt]	Bewerber/in	
	as [æz]	weil, da	= because
	valuable ['væljuəbl]	wertvoll; nützlich	This book only cost £1 but is far more ~ to me. Thank you, that was very ~ help.
	to date	bis heute	We need ten people to help with the party, but ~ ~ only six have volunteered.
	secondary school ['sekəndri]	weiterführende Schule	(F) l'école *(f)* secondaire
	primary school ['praɪməri] *(BE)*	Grundschule *in GB, von 4 oder 5 bis 11 Jahren*	= elementary school *(AE)* (F) l'école *(f)* primaire
	badge [bædʒ]	Abzeichen, Button	**badges**

a **button** (Knopf)

basic ['beɪsɪk]	Grund-, grundlegend; einfach, elementar	the **Basic Law** of Germany = das Grundgesetz Sorry, my French is very ~: what does *ami* mean?
written ['rɪtn]	schriftliche(r, s)	We're doing a three-hour ~ test in Maths tomorrow.
spoken ['spəʊkn]	mündliche(r, s)	**Spoken** language is often more informal than written language.
placement ['pleɪsmənt]	Praktikum	Students often do a ~ to get work experience.
reference ['refrəns]	Referenz, Empfehlung	! stress: **reference** ['--] I got a ~ when my placement finished.
request [rɪ'kwest]	Bitte, Wunsch	**on request** = auf Anfrage
p. 39 **candidate** ['kændɪdət]	Kandidat/in; Bewerber/in	! stress: **candidate** ['---] (F) le/la candidat,e (L) candidatus
effective [ɪ'fektɪv]	effektiv, wirksam, wirkungsvoll	! stress: **effective** [-'--] noun: **effect** – adjective: **effective**
employer [ɪm'plɔɪə]	Arbeitgeber/in	(F) l'employeur, -euse
employee [ɪm'plɔɪi:]	Arbeitnehmer/in	(F) l'employé,e
nationality [ˌnæʃə'nælətɪ]	Staatsangehörigkeit, Nationalität	! stress: **nationality** [ˌ--'---] My parents **are** different **nationalities**. Dad's French and Mum's Canadian.
suitable ['su:təbl]	geeignet, passend	Jeans aren't ~ clothes for a job interview. Dress **suitably** when you go for a job interview.
(to) **deserve** [dɪ'zɜ:v]	verdienen *(zu Recht bekommen)*	! pronunciation: (to) **deserve** [dɪ'zɜ:v]
successful [sək'sesfəl]	erfolgreich	
achievement [ə'tʃi:vmənt]	Leistung, Errungenschaft	verb: (to) **achieve** – noun: **achievement**
recent ['ri:snt]	jüngst, aktuell	Their most ~ CD was released last month. This news is very ~: the event happened a minute ago. (F) récent,e (L) recens
recently ['ri:sntli]	vor kurzem, kürzlich, neulich; in letzter Zeit	I met my old English teacher in London ~. I haven't done much sport ~. (F) récemment
certificate [sə'tɪfɪkət]	Urkunde, Zeugnis, Bescheinigung	Do you get a ~ at the end of the course?
award [ə'wɔ:d]	Auszeichnung, Preis	
brief [bri:f]	kurz (gefasst), knapp, von kurzer Dauer	Please be **brief**. = Fasse dich bitte kurz. He died after a ~ illness at the age of 23. (F) bref, brève (L) brevis
membership (of sth.) ['membəʃɪp]	Mitgliedschaft (in etwas)	What does ~ **of** the golf club cost?
responsibility (for) [rɪˌspɒnsə'bɪləti]	Verantwortung (für)	The car driver **took ~ for** the accident. *(übernahm die Verantwortung)* (F) la responsabilité
responsible (for) [rɪ'spɒnsəbl]	verantwortlich (für)	(F) responsable

HA für 11.12.

driving licence ['draɪvɪŋ ˌlaɪsəns]	Führerschein, Fahrerlaubnis	In the UK you can have a **driving ~** for a car at the age of 17.
foreign ['fɒrɪn]	ausländisch	a ~ language = eine Fremdsprache
foreigner ['fɒrɪnə]	Ausländer/in	
intermediate [ˌɪntə'miːdiət]	Mittel-, für fortgeschrittene Anfänger/innen	My mum did a Polish course for beginners last year, and this year she'll do the ~ course.
positive ['pɒzətɪv]	positiv	Jenny is always happy and has a very ~ attitude. ! stress: **positive** ['---]
negative ['negətɪv]	negativ	! stress: **negative** ['---] **negative** ◄► **positive**
(to) **avoid** [ə'vɔɪd]	vermeiden	This area is dangerous and should be **~ed**.
spelling ['spelɪŋ]	Rechtschreibung	Some peeple make lots of misstakes with there spelling.
format ['fɔːmæt]	Format	! stress: **format** ['--]
font [fɒnt]	Schrift(art)	Times, *Shelley Script* and **STENCIL** are all **~s**.
bold (type) [ˌbəʊld 'taɪp]	Fettdruck	To show a word is important, print it in ~.
p. 40 **formal** ['fɔːml]	formell, förmlich	! stress: **formal** ['--]
informal [ɪn'fɔːml]	informell; umgangssprachlich	**formal** ◄► **informal**
typical (of) ['tɪpɪkl]	typisch (für)	! That's **typical of** you = Das ist typisch für dich.
opportunity [ˌɒpə'tjuːnəti]	Gelegenheit, Chance, Möglichkeit	(F) l'opportunité *(f)* (L) opportunitas

German „Möglichkeit“

There are several ways to translate the word „Möglichkeit“.

The word **possibility** is used when „Möglichkeit“ means „nicht sicher, unwahrscheinlich“.

There is a	**possibility**	of snow in May, but it's very unlikely.
Is there a	**possibility**	of seeing the Queen when we go to London?
Have you thought about the	**possibility**	that I might be right?

German learners often use **possibility** too much. If „Möglichkeit“ means „Gelegenheit, Zeit“, we can use **chance** or **opportunity** (**opportunity** is a little more formal).

Did you find the	**chance/opportunity**	of finishing / to finish	your book?
My dad says he has a better	**chance/opportunity**	of getting / to get	a job if he moves abroad.
I have been given the	**chance/opportunity**	of going / to go	to Australia for a year.

If „Möglichkeit“ means „Art und Weise“, we can also use **way**.

There are several	**ways**	of translating / to translate	„Möglichkeit“.
There's no other	**way**	of solving / to solve	this problem.

electrical engineer [ɪˌlektrɪkəl‿ˌendʒɪ'nɪə]	Elektrotechniker/in	
(to) **remember doing** sth. ['rɪ'membə]	sich daran erinnern, etwas getan zu haben	

Same verb, different meaning

Some verbs can be used with the gerund *and* the infinitive, but the meaning is different:

Please **remember to buy** water tomorrow.	Denk daran, morgen Wasser zu kaufen.
I **remember buying** it, but I left it in the shop.	Ich erinnere mich daran, dass ich es gekauft habe, ...
Don't **forget to visit** John tomorrow.	Vergiss nicht, morgen John zu besuchen.
I'll never **forget visiting** John for the first time.	Ich werde nie vergessen, wie ich John zum ersten Mal besucht habe.
I think you should **stop buying** so many CDs.	Ich denke, du solltest aufhören, so viele CDs zu kaufen.
Look, a petrol station: let's **stop to buy** some drinks.	Guck, eine Tankstelle: halten wir an, um Getränke zu kaufen.
The phone rang but Pete **went on reading.**	Das Telefon klingelte aber Pete las weiter.
After finishing the *Harry Potter* series, Pete **went on to read** a book by Philip Pullman.	... las er dann (als Nächstes) ein Buch von Philip Pullman.
If you can't play an instrument, **try singing**.	..., probiere es mal mit Singen.
I **tried to sing** the song but had forgotten the words.	Ich versuchte, das Lied zu singen ...

	grateful ['greɪtfl]	dankbar	Thank you: I'm very ~ to you all for your help.
	interest ['ɪntrəst]	Interesse	verb: (to) **interest** – noun: **interest**
	community [kə'mju:nəti]	Gemeinde, Gemeinschaft	The Asian ~ makes up 4 % of the UK population. MySpace and Facebook are online **communities**. (F) la communauté (L) communitas
	by asking	indem du fragst	I got his number **by looking** on the internet. *(indem ich gesucht habe; durch Suchen)* **learning by doing** = Lernen durch Handeln/Tun
p. 41/P 1	**orchestra** ['ɔ:kɪstrə]	Orchester	! stress: **orchestra** ['---]

	advertisement [əd'vɜ:tɪsmənt, *AE:* ˌædvə'taɪzmənt] (*infml:* **ad** [æd], *BE auch:* **advert** ['ædvɜ:t])	Anzeige, Inserat; *(im Fernsehen)* Werbespot	You find job **~s** in newspapers or on the internet. Lots of people change channels during the **~s**.
	(to) **advertise** ['ædvətaɪz]	Werbung machen (für); inserieren	! English: (to) **advertise** clothes/cars/furniture German: **für** Kleidung/Autos/Möbel **werben**
	advertising ['ædvətaɪzɪŋ] *(no pl)*	Werbung	The company spends millions on ~ so that people will buy their products.
	advertiser ['ædvətaɪzə]	Inserent/in; Werbekunde/-kundin	
	(to) **enclose** [ɪn'kləʊz]	etwas *(einem Brief)* beilegen	I **enclose** my CV. *or* My CV **is enclosed**.
	interview ['ɪntəvju:]	Vorstellungsgespräch	! **interview** = **1.** Interview *(TV, Zeitung usw.)* **2.** Vorstellungsgespräch
p. 42/P 3	**mind** [maɪnd]	Verstand, Kopf	Grandpa is very old but his ~ is still very active.

p.42/P 5	**committee** [kəˈmɪti]	Ausschuss, Komitee	! spelling: **committee**

Collective nouns („Sammelnamen")

Collective nouns like *band, class* and *family* describe a *group of people.*

After a **collective noun** in the *singular*, the **verb** can be in the *singular* or the *plural* without much difference in meaning.

The orchestra **is** very good.
The orchestra **are** very good.

Examples:

band	My favourite band **is/are** Coldplay. *also:* Coldplay **is/are** my favourite band.	**family**	My family **doesn't/don't live** in London any more.
class	9 GE **is/are** probably the best class in the school.	**government**	The government **looks/look** after the population very well.
club	The drama club **is/are** looking for actors. *also*: Spurs **is/are** the best club in England.	**group**	A group of teenagers **was/were** standing in front of the building.
committee	What **has/have** the committee decided to do?	**staff**	The staff **doesn't/don't earn** much.
		team	The team **hopes/hope** to win.

We use a singular verb if we mean the group as a *whole group*:
The orchestra **has played** five times in four days and **is flying** home tomorrow.

We use a plural verb if we mean the *members of the group*:
The orchestra **have picked up** their instruments and **are leaving** the theatre.

p.43/P 6	**table of contents** [ˈkɒntents]	Inhaltsverzeichnis	The **table of** ~ is usually at the front of a book ...
	index [ˈɪndeks]	Index, Register	... and the ~ is usually at the back.

PART C The business: A reality TV show

p.44	(to) **impress** [ɪmˈpres]	beeindrucken	(F) impressionner (L) imprimere
	weakness [ˈwiːknəs]	Schwäche, Schwachpunkt	A typical interview question is 'What are your strengths and **~es**?'
	assessment [əˈsesmənt]	Einschätzung, Beurteilung	Here is my ~ of the situation: ...
	(to) **assess** [əˈses]	einschätzen, beurteilen	Interviewers try to ~ a candidate's qualities.
	sheet [ʃiːt]	Blatt, Bogen *(Papier)*	**sheets** of paper

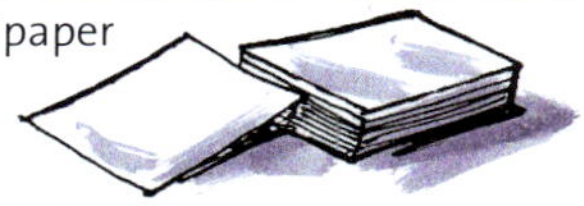

p.45/P 1	**visual aids** *(pl)* [ˌvɪʒuəl‿ˈeɪdz]	Anschauungsmaterialien	
	transparency [trænsˈpærənsi]	Folie	
	overhead projector, OHP [ˌəʊvəhed prəˈdʒektə, ˌəʊ‿eɪtʃ ˈpiː]	Tageslichtprojektor, Polylux	
	video projector [ˈvɪdiəʊ prəˌdʒektə]	Videoprojektor, Beamer	! 'beamer' does not exist in English
	slide [slaɪd]	Folie *(bei Präsentationsprogrammen)*	

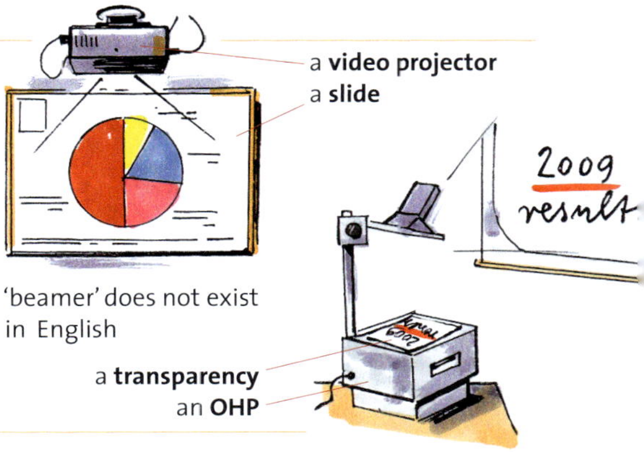

(to) **focus (on)** ['fəʊkəs]	sich konzentrieren (auf)	You're getting sidetracked again. Try to ~!
focus ['fəʊkəs]	Schwer-, Mittel-, Hauptpunkt	The ~ of tomorrow's lesson will be grammar.
audience ['ɔːdɪəns]	Zuschauer/innen, Zuhörer/innen, Publikum	At the end of the concert, the ~ stood up and clapped for five minutes. (F) l'audience *(f)* (L) audiens
one by one	eins nach dem anderen	I explained my reasons slowly and ~ by ~.

PART D How to be a teenage millionaire

p.46 (to) **earn (money)** [ɜːn]	(Geld) verdienen	! verdienen = **1.** (to) **deserve** *(what you should get)* **2.** (to) **earn** *(what you actually get)*
(to) **vote** [vəʊt]	zur Wahl gehen, wählen	Only 23 % of the population **~d** in the elections. ! (to) **vote for** sb. = für jn. stimmen (F) voter
design [dɪ'zaɪn]	Muster, Entwurf; Design, Gestaltung	This website has free **~s** for dresses and skirts. After school he wants to study ~ at art college.
(to) **set** sth. **up (-tt-), set, set** [set]	etwas gründen	The company was ~ **up** in 1906 by Henry Royce and Charles Rolls.
within [wɪ'ðɪn]	innerhalb (von)	We were asked to finish our project ~ four weeks, but I had already done it after one day.
p.47 (to) **trust** [trʌst]	trauen, vertrauen	He isn't honest, you know. You can't ~ him at all.
adviser [əd'vaɪzə]	Berater/in	The president has many **~s** to help him.
(to) **advise** sb. [əd'vaɪz]	jn. beraten	! (to) **advise** sb. **to do** sth. = jm. raten, etwas zu tun
advice *(no pl)* [əd'vaɪs]	Rat, Ratschlag, Ratschläge	Take my ~: go and see a doctor. (Hör auf meinen Rat: ...) ! She gave me **some** / **lots of** / **a piece of advice**. *Never:* She gave me ~~an advice~~ / lots of ~~advices~~.
(to) **get along (with** sb.**)**	gut (mit jm.) auskommen	We hated each other for a while, but now we **get ~ with** each other again.
set [set]	Reihe, Set, Satz	
minimum ['mɪnɪməm]	Minimum	Will says he needs **a ~ of** *(= at least)* £100 pocket money a month to survive.
maximum ['mæksɪməm]	Maximum	Will's parents say their ~ is £40.
ambition [æm'bɪʃn]	Ehrgeiz	My ~ is to be a famous author. (F) l'ambition *(f)* (L) ambitio
ambitious [æm'bɪʃəs]	ehrgeizig	Her dad is very ~ for her and helps her a lot. (F) ambitieux, -euse (L) ambitiosus
determination [dɪˌtɜːmɪ'neɪʃn]	Entschlossenheit	We admired his ~ to beat his illness. (F) la détermination
determined [dɪ'tɜːmɪnd]	(fest) entschlossen	Nothing will stop me: I am ~ to win.
faith (in sb./sth.**)** [feɪθ]	Vertrauen (in jn./etwas); Glaube	I have no ~ **in** you: I don't trust you at all. Do you have a ~? – Yes, I'm Jewish.
stressful ['stresfl]	anstrengend, stressig	Having a bath is nice at the end of a ~ day.
(to) **point** sth. **out (to** sb.**)** [ˌpɔɪnt‿'aʊt]	(jm.) etwas zeigen; (jn.) auf etwas hinweisen	He **~ed out** his brothers in the photo. May I ~ it **out** that this book was very expensive? Please be careful!

Phrasal verbs

Phrasal verbs are made up of a verb and an adverb: *write down, put on, give up, ...*

1 If the object of a phrasal verb is a **noun**, it can come before the adverb or after it. Compare:

Write your ideas **down**.	*or*	**Write down** your ideas.
She **put** a funny hat **on**.		She **put on** a funny hat.
Hans Richter **set** his business **up** in Bonn.		Hans Richter **set up** his business in Bonn.
Rick's never going to **give** his girlfriend **up**.		Rick's never going to **give up** his girlfriend.

2 But if the object is a **pronoun**, it has to come before the adverb:

Write them **down**.	! *not:*	~~**Write down** them.~~
She **put** it **on**.		~~She **put on** it.~~
Richter **set** it **up** in Bonn.		~~Richter **set up** it in Bonn.~~
Rick's never going to **give** her **up**.		~~Rick's never going to **give up** her.~~

	definite ['defɪnət]	fest, bestimmt; endgültig, eindeutig	Have you got any ~ plans for the future? I need a ~ answer by tomorrow (L) definitus
p.48	**formula** ['fɔːmjələ]	Formel	The ~ to work out the area of a circle is πr^2.
	role model ['rəʊl ˌmɒdl]	Vorbild	Doctors who smoke are bad ~ **models**.
p.49	**state** [steɪt]	Zustand	My brother's room is always in a terrible ~.
	in progress ['prəʊgres] *(fml)*	im Gange, im Verlauf	The meeting was already **in** ~ when I arrived.
	(to) **express** [ɪk'spres]	äußern, zum Ausdruck bringen, ausdrücken	John always **~es** his opinion in a very direct way. I **~ed** sadness at the news of his wife's death. He's not good at English so he can't ~ himself well. (F) exprimer (L) exprimere
	cashpoint ['kæʃpɔɪnt]	Geldautomat	Nowadays most people get money from a ~.

Unit 3 – Stand up for your rights

p.50	(to) **stand up for** sth./sb.	eintreten / sich einsetzen für etwas/jn.	If children don't learn to ~ **up for** themselves, they are sometimes bullied.
	(to) **pass** [pɑːs]	genehmigen, verabschieden *(Gesetz usw.)*	The law was **~ed** by the British parliament. (F) passer
	declaration [ˌdeklə'reɪʃn]	Erklärung	! Erklärung = **1. explanation** *(Erläuterung)* **2. declaration** *(Mitteilung)* (F) déclaration
	symbol (of sth.) ['sɪmbəl]	Symbol (für etwas)	Red roses are the ~ **of** love. ! stress: **symbol** ['--] (F) le symbole

Religions

Religion	Person	Adjective	Building
Buddhism ['bʊdɪzm]	**Buddhist** ['bʊdɪst]	**Buddhist**	**temple** ['templ]
Christianity [ˌkrɪsti'ænəti]	**Christian** ['krɪstʃən]	**Christian**	**church, chapel** ['tʃæpl]
Hinduism ['hɪnduːɪzm]	**Hindu** ['hɪnduː]	**Hindu**	**temple**
Islam ['ɪzlɑːm]	**Muslim** ['mʊzlɪm]	**Muslim**	**mosque**
Judaism ['dʒuːdeɪɪzm]	**Jew** [dʒuː]	**Jewish**	**synagogue**
atheism ['eɪθiɪzəm]	**atheist** ['eɪθiɪst]	**atheistic** [ˌeɪθi'ɪstɪk]	

PART A First Amendment

p. 52 **amendment (to** sth.**)** [ə'mendmənt]	(Ab-)Änderung (einer Sache); *(oft* **A~***)* Verfassungszusatz *(zur Verfassung der USA)*	If we make a small **~ to** this document, it will be perfect. The 18th **Amendment** made alcohol illegal.
(to) **explode** [ɪk'spləʊd]	explodieren, ausrasten	A bomb has **~d**, killing 33 people. When my mum saw my bedroom, she **~d**.
tax (on) [tæks]	Steuer (auf)	The **~ on** petrol is about 70 % of the price.
bubble ['bʌbl]	(Luft-)Blase	a **speech ~** a **thought ~** 
(to) **ignore** [ɪg'nɔː]	ignorieren, nicht beachten	(F) ignorer
(to) **complain (to** sb. **about** sth./sb.**)** [kəm'pleɪn]	sich (bei jm. über etwas/jn.) beklagen/beschweren	My mum had to **~ to** the waiter **about** the quality of the food.
awake [ə'weɪk]	wach	**awake ◄► asleep**
sympathetic [ˌsɪmpə'θetɪk]	mitfühlend, verständnisvoll, wohlwollend	**!** sympathisch ≠ **sympathetic** sympathisch = nice, friendly
(to) **concentrate (on** sth.**)** ['kɒnsəntreɪt]	sich (auf etwas) konzentrieren	Be quiet, I can't **~ on** my homework! (F) se concentrer
backwards ['bækwədz], **backward** ['bækwəd] *(bes. AE)*	rückwärts	My dream is to travel **~** through time and see my grandfather as a little boy.
forwards ['fɔːwədz], **forward** ['fɔːwəd] *(bes. AE)*	vorwärts	It's easier to count **forwards** from 1 to 100 than to count **backwards** from 100 to 1.
(to) **figure** sth. **out** ['fɪgə]	etwas ausrechnen; etwas herausfinden *(oft mit Zahlen)*	I can't **~ out** how this machine works.
district ['dɪstrɪkt]	Gegend, Bezirk	Sophie lives in the Cotham **~** of Bristol.
argument ['ɑːgjumənt]	Argument	He listed five **~s** against my idea. **!** stress: **argument** ['---] **argument** = **1.** Streit, Auseinandersetzung **2.** Argument
disagreement [ˌdɪsə'griːmənt]	Uneinigkeit, Streit	We all knew he was rich. But there was **~** about exactly how much money he had. My parents had a little **~** last Monday and haven't talked to each other since then.
agreement [ə'griːmənt]	Einigung	We **reached ~** after a long discussion. *(= Wir haben uns geeinigt.)*
(to) **challenge** sb. **(to** sth.**)** ['tʃælɪndʒ]	jn. (zu etwas) herausfordern; für jn. eine Herausforderung sein	He **~d** me **to** a fight in the park after school. Maths doesn't really **~** me at the moment.

lazy ['leɪzi]	faul	
no matter what ['mætə]	ganz gleich, was	I don't want to see him ... **no** ~ who he is, **no** ~ where he has come from, **no** ~ why he is here, and **no** ~ how often he says he loves me.
(to) **make** sb. **do** sth.	jn. zwingen, etwas zu tun; jn. dazu bringen, etwas zu tun	I didn't want to go to Grandma's party, but my dad **made** me **go**.
p. 53 **pressure** ['preʃə]	Druck, Belastung	We're always under a lot of ~ just before a test. (L) pressus
(to) **debate (sth.)** [dɪ'beɪt]	(über etwas) debattieren; hin und her überlegen	We **~d** the topic of bringing mobiles to school. Our visitors **~d** whether to go or stay.
constitution [ˌkɒnstɪ'tju:ʃn]	Verfassung	(F) la constitution (L) constitutio
citizenship ['sɪtɪzənʃɪp]	Staatsangehörigkeit	My uncle immigrated to the UK 20 years ago and has now applied for British ~.
citizen ['sɪtɪzən]	(Staats-)Bürger/in	If they say yes, my uncle will become a British ~.
xenophobic [ˌzenə'fəʊbɪk]	fremdenfeindlich, xenophob	(F) xénophobe
(to) **turn** sb./sth. **into** sth.	jn./etwas in etwas verwandeln	He **~ed** the rabbit **into** a bird. It was magic!
(to) **stare (at** sb./sth.**)** [steə]	(jn./etwas an)starren	You mustn't ~ **at** people. It's rude.
silence ['saɪləns]	Stille, Schweigen	The orchestra finished playing, there was ~ for five seconds, then everybody cheered. (F) le silence (L) silentium
power ['paʊə]	Macht; Stärke	A new government came to ~ after the election. Electric cars don't have the ~ to drive very fast.
on the one hand ... on the other (hand) ...	auf der einen Seite ... auf der anderen Seite ...	**On the one ~**, I'd like a city holiday. **On the ~**, I love the mountains. What shall I do?
Congress ['kɒŋgres]	Kongress *(das Parlament der USA)*	What's on in Washington next week? – Well, there is an important debate in **Congress**. ! stress: **Congress** ['--]
democracy [dɪ'mɒkrəsi]	Demokratie	! stress: **democracy** [-'---] (F) la démocratie
democrat ['deməkræt]	Demokrat/in	! stress: **democrat** ['---] (F) un démocrat
democratic [ˌdemə'krætɪk]	demokratisch	(F) démocratique

Different forms of government

Name:	The power is with:
absolute monarchy ['mɒnəki]	a **monarch** ['mɒnək], who has absolute power
anarchy ['ænəki]	no one
constitutional monarchy [ˌkɒnstɪ'tju:ʃənl]	a monarch (but with little power)
democracy	the citizens ►►►

Different forms of government

Name:	The power is with:
dictatorship [ˌdɪk'teɪtəʃɪp]	a single person, a **dictator** [dɪk'teɪtə]
junta ['dʒʌntə, 'hʊntə]	the army
oligarchy ['ɒlɪgɑːki]	a small number of people
plutocracy [pluː'tɒkrəsi]	the rich people
theocracy [θi'ɒkrəsi]	religious leaders

	(to) **influence** ['ɪnfluəns]	beeinflussen	
	(to) **guarantee** [ˌgærən'tiː]	garantieren	The Constitution **~s** these rights. ! My watch is **~d** for three years. *(= hat drei Jahre Garantie)* (F) garantir
	the press [pres]	die Presse, Zeitungen	His death was a big story on TV and in **the ~**.
	assembly [ə'sembli]	Versammlung	Has Obama made his speech to the UN General **Assembly**? (F) l'assemblée *(f)*
p. 54	**review** [rɪ'vjuː]	(Buch-, Film-)Besprechung, Rezension	I always like to read a ~ of a film before I see it in the cinema.
	(to) **break** sth. **up** [ˌbreɪk‿'ʌp], **broke, broken**	etwas auflösen	The fight was **broken ~** by a teacher.
	(to) **refuse to do** sth. [rɪ'fjuːz]	sich weigern, etwas zu tun	It was very cold but he still **~d** to wear a hat.
	(to) **encourage** [ɪn'kʌrɪdʒ]	*(jn.)* ermutigen, ermuntern; *(etwas)* fördern	My parents **~d** me to apply for the job. We'd like to ~ interest in local history.
	heart-warming ['hɑːtwɔːmɪŋ]	herzerwärmend	
p. 56/P 3	(to) **defend** sb./sth. **(against** sb./sth.**)** [dɪ'fend]	jn./etwas (gegen jn./etwas) verteidigen	He was able to ~ himself **against** his attacker. (F) défendre (L) defendere
	(to) **arrest** sb. **(for** sth.**)** [ə'rest]	jn. (wegen einer Sache) verhaften/festnehmen	The man was **~ed for** the murder of three tourists. (F) arrêter.
p. 56/P 4	**police officer** [pə'liːs‿ɒfɪsə]	Polizist/in	
p. 57/P 6	**screenplay** ['skriːnpleɪ]	Drehbuch	The plot of the ~ is different from the novel.
p. 58/P 7	**dialogue** ['daɪəlɒg]	Dialog	! stress: **di̲alogue** ['---] (F) le dialogue
p. 59/P 10	**stripe** [straɪp]	Streifen	A zebra has black and white **~s**.
	(to) **fly** [flaɪ], **flew** [fluː], **flown** [fləʊn]	*(Fahne)* wehen; wehen lassen	 When the Queen is at home, her flag **flies** over Buckingham Palace. (L) flare
	loyal (to sb./sth.**)** ['lɔɪəl]	(jm./etwas) treu; (jm./etwas gegenüber) loyal	My grandpa has been a ~ Schalke fan for 50 years. (F) loyal,e
	(to) **represent** sth. [ˌreprɪ'zent]	*(stellvertretend)* für etwas stehen, etwas repräsentieren	In this Vocabulary, the symbol ◄► **~s** 'opposite'. (F) représenter

(to) **increase** [ɪn'kri:s]	wachsen, zunehmen, steigen		The number of kids in my class has **~d** to 30. Ⓛ increscere
increase (in sth.**)** ['ɪŋkri:s]	Zunahme, Steigerung, Erhöhung	!	There has been a 30 % **increase** in crime. stress: **increase** *(noun)* ['--] **increase** *(verb)* [-'-]

PART B Running for office

p.60	(to) **run (for** sth.**) (-nn-)** *(bes. AE)*, (to) **stand (for** sth.**)** *(bes. BE)*	(als/für etwas) kandidieren	She first **ran ~** Congress in 2008. He's **standing ~** parliament in London.

(to) run

He can **run** a mile in under five minutes.	laufen, rennen
She **ran away** from home when she was 14.	weglaufen, davonlaufen
My aunt **runs** a home for old people.	leiten
Abraham Lincoln **ran for** president in 1860.	kandidieren als
The border **runs** from west to east through this wood.	verlaufen
The River Thames **runs** through Oxford.	fließen
Your nose is **running**. Would you like a handkerchief?	laufen
How is your car **running** these days?	fahren
I **ran across** an old friend from kindergarten yesterday.	zufällig treffen
That car just **ran** a dog **over** and the driver didn't even stop.	überfahren

office ['ɒfɪs]	Amt; Büro	!	He died in **office**. = Er starb im Amt. He died in the **office**. = Er starb im Büro. Ⓛ officium
official [ə'fɪʃl]	Amts-, amtliche(r, s); offiziell	!	Canada's ~ languages are English and French. stress: **official** [-'--] Ⓕ officiel, le Ⓛ officialis
of his own [əʊn]	eine eigene / seine eigene	!	My older sister would like a flat **of her own**. *As you know, you can't say* ~~an own flat~~. *If you want to express „eine eigene", use* **of ... own**.
(city) council ['kaʊnsəl]	(Stadt-)Rat		He's **on** the **city council** (**im** Stadtrat). Ⓛ consilium
(to) **take** sth. **up**	etwas in Anspruch nehmen *(Zeit, Platz)*		This discussion is **taking ~** too much time.
economic [ˌi:kə'nɒmɪk]	wirtschaftliche(r, s); Wirtschafts-		Can the government solve our ~ problems? Ⓕ économique
development [dɪ'veləpmənt]	Entwicklung		Ⓕ le développement
agenda [ə'dʒendə]	Tagesordnung		We have a very long ~ at tonight's meeting.
item ['aɪtəm]	Punkt *(auf einer Liste)*; Gegenstand	!	There were only three **~s** on my shopping list. *You can use* **items** *with nouns that don't have a plural:* **items** of clothing, furniture, news, *etc.*
budget ['bʌdʒɪt]	Etat, Budget		Our ~ just isn't big enough for a holiday this year. Ⓕ le budget
proposal [prə'pəʊzl]	(offizieller) Vorschlag		The government's ~ will not be popular with lots of people. Ⓛ propositum

	income ['ɪnkʌm]	Einkommen	= all the money sb. receives from their job and other sources
	annual ['ænjuəl]	jährlich	My mum's company has an ~ summer party. (F) annuel,le (L) annuus
	term (of office) [tɜːm]	Amtsperiode	The president is allowed only two **~s of office**. Each lasts four years.
	messy ['mesi]	schmutzig, unordentlich	
p. 61	(to) **summarize** ['sʌməraɪz]	zusammenfassen	Can you ~ the main points of the book?
	(to) **mention** sth. **(to** sb.**)** ['menʃn]	etwas (jm. gegenüber) erwähnen	Uncle John **~ed** that he had a new job, but didn't give us any details. (F) mentionner
	order ['ɔːdə]	Reihenfolge	Put these numbers into the right ~: 5 3 6 2 4. (F) l'ordre *(m)* (L) ordo
p. 62/P 1	**political** [pə'lɪtɪkl]	politisch	(F) politique
p. 62/P 2	**policy (on** sth.**)** ['pɒləsi]	Politik *(in Bezug auf etwas)*	! Politik = **1. politics** *(no pl) (politisches Leben / Geschehen)*: I'm not very interested in **politics**. **2. policy,** *pl* **policies** *(politische Maßnahmen, Linie)*: economic **policies**, **policy on** education.
	party ['pɑːti]	Partei	! **party** = **1.** Party; **2.** Partei
p. 63/P 3	(to) **possess** [pə'zes] *(fml)*	besitzen, haben	Everything they **~ed** was destroyed in the fire. (F) posséder (L) possidere
	alcoholic [ˌælkə'hɒlɪk]	alkoholisch	**Alcoholic** drinks can make you drunk. (F) alcoolique
	(to) **oppose** sb./sth. [ə'pəʊz]	sich jm./etwas widersetzen; jn./etwas ablehnen	Our group **~s** the building of the new airport. (F) s'opposer à qn./qc. (L) opponere
	(to) **depend on** sth. [dɪ'pend]	von etwas abhängen	Are you coming to the cinema with us? – It **~s on** the film. (F) dépendre (L) dependere
	individual [ˌɪndɪ'vɪdʒuəl]	einzeln	13 ~ states formed the USA. (F) individuel,le
	(to) **ban (-nn-)** [bæn]	verbieten; sperren; ein (Aufenthalts-)Verbot erteilen	The British parliament **~ned** slavery in 1807. He was **~ned** from racing as he had taken drugs. The song has been **~ned** because of its lyrics.
	medical ['medɪkl]	medizinisch	If a person's heart stops, they need ~ help immediately.
p. 64/P 4	**judge** [dʒʌdʒ]	Richter/in	a **judge**  (F) le/la juge (L) iudex
	balcony ['bælkəni]	Balkon	(F) le balcon

	(to) **demonstrate** ['demənstreɪt]	demonstrieren	In London yesterday, 20,000 people **~d** against the war.
p.64/P 5	(to) **march** [mɑːtʃ]	marschieren; demonstrieren	(F) marcher
	(to) **injure** ['ɪndʒə]	verletzen	**!** verletzen = **1.** (to) **hurt** *(cause pain)* **2.** (to) **injure** *(break, cut, etc. a part of the body)*
	peaceful ['piːsfl]	friedlich	(L) pacificus
	(to) **limit** sth. **(to** sth.**)** ['lɪmɪt]	etwas einschränken; etwas (auf etwas) beschränken/begrenzen	This new law **~s** our human rights. The audience was **~ed to** 500 people. (L) limiter
p.65/P 6	**oral** ['ɔːrəl]	mündlich	an ~ exam, an ~ summary, ~ history (F) oral, e
	(to) **persuade** [pə'sweɪd]	überreden	I tried very hard but couldn't ~ Jo to go to the musical with me. (F) persuader (L) persuadere
	(to) **register** ['redʒɪstə]	sich anmelden; sich eintragen *(z.B. in die Wahlliste)*	If a person moves to Germany, they have to ~ at the *Einwohnermeldeamt*. They **~ed** at the hotel as Mr and Mrs Smith.
	(to) **get** sth. **across (to** sb.**)** [ə'krɒs]	(jm.) etwas klarmachen, rüberbringen	I tried hard to **get** it **~ to** her that she was wrong, but she refused to understand.
	tone of voice [təʊn]	Ton(fall)	He said 'OK', but from his **~ of ~** he meant 'No'.
	(to) **stress** [stres]	betonen	**!** noun: **stress** – verb: (to) **stress**
	clip [klɪp]	(Film-)Ausschnitt	We watched a ~ that we found on the internet.

PART C Free and equal

p.66	(to) **remove** [rɪ'muːv]	entfernen, wegnehmen; herausnehmen	Boil the potatoes for 10 minutes, then ~ them from the water. (L) removere
	approximate [ə'prɒksɪmət]	ungefähre(r, s)	The ~ height of the building is 120 metres. **approximately** *(adv)* = about
	(to) **combine** [kəm'baɪn]	vermischen; verbinden	**Combine** the apples, oranges and bananas with a little lemon juice and some sugar. We **~d** the visit to Granny with an afternoon out in London. (F) combiner (L) combinare
	fresh [freʃ]	frisch	Is ~ food healthier than food in tins?
	melting pot ['meltɪŋ pɒt]	Schmelztiegel	The USA has been called a **~ pot** of nationalities.
	ingredient [ɪn'griːdiənt]	Zutat	For this dish you will need the following **~s**: ... (F) l'ingrédient *(m)*
	unity ['juːnəti]	Einheit	Will there ever be real ~ among European countries? (F) l'unité *(f)* (L) unitas
	understanding [ˌʌndə'stændɪŋ]	Verständnis, Verständigung	My teacher was full of ~ for my problem. The Olympics lead to greater ~ among nations.
	justice ['dʒʌstɪs]	Gerechtigkeit	The marchers were demonstrating for ~ for political prisoners. (F) la justice (L) iustitia
	(to) **treat** [triːt]	behandeln	Minority cultures should be **~ed** with respect. (F) traiter (L) tractare
	bitter ['bɪtə]	bitter	We know four tastes: sweet, sour, **salty** *(= salzig)* and ~.

(to) **damage** ['dæmɪdʒ]	beschädigen, schaden	My dad crashed into a tree, injuring himself and **damaging** the car.

Verbs and nouns with the same form

(to) **ban** **ban**	verbieten Verbot	(to) **increase** [-'-] **increase** ['--]	wachsen, zunehmen, steigen Zunahme, Steigerung, Erhöhung
(to) **challenge** **challenge**	herausfordern Herausforderung	(to) **interest** **interest**	interessieren Interesse
(to) **damage** **damage**	beschädigen, schaden Schaden, Beschädigung	(to) **judge** **judge**	(be)urteilen Richter/in
(to) **design** **design**	entwerfen, entwickeln Design, Gestaltung	(to) **limit** **limit**	ein-/beschränken, begrenzen Begrenzung, Beschränkung
(to) **figure out** **figure**	ausrechnen Zahl, Ziffer, Betrag	(to) **order** **order**	bestellen; ordnen Bestellung; Reihenfolge
(to) **focus (on)** **focus**	sich konzentrieren (auf) Schwer-, Mittel-, Hauptpunkt	(to) **tax** **tax**	besteuern Steuer
(to) **guarantee** **guarantee**	garantieren Garantie	(to) **trust** **trust (in)**	trauen, vertrauen Vertrauen (zu)

	equality [i'kwɒləti]	Gleichheit, Gleichberechtigung	adjective: **equal** – adjective: **equality** (F) l'égalité *(f)* (L) aequalitas
p.69/P 2	(to) **read** sth. **aloud** [ə'laʊd]	etwas vorlesen	I get nervous when I have to **read** anything ~ to the whole class.
	knowledge *(no pl)* ['nɒlɪdʒ]	Wissen, Kenntnisse	
	wisdom *(no pl)* ['wɪzdəm]	Weisheit, Klugheit	

Sir Francis Bacon (1561–1626)

Jimi Hendrix (1942–1970)

Unit 4 – Teen world

PART A Mobile life and love

p.80	**behaviour** [bɪ'heɪvjə]	Verhalten, Benehmen	He used to make trouble in class but his ~ is improving now.
	(to) **behave** [bɪ'heɪv]	sich verhalten, sich benehmen	He **~d** as if he hadn't seen me. **Behave** yourself, or you can go to your room.
	questionnaire (on sth.**)** [ˌkwestʃə'neə]	Fragebogen (zu etwas)	Our teacher asked us to complete a **~ on** fashion. (F) le questionnaire
	secretly ['siːkrətli]	heimlich, insgeheim	*(adv)* She **secretly** put some poison into his tea. *(adj)* We had a **secret** meeting. *(geheim)* *(n)* I can't tell you. It's a **secret**. *(Geheimnis)* (F) en secret

	(to) **ask** sb. **out (on a date)**	sich mit jm. verabreden; jn. einladen, mit ihr/ihm auszugehen	If you really like him, why don't you ~ him **out**?
	date [deɪt]	Verabredung, Date	(to) **go on a ~** with sb. *(mit jm. ausgehen)*
	(to) **end** sth. [end]	etwas beenden	! (to) **end** = **1.** zu Ende gehen; **2.** beenden
	relationship [rɪ'leɪʃnʃɪp]	Verhältnis, Beziehung	to **end a ~** *(= Schluss machen)*
	unwanted [ˌʌn'wɒntɪd]	unerwünscht, ungewollt	If you don't ask him to join you, he'll feel ~. an **unwanted** baby *(ein ungewolltes Baby)*
	(to) **go by**	vergehen, vorübergehen *(Zeit)*	She said she'd be back in a minute, but a whole hour **went ~** before she came.
	out of order	außer Betrieb; *(infml)* nicht in Ordnung	The lift was **~ of ~** so we had to take the stairs. He's so rude: his behaviour is completely **~ of ~**.
	(to) **chuck** *(infml, bes. BE)* [tʃʌk]	werfen, schmeißen	= (to) throw
	(to) **chuck** sb. *(infml, bes. BE)*	mit jm. Schluss machen	Jack and Olivia aren't together any more. – Who **~ed** who?
	(to) **ruin** ['ruːɪn]	verderben; ruinieren	Too much rain can ~ camping trips. He was **~ed** in the economic crisis. (F) ruiner
	(to) **cheat** sb. [tʃiːt]	jn. betrügen	A thief **~ed** me and stole all my money.
	(to) **cheat on** sb. *(infml)*	jn. betrügen, jm. untreu sein	He **~ed on** his wife twice before she left him.
p. 82/P 1	**argumentative writing** *(no pl)* [ˌɑːgju'mentətɪv]	Erörterung	
	opposite ['ɒpəzɪt]	entgegengesetzt; gegenüberliegende(r, s)	You're going the wrong way. You have to go in the ~ direction. She lives on the ~ side of the street.
	(to) **sum** sth. **up (-mm-)** [ˌsʌm_'ʌp]	(etwas) zusammenfassen	**To sum up**, this is what we have learned: ... *(Ich fasse zusammen:)*
	(to) **rate** [reɪt]	bewerten, einschätzen	How do you ~ your spoken English?
p. 83/P 2	(to) **stop** sb./sth. **doing** sth. **(-pp-)** [stɒp]	jn./etwas daran hindern etwas zu tun	I wanted to visit the Queen but a guard **~ped** me **getting** into the palace.
p. 83/P 3	**handsome** ['hænsəm]	attraktiv, gut aussehend	

German „schön“ etc.

attractive [ə'træktɪv]	used to describe a place or a person (the way they look *and* their personality)
beautiful	used to describe a place, a woman or a girl (but not usually a man)
good-looking	used to describe a person (the way they look but *not* their personality)
gorgeous	used informally to describe a very attractive person
handsome	usually only used to describe a man
lovely	used to describe a place, situation or a person. If you are describing a person, it often shows you like or love them.
pretty	used to describe a place and a baby or a girl – or a woman who looks like a girl

(to) be/feel **flattered** ['flætəd]	sich geschmeichelt fühlen	When I said he was handsome, he was both ~ and embarrassed.

PART B Teens in trouble

p.84 **troublemaker** ['trʌbl,meɪkə]	Unruhestifter/in	
social ['səʊʃl]	sozial, Sozial-, gesellschaftlich	! stress: **social** ['--] (F) social,e
order ['ɔːdə]	Befehl, Anweisung, Anordnung	(F) l'ordre *(m)*
(to) **order** ['ɔːdə]	befehlen	The soldier **~ed** me to get out of the car. (L) ordinare
(to) **be supposed to do** sth. [sə'pəʊzd]	etwas tun sollen	

German „sollen"

There are different ways of expressing the German word „sollen".

- We use **should** to say what is or was the right thing to do.
  We **should** buy a map. — Wir sollten einen Stadtplan kaufen.
  We **should** have bought a map. — Wir hätten einen Stadtplan kaufen sollen.
- We also use **had better** to say what is the best thing to do. **Had better** is stronger than **should**.
  It's cold. We**'d better** (= We **had better**) take our pullovers. — Wir sollten lieber unsere Pullover mitnehmen.
  I**'d better** go now. — Ich sollte jetzt besser gehen.
- We use **shall** and **should** when making a suggestion or asking what to do.
  Shall/Should we wait for the others? — Sollen wir auf die anderen warten?
  What **shall/should** I do now? — Was sollen wir jetzt tun?
- We use **be supposed to** or **be to** to say what other people are expected to do, e.g. because of a rule.
  We**'re supposed to** turn off our mobiles at school. — Wir sollen unsere Handys ... ausschalten.
  Mum says I**'m to** be back before ten. — Mutter sagt, ich soll vor zehn zu Hause sein.
- We use **be said to** or **be supposed to** to report what people say or think.
  Mr Jones **is said to** be very rich; he**'s supposed to** have four houses. — Herr Jones soll (angeblich) sehr reich sein und vier Häuser besitzen.

(to) **train as ...** [treɪn]	eine Ausbildung machen zu ...	She has **~ed as** a hairdresser and is looking for a job now.
builder ['bɪldə]	Bauarbeiter/in	
(to) **straighten** sth. **up** [,streɪtn_'ʌp]	etwas aufräumen, etwas in Ordnung bringen	We'll have to **~ up** the flat before the guests arrive. Give up smoking and drinking and try to **~ up** your life.
(to) **punish** ['pʌnɪʃ]	bestrafen	When you did something wrong as a child, how were you **~ed**? (F) punir (L) punire
punishment ['pʌnɪʃmənt]	Bestrafung, Strafe	Feeling sick was a kind of **~** for eating too much. (F) la punition (L) punitio
under age [,ʌndər_'eɪdʒ]	minderjährig	

	vandalism ['vændəlɪzəm]	Vandalismus, Zerstörungswut	! stress: **vandalism** ['----] (F) le vandalisme
	(to) **vandalize** ['vændəlaɪz]	mutwillig beschädigen, mutwillig zerstören	Cars and shop windows in the city centre have been **~d** again. 
p.85	**boot camp** ['bu:t kæmp]	Erziehungslager *(für junge Straftäter/innen)*	
	eagle ['i:gl]	Adler	
	military ['mɪlətri]	militärisch, Militär-	**military-style** fashion *(Mode im Militärstil)* (F) militaire (L) militaris 
	discipline ['dɪsəplɪn]	Disziplin	! stress: **discipline** ['---] (F) la discipline (L) disciplina
	clarification [,klærəfɪ'keɪʃn]	Klarstellung, Klärung	
	unless [ən'les]	es sei denn; außer (wenn)	You'll get into trouble with your parents ~ you work harder. (= ... if you don't work harder)
p.87/P3	**mph** [,em pi:‿'eɪtʃ] **(miles per hour)**	Meilen pro Stunde *(100 mph entspricht ca. 160 km/h)*	
p.87/P4	(to) **do** sth. **wrong**	etwas Verbotenes tun	I didn't **do** anything ~. It was an accident.

PART C Get involved

p.88	**along with** sb./sth. [ə'lɒŋ]	neben jm./etwas, (zusammen) mit jm./etwas	We walked onto the ferry ~ **with** hundreds of other travellers.
	diver ['daɪvə]	Taucher/in	The body was found in a canal by **~s**.
	trash *(AE)* [træʃ]	Abfall, Müll	= *BE* rubbish
	(bottle) cap [kæp]	(Flaschen-)Deckel	! **cap** = **1.** Mütze, Kappe; **2.** Deckel
	(to) **happen to** be/do sth. ['hæpn]	etwas zufällig sein/tun	He **~ed to** be in London at the same time. *(Er war zufällig zur selben Zeit in London.)* Do you **~ to** know why he was there? *(Weißt du zufällig, ...?)*
	turtle ['tɜ:tl]	Wasserschildkröte	a **turtle** 
	by far [baɪ 'fɑ:]	bei weitem; mit Abstand	Of the whole class, he got **by ~** the best marks.
	(to) **donate** [dəʊ'neɪt]	spenden, schenken	My dad **~s** blood every six months. Our neighbours have **~d** their old clothes to Oxfam. (F) donner (L) donare

	coin [kɔɪn]	Münze	 some **coins** and **bills** *(AE)* / **notes** *(BE)*
	bill *(AE)* [bɪl], **note** *(BE)* [nəʊt]	(Geld-)Schein, Banknote	
	altogether [ˌɔ:ltəˈgeðə]	insgesamt	£3.75 for the postcards and £5.50 for the stamps. That's £9.25 ~.
	the hungry [ˈhʌŋgri]	die Hungernden	

the rich, the poor, etc.

We can use **the + adjective** to talk about whole groups of people, e.g. the rich, the poor, etc.

The old are less active than **the young**.
Here, **The old** means 'all old people', so we could also say: **Old people** are less active than **young people**.

Compare:
The rich have more power than **the poor**. = **Rich people** have more power than **poor people**.
We should help **the homeless** more. = We should help **homeless people** more.

But when we talk about one person or about a few people, we use *woman*, *man*, *people*, etc.
I bought a magazine from **a homeless woman**. (not: ...from ~~a homeless~~.)
The homeless man spent the night in the park. (not: ~~The homeless~~ spent ...)
The homeless people got on the bus in front of the hostel. (not: ~~The homeless~~ got on ...)

	store *(AE)* [stɔ:]	Laden	= *BE* shop
	beef [bi:f]	Rindfleisch	  Ⓕ le boeuf **beef** a **cow**
	(to) **have** sth. **done** (by sb.)	etwas (von jm.) machen lassen	You hair looks nice. Did you ~ it **cut** or did you cut it yourself?
p. 89	**community service** [kəˈmju:nəti ˌsɜ:vɪs]	gemeinnützige Arbeit	Naomi wasn't sent to prison. Instead, her punishment was to do 200 hours' ~ **service**.
	(to) **require** sb. **to do** sth. [rɪˈkwaɪə]	von jm. verlangen, etwas zu tun	STUDENTS ARE REQUIRED TO TURN OFF THEIR MOBILES DURING LESSONS. Ⓛ requirere
p. 90	**monolingual** [ˌmɒnəˈlɪŋgwəl]	einsprachig	**monolingual** ◄► **bilingual**
p. 92/P 1	**privilege** [ˈprɪvəlɪdʒ]	Privileg	! stress: **privilege** [ˈ---] Ⓕ le privilège
	(to) **do a paper round** [ˈpeɪpə raʊnd]	Zeitungen austragen	He **does a paper** ~ every morning before school to earn a bit of money.
	(to) **walk** the dog [wɔ:k]	den Hund ausführen	Dogs should be **~ed** three times a day.

PART D The caller

p. 94	**ugly** [ˈʌgli]	hässlich	**ugly** ◄► **beautiful**
	(to) **bump into** sb./sth. [bʌmp]	sich an etwas stoßen; gegen jn. stoßen	It was dark and I **~ed into** my desk. A man **~ed into** me in the street and I fell down.

	lady ['leɪdi]	Dame	
	gentleman ['dʒentlmən], *pl* **-men** ['dʒentlmən]	Herr	**Ladies** and **gentlemen** = Meine Damen und Herren
	impatient [ɪm'peɪʃnt]	ungeduldig	I get ~ when I have to wait for a long time. (F) impatient, e (L) impatiens
	patient ['peɪʃənt]	geduldig	Be ~, I'm doing it as fast as I can. (L) patiens
	(to) **lie (to** sb.**)** [laɪ]	(jn. an)lügen	! (to) **lie, lay, lain** = liegen (to) **lie, lied, lied** = lügen
	diamond ['daɪəmənd]	Diamant	! stress: **diamond** ['---]
	darling ['dɑ:lɪŋ]	Liebling, Schatz	= dear, love, sweetheart
	(to) **search** sth./sb. **(for** sth./sb.**)** [sɜ:tʃ]	etwas/jn. (nach etwas/jm.) durchsuchen	The police **~ed** the flat **for** the dealers and their drugs.
	mood [mu:d]	Laune, Stimmung	The ~ of the meeting got angry after a while.
	(to) **be in a** good/bad **mood** [mu:d]	gute/schlechte Laune haben	Natalie **is in a** terrible ~ every Monday morning.
p. 95	(to) **pretend** [prɪ'tend]	so tun, als ob	He **~ed** to be ill so that he could miss school. (F) prétendre (L) praetendere
	ghost [gəʊst]	Gespenst, Geist	You look scared, as if you've just seen a ~.
	Anyway, ... ['eniweɪ]	Aber egal, ... / Wie dem auch sei, ...	Sorry, I still don't agree. **Anyway,** let's talk about something else.
p. 96	**muddy** ['mʌdi]	schlammig, matschig	
	mud [mʌd]	Schlamm, Matsch	
p. 97	**suspense** [sə'spens]	Spannung	(F) le suspense
	repetition [,repə'tɪʃn]	Wiederholung	verb: (to) **repeat** – noun: **repetition** (F) la répétition (L) repetitio
	climax ['klaɪmæks]	Höhepunkt	! Höhepunkt = **1. highlight** *(schönster Teil von etwas)* **2. climax** *(spannendster Moment in einem Roman, Film usw.)*
	quotation [kwəʊ'teɪʃn]	Zitat	My favourite ~ is by George Bernard Shaw: 'Youth is a wonderful thing. What a crime to waste it on children.'

Das **Dictionary** (S. 211–252) enthält den Wortschatz der Bände 1 bis 5 von *English G 21*.
Wenn du wissen möchtest, was ein Wort bedeutet, wie man es ausspricht oder wie es genau geschrieben wird, kannst du hier nachschlagen.

Im **Dictionary** werden folgende **Abkürzungen und Symbole** verwendet:

jm. = jemandem	sb. = somebody	*pl = plural*	*AE = American English*
jn. = jemanden	sth. = something	*no pl = no plural*	*infml = informal*

° Mit diesem Kringel sind Wörter markiert, die nicht zum Lernwortschatz gehören.
► Der Pfeil verweist auf Kästchen im **Vocabulary** (S. 181–210), in denen du weitere Informationen zu diesem Wort findest.

Die **Fundstellenangaben** zeigen, wo ein Wort zum ersten Mal vorkommt.
Die Ziffern in Klammern bezeichnen Seitenzahlen:

I = Band A1 • II = Band A2 • III = Band A3 • IV = Band A4 • V = Band A5
V 1 (15) = Band 5, Unit 1, Seite 15
V 1 (29/200) = Band 5, Unit 1, Seite 200 (im Vocabulary, zu Seite 29)

Tipps zur Arbeit mit einem Wörterbuch findest du im Skills File auf Seite 124.

Tipp

Auf der **Audio-CD im Workbook** findest du sowohl dieses englisch-deutsche Wörterverzeichnis als auch ein deutsch-englisches Wörterverzeichnis mit dem Lernwortschatz der Bände 1–5.

1

1950s [ˌnaɪntiːn'fɪftiz] die Fünfzigerjahre (des 20. Jahrhunderts) III
°**911** [ˌnaɪn ˌwʌn 'wʌn] die Notrufnummer in Nordamerika *(entspricht 112 in Europa)*
9/11 [ˌnaɪn‿ɪ'levn] Nine Eleven *(der Terroranschlag am 11. September 2001)* IV

A

a [ə]
1. ein, eine I
2. once/twice a week einmal/zweimal pro Woche III • **a bit** ein bisschen, etwas II • **a few** ein paar, einige II • **a lot (of)** eine Menge, viel, viele II • **He likes her a lot.** Er mag sie sehr. I
abbey ['æbi] Abtei II
abbreviation [əˌbriːvi'eɪʃn] Abkürzung IV
able ['eɪbl]: **be able to do sth.** etwas tun können; fähig sein/in der Lage sein, etwas zu tun II
Aboriginal [ˌæbə'rɪdʒənəl] Aborigine- *(die Ureinwohner/innen Australiens betreffend)* V 1 (8/183) • **the Aboriginal people** *die Ureinwohner/innen Australiens* V 1 (8/183)
Aborigine [ˌæbə'rɪdʒəni] *Ureinwohner/in Australiens* V 1 (8)
about [ə'baʊt]
1. über I
2. ungefähr II
ask about sth. nach etwas fragen I • **know about sth.** von etwas wissen; über etwas Bescheid wissen II • **learn about sth.** etwas über etwas erfahren, etwas über etwas herausfinden II • **This is about Mr Green.** Es geht um Mr Green. I • **What about ...? 1.** Was ist mit ...? / Und ...? I; **2.** Wie wär's mit ...? I • **What are you talking about?** Wovon redest du? I
What was the best thing about ...? Was war das Beste an ...? II
above [ə'bʌv] über, oberhalb (von) III
abroad [ə'brɔːd] im Ausland II
go abroad ins Ausland gehen/fahren II
absolute ['æbsəluːt] absolut V 3 (53/200)
absolutely [ˌæbsə'luːt] absolut, völlig IV
°**academy** [ə'kædəmi] Akademie
accent ['æksənt] Akzent II
°**accept** [ək'sept] *(Immigranten)* aufnehmen
accident ['æksɪdənt] Unfall II
accommodation [əˌkɒmə'deɪʃn] Unterkunft IV
accurate ['ækjərət] genau, akkurat III
°**ac/dc** [ˌeɪ siː 'diː siː] *(infml)* Strom
achieve [ə'tʃiːv] erreichen, erzielen, zustande bringen IV • **achieve an end** ein Ziel erreichen IV
achievement [ə'tʃiːvmənt] Leistung, Errungenschaft V 2 (39)
acid ['æsɪd] Säure IV
acrobat ['ækrəbæt] Akrobat/in III
across [ə'krɒs]
1. (quer) über II
2. hinüber, herüber III
act [ækt] aufführen, spielen I
°**acting** ['æktɪŋ] Schauspielerei
action ['ækʃn] Action; Handlung, Tat III
active ['æktɪv] aktiv III
activist ['æktəvɪst] Aktivist/in IV
activity [æk'tɪvəti] Aktivität, Tätigkeit I
actor ['æktə] Schauspieler/in II
actually ['æktʃuəli] eigentlich, tatsächlich, übrigens, zwar IV
ad [æd] Anzeige, Inserat; *(im Fernsehen)* Werbespot IV
AD [ˌeɪ 'diː] *(from Latin: Anno Domini)* nach Christus III
°**adapt** [ə'dæpt] adaptieren
add (to) [æd] hinzufügen, ergänzen, addieren (zu) I • °**Added to that ...** Hinzu kommt, dass ...
address [ə'dres] Anschrift, Adresse II
adjust (to sth.) [ə'dʒʌst] sich (an etwas) gewöhnen, sich (auf etwas) einstellen IV
admire [əd'maɪə] bewundern IV
adult ['ædʌlt] Erwachsene(r) III
adult life das Leben als Erwachsene(r) III
advanced [əd'vɑːnst] fortgeschritten; für Fortgeschrittene V 2 (32/189)
advantage (over sb./sth.) [əd'vɑːntɪdʒ] Vorteil (gegenüber jm./etwas) IV
adventure [əd'ventʃə] Abenteuer II
advert ['ædvɜːt] Anzeige, Inserat; *(im Fernsehen)* Werbespot II
advertise ['ædvətaɪz] Werbung machen (für); inserieren V 2 (41)
advertisement [əd'vɜːtɪsmənt] Anzeige; Inserat; *(im Fernsehen)* Werbespot V 2 (41)

advertiser ['ædvətaɪzə] Inserent/in; Werbekunde/-kundin V 2 (46)
advertising ['ædvətaɪzə] Werbung V 2 (41) • **advertising company** Werbefirma
advice *(no pl)* [əd'vaɪs] Rat, Ratschlag, Ratschläge V 2 (47) • **Take my advice.** Hör auf meinen Rat. V 2 (47/197)
advise sb. [əd'vaɪz] jn. beraten V 2 (47)
adviser [əd'vaɪzə] Berater/in V 2 (47)
°**afar** [ə'fɑː]: **from afar** von weitem
afraid [ə'freɪd]
1. be afraid (of) Angst haben (vor) I
2. I'm afraid leider II
after ['ɑːftə] nach *(zeitlich)* I
after that danach I • **after-school** nach dem Unterricht stattfindende(r, s) V 2 (38)
after ['ɑːftə] nachdem II
afternoon [ˌɑːftə'nuːn] Nachmittag I • **in the afternoon** nachmittags, am Nachmittag I • **on Friday afternoon** freitagnachmittags, am Freitagnachmittag I
again [ə'gen] wieder; noch einmal I
now and again ab und zu, von Zeit zu Zeit III
against [ə'genst] gegen I
age [eɪdʒ] Alter III • **age discrimination** Diskriminierung aufgrund des Alters V 3 (63) • **at (the age of) 16** mit 16; im Alter von 16 III
she's my age sie ist in meinem Alter V 2 (47) • **under age** minderjährig V 4 (84)
agency ['eɪdʒənsi]: **news agency** Nachrichtenagentur IV
agenda [ə'dʒendə] Tagesordnung V 3 (60)
ago [ə'gəʊ]: **a minute ago** vor einer Minute I
agree [ə'griː]: **agree (on)** sich einigen (auf) I • **agree (with sb.)** (jm.) zustimmen I
agreement [ə'griːmənt] Einigung V 3 (52) • **reach agreement** sich einigen V 3 (52/199)
agriculture ['ægrɪkʌltʃə] Landwirtschaft IV
ahead (of sb./sth.) [ə'hed] (jm./etwas) voraus V 2 (32) • **the road ahead** die Straße vor uns V 2 (32)
aim [eɪm] Ziel III
air [eə] Luft II
airport ['eəpɔːt] Flughafen III
alarm clock [ə'lɑːm klɒk] Wecker I
album ['ælbəm] Album II
alcohol ['ælkəhɒl] Alkohol III
alcoholic [ˌælkə'hɒlɪk] alkoholisch V 3 (63)

A-level exams, A-levels *(pl)* ['eɪ ˌlevl] *die höchsten Abschlussprüfungen des Schulsystems in England, Wales und Nordirland* V 2 (32)
alive [ə'laɪv]: **be alive** leben, am Leben sein IV • °**come alive** lebendig werden • **keep sth. alive** etwas am Leben halten IV
all [ɔːl] alle; alles I • **2 all** 2 beide (2:2 unentschieden) III • **all day** den ganzen Tag (lang) I • **all over the world** auf der ganzen Welt III
all right [ɔːl 'raɪt] gut, in Ordnung II • **All the best** Viele Grüße IV
all the time die ganze Zeit I • **all we have to do now ...** alles, was wir jetzt (noch) tun müssen, ... II
from all over the world aus der ganzen Welt II • **This is all wrong.** Das ist ganz falsch. I • **all year round** das ganze Jahr hindurch IV
allergic (to sth.) [ə'lɜːdʒɪk] allergisch (gegen etwas) III
allow [ə'laʊ] erlauben, zulassen II
be allowed to do sth. [ə'laʊd] etwas tun dürfen II
almost ['ɔːlməʊst] fast, beinahe II
alone [ə'ləʊn] allein I
along [ə'lɒŋ]: **along the road** entlang der Straße / die Straße entlang II • **get along** zurechtkommen IV; gut (mit jm.) auskommen V 2 (47)
along with sb./sth. [ə'lɒŋ] neben jm./etwas, (zusammen) mit jm./etwas V 4 (88)
alphabet ['ælfəbet] Alphabet I
already [ɔːl'redi] schon, bereits II
also ['ɔːlsəʊ] auch IV • **not only ... but also ...** nicht nur ... sondern auch ... IV
although [ɔːl'ðəʊ] obwohl III
altogether [ˌɔːltə'geðə] insgesamt V 4 (88)
always ['ɔːlweɪz] immer I
am [ˌeɪ‿'em]: **7 am** 7 Uhr morgens/vormittags I
amazing [ə'meɪzɪŋ] erstaunlich, unglaublich II
ambition [æm'bɪʃn] Ehrgeiz V 2 (47)
ambitious [æm'bɪʃəs] ehrgeizig V 2 (47)
ambulance ['æmbjələns] Krankenwagen III
amendment (to sth.) [ə'mendmənt] (Ab)Änderung (einer Sache); *(oft* **Amendment***)* Verfassungszusatz *(zur Verfassung der USA)* V 3 (52)
°**make an amendment to sth.** eine Änderung/Ergänzung vornehmen
American football [əˌmerɪkən 'fʊtbɔːl] Football I

among [ə'mʌŋ] unter, zwischen *(mehreren Personen oder Dingen)* IV
an [ən] ein, eine I
anarchy ['ænəki] Anarchie V 3 (53/200)
► S.200 Different forms of government
ancestor ['ænsestə] Vorfahr/in IV
and [ənd, ænd] und I • **and now for** und jetzt ... *(kündigt ein neues Thema an)* III • **nice and cool/clean/...** schön kühl/sauber/... I
angel ['eɪndʒl] Engel II
°**Angles** *(pl)* ['æŋglz] die Angeln *(Volk)* V 3 (67)
°**Anglo-Saxons** *(pl)* [ˌæŋglo'sæksnz] die Angelsachsen
angry (about sth./with sb.) ['æŋgri] wütend, böse (über etwas/auf jn.) II
animal ['ænɪml] Tier I
°**annex** ['æneks] Nebengebäude
anniversary [ˌænɪ'vɜːsəri] Jahrestag IV • **anniversary of sb.'s death** Todestag IV
announce [ə'naʊns] bekanntgeben III
announcement [ə'naʊnsmənt] Bekanntgabe, Ankündigung; Durchsage; Ansage III
annoy [ə'nɔɪ] ärgern, verärgern V 2 (35) • **be/get annoyed (with sb., about sth.)** sich (über jn./etwas) ärgern V 2 (35)
annoying [ə'nɔɪɪŋ] ärgerlich, lästig V 2 (35)
annual ['ænjuəl] jährlich V 3 (60)
anorak ['ænəræk] Anorak, Windjacke III
another [ə'nʌðə] ein(e) andere(r, s); noch ein(e) I • **another 70 metres** weitere 70 Meter, noch 70 Meter II
answer ['ɑːnsə] (be)antworten I
answer (the phone) rangehen *(ans Telefon)* IV
answer (to) ['ɑːnsə] Antwort (auf) I
anti-social [ˌænti'səʊʃl] asozial, antisozial V 4 (84)
antonym ['æntənɪm] Antonym IV
any ['eni]: **any ...?** (irgend)welche ...? I • **not (...) any** kein(e) I • **not (...) any more** nicht mehr II • **any** irgendeine(r) V 2 (35/191)
anybody ['enibɒdi]: **anybody?** (irgend)jemand? II • **not (...) anybody** niemand II • **anybody** jede(r) (beliebige) V 2 (35)
anyone ['eniwʌn]: **anyone?** (irgend) jemand? III • **not (...) anyone** niemand III • **anyone** jede(r) (beliebige) V 2 (35)
anything ['eniθɪŋ]: **anything?** (irgend)etwas? II • **Did you do any-**

thing special? Habt ihr irgendetwas Besonderes gemacht? I
not (...) anything nichts II • **anything** alles, egal was V 2 (35/191)
► S.191 any, anyone, etc.
anyway ['eniweɪ]
1. sowieso I
2. trotzdem II
Anyway, ... ['eniweɪ] Aber egal, ... / Wie dem auch sei, ... V 4 (95)
anywhere ['eniweə]**: anywhere?** irgendwo(hin)? II • **not (...) anywhere** nirgendwo(hin) II • **anywhere** überall hin V 2 (35/191)
► S.191 any, anyone, etc.
apart [ə'pɑːt] voneinander getrennt, auseinander IV
apart from [ə'pɑːt] außer V 1 (23)
apartment [ə'pɑːtmənt] Wohnung IV
apologize (to sb. for sth.) [ə'pɒlədʒaɪz] sich (bei jm. für etwas) entschuldigen V 1 (17)
appear [ə'pɪə] erscheinen, auftauchen III
appetite ['æpɪtaɪt] Appetit III
apple ['æpl] Apfel I
applicant ['æplɪkənt] Bewerber/in V 2 (39)
application [ˌæplɪ'keɪʃn] Bewerbung V 2 (38) • **letter of application** Bewerbungsschreiben V 2 (38/192)
apply for [ə'plaɪ] sich bewerben (um/für etwas); etwas beantragen IV
appointment [ə'pɔɪntmənt] Termin, Verabredung I
°**approve** [ə'pruːv] *(Gesetz usw.)* ratifizieren
approximate [ə'prɒksɪmət] ungefähre(r, s) V 3 (66)
April ['eɪprəl] April I
°**archery** ['ɑːtʃəri] Bogenschießen
architect ['ɑːkɪtekt] Architekt/in III
archive ['ɑːkaɪv] Archiv IV
are [ɑː] bist; sind; seid I • **How are you?** Wie geht es dir/Ihnen/euch? II • **The pencils are 35 p.** Die Bleistifte kosten 35 Pence. I
area ['eəriə] Gebiet, Gegend; Bereich III
argue ['ɑːgjuː] sich streiten, sich zanken I
argument ['ɑːgjumənt]
1. Streit, Auseinandersetzung II
have an argument eine Auseinandersetzung haben, sich streiten II
2. Argument V 3 (52)
argumentative writing [ˌɑːgju'mentətɪv] Erörterung V 4 (82)
arm [ɑːm] Arm I
armchair ['ɑːmtʃeə] Sessel I
army ['ɑːmi] Armee, Heer IV
around [ə'raʊnd] in ... umher, durch, um ... (herum) III • **around six** um sechs Uhr herum, gegen sechs III
around the lake um den See (herum) III • **around the town** in der Stadt umher, durch die Stadt III • **look around** sich umsehen III
turn around sich umdrehen IV
walk/run/jump around herumgehen/-rennen/-springen, umhergehen/-rennen/-springen III
°**arrange a date** [ə'reɪndʒ] eine Verabredung planen
arrest sb. (for sth.) [ə'rest] jn. (wegen einer Sache) verhaften/festnehmen V 3 (56)
arrival [ə'raɪvl] Ankunft III
arrive [ə'raɪv] ankommen, eintreffen II
arrow ['ærəʊ] Pfeil IV • **bow and arrow** Pfeil und Bogen IV
art [ɑːt] Kunst I • **rock art** *(no pl)* Felsmalerei(en) V 1 (8)
article ['ɑːtɪkl] (Zeitungs-)Artikel I
artificial [ˌɑːtɪ'fɪʃl] künstlich, Kunst- III
as [əz, æz]
1. als, während II
2. wie II • **as you know** wie du weißt II
3. **as nice/big/exciting as** so schön/groß/aufregend wie II
just as ... as ebenso ... wie IV
as soon as sobald, sowie II
4. weil V 2 (38)
°**ASBO** ['æzbəʊ] einstweilige Verfügung wegen asozialen Verhaltens
as if [əz‿'ɪf] als ob IV
ask [ɑːsk] fragen I • **ask about sth.** nach etwas fragen I • **ask questions** Fragen stellen I • **ask sb. for sth.** jn. um etwas bitten II • **ask someone out (on a date)** sich mit jm. verabreden; jn. einladen, mit ihr/ihm auszugehen V 4 (80) • **ask sb. the way** jn. nach dem Weg fragen II
asleep [ə'sliːp]**: be asleep** schlafen II • **fall asleep** einschlafen V 1 (21)
°**aspect** ['æspekt] Aspekt
assembly [ə'sembli] Versammlung V 3 (53)
assess [ə'ses] einschätzen, beurteilen V 2 (44)
assessment [ə'sesmənt] Einschätzung, Beurteilung V 2 (44)
assignment [ə'saɪnmənt] *(AE)* Hausaufgabe IV
assistant [ə'sɪstənt] Verkäufer/in I
°**association** [əˌsəʊsi'eɪʃn] Bund
°**asylum seeker** [ə'saɪləm ˌsiːkə] Asylbewerber/in, Asylant/in
at [ət, æt]**: at 7 Hamilton Street** in der Hamiltonstraße 7 I • **at 8.45** um 8.45 I • **at (the age of) 16** mit 16; im Alter von 16 III • **at break** in der Pause *(zwischen Schulstunden)* II • **at home** zu Hause, daheim I • **at last** endlich, schließlich I • **at least** zumindest, wenigstens I • **at night** nachts, in der Nacht I • **at school** in der Schule I • **at sea** auf See II • **at that table** an dem Tisch (dort) / an den Tisch (dort) I • **at the back (of the room)** hinten, im hinteren Teil (des Zimmers) II • **at the bottom (of)** unten, am unteren Ende (von) II • **at the chemist's/doctor's/hairdresser's** beim Apotheker/Arzt/Friseur III • **at the end (of)** am Ende (von) I • **at the moment** im Moment, gerade, zurzeit I • **at the Shaws' house** im Haus der Shaws, bei den Shaws zu Hause I • **at the station** am Bahnhof I • **at the top (of)** oben, am oberen Ende, an der Spitze (von) I • **at the weekend** am Wochenende I • **at work** bei der Arbeit / am Arbeitsplatz I
go at 50 mph 50 Meilen pro Stunde fahren V 4 (87)
ate [et, eɪt] *siehe* **eat**
atheism ['eɪθiɪzəm] Atheismus V 3 (50/198)
atheist ['eɪθiɪst] Atheist(in) V 3 (50/198)
atheistic [ˌeɪθi'ɪstɪk] atheistisch V 3 (50/198)
► S.198 Religions
athletics [æθ'letɪks] Leichtathletik III
atmosphere ['ætməsfɪə] Atmosphäre; Stimmung V 1 (9)
°**atom** ['ætəm] Atom
attach to [ə'tætʃ] anhängen, anheften (an) *(an Brief, Mail)* V 1 (12)
attack [ə'tæk] Angriff III • **heart attack** Herzinfarkt IV
attack [ə'tæk] angreifen III
°**attention** [ə'tenʃn]**: attract sb.'s attention** jm. ins Auge fallen
attitude to/towards ['ætɪtjuːd] Haltung gegenüber, Einstellung zu IV
°**attract sb.'s attention** [ə'trækt] jm. ins Auge fallen
attractive [ə'træktɪv] attraktiv, verlockend V 3 (83/206)
► S.206 German „schön" etc.
audience ['ɔːdiəns] Zuschauer/innen, Zuhörer/innen, Publikum V 2 (45)

August ['ɔ:gəst] August I
aunt [ɑ:nt] Tante I • **auntie** ['ɑ:nti] Tante II
°**Aussie** ['ɒzi] *(infml)* Australier/in; australisch
°**Aussie rules football** Australian Football
author ['ɔ:θə] Autor/in V 1 (25)
auto ['ɔ:təʊ] *(AE)* Auto, PKW IV
autobiography [,ɔ:təʊbaɪ'ɒgrəfi] Autobiografie IV
autumn ['ɔ:təm] Herbst I
available [ə'veɪləbl] erhältlich; vorrätig IV
avenue ['ævənju:] Allee, Boulevard IV
average ['ævərɪdʒ] Durchschnitt; durchschnittlich IV
avoid [ə'vɔɪd] vermeiden V 2 (39)
awake [ə'weɪk] wach V 3 (52)
award [ə'wɔ:d] Auszeichnung, Preis V 2 (39)
away [ə'weɪ] weg, fort I • **get away from sth./sb.** von etwas/ jm. weggehen, sich entfernen III **put sth. away** wegräumen IV
awesome ['ɔ:səm] *(AE, infml)* klasse, großartig IV
awful ['ɔ:fl] furchtbar, schrecklich II
°**axis** ['æksɪs] Achse

B

baby ['beɪbi] Baby I • **have a baby** ein Baby/Kind bekommen II
back [bæk]: **at the back (of the room)** hinten, im hinteren Teil (des Zimmers) II • **back home** zurück zu Hause IV • **go back** zurückgehen, -fahren V 2 (47)
°**back and forth** [fɔ:θ] hin und her
back door [,bæk 'dɔ:] Hintertür II
background ['bækgraʊnd] Hintergrund II • **background file** *etwa:* Hintergrundinformation II
backwards ['bækwədz], **backward** ['bækwəd] *(bes. AE)* rückwärts V 3 (52)
bacon ['beɪkən] Schinkenspeck II
bacteria *(pl)* [bæk'tɪəriə] Bakterien IV
bad [bæd] schlecht, schlimm I **bad timing** schlechtes Timing, schlechte Wahl des Zeitpunkts III
badge [bædʒ] Abzeichen, Button V 2 (38)
badminton ['bædmɪntən] Badminton, Federball I • **badminton racket** Federballschläger III

bag [bæg] Tasche, Beutel, Tüte I; Handtasche III
bagel ['beɪgl] Bagel *(ringförmiges Brötchen)* IV
°**Bajan** ['beɪdʒn] *Sprache und Bewohner/in von Barbados*
balcony ['bælkəni] Balkon V 3 (64)
ball [bɔ:l]
1. Ball *(zum Sport)* I
2. Ball *(Tanz)* II
balloon [bə'lu:n] Heißluftballon; Luftballon II
°**ballot box** ['bælət bɒks] Wahlurne
ban (-nn-) [bæn] verbieten; sperren; ein (Aufenthalts-)Verbot erteilen V 3 (63)
ban [bæn] Verbot V 3 (66/205)
► S.205 Verbs & nouns with the same form
banana [bə'nɑ:nə] Banane I
band [bænd] Band, (Musik-)Gruppe I
► S.196 Collective nouns
banjo ['bændʒəʊ] Banjo III
bank [bæŋk] Bank, Sparkasse I **bank robber** ['bæŋk ,rɒbə] Bankräuber/in I
bar [bɑ:] Bar II
bar chart ['bɑ: tʃɑ:t] Balkendiagramm V 1 (10)
barbecue ['bɑ:bɪkju:] Grillfest, Grillparty V 1 (6)
°**barbie** ['bɑ:bi] *(infml)* Grillfest, Grillparty
bark [bɑ:k] bellen II
baseball ['beɪsbɔ:l] Baseball I **baseball cap** Baseballmütze II
basic ['beɪsɪk] grundlegend, Grund-; einfach, elementar V 2 (38) **Basic Law** Grundgesetz V 2 (38/193)
basket ['bɑ:skɪt] Korb I • **a basket of apples** ein Korb Äpfel I
basketball ['bɑ:skɪtbɔ:l] Basketball I
bass [beɪs] Kontrabass; Bassgitarre III • **bass guitar** Bassgitarre III **double bass** Kontrabass III
bat [bæt]: **table tennis bat** Tischtennisschläger III
bath [bɑ:θ] Bad, Badewanne II **have a bath** baden, ein Bad nehmen II
bathroom ['bɑ:θru:m; 'bɑ:θrʊm] Badezimmer I
°**baton** ['bætɒn] Schlagstock
bay [beɪ] Bucht III
BC [,bi: 'si:] v. Chr. IV
be [bi:], **was/were, been** sein I • **be into sth.** *(infml)* etwas mögen III **be a farmer, a teacher, ...** Bauer/ Bäuerin, Lehrer/in, ... werden IV
beach [bi:tʃ] Strand II • **on the beach** [bi:tʃ] am Strand II

bean [bi:n] Bohne IV
bear [beə] Bär II • **teddy bear** Teddybär III
beat [bi:t], **beat, beaten** schlagen; besiegen III
beaten ['bi:tn] *siehe* **beat**
beautiful ['bju:tɪfl] schön I
► S.206 German „schön" etc.
beauty ['bju:ti] Schönheit III
became [bɪ'keɪm] *siehe* **become**
because [bɪ'kɒz] weil I
because of [bɪ'kɒz_əv] wegen IV
become [bɪ'kʌm], **became, become** werden II • °**become law** Rechtskraft erlangen
bed [bed] Bett I • **Bed and Breakfast (B&B)** [,bed_ən 'brekfəst] Frühstückspension I • **go to bed** ins Bett gehen I • **put sb. to bed** jn. ins Bett bringen III
bedroom ['bedru:m; 'bedrʊm] Schlafzimmer I
beef [bi:f] Rindfleisch V 4 (88)
been [bi:n] *siehe* **be**
before [bɪ'fɔ:] vor *(zeitlich)* I • **the day before yesterday** vorgestern II
before [bɪ'fɔ:] bevor II
before [bɪ'fɔ:] (vorher) schon mal II
began [bɪ'gæn] *siehe* **begin**
begin (-nn-) [bɪ'gɪn], **began, begun** beginnen, anfangen (mit) I
beginner [bɪ'gɪnə] Anfänger/in V 1 (15)
beginning [bɪ'gɪnɪŋ] Anfang, Beginn III
begun [bɪ'gʌn] *siehe* **begin**
behave [bɪ'heɪv] sich verhalten, sich benehmen V 4 (80)
behaviour [bɪ'heɪvjə] Verhalten, Benehmen V 4 (80)
behind [bɪ'haɪnd] hinter I • **leave behind** zurücklassen IV
bell [bel] Klingel, Glocke I
believe [bɪ'li:v] glauben III **believe in sth.** an etwas glauben IV • **She couldn't believe her eyes.** Sie traute ihren Augen kaum. III
belong (to) [bɪ'lɒŋ] gehören (zu) II
below [bɪ'ləʊ] unter, unterhalb (von) III
beside [bɪ'saɪd] neben V 1 (21)
besides [bɪ'saɪdz] außerdem IV
best [best] am besten II • **All the best** Viele Grüße IV **Best wishes** Viele Grüße IV • **the best** ... der/ die/das beste ...; die besten ... I **What was the best thing about ...?** Was war das Beste an ...? II
bet (-tt-) [bet], **bet, bet** wetten III **You bet!** *(infml)* Aber klar! / Und ob! IV

better ['betə] besser I • **like sth. better** etwas lieber mögen II • **I'd (= I had) better go.** Ich sollte (besser) gehen. V 1 (84/207)
► S.207 German „sollen"
between [bɪ'twi:n] zwischen II
°**beyond** [bɪ'jɒnd] jenseits (von), über ... hinaus
Bible ['baɪbl] Bibel IV
big [bɪg] groß I • **big wheel** Riesenrad III
°**big time** ['bɪg taɪm] *(adv, infml)* groß, richtig
bike [baɪk] Fahrrad I • **bike tour** Radtour II • **ride a bike** Rad fahren I
bilingual [ˌbaɪ'lɪŋgwəl] zweisprachig IV
bill [bɪl] *(AE)* (Geld-)Schein, Banknote V 4 (88)
°**Bill of Rights** [bɪl] *Zusatzartikel 1–10 zu den Grundrechten der USA*
bin [bɪn] Mülltonne II
binoculars *(pl)* [bɪ'nɒkjuləz] Fernglas IV
biography [baɪ'ɒgrəfi] Biografie III
biological [ˌbaɪə'lɒdʒɪkl] biologisch IV
biology [baɪ'ɒlədʒi] Biologie I
bird [bɜ:d] Vogel I
birth [bɜ:θ] Geburt IV • **birth rate** Geburtsrate V 1 (9/183) • **date of birth** Geburtsdatum IV • °**give birth to sb.** jn. gebären
birthday ['bɜ:θdeɪ] Geburtstag I **Happy birthday.** Herzlichen Glückwunsch zum Geburtstag. I • **My birthday is in May.** Ich habe im Mai Geburtstag. I • **My birthday is on 13th June.** Ich habe am 13. Juni Geburtstag. I • **When's your birthday?** Wann hast du Geburtstag? I • **for his birthday** zu seinem Geburtstag III
biscuit ['bɪskɪt] Keks, Plätzchen I
bit [bɪt]**: a bit** ein bisschen, etwas II
bitter ['bɪtə] bitter V 3 (66)
black [blæk] schwarz I
°**black** [blæk] Schwarze(r)
blame sb. (for) [bleɪm] jm. die Schuld geben (an); jm. Vorwürfe machen (wegen) III
blanket ['blæŋkɪt] Decke *(zum Zudecken)* V 1 (17)
bled [bled] *siehe* **bleed**
bleed [bli:d]**, bled, bled** bluten IV
bleep [bli:p] piepsen II
bleep [bli:p] Piepton II
blessing ['blesɪŋ] Segen IV
blew [blu:] *siehe* **blow**
blind [blaɪnd] blind III

block [blɒk] blockieren, (ver)sperren IV
block [blɒk] (Häuser-, Wohn-)Block IV
blog [blɒg] Blog *(Weblog, digitales Tagebuch)* IV
blond *(bei Frauen oft:* **blonde***)* [blɒnd] blond IV
blood [blʌd] Blut III
blouse [blaʊz] Bluse II
blow [bləʊ]**, blew, blown** pusten, blasen; wehen III
blown [bləʊn] *siehe* **blow**
blue [blu:] blau I
blues [blu:z] Blues III
board [bɔ:d] (Wand-)Tafel I • **on the board** an der/die Tafel I
boat [bəʊt] Boot, Schiff I
body ['bɒdi] Körper I
bodyguard ['bɒdigɑ:d] Bodyguard, Leibwächter/in, Leibwache IV
boil [bɔɪl] kochen *(Flüssigkeit, Speise)* IV
°**bold** [bəʊld] kräftig, auffallend
bold (type) [ˌbəʊld 'taɪp] Fettdruck V 2 (39)
bone [bəʊn] Knochen IV
bomb [bɒm] Bombe IV
book [bʊk] Buch I
booklet ['bʊklət] Broschüre II
boot [bu:t] Stiefel I
boot camp ['bu:t kæmp] Erziehungslager *(für junge Straftäter/innen)* V 4 (85)
border ['bɔ:də] Grenze IV
bored [bɔ:d]**: get bored** sich langweilen; gelangweilt sein IV
boring ['bɔ:rɪŋ] langweilig I
born [bɔ:n]**: be born** geboren sein/werden II
borough ['bʌrə, *AE:* 'bɜ:roʊ] (Stadt-)Bezirk III
borrow sth. ['bɒrəʊ] sich etwas (aus)leihen, etwas entleihen II
boss [bɒs] Boss, Chef/in I
both [bəʊθ] beide I
bottle ['bɒtl] Flasche I • **a bottle of milk** eine Flasche Milch I **bottle cap** (Flaschen-)Deckel V 4 (88)
bottom ['bɒtəm] unteres Ende II **at the bottom (of)** unten, am unteren Ende (von) II
bought [bɔ:t] *siehe* **buy**
bow [bəʊ] Bogen *(Waffe und zum Musizieren)* IV • **bow and arrow** Pfeil und Bogen IV
bowl [bəʊl] Schüssel I • **a bowl of cornflakes** eine Schale Cornflakes I
box [bɒks] Kasten, Kästchen, Kiste I

box office ['bɒks‿ˌɒfɪs] (Theater-, Kino-)Kasse III
boy [bɔɪ] Junge I • **boy!** *(AE, infml)* Mann! Mensch! III
boycott ['bɔɪkɒt] Boykott IV
bracket ['brækɪt] Klammer *(in Texten)* IV • **round brackets** runde Klammern IV • **square brackets** eckige Klammern IV
brainstorm ['breɪnstɔ:m] brainstormen *(so viele Ideen wie möglich sammeln)* III
°**branch** [brɑ:ntʃ] Ast, Zweig
brave [breɪv] tapfer, mutig IV
bread *(no pl)* [bred] Brot I
break [breɪk]**, broke, broken** (zer)brechen; kaputt machen; kaputt gehen II • **break a rule/order** gegen eine Regel/Anordnung verstoßen IV • **break sth. open** etwas aufbrechen IV • **break sth. up** etwas auflösen V 3 (53)
break [breɪk] Pause I • **at break** in der Pause *(zwischen Schulstunden)* II • **take a break** eine Pause machen IV
break down [ˌbreɪk 'daʊn]
1. eine Panne haben V 1 (20)
2. zusammenbrechen V 1 (20)
breakfast ['brekfəst] Frühstück I **have breakfast** frühstücken I
breathe [bri:ð] atmen IV
bridge [brɪdʒ] Brücke I
bridle path ['braɪdl ˌpɑ:θ] Reitweg III
bright [braɪt] hell, leuchtend II
brief [bri:f] kurz (gefasst), knapp, von kurzer Dauer V 2 (39) • **be brief** sich kurz fassen V 2 (39/193)
°**brilliant** ['brɪliənt] glänzend; strahlend
bring [brɪŋ]**, brought, brought** (mit-, her)bringen I • °**bring in** einbringen
British ['brɪtɪʃ] britisch II
°**Britons** *(pl)* ['brɪtn] die Britannier
broadcast ['brɔ:dkɑ:st]**, broadcast broadcast** senden; *(eine Sendung)* ausstrahlen IV
broke [brəʊk] *siehe* **break**
broken ['brəʊkən] *siehe* **break**
broken ['brəʊkən] gebrochen; zerbrochen, kaputt II
brother ['brʌðə] Bruder I
brought [brɔ:t] *siehe* **bring**
brown [braʊn] braun I
bubble ['bʌbl] (Luft-)Blase V 3 (52) **speech bubble** Sprechblase V 3 (50/199) • **thought bubble** Denkblase V 3 (50/199)
Buddhism ['bʊdɪzm] Buddhismus V 3 (50/198)

Buddhist ['bʊdɪst] Buddhist/in, buddhistisch V 3 (50/198)
► S.198 Religions
budget ['bʌdʒɪt] Etat, Budget V 3 (60)
budgie ['bʌdʒi] Wellensittich I
°**bug** [bʌg] (Programm)fehler
build [bɪld], **built, built** bauen II
the ship was built in Bristol das Schiff wurde in Bristol gebaut II
builder ['bɪldə] Bauarbeiter/in V 4 (84)
building ['bɪldɪŋ] Gebäude II
built [bɪlt] *siehe* **build**
bulletin board ['bʊlətɪn bɔ:d] schwarzes Brett, Anschlagtafel IV
bully ['bʊli] einschüchtern, tyrannisieren II
bully ['bʊli] (Schul-)Tyrann III
bummer ['bʌmə]: **What a bummer!** *(infml)* So ein Mist! Wie schade! III
bump into sb./sth. [bʌmp] sich an etwas stoßen; gegen jn. stoßen V 4 (94)
bunk (bed) [bʌŋk] Etagenbett, Koje II
°**bunsen burner** [ˌbʌnsn 'bɜ:nə] Bunsenbrenner
burn [bɜ:n] brennen; verbrennen IV
bury ['beri] begraben, vergraben; beerdigen IV
bus [bʌs] Bus I • °**bus driver** Busfahrer/in
bush [bʊʃ] Busch, Strauch V 1 (6)
bus pass ['bʌs pɑ:s] Bus-Monatskarte III
bus stop ['bʌs stɒp] Bushaltestelle III
bush [bʊʃ]: **the bush** der Busch *(unkultiviertes, „wildes“ Land in Australien, Afrika)* V 1 (6)
business ['bɪznəs] Unternehmen; Geschäfte V 1 (8) • **do business (with)** Geschäfte machen (mit); Handel treiben (mit) V 1 (8) • °**get down to business** an die Arbeit gehen • **Mind your own business.** Das geht dich nichts an! / Kümmere dich um deine eigenen Angelegenheiten! II
°**businesswoman** ['bɪznəswʊmən], *pl* **businesswomen** Geschäftsfrau
busy ['bɪzi]
1. beschäftigt I
2. belebt, verkehrsreich; hektisch III
but [bət, bʌt]
1. aber I
2. sondern IV • **not only ... but also ...** nicht nur ... sondern auch ... IV
°**butt** [bʌt] *(infml)* Hinterteil
butter ['bʌtə] Butter IV
button ['bʌtn] Knopf III
buy [baɪ], **bought, bought** kaufen I
by [baɪ]
1. von I
2. an; (nahe) bei II
3. **by two degrees/ten per cent** um zwei Grad/zehn Prozent V 1 (9)
°4. neben
by asking indem du fragst V 2 (40) • **by car/bike/...** mit dem Auto/Rad/... II • **by far** bei weitem; mit Abstand V 4 (88) • **by the end of the song** (spätestens) bis zum Ende des Lieds III • **by the way** übrigens; nebenbei (bemerkt) III
Bye. [baɪ] Tschüs! I

C

cabin ['kæbɪn] Hütte III
café ['kæfeɪ] *(kleines)* Restaurant, Imbissstube, Café I
cafeteria [ˌkæfə'tɪəriə] Cafeteria, Selbstbedienungsrestaurant II
cage [keɪdʒ] Käfig I
cake [keɪk] Kuchen, Torte I
calendar ['kælɪndə] Kalender I
call [kɔ:l] rufen; anrufen; nennen I
be called heißen, genannt werden II • **call for help** um Hilfe rufen V 4 (96) • **call sb. names** jn. mit Schimpfwörtern hänseln, jm. Schimpfwörter nachrufen III
call [kɔ:l] Ruf, Schrei; Anruf II
give sb. a call jn. anrufen V 4 (83)
make a call ein Telefongespräch führen, telefonieren II
calm [kɑ:m] ruhig, still V 2 (35)
keep calm ruhig/still bleiben; Ruhe bewahren V 2 (35/191)
calm down [ˌkɑ:m 'daʊn] sich beruhigen II • **calm sb. down** jn. beruhigen II
came [keɪm] *siehe* **come**
camel ['kæml] Kamel II
camera ['kæmərə] Kamera, Fotoapparat I
camp [kæmp] zelten III
camp [kæmp] Camp, Lager IV
campground ['kæmpˌgraʊnd] *(AE)* Zeltplatz III
camping gear ['kæmpɪŋ ˌgɪə] Campingausrüstung IV
campsite ['kæmpsaɪt] Zeltplatz III
can [kæn] Dose V 1 (21)
can [kən, kæn]
1. können I
2. dürfen I
Can I help you? Kann ich Ihnen helfen? / Was kann ich für Sie tun? *(im Geschäft)* I
canal [kə'næl] Kanal III
cancel ['kænsəl] absagen V 2 (34)
cancer ['kænsə] Krebs *(Krankheit)* V 1 (9)
candidate ['kændɪdət] Kandidat/in; Bewerber/in V 2 (39)
candle ['kændl] Kerze IV
cannot [kæ'nɒt] kann nicht IV
canoe [kə'nu:] Kanu III
canoe [kə'nu:] paddeln, Kanu fahren III
canyon ['kænjən] Cañon IV
cap [kæp] Mütze, Kappe II
capital ['kæpɪtl] Hauptstadt III
capital letter [ˌkæpɪtl 'letə] Großbuchstabe III
captain ['kæptɪn] Kapitän/in III
caption ['kæpʃn] Bildunterschrift IV
car [kɑ:] Auto I
car park ['kɑ: pɑ:k] Parkplatz III
caravan ['kærəvæn] Wohnwagen II
card [kɑ:d] (Spiel-, Post-)Karte I
care (about) [keə] sich interessieren (für); sich kümmern (um); wichtig nehmen III • **I care about the environment.** Die Umwelt liegt mir am Herzen. III • **I don't care about money.** Geld ist mir egal. III • **Who cares?** Ist doch egal! / Na und? III
care [keə]: **take care of sth.** sich um etwas kümmern III
career [kə'rɪə] Karriere III
careful ['keəfl] vorsichtig I
caretaker ['keəteɪkə] Hausmeister/in II
carrot ['kærət] Möhre, Karotte I
carry ['kæri] tragen V 1 (6)
cart [kɑ:t] Wagen, Karren IV
cartoon [kɑ:'tu:n] Cartoon (Zeichentrickfilm; Bilderwitz) II
case [keɪs] Fall II
cashpoint ['kæʃpɔɪnt] Geldautomat V 2 (49)
casino [kə'si:nəʊ] (Spiel)kasino IV
castle ['kɑ:sl] Burg, Schloss II
cat [kæt] Katze I
catch [kætʃ], **caught, caught** fangen; erwischen II • **be catching** ansteckend sein V 1 (6)
cathedral [kə'θi:drəl] Kathedrale, Dom III
°**Catholic** [kæθlɪk] katholisch
cattle *(pl)* ['kætl] Vieh, Rinder IV
caught [kɔ:t] *siehe* **catch**
cause [kɔ:z] verursachen IV
cause [kɔ:z] Ursache IV
cave [keɪv] Höhle V 1 (16)

CD [ˌsiːˈdiː] CD I • **CD player** CD-Spieler I
ceilidh [ˈkeɪli] *Musik- und Tanzveranstaltung, vor allem in Schottland und Irland* III
celebrate [ˈselɪbreɪt] feiern IV
celebration [ˌseləˈbreɪʃn] Feier IV
celebrity [səˈlebrəti] berühmte Persönlichkeit, Prominente(r) III
cello [ˈtʃeləʊ] Cello III
cellphone [ˈselfəʊn] *(AE)* Mobiltelefon, Handy III
°**Celts** *(pl)* [kelts] die Kelten
cent (c) [sent] Cent I
cent: per cent [pəˈsent] Prozent III
centimetre (cm) [ˈsentɪmiːtə] Zentimeter III
central [ˈsentrəl] Zentral-, Mittel- III
centre [ˈsentə] Zentrum, Mitte I
century [ˈsentʃəri] Jahrhundert II
certificate [səˈtɪfɪkət] Urkunde, Zeugnis, Bescheinigung V 2 (39)
chair [tʃeə] Stuhl I
challenge sb. (to sth.) [ˈtʃælɪndʒ] jn. (zu etwas) herausfordern; für jn. eine Herausforderung sein V 3 (52)
challenge [ˈtʃælɪndʒ] Herausforderung V 3 (66/205)
► S.205 Verbs & nouns with the same form
champion [ˈtʃæmpiən] Meister/in, Champion I
championship [ˈtʃæmpiənʃɪp] Meisterschaft III
chance [tʃɑːns] Chance II
► S.194 German „Möglichkeit"
change [tʃeɪndʒ]
1. Wechselgeld I
2. (Ver-)Änderung, Wechsel IV
change [tʃeɪndʒ]
1. umsteigen III
2. (sich) (ver-)ändern IV
3. wechseln IV
4. umtauschen IV
5. umwandeln IV
6. **change stations** *(Radio)* umschalten IV
7. sich umziehen IV
chapel [ˈtʃæpl] Kapelle, Kirche *(für manche protestantische Gemeinden)* V 3 (50/198)
► S.198 Religions
°**chapter** [ˈtʃæptə] Kapitel
character [ˈkærəktə] Charakter, Persönlichkeit IV
characteristic [ˌkærəktəˈrɪstɪk] (charakteristisches) Merkmal IV
charge (at sb.) [tʃɑːdʒ] stürmen; (jn.) angreifen IV
charge [tʃɑːdʒ]**: be in charge of sth./sb.** für etwas/jn. verantwortlich sein; etwas leiten V 2 (34)
charity [ˈtʃærəti] Wohlfahrtsorganisation II
chase sb. [tʃeɪs] jn. jagen; jm. hinterherjagen IV
chat (-tt-) [tʃæt] chatten, plaudern II
chat [tʃæt] Chat, Unterhaltung II
chat room [ˈtʃæt ruːm] Chatroom III
chat show Talkshow II
cheap [tʃiːp] billig, preiswert II
cheat [tʃiːt]**: cheat sb.** jn. betrügen V 4 (80) • **cheat on sb.** jn. betrügen, jm. untreu sein V 4 (80)
check [tʃek] (über)prüfen, kontrollieren I
checklist [ˈtʃeklɪst] Checkliste III
check out (of a hotel) [ˌtʃek‿ˈaʊt] (aus einem Hotel) auschecken, abreisen V 1 (18)
checkpoint [ˈtʃekpɔɪnt] Kontrollpunkt *(zur Selbstüberprüfung)* I
°**cheeky** [ˈtʃiːki] *(BE, infml)* frech
cheer [tʃɪə] jubeln II
cheerleader [ˈtʃɪəliːdə] Cheerleader *(Stimmungsanheizer/in bei Sportereignissen)* IV
cheese [tʃiːz] Käse I
chemist [ˈkemɪst] Drogerie, Apotheke II • **at the chemist's** beim Apotheker III
°**cheque (for)** [tʃek] Scheck (über)
chicken [ˈtʃɪkɪn] Huhn; (Brat-)Hähnchen I
chief [tʃiːf] Häuptling IV
child [tʃaɪld], *pl* **children** [ˈtʃɪldrən] Kind I • **children's home** Kinderheim V 1 (19)
childproof [ˈtʃaɪldpruːf] kindersicher V 1 (17/187)
chill out [ˌtʃɪl‿ˈaʊt] *(infml)* sich entspannen, relaxen III
Chinese [tʃaɪˈniːz] chinesisch IV
chips *(pl)* [tʃɪps]
1. *(BE)* Pommes frites I
2. *(AE)* Chips IV
chocolate [ˈtʃɒklət] Schokolade I
°**choice** [tʃɔɪs] (Aus-)Wahl
choir [ˈkwaɪə] Chor I
choose [tʃuːz]**, chose, chosen** (sich) aussuchen, (aus)wählen I
°**chorus** [ˈkɔːrəs] Refrain
chose [tʃəʊz] *siehe* **choose**
chosen [ˈtʃəʊzn] *siehe* **choose**
Christ [kraɪst] Christus IV
Christian [ˈkrɪstʃən] Christ/in, christlich V 3 (50/198)
Christianity [ˌkrɪstiˈænəti] Christentum V 3 (50/198)
► S.198 Religions
Christmas [ˈkrɪsməs] Weihnachten V 2 (34) • **at Christmas** an/zu Weihnachten V 2 (34/190) • **Christmas tree** Christ-, Weihnachtsbaum V 2 (34/190) • **for Christmas** zu Weihnachten V 2 (34/190)
chuck sb. [tʃʌk] *(infml)* mit jm. Schluss machen V 4 (80)
church [tʃɜːtʃ] Kirche I • **go to church** in die Kirche gehen III
► S.198 Religions
cinema [ˈsɪnəmə] Kino II • **go to the cinema** ins Kino gehen II
circle [ˈsɜːkl] Kreis III • °**double circle** Doppelkreis
circus [ˈsɜːkəs] (runder) Platz III
citizen [ˈsɪtɪzən] (Staats)Bürger/in V 3 (53)
citizenship [ˈsɪtɪzənʃɪp] Staatsbürgerschaft V 3 (53)
city [ˈsɪti] Stadt, Großstadt I
city centre [ˌsɪti ˈsentə] Stadtzentrum, Innenstadt I • **city council** (Stadt-)Rat V 3 (60)
civilization [ˌsɪvəlaɪˈzeɪʃn] Zivilisation V 2 (34)
civil rights *(pl)* [ˌsɪvl ˈraɪts] Bürgerrechte IV
civil war [ˌsɪvl ˈwɔː] Bürgerkrieg IV
°**claim sth. (for sb.)** [kleɪm] etwas in Besitz nehmen (für jn.)
clap (-pp-) [klæp] (Beifall) klatschen IV
clarification [ˌklærəfɪˈkeɪʃn] Klarstellung, Klärung V 4 (86)
clarinet [ˌklærɪˈnet] Klarinette III
class [klɑːs]
1. (Schul-)Klasse I • **class teacher** Klassenlehrer/in I
► S.196 Collective nouns
2. Unterricht; Kurs IV
classic [ˈklæsɪk] klassisch III
classical [ˈklæsɪkl] klassisch III
classmate [ˈklɑːsmeɪt] Klassenkamerad/in, Mitschüler/in I
classroom [ˈklɑːsruːm; ˈklɑːsrʊm] Klassenzimmer I
clause [klɔːz] (Teil-, Glied-)Satz III
clean [kliːn] sauber II
clean [kliːn] sauber machen, putzen I • **clean one's teeth** sich die Zähne putzen III
cleaner [ˈkliːnə] Putzfrau, -mann II
°**clean-up** [ˈkliːnʌp] Säuberung
clear [klɪə] klar, deutlich I
°**clerk** *(BE)* [klɑːk]**,** *(AE)* [klɜːk] Schriftführer/in; Protokollant/in
clever [ˈklevə] klug, schlau I
cleverness [ˈklevənəs] Klugheit, Schlauheit IV
click on sth. [klɪk] etwas anklicken II
°**client** [ˈklaɪənt] Kunde, Kundin
cliff [klɪf] Klippe III
climate [ˈklaɪmət] Klima V 1 (9)

climax ['klaɪmæks] Höhepunkt V 4 (97)
climb [klaɪm] klettern; hinaufklettern (auf) I • **Climb a tree.** Klettere auf einen Baum. I
clinic ['klɪnɪk] Klinik II
clip [klɪp] (Film-)Ausschnitt V 3 (65)
clock [klɒk] (Wand-, Stand-, Turm-) Uhr I
°**clockwise** ['klɒkwaɪz] im Uhrzeigersinn
close (to) [kləʊs]
1. nahe (bei, an) III
2. eng V 1 (8)
That was close. Das war knapp. II
close [kləʊz] schließen, zumachen I
closely ['kləʊsli]: **look closely at sth.** etw. genau anschauen III
closed [kləʊzd] geschlossen II
clothes *(pl)* [kləʊðz, kləʊz] Kleider, Kleidungsstücke I
clothing ['kləʊðɪŋ] Kleidung IV
piece of clothing Kleidungsstück IV
cloud [klaʊd] Wolke II • °**with one's head in the clouds** mit seinen Gedanken ganz woanders
cloudy ['klaʊdi] bewölkt II
clown [klaʊn] Clown/in I
club [klʌb] Klub; Verein I
► S.196 Collective nouns
coach [kəʊtʃ] Trainer/in III • **life coach** Lebensberater/in V 2 (44)
coast [kəʊst] Küste II
coffee ['kɒfi] Kaffee IV • **coffee to go** Kaffee zum Mitnehmen IV
coin [kɔɪn] Münze V 4 (88)
cola ['kəʊlə] Cola I
cold [kəʊld] kalt I • **be cold** frieren I
cold [kəʊld] Erkältung II • **have a cold** erkältet sein, eine Erkältung haben II
collapse [kə'læps] zusammenbrechen; einstürzen IV
collect [kə'lekt] sammeln I
collection [kə'lekʃn] Sammlung IV
collector [kə'lektə] Sammler/in II
college ['kɒlɪdʒ] Hochschule, Fachschule III
collocation [ˌkɒlə'keɪʃn] Kollokation *(Wörter, die oft zusammen vorkommen)* IV
colonist ['kɒlənɪst] Kolonist/in; Siedler/in IV
colony ['kɒləni] Kolonie IV
colour ['kʌlə] Farbe I • **What colour is ...?** Welche Farbe hat ...? I
colourful ['kʌləfl] bunt IV
column ['kɒləm] Säule III

combine [kəm'baɪn] verbinden; vermischen V 3 (66)
come [kʌm], **came, come** kommen I • °**come across sth.** etwas finden
°**come alive** lebendig werden
come from stammen von/aus IV
come home nach Hause kommen I • **come in** hereinkommen I
Come on. 1. Na los, komm. II; **2.** Ach komm! / Na hör mal! II
come together zusammenkommen IV • **come true** wahr werden II • **come up with sth.** sich etwas ausdenken, sich etwas einfallen lassen IV
comedy ['kɒmədi] Comedyshow, Komödie II
comfort ['kʌmfət] trösten IV
comfortable ['kʌmftəbl] bequem I
comic ['kɒmɪk] Comic-Heft I
comment ['kɒment] Kommentar IV
°**comment on sth.** ['kɒment] zu etwas einen Kommentar abgeben
commit (-tt-) [kə'mɪt]: **commit a crime** ein Verbrechen begehen IV
committee [kə'mɪti] Ausschuss, Komitee V 2 (42) • °**Head of the Committee** Ausschussvorsitzende(r)
► S.196 Collective nouns
Commonwealth ['kɒmənwelθ]: **the Commonwealth** *Gemeinschaft der Länder des ehemaligen Britischen Weltreichs* III
community [kə'mju:nəti] Gemeinschaft, Gemeinde V 2 (40) • **community hall** Gemeinschaftshalle, -saal / Gemeindehalle, -saal III
community service gemeinnützige Arbeit V 4 (89)
company ['kʌmpəni] Firma, Gesellschaft III
compare [kəm'peə] vergleichen II
comparison [kəm'pærɪsn] Steigerung; Vergleich II
competition [ˌkɒmpə'tɪʃn] Wettbewerb III
complain (to sb. about sth./sb.) [kəm'pleɪn] sich (bei jm. über etwas/jn.) beklagen, beschweren V 3 (52)
complete [kəm'pli:t] komplett, vollständig V 1 (6)
complete [kəm'pli:t] vervollständigen; abschließen, beenden V 1 (6)
computer [kəm'pju:tə] Computer I
°**computer geek** [gi:k] *(bes. AE, infml)* Computerfreak • **computer science** Computerwissenschaft, Informatik III
°**con** [kɒn]: **pros and cons** *(pl)* Vor- und Nachteile

concentrate (on sth.) ['kɒnsəntreɪt] sich (auf etwas) konzentrieren V 3 (52)
concern [kən'sɜ:n]: **To whom it may concern** *(bes. AE)* Sehr geehrte Damen und Herren IV
concert ['kɒnsət] Konzert II
conclude (sth. from sth.) [kən'klu:d] (etwas aus etwas) schließen V 1 (10)
conclusion [kən'klu:ʒn] Schluss(folgerung) V 1 (10) • **draw a conclusion** einen Schluss ziehen V 1 (10/185)
confident ['kɒnfɪdənt] selbstbewusst, (selbst)sicher V 2 (35)
confirm [kən'fɜ:m] bestätigen V 2 (37)
confuse [kən'fju:z] verwirren IV
confusion [kən'fju:ʒn] Verwirrung IV
Congratulations! [kənˌgrætʃu'leɪʃnz] Herzlichen Glückwunsch! III
Congress ['kɒŋgres] Kongress *(Parlament der USA)* V 3 (53)
connect A with/to B [kə'nekt] A mit B verbinden V 1 (10)
connection [kə'nekʃn] Verbindung V 1 (10)
°**conquer** ['kɒŋkə] erobern
°**Conqueror** ['kɒŋkərə] Eroberer/in
conscious ['kɒnʃəs] bei Bewusstsein V 1 (23) • **conscious of sth.** sich einer Sache bewusst V 1 (23)
consequence ['kɒnsɪkwəns] Folge, Konsequenz IV
°**consider** [kən'sɪdə] nachdenken über, berücksichtigen, in Betracht ziehen
console ['kɒnsəʊl]: **game console** Spielkonsole V 2 (34)
constitution [ˌkɒnstɪ'tju:ʃn] Verfassung V 3 (53)
constitutional monarchy [ˌkɒnstɪ'tju:ʃənl] konstitutionelle Monarchie V 3 (53/200)
► S.200 Different forms of government
contact sb. ['kɒntækt] sich mit jm. in Verbindung setzen; mit jm. Kontakt aufnehmen III
contact ['kɒntækt] Kontakt IV
contact details Kontaktdaten V 2 (39)
context ['kɒntekst] Zusammenhang, Kontext IV
continent ['kɒntɪnənt] Kontinent IV
continue [kən'tɪnju:] weitermachen (mit); weiterreden; weitergehen II
contrast (to/with sth., between two things) ['kɒntrɑ:st] Gegensatz (zu) V 1 (10)
contrast sth. and/with sth. [kən'trɑ:st] A mit B kontrastieren *(die Unterschiede aufzeigen)* V 1 (10)

control [kən'trəʊl]: **under control** unter Kontrolle IV • **°take control** die Kontrolle übernehmen
conversation [ˌkɒnvə'seɪʃn] Gespräch, Unterhaltung II
convict ['kɒnvɪkt] Sträfling, Strafgefangene(r) V 1 (8)
cook [kʊk] kochen, zubereiten II
cook [kʊk] Koch, Köchin II
cooker ['kʊkə] Herd I
cookie ['kʊki] *(AE)* Keks IV
cool [ku:l]
1. kühl I
2. cool I
copy ['kɒpi] kopieren II
copy ['kɒpi] Kopie, Abschrift IV
°coral ['kɒrəl] Koralle
corner ['kɔ:nə] Ecke I • **on the corner of Sand Street and London Road** Sand Street, Ecke London Road II • **°from all corners of the empire** aus dem ganzen Weltreich
corn [kɔ:n] *(AE, no pl)* Mais IV
cornflakes ['kɔ:nfleɪks] Cornflakes I
correct [kə'rekt] korrigieren, verbessern II
correct [kə'rekt] richtig, korrekt II
correction [kə'rekʃn] Korrektur, Berichtigung IV
°correspond with sth. [ˌkɒrə'spɒnd] mit etwas übereinstimmen
cost [kɒst], **cost, cost** kosten III
cost [kɒst] Preis, Kosten IV
costume ['kɒstju:m] Kostüm, Verkleidung I
cotton ['kɒtn] Baumwolle IV
°couch potato ['kaʊtʃ pəˌteɪtəʊ] Dauerglotzer/in
could [kəd, kʊd]: **he could ...** er konnte ... II
could [kəd, kʊd]: **we could ...** wir könnten ... II
°could [kəd, kʊd]: **°it could have cut ...** es hätte ... schneiden können
council ['kaʊnsəl]: **(city) council** (Stadt-)Rat V 3 (60)
°Councilman ['kaʊnsəlmən] Mitglied des Stadtrats
count [kaʊnt] zählen II
countdown ['kaʊntdaʊn] Countdown III
counter ['kaʊntə]
1. Spielstein II
2. Theke, Ladentisch IV
country ['kʌntri] Land *(auch als Gegensatz zur Stadt)* II • **in the country** auf dem Land II
couple ['kʌpl]: **a couple of** ein paar/Paar III
course [kɔ:s] Kurs, Lehrgang III
course: of course [əv 'kɔ:s] natürlich, selbstverständlich I
court [kɔ:t]
1. Platz, Court III
2. Gericht(shof) IV
cousin ['kʌzn] Cousin, Cousine I
cover ['kʌvə]
1. zudecken, bedecken IV
°2. sich erstrecken über
cover ['kʌvə] (CD-)Hülle I
°covering letter ['kʌvərɪŋ] Begleitbrief
cow [kaʊ] Kuh II
°coz [kəz] = **because**
crash [kræʃ] abstürzen III • **crash in(to) sth.** gegen etwas fahren/laufen V 1 (20)
crazy ['kreɪzi] verrückt III
cream [kri:m] Sahne; Creme IV
cream cheese [ˌkri:m 'tʃi:z] Frischkäse IV
create [kri'eɪt] (er)schaffen, kreieren V 1 (8)
creative [kri'eɪtɪv] kreativ, einfallsreich IV
crew [kru:] Crew, (Schiffs-)Mannschaft III
cricket ['krɪkɪt] Kricket III
crime [kraɪm] Verbrechen; Kriminalität IV • **commit a crime** ein Verbrechen begehen IV • **crime film** Krimi IV • **crime story** Krimi IV
crisis ['kraɪsɪs] Krise IV
crisps *(pl)* [krɪsps] Kartoffelchips I
critic ['krɪtɪk] Kritiker/in IV
crocodile ['krɒkədaɪl] Krokodil II
cross [krɒs] überqueren; (sich) kreuzen II
crosswalk ['krɒswɔ:k] *(AE)* Fußgängerüberweg IV
crowd [kraʊd] (Menschen-)Menge III
crowded ['kraʊdɪd] voller Menschen, überfüllt III
°crown [kraʊn] Krone • **the jewel in the crown** das Prunkstück
°crown-of-thorns starfish [kraʊn‿əv ˌθɔ:nz 'stɑ:fɪʃ] Dornenkronenseestern
cruel ['kru:əl] grausam IV
cry [kraɪ]
1. schreien I • **cry in pain** vor Schmerzen schreien I
2. weinen III
°crystal-clear [ˌkrɪstəl 'klɪə] kristallklar
culture ['kʌltʃə] Kultur V 1 (16)
cup [kʌp]
1. Tasse II • **a cup of tea** eine Tasse Tee II
2. Pokal III
cupboard ['kʌbəd] Schrank I
°curfew ['kɜ:fju:] Ausgangssperre, Ausgehverbot
curriculum vitae [kəˌrɪkjələm 'vi:taɪ] *(BE)* Lebenslauf V 2 (38)
cut (-tt-) [kʌt], **cut, cut** schneiden II
cut sth. off etwas abschneiden, abtrennen III • **cut sth. out** ausschneiden III • **cut the grass** Rasen mähen IV
cut [kʌt] Schnitt IV
CV [ˌsi: 'vi:] *(BE)* Lebenslauf V 2 (38)
cycle ['saɪkl] (mit dem) Rad fahren II
cycle path ['saɪkl pɑ:θ] Radweg II

D

dad [dæd] Papa, Vati; Vater I
daily ['deɪli] täglich IV
damage ['dæmɪdʒ] beschädigen, schaden V 3 (66)
damage ['dæmɪdʒ] Beschädigung, Schaden V 3 (66/205)
► S.205 Verbs & nouns with the same form
damn [dæm] verdammt IV
dance [dɑ:ns] tanzen I
dance [dɑ:ns] Tanz I • **dance floor** Tanzfläche III
dancer ['dɑ:nsə] Tänzer/in II
dancing ['dɑ:nsɪŋ] Tanzen I
dancing lessons Tanzstunden, Tanzunterricht I
danger (to) ['deɪndʒə] Gefahr (für) I
°stop a danger einer Gefahr Einhalt gebieten
dangerous ['deɪndʒərəs] gefährlich II
dark [dɑ:k]
1. dunkel I
2. dunkelhaarig V 1 (9)
dark [dɑ:k]: **after dark** nach Einbruch der Dunkelheit IV
darling ['dɑ:lɪŋ] Liebling, Schatz V 4 (94)
date [deɪt]
1. Datum I • **date of birth** Geburtsdatum IV • **to date** bis heute, bis dato V 2 (38)
2. Verabredung, Date V 4 (80) • **to go on a date with sb.** mit jm. ausgehen V 4 (80/206)
date [deɪt] *(bes. AE)* mit jm. (aus)gehen; sich (regelmäßig) mit jm. treffen III
daughter ['dɔ:tə] Tochter I
°dawn [dɔ:n] Sonnenaufgang
day [deɪ] Tag I • **one day** eines Tages I • **days of the week** Wochentage I • **the day before yesterday** vorgestern II • **that day** an jenem Tag III
dead [ded] tot I
deaf [def] taub, gehörlos III

deal with sb./sth. [di:l], **dealt, dealt** sich mit jm./etwas beschäftigen; handeln von etwas IV • °**deal drugs** mit Drogen handeln
deal [di:l] Angebot IV • **make a deal** ein Abkommen/eine Abmachung treffen III • **It's a deal!** Abgemacht! III
dealt [delt] *siehe* **deal**
dear [dɪə] Schatz, Liebling I • **Oh dear!** Oje! II
dear [dɪə]: **Dear Jay ...** Lieber Jay, ... I **Dear Sir or Madam ...** Sehr geehrte Damen und Herren IV
death [deθ] Tod IV • **death rate** Sterberate V 1 (9/183) • **death sentence** Todesstrafe IV • **fall to one's death** zu Tode stürzen IV
debate [dɪ'beɪt] Debatte V 1 (6)
debate (sth.) [dɪ'beɪt] (über etwas) debattieren; hin und her überlegen V 3 (53)
debts *(pl)* [dets] Schulden IV
December [dɪ'sembə] Dezember I
decide (on sth.) [dɪ'saɪd] sich entscheiden (für etwas), (etwas) beschließen II
°**decision** [dɪ'sɪʒn] Entscheidung
declaration [ˌdeklə'reɪʃn] Erklärung V 3 (50)
deep [di:p] tief IV
deer, *pl* **deer** [dɪə] Reh, Hirsch II
°**defeat** [dɪ'fi:t] besiegen
defence [dɪ'fens] Verteidigung III
defend sb./sth. (against sb./sth.) [dɪ'fend] jn./etwas (gegen jn./etwas) verteidigen V 3 (56)
definite ['defɪnət] fest, bestimmt; endgültig, eindeutig V 2 (47)
degree [dɪ'gri:] Grad II
delay [dɪ'leɪ] aufhalten IV
delay [dɪ'leɪ] Verspätung IV
deli ['deli] Deli *(Lebensmittelgeschäft mit Fastfoodrestaurant)* IV
delicious [dɪ'lɪʃəs] köstlich, lecker II
deliver [dɪ'lɪvə] (aus)liefern, austragen IV
democracy [dɪ'mɒkrəsi] Demokratie; demokratischer Staat V 3 (53)
► S.200 Different forms of government
democrat ['deməkræt] Demokrat/in V 3 (53)
democratic [ˌdemə'krætɪk] demokratisch V 3 (53)
demonstrate ['demənstreɪt] demonstrieren V 3 (64)
°**demonstration** [ˌdemən'streɪʃn] Demonstration, Marsch
dentist ['dentɪst] Zahnarzt, -ärztin IV
°**department** [dɪ'pɑ:tmənt] Abteilung
department store [dɪ'pɑ:tmənt stɔ:] Kaufhaus II
departure [dɪ'pɑ:tʃə] Abfahrt; Abflug IV
depend on sth./sb. [dɪ'pend] **1.** sich auf etwas/jn verlassen IV **2.** von etwas abhängen V 3 (63)
dependable [dɪ'pendəbl] zuverlässig IV
describe sth. (to sb.) [dɪ'skraɪb] (jm.) etwas beschreiben II
description [dɪ'skrɪpʃn] Beschreibung II
desert ['dezət] Wüste IV
deserve [dɪ'zɜ:v] verdienen *(zu Recht bekommen)* V 2 (39)
design [dɪ'zaɪn] Muster, Entwurf; Design, Gestaltung V 2 (46) **design school** Kunsthochschule V 2 (47)
design [dɪ'zaɪn] entwickeln, entwerfen I
► S.205 Verbs & nouns with the same form
desk [desk] Schreibtisch I
despite [dɪ'spaɪt] trotz V 1 (8)
destroy [dɪ'strɔɪ] zerstören III
detail ['di:teɪl] Detail, Einzelheit III **contact details** Kontaktdaten V 2 (39)
detailed ['di:teɪld] ausführlich, detailliert V 1 (10)
detective [dɪ'tektɪv] Detektiv/in I
determination [dɪˌtɜ:mɪ'neɪʃn] Entschlossenheit V 2 (47)
determined [dɪ'tɜ:mɪnd] (fest) entschlossen V 2 (47)
develop (from ... into ...) [dɪ'veləp] entwickeln; sich (aus ... zu ...) entwickeln V 1 (8)
development [dɪ'veləpmənt] Entwicklung V 3 (60)
diagonal [daɪ'ægənəl] diagonal, schräg IV
dial (-ll-) ['daɪəl] wählen *(Telefonnummer)* II
dialogue ['daɪəlɒg] Dialog V 3 (58)
diamond ['daɪəmənd] Diamant V 4 (94)
diary ['daɪəri] Tagebuch; Terminkalender I
dice, *pl* **dice** [daɪs] Würfel II **throw the dice** würfeln II
dictator [dɪk'teɪtə] Diktator/in V 3 (53/201)
dictatorship [ˌdɪk'teɪtəʃɪp] Diktatur V 3 (53/201)
► S.200 Different forms of government
dictionary ['dɪkʃənri] Wörterbuch, *(alphabetisches)* Wörterverzeichnis I
did [dɪd] *siehe* **do** • **Did you go?** Bist du gegangen? / Gingst du? I
we didn't go ['dɪdnt] wir sind nicht gegangen/wir gingen nicht I
die (of) *(-ing form:* **dying***)* [daɪ] sterben (an) II
difference ['dɪfrəns] Unterschied III
different (from) ['dɪfrənt] verschieden, unterschiedlich; anders (als) I
difficult ['dɪfɪkəlt] schwierig, schwer I
dining room ['daɪnɪŋ ru:m; 'daɪnɪŋ rʊm] Esszimmer I
dinner ['dɪnə] Abendessen, Abendbrot I • **have dinner** Abendbrot essen I
dinosaur ['daɪnəsɔ:] Dinosaurier IV
direct [də'rekt] direkt V 2 (37)
direct [də'rekt] Regie führen III
direct speech [də'rekt] direkte Rede III
directions *(pl)* [də'rekʃnz] Wegbeschreibung(en) II
director [də'rektə] Regisseur/in III
dirt [dɜ:t] Schmutz, Dreck V 1 (12)
dirt bike ['dɜ:t baɪk] Geländemotorrad V 1 (12)
dirt road ['dɜ:t rəʊd] unbefestigte Straße V 1 (6)
dirty ['dɜ:ti] schmutzig II
disabled [dɪs'eɪbld] (körper)behindert III
disadvantage [ˌdɪsəd'vɑ:ntɪdʒ] Nachteil IV
disagree (with) [ˌdɪsə'gri:] anderer Meinung sein (als), nicht übereinstimmen (mit) II
disagreement [ˌdɪsə'gri:mənt] Uneinigkeit, Streit V 3 (52)
disappear [ˌdɪsə'pɪə] verschwinden II
disappoint sb. [ˌdɪsə'pɔɪnt] jn. enttäuschen IV
disappointed (with/in sb., with/about sth.) [ˌdɪsə'pɔɪntɪd] enttäuscht (von jm./etwas) IV
discipline ['dɪsəplɪn] Disziplin V 4 (85)
disc jockey ['dɪsk dʒɒki] Diskjockey III
disco ['dɪskəʊ] Disko I
discover [dɪ'skʌvə] entdecken; herausfinden II
discriminate against sb. [dɪ'skrɪmɪneɪt] jn. diskriminieren, jn. benachteiligen IV
discrimination (against) [dɪˌskrɪmɪ'neɪʃn] Diskriminierung (von), Benachteiligung (von) IV **age discrimination** Diskriminierung aufgrund des Alters V 3 (63) °**race discrimination** Diskriminierung aufgrund der Rasse
discussion [dɪ'skʌʃn] Diskussion II

disease [dɪ'zi:z] *(ansteckende)* Krankheit IV
dish [dɪʃ] Gericht *(Speise)* III
dishes *(pl)* ['dɪʃɪz] Geschirr I • **do the dishes** das Geschirr abwaschen I
dishwasher ['dɪʃwɒʃə] Geschirrspülmaschine I
display [dɪs'pleɪ] Display IV • **be on display** ausgestellt sein IV
distance ['dɪstəns] Entfernung IV
district ['dɪstrɪkt] Gegend, Bezirk V 3 (52)
diver ['daɪvə] Taucher/in V 4 (88)
divide (into) [dɪ'vaɪd] (sich) teilen (in), (sich) aufteilen (in) II
divorced [dɪ'vɔ:st] geschieden I
DJ ['di:dʒeɪ] Diskjockey III
DJ ['di:dʒeɪ] (Musik/CDs/Platten) auflegen *(in der Disko)* III
do [du:], **did, done** tun, machen I **do a gig** einen Auftritt haben, ein Konzert geben III • **do a good job** gute Arbeit leisten II • **do an exercise** eine Übung machen II **do a project** ein Projekt machen, durchführen II • **do sb. a favour** jm. einen Gefallen tun IV • **do sport** Sport treiben I • **do sth. wrong** etwas Verbotenes tun V 4 (87) • **do the dishes** das Geschirr abwaschen I • **How am I doing?** Wie komme ich voran? (Wie sind meine Fortschritte?) III **learning by doing** Lernen durch Handeln/Tun V 2 (40/195)
doctor ['dɒktə] Arzt/Ärztin, Doktor I • **at/to the doctor's** beim/zum Arzt III
documentary [ˌdɒkju'mentri] Dokumentarfilm II
dog [dɒg] Hund I • **walk the dog** den Hund ausführen V 4 (92)
doll [dɒl] Puppe IV
dollar ($) ['dɒlə] Dollar IV
dolphin ['dɒlfɪn] Delfin V 1 (9)
°**domain** [də'meɪn] Domain, Domäne
donate [dəʊ'neɪt] spenden, schenken V 4 (88)
done [dʌn] *siehe* **do**
don't [dəʊnt]**: Don't listen to Dan.** Hör/Hört nicht auf Dan. I • **I don't like ...** Ich mag ... nicht. / Ich mag kein(e) ... I
door [dɔ:] Tür I
doorbell ['dɔ:bel] Türklingel I
dossier ['dɒsieɪ] Mappe, Dossier *(des Sprachenportfolios)* I
double ['dʌbl] zweimal, doppelt, Doppel- I • °**double circle** Doppelkreis
double bass [ˌdʌbl 'beɪs] Kontrabass III
dough [dəʊ] Teig IV
down [daʊn] hinunter, herunter, nach unten I • **down there** (nach) dort unten II
download [ˌdaʊn'ləʊd] runterladen, downloaden II
downstairs [ˌdaʊn'steəz] unten; nach unten I
downtown ['daʊntaʊn] Stadtzentrum IV • **downtown bus** *(AE)* Bus in Richtung Stadtzentrum IV
°**Down Under** [ˌdaʊn'ʌndə] *umgangssprachliche Bezeichnung für Australien*
Dr., Dr ['dɒktə] Dr. IV
draft [drɑ:ft] Entwurf IV
dragon ['drægən] Drache III
drama ['drɑ:mə]
1. Schauspiel, darstellende Kunst I
2. Fernsehspiel; Drama IV
drank [dræŋk] *siehe* **drink**
draw [drɔ:], **drew, drawn** zeichnen III
draw a conclusion [drɔ:] einen Schluss ziehen V 1 (10/185)
draw [drɔ:] Unentschieden III
drawing ['drɔ:ɪŋ] Zeichnung III
drawn [drɔ:n] *siehe* **draw**
dream [dri:m] Traum I • **dream house** Traumhaus I
dream (of, about) [dri:m] träumen (von) III • **dream on** weiterträumen III • °**the Dreaming** die Traumzeit
dress [dres] sich kleiden, sich anziehen IV
dress [dres] Kleid I
dressed [drest]**: get dressed** sich anziehen I
drew [dru:] *siehe* **draw**
°**drill** [drɪl] Waffendrill
drink [drɪŋk] Getränk I
drink [drɪŋk], **drank, drunk** trinken I
drive [draɪv], **drove, driven** *(ein Auto / mit dem Auto)* fahren II **driving instructor** Fahrlehrer/in V 1 (6/182)
drive [draɪv] (Auto)fahrt IV
driven ['drɪvn] *siehe* **drive**
driver ['draɪvə] Fahrer/in II
driving licence ['draɪvɪŋ ˌlaɪsəns] Führerschein, Fahrerlaubnis V 2 (39)
drop (-pp-) [drɒp]
1. fallen lassen I
2. fallen I
drop sb. off jn. absetzen (aussteigen lassen) IV
drove [drəʊv] *siehe* **drive**
drown [draʊn] ertrinken IV
drum [drʌm] Trommel; Schlagzeug III • **drumstick** Trommelstock III **play the drums** Schlagzeug spielen III
drunk *siehe* **drink**
drunk [drʌŋk] betrunken IV
dry [draɪ] trocken III
°**Dunno.** [də'nəʊ] *(infml)* = **I don't know.**
during *(prep)* ['djʊərɪŋ] während III
dust [dʌst] Staub IV
dustbin ['dʌstbɪn] Mülltonne II
DVD [ˌdi: vi: 'di:] DVD I

E

each [i:tʃ] jeder, jede, jedes (einzelne) I • **each other** einander, sich (gegenseitig) III
eagle ['i:gl] Adler V 4 (85)
ear [ɪə] Ohr I
earache ['ɪəreɪk] Ohrenschmerzen II
early ['ɜ:li] früh I
earn money [ɜ:n] Geld verdienen V 2 (46)
earring ['ɪərɪŋ] Ohrring I
earth [ɜ:θ] Erde V 1 (9)
earthquake ['ɜ:θkweɪk] Erdbeben IV
earthworm ['ɜ:θwɜ:m] Regenwurm IV
east [i:st] Osten; nach Osten; östlich II • **eastbound** ['i:stbaʊnd] Richtung Osten III • **eastern** ['i:stən] östlich, Ost- III
easy ['i:zi] leicht, einfach I • **easy-to-read** leicht zu lesende(r, s) V 2 (39)
easy-going [ˌi:zi 'gəʊɪŋ] gelassen, unbeschwert V 1 (25)
eat [i:t], **ate, eaten** essen I
eaten ['i:tn] *siehe* **eat**
economic [ˌi:kə'nɒmɪk] wirtschaftliche(r, s); Wirtschafts- V 3 (60)
edit ['edɪt] redigieren III
editor ['edɪtə] Redakteur/in III
education [ˌedʒu'keɪʃn] (Schul-, Aus-)Bildung; Erziehung IV
effect (on) [ɪ'fekt] Wirkung, Auswirkung (auf) IV
effective [ɪ'fektɪv] effektiv, wirksam, wirkungsvoll V 2 (39)
e-friend ['i:frend] Brieffreund/in *(im Internet)* I
egg [eg] Ei I
eightish ['eɪtɪʃ] ungefähr acht (Jahre/Uhr) IV
either ['aɪðə, 'i:ðə]**: either ... or ...** entweder ... oder ... V 1 (8) • **not (...) either** auch nicht II
► S.190 neither

°**elder** ['eldə] Stammesälteste(r)
elect sb. sth. [ɪ'lekt] jn. zu etwas wählen IV
election [ɪ'lekʃn] Wahl *(von Kandidaten bei einer Abstimmung)* IV
electric [ɪ'lektrɪk] elektrisch, Elektro- III
electrical engineer [ɪˌlektrɪkəl ˌendʒɪ'nɪə] Elektrotechniker/in V 2 (40)
electricity [ɪˌlek'trɪsəti] Strom, Elektrizität III • **static electricity** elektrische Aufladung IV
electronic [ɪˌlek'trɒnɪk] elektronisch III
elementary school [ˌelɪ'mentri sku:l] *(USA) Grundschule (für 6- bis 11-Jährige)* IV
elephant ['elɪfənt] Elefant I
elevator ['elɪveɪtə] *(AE)* Fahrstuhl, Aufzug II
°**eloquent** ['eləkwənt] eloquent, gewandt
else [els]**: anybody/anything else** sonst (noch) jemand/etwas **anywhere else** sonst (noch) irgendwo(hin) • **somebody else** jemand anders • **something else** etwas anderes • **somewhere else** woanders(hin) • **who/what/where/why/... else?** wer/was/wo/warum/... (sonst) noch? III
e-mail ['i:meɪl] E-Mail I
embarrassed [ɪm'bærəst] verlegen IV
embarrassing [ɪm'bærəsɪŋ] peinlich IV
emergency [ɪ'mɜ:dʒənsi] Notfall, Not- IV
°**empire** ['empaɪə] (Welt-)Reich
employer [ɪm'plɔɪə] Arbeitgeber/in V 2 (39)
empty ['empti] leer I
emu ['i:mju:] Emu V 1 (9)
enclose [ɪn'kləʊz] etwas *(einem Brief)* beilegen V 2 (41)
encourage [ɪn'kʌrɪdʒ] *(jn.)* ermutigen, ermuntern; *(etwas)* fördern V 3 (54)
encyclopedia [ɪnˌsaɪklə'pi:diə] Enzyklopädie, Lexikon II
end [end] Ende; Schluss I • **at the end (of)** am Ende (von) I • **achieve an end** ein Ziel erreichen IV
end [end]
1. zu Ende gehen IV]
2. (etwas) beenden V 4 (80) • **end a relationship** mit jm. Schluss machen V 4 (80/206)
ending ['endɪŋ] Ende, (Ab-)Schluss *(einer Geschichte, eines Films usw.)* III • **happy ending** Happyend II
endless ['endləs] endlos V 1 (6)
enemy ['enəmi] Feind/in II
energetic [ˌenə'dʒetɪk] dynamisch, tatkräftig, energisch V 2 (35)
engineer [ˌendʒɪ'nɪə] Ingenieur/in II
English ['ɪŋglɪʃ] Englisch; englisch I
enjoy [ɪn'dʒɔɪ] genießen I
enough [ɪ'nʌf] genug I
enroll for/in/on sth. [ɪn'rəʊl] sich (für etwas) anmelden IV
enter ['entə]
1. betreten IV • **enter a country** in ein Land einreisen IV
2. eingeben, eintragen II
entertain sb. [ˌentə'teɪn] jn. unterhalten IV
entertainment [ˌentə'teɪnmənt] Unterhaltung (Vergnügen) IV
entry ['entri]
1. Eintrag, Eintragung *(im Wörterbuch/Tagebuch)* III
2. Einsendung, Beitrag *(zu einem Wettbewerb)* III
environment [ɪn'vaɪrənmənt] Umwelt IV
environmental [ɪnˌvaɪrən'mentl] Umwelt- IV
equal ['i:kwəl] gleich IV
equality [i'kwɒləti] Gleichheit, Gleichberechtigung V 3 (66)
equalize ['i:kwəlaɪz] ausgleichen; das Ausgleichstor erzielen III
equator [ɪ'kweɪtə] Äquator V 1 (9)
equipment [ɪ'kwɪpmənt] Ausrüstung III
eraser [ɪ'reɪzə(r), ɪ'reɪsə(r)] *(AE)* Radiergummi IV
escape from sb./sth. [ɪ'skeɪp] vor jm./aus etwas fliehen; entkommen IV
°**especially** [ɪ'speʃli] besonders
essay (about, on) ['eseɪ] Aufsatz (über) I
etc. (et cetera) [et'setərə] usw. (und so weiter) IV
ethnic ['eθnɪk] ethnisch, Volks- IV
euro (€) ['jʊərəʊ] Euro I
even ['i:vn]
1. sogar II
2. (sogar) schon III
evening ['i:vnɪŋ] Abend I • **in the evening** abends, am Abend I **on Friday evening** freitagabends, am Freitagabend I
event [ɪ'vent] Ereignis II
ever ['evə] je, jemals III • **ever?** je? / jemals? / schon mal? II
every ['evri] jeder, jede, jedes I
everybody ['evribɒdi] jeder, alle II
everyday *(adj)* ['evrideɪ] Alltags-; alltäglich III
everyone ['evriwʌn] jeder; alle III
everything ['evriθɪŋ] alles I
everywhere ['evriweə] überall I
exact [ɪg'zækt] genau III
exam [ɪg'zæm] Prüfung V 2 (32)
example (of) [ɪg'zɑ:mpl] Beispiel (für) I • **for example** zum Beispiel I
excellent ['eksələnt] ausgezeichnet, hervorragend IV
except [ɪk'sept] außer, bis auf IV
exchange [ɪks'tʃeɪndʒ] (Schüler-)Austausch III
exchange [ɪks'tʃeɪndʒ] aus-, umtauschen III; *(Geld)* wechseln III
excited [ɪk'saɪtɪd] *(positiv)* aufgeregt, begeistert II
exciting [ɪk'saɪtɪŋ] aufregend, spannend II
Excuse me, ... [ɪk'skju:z mi:] Entschuldigung, ... / Entschuldigen Sie, ... I
execution [ˌeksɪ'kju:ʃn] Hinrichtung IV
exercise ['eksəsaɪz] Übung, Aufgabe I • **do an exercise** eine Übung machen II • **exercise book** Schulheft, Übungsheft I • **prewriting exercise** Übung vor dem Schreiben III
exhibition (on) [ˌeksɪ'bɪʃn] Ausstellung (über) IV
exist [ɪg'zɪst] existieren V 1 (16)
°**expand** [ɪk'spænd] erweitern
expect [ɪk'spekt] erwarten, annehmen, vermuten IV
expensive [ɪk'spensɪv] teuer I
experience [ɪk'spɪəriəns] Erfahrung; Erlebnis IV • **work experience** *(no pl)* Arbeits-, Praxiserfahrung(en) V 2 (38)
experienced [ɪk'spɪəriənst] erfahren IV
explain sth. to sb. [ɪk'spleɪn] jm. etwas erklären, erläutern II
explanation [ˌeksplə'neɪʃn] Erklärung II
explode [ɪk'spləʊd] explodieren, ausrasten V 3 (52)
explore [ɪk'splɔ:] erkunden, erforschen I
explorer [ɪk'splɔ:rə] Entdecker/in, Forscher/in II
explosion [ɪk'spləʊʒn] Explosion IV
express [ɪk'spres] äußern, zum Ausdruck bringen, ausdrücken V 2 (49)
expression [ɪk'spreʃn] Ausdruck III
extra ['ekstrə] zusätzlich I
°**extract** ['ekstrækt] Auszug *(aus einem Buch, Text, Film usw.)*
extracurricular activities *(kurz:* **extracurriculars***)* [ˌekstrəkə'rɪkjələz]

schulische Angebote außerhalb des regulären Unterrichts, oft als Arbeitsgemeinschaften IV
extraordinary [ɪk'strɔːdnri] außergewöhnlich IV
°**extreme** [ɪk'striːm] extrem
eye [aɪ] Auge I • **keep an eye on sth./ sb.** nach jm./etwas Ausschau halten IV • **She couldn't believe her eyes.** Sie traute ihren Augen kaum. III

F

face [feɪs] Gesicht I
fact [fækt] Tatsache, Fakt III
factory ['fæktri] Fabrik II
factual text ['fæktʃuːl] Sachtext IV
failure ['feɪljə] ungenügend IV
fair [feə]
1. fair, gerecht II
2. hell *(Haut; Haare)* V 1 (9)
°**fair dinkum** [ˌfeə 'dɪŋkəm] *(Australisches E)* echt, wahr(haftig)
faith (in sb./sth.) [feɪθ] Vertrauen (in jn./etwas); Glaube V 2 (47)
faithfully ['feɪθfəli]**: Yours faithfully** *(BE)* mit freundlichen Grüßen IV
fall [fɔːl]**, fell, fallen** fallen, stürzen; hinfallen II • **fall asleep** einschlafen V 1 (21) • **fall down** runterfallen; hinfallen II • **fall in love (with sb.)** sich verlieben (in jn.) IV • **fall off** herunterfallen (von) II • **fall to one's death** zu Tode stürzen IV
fallen ['fɔːlən] *siehe* **fall**
family ['fæməli] Familie I • **family man** Familienmensch IV • **family tree** (Familien-)Stammbaum I
► S.196 Collective nouns
famous (for) ['feɪməs] berühmt (für, wegen) II
fan [fæn] Fan, Anhänger/in III
fantastic [fæn'tæstɪk] fantastisch, toll I
fantasy ['fæntəsi] Fantasy *(Genre)* V 2 (34)
far [fɑː] weit (entfernt) I • **by far** bei weitem; mit Abstand V 4 (88)
far and wide weit und breit IV
so far bis jetzt, bis hierher III
faraway ['fɑːrəweɪ] abgelegen III
farm [fɑːm] Bauernhof, Farm II
farmer ['fɑːmə] Bauer/Bäuerin, Landwirt/in; (Fisch-)Züchter/in III
farmhouse ['fɑːmhaʊs] Bauernhaus III
fashion ['fæʃn] Mode II • **military-style fashion** Mode im Militärstil V 4 (85/207)
fast [fɑːst] schnell II
fat [fæt] dick IV
father ['fɑːðə] Vater I
fault [fɔːlt] Schuld, Fehler IV • **it's your fault** du hast Schuld IV
favour ['feɪvə]**: do sb. a favour** jm. einen Gefallen tun IV
favourite ['feɪvərɪt] Lieblings- I
my favourite colour meine Lieblingsfarbe I
favourite ['feɪvərɪt] Favorit/in; Liebling III
fear (of) ['fɪə] Furcht, Angst (vor) III
°**feature** ['fiːtʃə] Merkmal
February ['februəri] Februar I
fed [fed] *siehe* **feed**
feed [fiːd]**, fed, fed** füttern I
feel [fiːl]**, felt, felt** fühlen; sich fühlen II; sich anfühlen II • **I feel sick.** Mir ist schlecht. IV
feeling ['fiːlɪŋ] Gefühl III
feet [fiːt] *Plural von „foot"* I
fell [fel] *siehe* **fall**
felt [felt] *siehe* **feel**
felt tip ['felt tɪp] Filzstift I
female ['fiːmeɪl] Weibchen II
fence [fens] Zaun IV
ferry ['feri] Fähre III
festival ['festɪvl] Fest, Festival II
fetch [fetʃ] holen, abholen IV
few [fjuː] wenige IV • **a few** ein paar, einige II
fewer ['fjuːə] weniger IV
fiction ['fɪkʃn] Belletristik; Prosaliteratur IV
fiddle ['fɪdl] *(infml)* Fiedel, Geige III • **play the fiddle** Geige spielen III
field [fiːld] Feld, Acker, Weide II
in the field auf dem Feld II
fight (for) [faɪt]**, fought, fought** kämpfen (für, um) III
fight [faɪt] Kampf IV
figure ['fɪgə] Zahl, Ziffer, Betrag V 1 (8)
figure sth. out ['fɪgə] etwas ausrechnen; etwas herausfinden *(oft mit Zahlen)* V 3 (52)
► S.205 Verbs & nouns with the same form
file [faɪl]**: background file** *etwa:* Hintergrundinformation II
grammar file *Grammatikanhang* I • **skills file** *Anhang mit Lern- und Arbeitstechniken* I
fill sth. (with sth.) [fɪl] etwas (mit etwas) (aus)füllen IV
filling ['fɪlɪŋ] (Brot-)Belag IV
film [fɪlm] Film I • **crime film** Krimi IV • **film star** Filmstar I
film [fɪlm] filmen III
final ['faɪnl] Finale, Endspiel III
final ['faɪnl] letzte(r, s); End- III
finally ['faɪnəli] endlich, schließlich IV
find [faɪnd]**, found, found** finden I
find out (about) herausfinden (über) I
°**finding** ['faɪndɪŋ] Ergebnis
fine [faɪn]
1. gut, ausgezeichnet; in Ordnung II
2. *(gesundheitlich)* gut II
I'm/He's fine. Es geht mir/ihm gut. II
fine [faɪn] Geldstrafe IV
finger ['fɪŋgə] Finger I
finish ['fɪnɪʃ] beenden, zu Ende machen; enden I
fire ['faɪə] Feuer, Brand II • **There's no smoke without fire.** Wo Rauch ist, ist auch Feuer. IV
firefighter ['faɪəfaɪtə] Feuerwehrmann, -frau IV
fireman ['faɪəmən] Feuerwehrmann II
fireproof ['faɪəpruːf] feuerbeständig, -fest V 1 (17/187)
firewoman ['faɪəˌwʊmən]**,** *pl* **firewomen** Feuerwehrfrau II
fire station ['faɪə ˌsteɪʃn] Feuerwache IV
first [fɜːst]
1. erste(r, s) I
2. zuerst, als Erstes I
be first der/die Erste sein I
°**come first** den Vorrang haben
for the first time zum ersten Mal II • **First Nations** die Ersten Nationen *(indianische Ureinwohner/innen Kanadas)* III
first floor [ˌfɜːst flɔː] erster Stock *(BE)* / Erdgeschoss *(AE)* IV
fish, *pl* **fish/fishes** [fɪʃ] Fisch I
fish [fɪʃ] fischen, angeln III
fisherman ['fɪʃəmən]**,** *pl* **fishermen** ['fɪʃəmən] Angler, Fischer III
fist [fɪst] Faust IV
fit (-tt-) [fɪt] passen I
flag [flæg] Fahne, Flagge V 1 (8)
flash [flæʃ] aufblitzen; leuchten IV
flash [flæʃ] Lichtblitz III
flashback ['flæʃbæk] Rückblende V 1 (24)
flat [flæt] Wohnung I
flat [flæt] flach, eben II
flattered ['flætəd]**: be/feel flattered** sich geschmeichelt fühlen V 4 (83)
flavour ['fleɪvə] Geschmack, Geschmacksrichtung II
flea market ['fliː ˌmɑːkɪt] Flohmarkt III
flew [fluː] *siehe* **fly**
flexible ['fleksəbl] flexibel, anpassungsfähig V 2 (35)

flight [flaɪt] Flug II
floor [flɔː]
1. Fußboden I • **dance floor** Tanzfläche III
2. Stock(werk) IV • **first floor** erster Stock *(BE)* / Erdgeschoss *(AE)* IV • **ground floor** *(BE)* Erdgeschoss IV • **on the second floor** im zweiten Stock *(BE)* / im ersten Stock *(AE)* IV
flow [fləʊ] fließen IV
flow chart ['fləʊ tʃɑːt] Flussdiagramm I
flower ['flaʊə] Blume; Blüte II
flown [fləʊn] *siehe* **fly**
flu [fluː] Grippe II
flute [fluːt] Querflöte III
fly [flaɪ], **flew, flown**
1. fliegen II
flying instructor Fluglehrer/in V 1 (6/182)
2. *(Fahne)* wehen (lassen) V 3 (59)
fly [flaɪ] Fliege V 1 (21)
flyer ['flaɪə] Flugblatt, Flyer IV
focus ['fəʊkəs] Schwerpunkt, Mittelpunkt, Hauptpunkt V 2 (45)
focus (on) ['fəʊkəs] sich konzentrieren (auf) V 2 (45)
► S.205 Verbs & nouns with the same form
fog [fɒg] Nebel II
foggy ['fɒgi] neblig II
folk (music) ['fəʊk ˌmjuːzɪk] Folk *(meist englischsprachige, volkstümliche Musik mit Elementen der Rockmusik)* III
folks [fəʊks] *(infml, bes. AE)* Leute III • °**old folks' home** *(infml)* Altenheim, Seniorenresidenz
follow ['fɒləʊ] folgen; verfolgen I
°**follow rules** ['fɒləʊ] sich an die Regeln halten • **the following ...** die folgenden ... III
font [fɒnt] Schrift(art) V 2 (39)
food [fuːd] Essen; Lebensmittel; Futter I
foot [fʊt], *pl* **feet** [fiːt]
1. Fuß I • **on foot** zu Fuß III
2. Fuß *(Längenmaß; ca. 30 cm)* IV
football ['fʊtbɔːl] Fußball I • **football boots** Fußballschuhe, -stiefel I • **football pitch** Fußballplatz, -feld II
footballer ['fʊtbɔːlə] Fußballspieler/in III
footnote ['fʊtnəʊt] Fußnote, Anmerkung IV
for [fə, fɔː] für I • **for a moment** einen Moment lang II • **for a while** eine Weile, einige Zeit IV **for breakfast/lunch/dinner** zum Frühstück/Mittagessen/Abendbrot I • **for example** zum Beispiel I **for his birthday** zu seinem Geburtstag III • **for lots of reasons** aus vielen Gründen I • **for miles** meilenweit II • **(in prison) for murder** (im Gefängnis) wegen Mordes IV • **for sale** *(auf Schild)* zu verkaufen IV • **for the first time** zum ersten Mal II • **for three days** drei Tage (lang) I • **for years** seit Jahren III • **just for fun** nur zum Spaß I • **What for?** [ˌwɒt 'fɔː] Wofür? II • **What's for homework?** Was haben wir als Hausaufgabe auf? I
force sb. to do sth. [fɔːs] jn. dazu bringen/jn. zwingen, etwas zu tun IV
foreground ['fɔːgraʊnd] Vordergrund II
forehead ['fɔːhed, 'fɒrɪd] Stirn IV
foreign ['fɒrɪn] ausländisch V 2 (39)
foreign language Fremdsprache V 2 (39)
foreigner ['fɒrɪnə] Ausländer/in V 2 (39)
forest ['fɒrɪst] Wald II
forever [fər'evə] endlos; ewig V 1 (6)
forgave [fə'geɪv] *siehe* **forgive**
forget (-tt-) [fə'get], **forgot, forgotten** vergessen III
► S.195 Same verb, different meaning
forgive sb. for sth. [fə'gɪv], **forgave, forgiven** jm. etwas vergeben, verzeihen IV
forgiven [fə'gɪvn] *siehe* **forgive**
forgot [fə'gɒt] *siehe* **forget**
forgotten [fə'gɒtn] *siehe* **forget**
fork [fɔːk] Gabel III
form [fɔːm] bilden IV
form [fɔːm] (Schul-)Klasse I • **form teacher** Klassenlehrer/in I
formal ['fɔːml] formell, förmlich V 2 (40)
format ['fɔːmæt] Format V 2 (39)
former ['fɔːmə] ehemalige(r, s), frühere(r, s) V 1 (8)
formula ['fɔːmjələ] Formel V 2 (48)
fort [fɔːt] Fort III
fortune ['fɔːtʃuːn] Vermögen; Glück V 2 (32)
forum ['fɔːrəm] Forum IV
forward ['fɔːwəd]: **look forward to sb./sth.** sich auf jn./etwas freuen IV
forwards ['fɔːwədz], **forward** *(bes. AE)* ['fɔːwəd] vorwärts V 3 (52)
fought [fɔːt] *siehe* **fight**
foul [faʊl] foulen III
found [faʊnd] *siehe* **find**
found [faʊnd] gründen IV
fox [fɒks] Fuchs II
freak out [ˌfriːk_'aʊt] ausflippen V 1 (6)
free [friː]
1. frei I • **free time** Freizeit, freie Zeit I • **free-time activities** Freizeitaktivitäten II
2. kostenlos I
freedom ['friːdəm] Freiheit V 2 (35)
freeway ['friːweɪ] *(USA, Australien)* Autobahn IV
°**freeze frame** ['friːz freɪm] Standbild
French [frentʃ] Französisch I
French fries [ˌfrentʃ 'fraɪz] *(bes. AE)* Pommes frites IV
fresh [freʃ] frisch V 3 (66)
°**freshwater** ['freʃwɔːtə] Süßwasser-
Friday ['fraɪdeɪ, 'fraɪdi] Freitag I
fridge [frɪdʒ] Kühlschrank I
friend [frend] Freund/in I • **make friends (with)** Freunde finden; sich anfreunden (mit) II
friendliness ['frendlinəs] Freundlichkeit IV
friendly ['frendli] freundlich II
°**friendship** ['frendʃɪp] Freundschaft
fries ['fraɪz]: **(French) fries** *(bes. AE)* Pommes frites IV
frighten ['fraɪtn] verängstigen, erschrecken V 1 (21)
frightening ['fraɪtnɪŋ] schrecklich, erschreckend V 1 (21)
frisbee ['frɪzbi] Frisbee IV
frog [frɒg] Frosch II
from [frəm, frɒm]
1. aus I
2. von I
dresses from the 60s Kleider aus den 60ern / aus den 60er Jahren II
from all over the UK / England aus dem gesamten Vereinigten Königreich / aus ganz England III
from all over the world aus der ganzen Welt II • **from Monday to Friday** von Montag bis Freitag III • **from my point of view** aus meiner Sicht; von meinem Standpunkt aus gesehen II • **I'm from ...** Ich komme/bin aus ... I • **Where are you from?** Wo kommst du her? I
front [frʌnt]: **at the front** vorne, im vorderen Teil III • **in front of** vor *(räumlich)* I • **to the front** nach vorn I • **front door** [ˌfrʌnt 'dɔː] Wohnungstür, Haustür I • **front page** Titelseite III
fruit [fruːt] Obst, Früchte; Frucht I
fruit salad Obstsalat I • **pick fruit** Obst pflücken IV
fry [fraɪ] braten III
full [fʊl] voll I

fun [fʌn]
1. Spaß I • **have fun** Spaß haben, sich amüsieren I • **Have fun!** Viel Spaß! I • **just for fun** nur zum Spaß I • **Riding is fun.** Reiten macht Spaß. I
2. lustige(r, s) V 4 (83)
funeral ['fju:nərəl] Trauerfeier IV
funny ['fʌni] witzig, komisch I
furniture *(no pl)* ['fɜ:nɪtʃə] Möbel III
future ['fju:tʃə] Zukunft I

G

gallery ['gæləri] Galerie III
game [geɪm] Spiel I • **a game of football** ein Fußballspiel II
game console Spielkonsole V 2 (34)
garage ['gærɑ:ʒ] Garage II
garbage ['gɑ:bɪdʒ] *(AE)* Müll, Abfall IV
garden ['gɑ:dn] Garten I
gas [gæs]
1. Gas IV
2. *(AE)* Benzin IV • **gas station** *(AE)* Tankstelle IV
gate [geɪt] Flugsteig III
gave [geɪv] *siehe* **give**
gear *(no pl)* [gɪə] Ausrüstung IV
camping gear Campingausrüstung IV • **sports gear** Sportausrüstung, Sportsachen II
°**geek** [gi:k]: **computer geek** *(bes. AE, infml)* Computerfreak
general ['genrəli] allgemeine(r, s) III
generally ['dʒenrəl] im Allgemeinen III
generation [ˌdʒenə'reɪʃn] Generation V 1 (17)
gentleman ['dʒentlmən], *pl* **gentlemen** ['dʒentlmən] Herr V 4 (94)
Ladies and gentlemen Meine Damen und Herren V 3 (94/210)
geography [dʒi'ɒgrəfi] Geografie, Erdkunde I
German ['dʒɜ:mən] Deutsch; deutsch; Deutsche(r) I
Germany ['dʒɜ:məni] Deutschland I
get (-tt-) [get], **got, got**
1. bekommen, kriegen II
2. holen, besorgen II
3. gelangen, (hin)kommen I
4. get angry/hot/... wütend/heiß/... werden II
5. get off (the train/bus) (aus dem Zug/Bus) aussteigen I • **get on (the train/bus)** (in den Zug/Bus) einsteigen I
6. get up aufstehen I
I don't get it. Das versteh ich nicht. / Das kapier ich nicht. II
get sth. across (to sb.) (jm.) etwas klarmachen/rüberbringen V 3 (65)
get along zurechtkommen IV; gut (mit jm.) auskommen V 2 (47)
get away from sth./sb. von etwas/jm. weggehen, sich entfernen III
get bored sich langweilen, gelangweilt sein IV • °**get down to business** an die Arbeit gehen • **get dressed** sich anziehen I • **get involved (in)** sich engagieren (für, bei); sich beteiligen (an) IV • **get lost** sich verlaufen III • **Get out of my sight.** Geh mir aus den Augen. IV • **get ready (for)** sich fertig machen (für), sich vorbereiten (auf) I
get sth. right etwas richtig machen III • **get sth. wrong** etwas falsch machen III • **get things ready** Dinge fertig machen, vorbereiten I • **get used to sth./sb.** sich gewöhnen an jn./etwas IV
What can I get you? Was kann/darf ich euch/Ihnen bringen? II
getting by in English [ˌgetɪŋ 'baɪ] *etwa:* auf Englisch zurechtkommen I
ghost [gəʊst] Gespenst, Geist V 4 (95)
giant ['dʒaɪənt] riesige(r, s), Riesen- IV
gig [gɪg] *(infml)* Gig, Auftritt III
do a gig einen Auftritt haben, ein Konzert geben III
giraffe [dʒə'rɑ:f] Giraffe II
girl [gɜ:l] Mädchen I
girlfriend ['gɜ:lfrend] Freundin III
gist [dʒɪst] das Wesentliche III
give [gɪv], **gave, given** geben I
give sth. back etwas zurückgeben I • **give sb. a call** jn. anrufen V 4 (83) • **give sb. a hug** jn. umarmen IV • **give information** Information(en) angeben V 2 (39)
give a smile lächeln IV • **give sb. a smile** jn. anlächeln IV • **give a source** eine Quelle angeben IV
give a speech eine Rede halten IV
give (sth./sb.) up (etwas/jn.) aufgeben V 2 (35)
given ['gɪvn] *siehe* **give**
glad [glæd] froh, dankbar IV
glass [glɑ:s] Glas I • **a glass of water** ein Glas Wasser I
glasses *(pl)* ['glɑ:sɪz] (eine) Brille I
gloves *(pl)* [glʌvz] Handschuhe II
glue [glu:] (auf-, ein)kleben II
glue [glu:] Klebstoff I • **glue stick** ['glu: stɪk] Klebestift I
go [gəʊ], **went, gone**
1. gehen I; fahren II
2. go hard/bad/deaf/blind/crazy/... hart/schlecht/taub/blind/verrückt/... werden III • **go red in the face** rot werden V 4 (94)
go abroad ins Ausland gehen/fahren II • **go ahead** in Führung gehen III • **go back** zurückgehen, -fahren V 2 (47) • **go by** vergehen, vorübergehen *(Zeit)* V 4 (80) • **go by car/bike/...** mit dem Auto/Rad/... fahren II • **go for a run** laufen gehen IV • **go for a walk** spazieren gehen, einen Spaziergang machen II • **go home** nach Hause gehen I • **go off 1.** losfahren, -gehen IV; **2.** *(Waffe)* losgehen; *(Bombe)* explodieren IV • **go on 1.** weitergehen; weiterreden III; **2.** angehen *(Licht)* III; °**3.** sich erstrecken • **go on a date with sb.** mit jm. ausgehen V 4 (80/206) • **go on a hike** eine Wanderung machen IV • **go on a trip** einen Ausflug machen II • **go on a walk** eine Wanderung / einen Spaziergang machen IV • **go on doing sth.** etwas weiter tun IV 2 (40/195)
go on holiday in Urlaub fahren II • **go on to do sth.** dann etwas tun IV 2 (40/195)
► S.195 Same verb, different meaning
go out weg-, raus-, ausgehen I
go out with sb. mit jm. (aus)gehen V 4 (83) • **go riding/shopping/swimming** reiten/einkaufen/schwimmen gehen I • **go skiing** Ski laufen/fahren III • **go surfing** wellenreiten gehen, surfen gehen II • **go to** führen nach *(Straße, Weg)* II • **go to bed** ins Bett gehen I
go to mass die Messe besuchen IV • **go to the cinema** ins Kino gehen II • **go to university** mit dem Studium anfangen V 2 (43) • **go well** gut (ver)laufen, gutgehen II
go with gehören zu, passen zu III
Let's go. Auf geht's! (*wörtlich:* Lass uns gehen.) I • **coffee to go** Kaffee zum Mitnehmen IV • **What are you going to do?** Was wirst du tun? / Was hast du vor zu tun? I
goal [gəʊl]
1. Tor *(im Sport)* III • **score a goal** ein Tor schießen, einen Treffer erzielen III
2. Ziel V 2 (35)
goalkeeper ['gəʊlki:pə] Torwart, Torfrau III
goat [gəʊt] Ziege IV
God [gɒd] Gott IV
gold [gəʊld] Gold III
gold [gəʊld] goldfarben V 3 (69)

gone [gɒn]
1. *siehe* **go**
2. be gone weg sein, nicht da sein II
°**gonna** ['gʌnə] *(infml)* = **going to**
good [gʊd]
1. gut I • **Good afternoon.** Guten Tag. *(nachmittags)* I • **Good luck (with ...)!** Viel Glück (bei/mit ...)! I **Good morning.** Guten Morgen. I
2. brav II
Goodbye. [ˌgʊd'baɪ] Auf Wiedersehen. I • **say goodbye** sich verabschieden I
good-looking [ˌgʊd'lʊkɪŋ] gut aussehend V 3 (50/206)
► S.206 German „schön" etc.
goods *(pl)* [gʊdz] Waren, Güter V 1 (8)
goose bumps *(pl)* ['gu:s ˌbʌmps] Gänsehaut *(AE)* IV
goose pimples *(pl)* ['gu:s 'pɪmpəlz] *(BE)* Gänsehaut IV
gorge [gɔ:dʒ] Schlucht IV
gorgeous ['gɔ:dʒəs] *(infml)* äußerst schön und attraktiv V 1 (6)
► S.206 German „schön" etc.
gorilla [gə'rɪlə] Gorilla IV
gossip ['gɒsɪp] schwatzen, klatschen, tratschen III
°**gossip** ['gɒsɪp] Klatsch (und Tratsch)
got [gɒt] *siehe* **get**
got [gɒt]: **I've got ...** Ich habe ... I **I haven't got a chair.** Ich habe keinen Stuhl. I
government ['gʌvənmənt] Regierung *(als Schulfach etwa:* Staatskunde*)* IV
► S.196 Collective nouns
governor ['gʌvənə] Gouverneur/in IV
grab (-bb-) [græb] schnappen, packen III
grade [greɪd]
1. *(AE)* Jahrgangsstufe, Klasse IV
2. (Schul-)Note, Zensur IV
graduate ['grædʒueɪt] *(AE)* den Schulabschluss machen IV *(BE)* den Hochschulabschluss machen IV
graffiti [grə'fi:ti] Graffiti V 4 (84)
grammar ['græmə] Grammatik I **grammar file** *Grammatikanhang* I **grammar school** Gymnasium III
grand [grænd] eindrucksvoll, beeindruckend IV
grandchild ['græntʃaɪld], *pl* **grandchildren** ['-tʃɪldrən] Enkel/in I
granddaughter ['grændɔ:tə] Enkelin II
grandfather ['grænfɑ:ðə] Großvater I
grandma ['grænmɑ:] Oma I
grandmother ['grænmʌðə] Großmutter I
grandpa ['grænpɑ:] Opa I
grandparents ['grænpeərənts] Großeltern I
grandson ['grænsʌn] Enkel II
granny ['græni] Oma II
grape [greɪp] Weintraube IV
grass [grɑ:s] Gras, Rasen IV • **cut the grass** Rasen mähen IV
grateful ['greɪtfl] dankbar V 2 (40)
great [greɪt] großartig, toll I
great-grandmother/-father [ˌgreɪt 'grænmʌðə], [ˌgreɪt 'grænfɑ:ðə] Urgroßmutter/-vater III
green [gri:n] grün I
greet [gri:t] begrüßen IV
grew [gru:] *siehe* **grow**
grey [greɪ] grau II
grid [grɪd] Gitter; Rechteckschema IV
ground [graʊnd] (Erd-)Boden III
ground floor [ˌgraʊnd 'flɔ:] *(BE)* Erdgeschoss IV
Ground Zero [ˌgraʊnd 'zɪərəʊ] Bodennullpunkt *(Bezeichnung für das zerstörte World Trade Center in New York)* IV
group [gru:p] Gruppe I • **group word** Oberbegriff II
► S.196 Collective nouns
grow [grəʊ], **grew, grown**
1. wachsen II • **grow up** erwachsen werden; aufwachsen III °**grow rich** reich werden
2. *(Getreide usw.)* anbauen, anpflanzen IV
grown [grəʊn] *siehe* **grow**
grumble ['grʌmbl] murren, nörgeln II
guarantee sth. [ˌgærən'ti:] garantieren V 3 (53)
guarantee [ˌgærən'ti:] Garantie V 3 (66/205)
► S.205 Verbs & nouns with the same form
guard [gɑ:d] Wachposten IV
guess [ges] raten, erraten, schätzen II • **Guess what!** [ˌges 'wɒt] Stell dir vor! / Stellt euch vor! II
guest [gest] Gast I
guide [gaɪd] Fremdenführer/in, Reiseleiter/in IV
guided tour [ˌgaɪdɪd 'tʊə] Führung IV
guinea pig ['gɪni pɪg] Meerschweinchen I
guitar [gɪ'tɑ:] Gitarre I • **play the guitar** Gitarre spielen I
gun [gʌn] Schusswaffe IV • °**fire a gun** [faɪə] mit einer Schusswaffe schießen
guy [gaɪ] Typ, Kerl II • **guys** *(pl)* Leute II
gym [dʒɪm] Sporthalle, Turnhalle; Fitnessstudio IV

H

had [hæd] *siehe* **have**
hair *(no pl)* [heə] Haar, Haare I
hairdresser ['heədresə] Friseur/in III **at the hairdresser's** beim Friseur III
half [hɑ:f], *pl* **halves** [hɑ:vz]
1. Hälfte III
2. Halbzeit III
half [hɑ:f] halbe(r, s) II • **half an hour** eine halbe Stunde II • **half past 11** halb zwölf (11.30 / 23.30) I **half-time** Halbzeit(pause) III **three and a half days/weeks** dreieinhalb Tage/Wochen IV
half-pipe ['hɑ:fpaɪp] Halfpipe *(halbierte Röhre für Inlineskater)* III
hall [hɔ:l]
1. Flur, Diele I
2. Halle, Saal III • **community hall** Gemeinschaftshalle, -saal III • **sports hall** Sporthalle III
hallway ['hɔ:lweɪ] *(AE)* Korridor, Gang IV
hamburger ['hæmbɜ:gə] Hamburger I
hamster ['hæmstə] Hamster I
hand sb. sth. [hænd] jm. etwas reichen IV
hand [hænd] Hand I • **on the one hand ... on the other (hand) ...** auf der einen Seite ... auf der anderen Seite ... V 3 (53) • °**put one's hand up, raise one's hand** sich melden **second-hand** gebraucht; aus zweiter Hand III
handkerchief ['hæŋkətʃi:f] Taschentuch IV
handout ['hændaʊt] Arbeitsblatt, Informationsblatt, Handout IV
handsome ['hænsəm] attraktiv, gut aussehend V 4 (83)
► S.206 German „schön" etc.
hang sb. [hæŋ] jn. hängen IV
hang sth. (up) [hæŋ], **hung, hung** etwas aufhängen IV
hang out [ˌhæŋ_'aʊt], **hung, hung** *(infml)* hängen, rumhängen, abhängen III
°**hang together** [ˌhæŋ tə'geðə] zusammenhängen, -passen
happen (to) ['hæpən] geschehen, passieren (mit) I • **happen to do/be sth.** etwas zufällig tun/sein V 4 (88)

happiness ['hæpinəs] Glück IV
happy ['hæpi] glücklich, froh I
Happy birthday. Herzlichen Glückwunsch zum Geburtstag. I • **happy ending** Happyend II
harbour ['hɑ:bə] Hafen III
hard [hɑ:d] hart; schwer, schwierig II • **work hard** hart arbeiten II
°**hard-hitting** [,hɑ:d'hɪtɪŋ] schonungslos, knallhart
harvest ['hɑ:vɪst] Ernte IV
hat [hæt] Hut I
hate [heɪt] hassen, gar nicht mögen I
have [həv, hæv], **had, had** haben, besitzen II • **have an argument** eine Auseinandersetzung haben, sich streiten II • **have a baby** ein Baby/Kind bekommen II • **have a bath** baden, ein Bad nehmen II **have a cold** erkältet sein, eine Erkältung haben II • **have a massage** sich massieren lassen II • **have a sauna** in die Sauna gehen II • **have a shower** (sich) duschen I • **have a sore throat** Halsschmerzen haben II • **have a temperature** Fieber haben II **have breakfast** frühstücken I **have dinner** Abendbrot essen I **have ... for breakfast** ... zum Frühstück essen/trinken I • **have fun** Spaß haben, sich amüsieren I **Have fun!** Viel Spaß! I • **have a good/great time** sich gut amüsieren III • **have sth. done (by sb.)** etwas machen lassen (von jm.) V 4 (88) • **have to do** tun müssen I
have got: I've got ... [aɪv 'gɒt] Ich habe ... I • **I haven't got a chair.** Ich habe keinen Stuhl. I
he [hi:] er I
head [hed] Kopf I • **nod (one's head)** (mit dem Kopf) nicken III **shake one's head** den Kopf schütteln III • °**with one's head in the clouds** mit seinen Gedanken ganz woanders • °**Head of the Committee** Ausschussvorsitzende(r)
head for/to/towards sth. [hed] auf etwas zugehen, -fahren, -steuern V 2 (34)
headache ['hedeɪk] Kopfschmerzen II
heading ['hedɪŋ] Überschrift IV
headline ['hed,laɪn] Schlagzeile III
headphones *(pl)* ['hedfəʊnz] Kopfhörer III
head teacher [,hed 'ti:tʃə] Schulleiter/in III
health [helθ] Gesundheit; Gesundheitslehre IV
healthy ['helθi] gesund II
hear [hɪə], **heard, heard** hören I
heard [hɜ:d] *siehe* **hear**
heart [hɑ:t] Herz I • **heart attack** Herzinfarkt IV • heart-warming herzerwärmend V 3 (54) • °**learn sth. by heart** etwas auswendig lernen
heat [hi:t] Hitze V 1 (21)
heaven ['hevn] Himmel *(im religiösen Sinn)* IV
heavy metal [,hevi 'metl] Heavymetal III
hedgehog ['hedʒhɒg] Igel II
°**height** [haɪt] Gipfel
held [held] *siehe* **hold**
helicopter ['helɪkɒptə] Hubschrauber, Helikopter II
°**hell** [hel]: **make sb.'s life hell** jm. das Leben zur Hölle machen
Hello. [hə'ləʊ] Hallo. / Guten Tag. I
helmet ['helmɪt] Helm III
help [help] helfen I • **Can I help you?** Kann ich Ihnen helfen? / Was kann ich für Sie tun? *(im Geschäft)* I • **help (sb.) out** (jm.) aushelfen V 4 (79)
help [help] Hilfe I
helpful ['helpfl] hilfreich, nützlich IV
helpless ['helpləs] hilflos IV
her [hə, hɜ:]
1. ihr, ihre I
2. sie; ihr I
herb [hɜ:b] (Gewürz-)Kraut III
here [hɪə]
1. hier I • **round here** hier (in der Gegend) IV
2. hierher I
Here you are. Bitte sehr. / Hier bitte. I
heritage ['herɪtɪdʒ] Erbe IV
hero ['hɪərəʊ], *pl* **heroes** ['hɪərəʊz] Held/in II
hers [hɜ:z] ihrer, ihre, ihrs II
herself [hɜ:'self]
1. sich III
2. selbst IV
Hey! [heɪ] Hallo! III
Hi! [haɪ] Hallo! I • **Say hi to your parents for me.** Grüß deine Eltern von mir. I
hid [hɪd] *siehe* **hide**
hidden ['hɪdn] *siehe* **hide**
hide [haɪd], **hid, hidden** sich verstecken; (etwas) verstecken I
high [haɪ] hoch III
highlight ['haɪ,laɪt] Höhepunkt III
high school ['haɪ sku:l] *(USA) Schule für 14- bis 18-Jährige* IV
highway ['haɪweɪ] *(USA)* Fernstraße *(oft mit vier oder mehr Spuren)* IV
hijacker ['haɪdʒækə] (Flugzeug-)Entführer/in IV
hike [haɪk] wandern IV
hike [haɪk] Wanderung, Marsch IV
hill [hɪl] Hügel II
hilly ['hɪli] hügelig III
him [hɪm] ihn; ihm I
himself [hɪm'self]
1. sich III
2. selbst IV
Hindu ['hɪndu:] Hindu; Hindu- V 3 (50/198)
Hinduism ['hɪndu:ɪzm] Hinduismus V 3 (50/198)
► S.198 Religions
hip hop ['hɪp ,hɒp] Hiphop IV
hippo ['hɪpəʊ] Flusspferd II
his [hɪz]
1. sein, seine I
2. seiner, seine, seins II
history ['hɪstri] Geschichte I
°**make history of one's own** selbst Geschichte machen
hit **(-tt-)** [hɪt], **hit, hit**
1. schlagen III
2. treffen IV
°**3. hit sb.** jn. angreifen
hobby ['hɒbi] Hobby I
hockey ['hɒki] Hockey I • **hockey pitch** Hockeyplatz, -feld II
hockey shoes Hockeyschuhe I
hold [həʊld], **held, held** halten II
hold a competition einen Wettbewerb veranstalten III • °**hold sth. in store** etwas bereithalten
hole [həʊl] Loch I
holiday(s) ['hɒlədeɪ] Ferien I • **be on holiday** in Urlaub sein II • **go on holiday** in Urlaub fahren II
holiday home Ferienhaus, -wohnung III
home [həʊm] Heim, Zuhause I
at home daheim, zu Hause I
children's home Kinderheim V 1 (19) • **come home** nach Hause kommen I • **get home** nach Hause kommen I • **go home** nach Hause gehen I • °**old folks' home** *(infml)* Altenheim, Seniorenresidenz • **old people's home** Altenheim, Seniorenresidenz V 1 (17/173)
homeland ['həʊmlænd] Heimat(land) IV
homeless ['həʊmləs] obdachlos IV
► S.209 the rich, the poor, etc.
homeowner ['həʊm,əʊnə] Eigenheimbesitzer/in IV
°**homestead** ['həʊmsted] Anwesen, Gehöft
hometown ['həʊm,taʊn] Heimat(stadt) IV

homework *(no pl)* ['həʊmwɜːk] Hausaufgabe(n) I • **do homework** die Hausaufgabe(n) machen I **What's for homework?** Was haben wir als Hausaufgabe auf? I
honest ['ɒnɪst] ehrlich V 1 (12)
Hooray! [hu'reɪ] Hurra! II
hope [həʊp] hoffen I • **I hope so.** Ich hoffe es. II
hope (of) [həʊp] Hoffnung (auf) III
hopeful ['həʊpfʊl] hoffnungsvoll IV
hopeless ['həʊpləs] hoffnungslos IV • **You're hopeless.** Dir ist nicht zu helfen. IV
°**horizontal** [ˌhɒrɪ'zɒntl] waagerecht
horrible ['hɒrəbl] scheußlich, grauenhaft II
horror ['hɒrə] Entsetzen, Grauen, Horror III
horse [hɔːs] Pferd I • **horse racing** Pferderennsport V 1 (12/186)
hose [həʊz] Schlauch IV
hospital ['hɒspɪtl] Krankenhaus II **He's gone to hospital.** Er ist ins Krankenhaus gegangen. III • **He's in hospital.** Er ist im Krankenhaus. III
host [həʊst] Gastgeber IV
hostess ['həʊstes] Gastgeberin *(in USA auch: Frau, die in einem Restaurant die Gäste in Empfang nimmt)* IV
hostel ['hɒstl] Herberge, Wohnheim III • **youth hostel** Jugendherberge III
hot [hɒt] heiß I • **hot chocolate** heiße Schokolade I • **hot-water bottle** Wärmflasche II
hotel [həʊ'tel] Hotel II
hotline ['hɒtlaɪn] Hotline II
hour ['aʊə] Stunde I • **half an hour** eine halbe Stunde II • **a 24-hour supermarket** ein Supermarkt, der 24 Stunden geöffnet ist III • **a two-hour operation** eine zweistündige Operation III
house [haʊs] Haus I • **at the Shaws' house** im Haus der Shaws / bei den Shaws zu Hause I
°**housing department** ['haʊzɪŋ] Wohnungsamt
how [haʊ] wie I • **How about you grabbing that table?** Wie wär's, wenn ihr den Tisch dort schnappt? IV • **How are you?** Wie geht es dir/Ihnen/euch? II • **How do you know ...?** Woher weißt/kennst du ...? I • **how many?** wie viele? I • **how much?** wie viel? I • **How much is/are ...?** Was kostet/kosten ...? / Wie viel kostet/kosten ...? I • **How old are you?** Wie alt bist du? I • **How was ...?** Wie war ...? I **How shall I put it?** Wie soll ich es formulieren/ausdrücken? IV **how to do sth.** wie man etwas tut / tun kann / tun soll IV
however [haʊ'evə] trotzdem IV
°**HTML** Hypertext-Auszeichnungssprache *(Formatierungssprache zur Erstellung von Hypertextseiten im WWW)*
hug (-gg-) [hʌg] umarmen IV
hug [hʌg] Umarmung IV • **give sb. a hug** jn. umarmen IV
huge [hjuːdʒ] riesig, sehr groß III
human ['hjuːmən] Mensch, menschliches Wesen IV • **human rights** Menschenrechte V 3 (50)
hundred ['hʌndrəd] hundert, Hundert I
hung [hʌŋ] *siehe* **hang**
hungry ['hʌŋgri] hungrig I • **be hungry** Hunger haben, hungrig sein I • **the hungry** die Hungernden V 4 (88)
► S.209 the rich, the poor, etc.
hunt [hʌnt] Jagd III
hunt [hʌnt] jagen III
hurry ['hʌri] eilen; sich beeilen II **hurry up** sich beeilen I
hurry ['hʌri]: **be in a hurry** in Eile sein, es eilig haben I
hurt [hɜːt], **hurt, hurt** wehtun; verletzen I
hurt [hɜːt] verletzt II
husband ['hʌzbənd] Ehemann II
hut [hʌt] Hütte IV
hutch [hʌtʃ] (Kaninchen-)Stall I

I

I [aɪ] ich I • **I'm** [aɪm] ich bin I **I'm from ...** Ich komme aus ... / Ich bin aus ... I • **I'm ... years old.** Ich bin ... Jahre alt. I • **I'm sorry.** Entschuldigung. / Tut mir leid. I
ice [aɪs] Eis II
ice cream [ˌaɪs 'kriːm] (Speise-)Eis I
ice hockey ['aɪs hɒki] Eishockey III
ice rink ['aɪs rɪŋk] Schlittschuhbahn II
ID [ˌaɪ 'diː] Ausweis IV
idea [aɪ'dɪə] Idee, Einfall I
ideal [aɪ'diːəl] Ideal, Idealvorstellung V 1 (17)
identification [aɪˌdentɪfɪ'keɪʃn] Ausweis IV
°**identify with** [aɪ'dentɪfaɪ] (sich) identifizieren (mit)
identity [aɪ'dentɪti] Identität IV
°**idiot** ['ɪdiət] Idiot/in • **Idiot's Guide to ...** *ähnlich wie die „... für Dummies"-Serie*
if [ɪf]
1. wenn, falls II
2. ob II
ignore [ɪg'nɔː] ignorieren, nicht beachten V 3 (52)
ill [ɪl] krank II
illegal [ɪ'liːgl] illegal, ungesetzlich IV
illness ['ɪlnəs] Krankheit IV
illustrate ['ɪləstreɪt] veranschaulichen, illustrieren IV
image ['ɪmɪdʒ] Bild V 1 (25)
imagery ['ɪmɪdʒəri] Metaphorik V 1 (25)
imagination [ɪˌmædʒɪ'neɪʃn] Fantasie, Vorstellung(skraft) IV
imagine sth. [ɪ'mædʒɪn] sich etwas vorstellen III
imitate ['ɪmɪteɪt] nachmachen III
immediately [ɪ'miːdiətli] sofort IV
immigrant ['ɪmɪgrənt] Einwanderer/Einwanderin IV
immigrate ['ɪmɪgreɪt] einwandern IV
immigration [ˌɪmɪ'greɪʃn] Einwanderung IV • °**immigration station** Einwanderungsstelle
impatient [ɪm'peɪʃnt] ungeduldig V 4 (94)
imperfect [ɪm'pɜːfɪkt] unvollkommen, mangelhaft V 2 (37/192)
impersonal [ɪm'pɜːsənl] unpersönlich V 2 (37/192)
impolite [ˌɪmpə'laɪt] unhöflich V 2 (37)
important [ɪm'pɔːtnt] wichtig II
impossible [ɪm'pɒsəbl] unmöglich II
impress [ɪm'pres] beeindrucken V 2 (44)
°**impression** [ɪm'preʃn] Eindruck
impressive [ɪm'presɪv] beeindruckend, eindrucksvoll III
improve [ɪm'pruːv] (sich) verbessern III
in [ɪn] in I • **the best view in the world** die beste Aussicht der Welt IV • **in 2050** im Jahr 2050 II • **in ... Street** in der ...straße I • **in English** auf Englisch I • **in front of** vor *(räumlich)* I • **in here** hier drinnen I • **in next to no time** im Nu III • **in other places** an anderen Orten, anderswo III • **in school** *(AE)* in der Schule IV • **in the afternoon** nachmittags, am Nachmittag I • **in the country** auf dem Land II • **in the evening** abends, am Abend I • **in the field**

auf dem Feld II • **in the morning** am Morgen, morgens I **in the photo/picture** auf dem Foto/Bild I • **in there** dort drinnen I • **in the sky** am Himmel II • **in the world** auf der Welt II • **in the yard** auf dem Hof II • **in time** [ɪn 'taɪm] rechtzeitig II

inaccurate [ɪn'ækjərət] ungenau V 2 (37/192)

inactive [ɪn'æktɪv] inaktiv, untätig V 2 (37/192)

include [ɪn'klu:d] einschließen IV

income ['ɪnkʌm] Einkommen V 3 (60)

incorrect [ˌɪnkə'rekt] inkorrekt, falsch V 2 (37/192)

increase [ɪn'kri:s] wachsen, zunehmen, steigen V 3 (59)

increase (in sth.) ['ɪŋkri:s] Zunahme, Steigerung, Erhöhung (einer Sache) V 3 (59)
► S.205 Verbs & nouns with the same form

incredible [ɪn'kredɪbl] unglaublich IV

°**independence** [ˌɪndɪ'pendəns] Unabhängigkeit

independent [ˌɪndɪ'pendənt] unabhängig V 1 (8)

index ['ɪndeks] Index, Register V 2 (43)

Indian ['ɪndiən]
1. Inder/in I
2. Indianer/in IV

indirect [ˌɪndə'rekt] indirekt V 2 (37/192) • **indirect speech** indirekte Rede III

individual [ˌɪndɪ'vɪdʒuəl] einzeln V 3 (63)

industrial [ɪn'dʌstriəl] industriell III

industry ['ɪndəstri] Industrie III

inexact [ˌɪnɪg'zækt] ungenau V 2 (37/192)

inexpensive [ˌɪnɪk'spensɪv] preiswert V 2 (37/192)

influence ['ɪnfluəns] beeinflussen V 3 (53)

infinitive [ɪn'fɪnətɪv] Infinitiv *(Grundform des Verbs)* I

inform sb. (about/of sth.) [ɪn'fɔ:m] jn. (über etwas) informieren IV

informal [ɪn'fɔ:ml] informell; umgangssprachlich V 2 (40)

information (about/on) *(no pl)* [ˌɪnfə'meɪʃn] Information(en) (über) I • **give information** Information(en) angeben V 2 (39)

ingredient [ɪn'gri:diənt] Zutat V 3 (66)

inherit sth. (from sb.) [ɪn'herɪt] etwas (von jm.) erben V 2 (32)

injure ['ɪndʒə] verletzen V 3 (64)

injury ['ɪndʒəri] Verletzung II

°**inland** [ˌɪn'lænd] ins Landesinnere

°**innit?** ['ɪnɪt] *(infml)* = **isn't it?**

innovation [ˌɪnə'veɪʃn] Innovation, Neuerung IV

insect ['ɪnsekt] Insekt IV

inside [ˌɪn'saɪd]
1. innen (drin), drinnen I; Innen- IV
2. nach drinnen II
3. inside the car ins Auto (hinein), ins Innere des Autos II

install [ɪn'stɔ:l] installieren, einrichten II

installation [ˌɪnstə'leɪʃn] Installation, Einrichtung II

instant message [ˌɪnstənt 'mesɪdʒ] *Nachricht, die man im Internet austauscht (in Echtzeit)* III

instead of [ɪn'sted‿əv] anstelle von, statt IV

instructions *(pl)* [ɪn'strʌkʃnz] (Gebrauchs-)Anweisung(en), Anleitung(en) II

instructor [ɪn'strʌktə] Lehrer/in, Ausbilder/in V 1 (6)

instrument ['ɪnstrəmənt] Instrument III

interest ['ɪntrəst] Interesse V 2 (40)

interest sb. ['ɪntrəst] jn. interessieren IV

interested [ɪntrəstɪd]**: be interested (in)** interessiert sein (an), sich interessieren (für) III

interesting ['ɪntrəstɪŋ] interessant I

intermediate [ˌɪntə'mi:diət] Mittel-, für fortgeschrittene Anfänger/innen V 2 (39)

international [ˌɪntə'næʃnəl] international II

internet ['ɪntənet] Internet I • **surf the internet** im Internet surfen II

interrupt [ˌɪntə'rʌpt] unterbrechen IV

interview ['ɪntəvju:] befragen, interviewen IV

interview ['ɪntəvju:] Vorstellungsgespräch V 2 (41)

°**interviewer** ['ɪntəvju:ə] jd., der ein Vorstellungsgespräch führt

into ['ɪntə, 'ɪntʊ]
1. in ... (hinein) I
2. be into sth. *(infml)* etwas mögen III

introduce sb. (to sb.) [ˌɪntrə'dju:s] jn. (jm.) vorstellen IV

introduce sb. to sth. [ˌɪntrə'dju:s] jn. in etwas einführen IV

introduction (to) [ˌɪntrə'dʌkʃn] Einführung (in) III

°**invade sth.** [ɪn'veɪd] in etwas einfallen

°**invader** [ɪn'veɪdə] Angreifer, Invasor

invent [ɪn'vent] erfinden III

inventor [ɪn'ventə] Erfinder/in III

invitation (to) [ˌɪnvɪ'teɪʃn] Einladung (zu) I

invite (to) [ɪn'vaɪt] einladen (zu) I

involved [ɪn'vɒlvd]**: get involved (in)** sich engagieren (für, bei); sich beteiligen (an) IV

°**iron filings** *(pl)* [ˌaɪən 'faɪlɪŋz] Eisenspäne

irregular [ɪ'regjələ] unregelmäßig III

is [ɪz] ist I

Islam ['ɪzlɑ:m] Islam V 3 (50/198)
► S.198 Religions

island ['aɪlənd] Insel II

it [ɪt] er/sie/es I • **It's £1.** Er/Sie/Es kostet 1 Pfund. I

IT [ˌaɪ 'ti:]**, information technology** IT (Informationstechnologie) II

item ['aɪtəm] Punkt *(auf einer Liste)*; Gegenstand V 3 (60)

itself [ɪt'self]
1. sich III
2. selbst IV

its [ɪts] sein/seine; ihr/ihre I

J

jacket ['dʒækɪt] Jacke, Jackett II

January ['dʒænjuəri] Januar I

jazz [dʒæz] Jazz III

jealous (of) ['dʒeləs] neidisch (auf); eifersüchtig (auf) V 1 (15)

jeans *(pl)* [dʒi:nz] Jeans I

jet lag ['jet ˌlæg] Jetlag IV

Jew [dʒu:] Jude/Jüdin V 3 (50/198)

°**jewel** ['dʒu:əl] Edelstein, Juwel **the jewel in the crown** das Prunkstück

Jewish ['dʒu:ɪʃ] jüdisch IV
► S.198 Religions

job [dʒɒb] Aufgabe, Job I • **do a good job** gute Arbeit leisten II

join sb./sth. [dʒɔɪn] sich jm. anschließen; bei jm./etwas mitmachen II

join in [ˌdʒɔɪn‿'ɪn] mitmachen III

joke [dʒəʊk] Witz I

joke [dʒəʊk] scherzen, Witze machen II

journalist ['dʒɜ:nəlɪst] Journalist/in IV

journey ['dʒɜ:ni] Reise, Fahrt III

Judaism ['dʒu:deɪɪzm] Judaismus V 3 (50/198)
► S.198 Religions

judge [dʒʌdʒ] Richter/in V 3 (64)

judge sb. (by) [dʒʌdʒ] jn. beurteilen, einschätzen (nach) IV
► S.205 Verbs & nouns with the same form

judo ['dʒuːdəʊ] Judo I • **do judo** Judo machen I
jug [dʒʌg] Krug I • **a jug of milk** ein Krug Milch I
juice [dʒuːs] Saft I
July [dʒu'laɪ] Juli I
jumble sale ['dʒʌmbl seɪl] Wohltätigkeitsbasar I
jump [dʒʌmp] springen II
June [dʒuːn] Juni I
jungle ['dʒʌŋgl] Dschungel IV
junior ['dʒuːniə]
1. Junioren-, Jugend- I
2. **junior (to sb.)** jm. untergeordnet IV
junta ['dʒʌntə, 'hʊntə] Junta V 3 (53/201)
► S.200 Different forms of government
just [dʒʌst]
1. (einfach) nur, bloß I
2. gerade (eben), soeben II
just then genau in dem Moment; gerade dann II
3. **just like you** genau wie du II
just as … as ebenso … wie IV
4. einfach III
justice ['dʒʌstɪs] Gerechtigkeit V 3 (66)
°**Jutes** *(pl)* [dʒuːts] die Jüten

K

kangaroo [ˌkæŋgə'ruː] Känguru II
keen to do sth. / on doing sth. [kiːn] wild darauf sein, etwas zu tun V 2 (35)
keep [kiːp], **kept, kept** (be)halten; aufbewahren III • **keep an eye on sth./sb.** nach jm./etwas Ausschau halten IV • **keep calm** ruhig/still bleiben; Ruhe bewahren V 2 (35/191)
keep (on) doing sth. etwas weiter tun; etwas ständig tun IV • **keep in touch** in Verbindung bleiben, Kontakt halten III • **keep quiet** still sein, leise sein IV • **keep sth. alive** etwas am Leben halten IV
keep sth. warm/cool/open/… etwas warm/kühl/offen/… halten II
keeper ['kiːpə] Torwart, Torfrau III
kept [kept] *siehe* **keep**
ketchup ['ketʃəp] Ketchup IV
key [kiː] Schlüssel I • **key word** Stichwort, Schlüsselwort I • **key ring** Schlüsselring IV
key [kiː] Haupt-, entscheidende(r, s) V 2 (39)
keyboard ['kiːbɔːd] Keyboard *(elektronisches Tasteninstrument)* III
kick [kɪk] *(mit dem Fuß)* treten (gegen) IV
kid [kɪd] Kind, Jugendliche(r) I
kill [kɪl] töten I
kilogram (kg) ['kɪləgræm], **kilo** ['kiːləʊ] Kilogramm, Kilo III • **a kilogram of oranges** ein Kilogramm Orangen III • **a 150-kilogram bear** ein 150 Kilogramm schwerer Bär III
kilometre (km) ['kɪləmiːtə] Kilometer III • **a ten-kilometre walk** eine Zehn-Kilometer-Wanderung III • **square kilometre** Quadratkilometer III
kind (of) [kaɪnd] Art (von) III
kind of scary *(infml)* irgendwie unheimlich III
kindergarten ['kɪndəgɑːtn] Kindergarten; *(USA)* Vorschule *(für 5- bis 6-Jährige)* IV
king [kɪŋ] König I
kiss [kɪs] (sich) küssen IV
kiss [kɪs] Kuss IV
kitchen ['kɪtʃɪn] Küche I
kite [kaɪt] Drachen I
knee [niː] Knie I
kneel (down) [niːl], **knelt, knelt** sich hinknien V 1 (21)
knelt [nelt] *siehe* **kneel**
knew [njuː] *siehe* **know**
knife [naɪf], *pl* **knives** [naɪvz] Messer III
knock (on) [nɒk] (an)klopfen (an) I
know [nəʊ], **knew, known**
1. wissen I
2. kennen I
How do you know …? Woher weißt du …?/Woher kennst du …? I • **know about sth.** von etwas wissen; über etwas Bescheid wissen II • **…, you know.** …, wissen Sie. / …, weißt du. I • **You know what, Sophie?** Weißt du was, Sophie? I
knowledge *(no pl)* ['nɒlɪdʒ] Wissen, Kenntnisse V 3 (69)
known [nəʊn]
1. *siehe* **know**
2. bekannt IV
koala [kəʊ'ɑːlə] Koala V 1 (9)
°**kookaburra** ['kʊkəbʌrə] Jägerliest, Lachender Hans *(australische Vogelart)*

L

ladder ['lædə] *(die)* Leiter IV
lady ['leɪdi] Dame V 4 (94) • **Ladies and gentlemen** Meine Damen und Herren V 4 (94/210)
laid [leɪd] *siehe* **lay**
lain [leɪn] *siehe* **lie**
lake [leɪk] (Binnen-)See II
lamp [læmp] Lampe I
land [lænd] landen II
land [lænd] Land III • **on land** auf dem Land III
landline ['lændlaɪn] Festnetzleitung V 2 (34)
landscape ['lændskeɪp] Landschaft V 1 (8)
lane [leɪn] Gasse, Weg III
language ['læŋgwɪdʒ] Sprache I
foreign language Fremdsprache V 2 (39)
laptop ['læptɒp] Laptop V 1 (12)
large [lɑːdʒ] groß III
lasagne [lə'zænjə] Lasagne I
last [lɑːst] letzte(r, s) I • **the last day** der letzte Tag I • **at last** endlich, schließlich I
last-minute: a last-minute shot [ˌlɑːst 'mɪnɪt] ein Schuss in der letzten Minute III
late [leɪt] spät; zu spät I • **be late** zu spät sein/kommen I • **late at night** spät abends V 4 (84) • **Sorry, I'm late.** Entschuldigung, dass ich zu spät bin/komme. I
later ['leɪtə] später I
latest ['leɪtɪst] neueste(r, s) III
laugh [lɑːf] lachen I • **laugh out loud** laut lachen II
laughter ['lɑːftə] Gelächter II
°**lavatory** ['lævətri] Toilette
law [lɔː] Gesetz IV • **Basic Law** Grundgesetz V 2 (38/193) • °**become law** Rechtskraft erlangen
lay [leɪ] *siehe* **lie**
lay the table [leɪ], **laid, laid** den Tisch decken I
layer ['leɪə] Schicht IV
°**layout** ['leɪaʊt] Anordnung, Layout
lazy ['leɪzi] faul V 3 (52)
lead (to sth.) [led], **led, led** (zu etwas) führen IV
leader ['liːdə] (An-)Führer/in, Leiter/in IV
learn [lɜːn] lernen I • **learn about sth.** etwas über etwas erfahren, etwas über etwas herausfinden II • °**learn sth. by heart** etwas auswendig lernen • **learning by doing** Lernen durch Handeln/Tun V 2 (40/195)
least [liːst] am wenigsten IV • **at least** zumindest, wenigstens I
leather ['leðə] Leder III
leave [liːv], **left, left**
1. (weg)gehen; abfahren II
2. verlassen II
3. **leave (behind)** zurücklassen IV
4. **leave sth. out** etwas auslassen V 3 (61)

led [led] *siehe* **lead**
left [left] *siehe* **leave** • **be left** übrig sein II
left [left] linke(r, s) I • **look left** nach links schauen I • **on the left** links, auf der linken Seite I • **take a left** *(AE)* nach links/rechts abbiegen IV • **to the left** nach links III • **turn left** (nach) links abbiegen II
leg [leg] Bein I
legal ['li:gl] legal IV
leisure centre ['leʒə sentə] Freizeitzentrum, -park II
lemonade [,lemə'neɪd] Limonade I
lend sb. sth. [lend], **lent, lent** jm. etwas leihen II
lent [lent] *siehe* **lend**
lentil ['lentəl] Linse *(Hülsenfrucht)* III
leotard ['li:ətɑ:d] Gymnastikanzug; Turnanzug III
less [les] weniger IV • **more or less** mehr oder weniger IV
lesson ['lesn] (Unterrichts-)Stunde I • **lessons** *(pl)* Unterricht I
let [let], **let, let** lassen II • **Let's ...** Lass uns ... / Lasst uns ... I • **Let's go.** Auf geht's! (*wörtlich:* Lass uns gehen.) I • **Let's look at the list.** Sehen wir uns die Liste an. / Lasst uns die Liste ansehen. I • **let sb. do sth.** jm. erlauben, etwas zu tun; zulassen, dass jd. etwas tut III
letter ['letə]
1. Buchstabe I • **capital letter** Großbuchstabe III • **small letter** Kleinbuchstabe III
2. letter (to) ['letə] Brief (an) II
°**covering letter** Begleitbrief
letter of application Bewerbungsschreiben V 2 (38/192)
lettuce ['letɪs] (Kopf-)Salat II
level ['levl] (Lern-)Stand, Niveau, Grad V 2 (32)
liberty ['lɪbəti] Freiheit IV
library ['laɪbrəri] Bibliothek, Bücherei I
license plate ['laɪsns pleɪt] *(AE)* Nummernschild IV
lie *(-ing form:* **lying***)* [laɪ], **lay, lain** liegen IV
lie (to sb.) [laɪ] jn (an)lügen V 4 (94)
life [laɪf], *pl* **lives** [laɪvz] Leben I
life coach Lebensberater/in V 2 (44)
life sentence lebenslängliche Haftstrafe IV • **way of life** Lebensart III
lift [lɪft] (an-, hoch)heben IV
lift [lɪft] Fahrstuhl, Aufzug II
light [laɪt] Licht III

like [laɪk]
1. wie I • **just like you** genau wie du II • **language like that** solche Sprache IV • **like what?** wie zum Beispiel? IV • **What was the weather like?** Wie war das Wetter? II
2. *(infml)* als ob III
°**3. He's like; I'm like** *(infml)* Er sagt(e); Ich sag(t)e
like [laɪk] mögen, gernhaben I
like sth. better etwas lieber mögen II • **like sth. very much** etwas sehr mögen II • **I like dancing/swimming...** Ich tanze/schwimme... gern. I • **I'd like ... (= I would like ...)** Ich hätte gern ... / Ich möchte gern ... I • **I'd like to go (= I would like to go)** Ich würde gern gehen / Ich möchte gehen I
I wouldn't like to go Ich würde nicht gern gehen / Ich möchte nicht gehen I • **Would you like ...?** Möchtest du ...? / Möchten Sie ...? I
limit ['lɪmɪt] Begrenzung, Beschränkung III • **speed limit** Geschwindigkeitsbegrenzung, -beschränkung III
limit sth. (to sth.) ['lɪmɪt] etwas einschränken; etwas (auf etwas) beschränken/begrenzen V 3 (64)
► S.205 Verbs & nouns with the same form
line [laɪn]
1. Zeile II
2. (U-Bahn-)Linie III
3. Schlange, Reihe *(wartender Menschen)* IV • **Line starts here.** Hier anstellen. IV • °**wait in line (for sth.)** sich (nach etwas) anstellen
line of work Beruf, berufliche Richtung IV • **be in a line of work** einen Beruf ausüben IV
°**line chart** ['laɪn tʃɑ:t] Liniendiagramm
link [lɪŋk] verbinden, verknüpfen I
link [lɪŋk] Verbindung III
linking word ['lɪŋkɪŋ wɜ:d] Bindewort II
lion ['laɪən] Löwe II
lip [lɪp] Lippe IV
list [lɪst] auflisten, aufzählen II
list [lɪst] Liste I • **put one's name on a list** sich eintragen IV
listen (to) ['lɪsn] zuhören; sich etwas anhören I • **listen for sth.** auf etwas horchen, achten III
listener ['lɪsnə] Zuhörer/in II
°**lit** [lɪt] *siehe* **light**
literature ['lɪtrətʃə] Literatur V 1 (24)
litter ['lɪtə] Abfälle zurücklassen IV
litter ['lɪtə] Abfall IV

little ['lɪtl]
1. klein I
2. wenig IV • **a little** ein bisschen, ein wenig IV
live [lɪv] leben, wohnen I
live [laɪv]**: live concert** Livekonzert III • **live music** Livemusik II
lives [laɪvz] *Plural von „life"* I
living-history museum Freilichtmuseum IV
living room ['lɪvɪŋ ru:m; rʊm] Wohnzimmer I
lizard ['lɪzəd] Eidechse V 1 (16)
load [ləʊd] beladen III
lobby ['lɒbi] Eingangshalle IV
local ['ləʊkl] örtlich, Lokal-; am/vom Ort III
location [ləʊ'keɪʃn] (Einsatz-)Ort, Platz III
loch [lɒx] (Binnen-)See in Schottland III
lock [lɒk] Schleuse III
lock [lɒk] abschließen, zuschließen I • **lock up** abschließen II
logical ['lɒdʒɪkl] logisch (denkend) V 2 (35)
logo ['ləʊgəʊ] Logo, Markenzeichen III
lonely ['ləʊnli] einsam V 1 (20)
long [lɒŋ] lang I • **a long way (from)** weit entfernt (von) I • **a long time** lange III
look [lʊk]
1. schauen, gucken I
2. look different/great/old anders/toll/alt aussehen I • **look after sth./sb.** sich um etwas/jn. kümmern; auf etwas/jn. aufpassen II • **look at** ansehen, anschauen I
look at sth. closely etwas genau anschauen III • **look for** suchen II • **look forward to sb./sth.** sich auf jn./etwas freuen IV • **look left and right** nach links und rechts schauen I • **look around/round** sich umsehen I • **look up (from)** hochsehen, aufschauen (von) II
look up to sb. zu jm. aufsehen IV
look words/information up Wörter/Informationen nachschlagen III
Lord [lɔ:d] Herr(gott) IV
lose [lu:z], **lost, lost** verlieren II
lost [lɒst]
1. *siehe* **lose**
2. get lost sich verlaufen III
lot [lɒt]**: a lot (of), lots of** eine Menge, viel, viele I / II • **He likes her a lot.** Er mag sie sehr. I • **lots more** viel mehr I • **Thanks a lot!** Vielen Dank! I
°**lottery** ['lɒtəri] Lotterie
loud [laʊd] laut I

love [lʌv] lieben, sehr mögen I
love sth. very much etwas sehr lieben II
love [lʌv]
1. Liebe II
2. „Liebes", „Liebling" III
fall in love (with sb.) sich verlieben (in jn.) IV • **be in love** verliebt sein V 4 (79)
Love ... Liebe Grüße, ... *(Grußformel am Ende eines Briefes)* I • **make love** miteinander schlafen, sich lieben V 1 (16)
lovely ['lʌvli] schön, hübsch, wunderbar II
► S.206 German „schön" etc.
loyal (to sb./sth.) ['lɔɪəl] (jm./etwas) treu; (jm./etwas gegenüber) loyal V 3 (59)
luck [lʌk]: **Good luck (with ...)!** Viel Glück (bei/mit ...)! I
luckily ['lʌkɪli] zum Glück, glücklicherweise II
lucky ['lʌki]: **be lucky** Glück haben III
lunch [lʌntʃ] Mittagessen I • **for lunch** zum Mittagessen III
lunch break Mittagspause I
lunchtime ['lʌntʃtaɪm] Mittagszeit III
°**Lutheran** ['lu:θərən] Lutheraner/in
lyrics *(pl)* ['lɪrɪks] Liedtext(e) III

M

machine [mə'ʃi:n] Maschine, Gerät II
mad [mæd] verrückt I • **mad about** verrückt nach III
madam ['mædəm]: **Dear Sir or Madam ...** Sehr geehrte Damen und Herren IV
made [meɪd]
1. *siehe* **make**
2. **be made of sth.** aus etwas (gemacht) sein III • **be made up of sth.** aus etwas bestehen V 1 (10/185)
magazine [,mægə'zi:n] Zeitschrift, Magazin I
magical ['mædʒɪkl] zauberhaft, wundervoll V 1 (6)
°**Maharashtrian** [,mɑ:hə'ræʃtriən] *Bewohner/in des indischen Bundesstaats Maharashtra*
mail sb. [meɪl] jn. anmailen II
mail sb. sth. jm. etwas schicken, senden *(vor allem per E-Mail)* III
main [meɪn] Haupt- III
mainly ['meɪnli] hauptsächlich, vorwiegend V 1 (6)
maize *(no pl)* [meɪz] *(BE)* Mais IV
majority [mə'dʒɒrəti] Mehrheit IV
make [meɪk], **made, made** machen; bauen I • **make a call** ein Telefongespräch führen, telefonieren II
make a deal ein Abkommen/eine Abmachung treffen III • **make a mess** alles durcheinanderbringen, alles in Unordnung bringen I
make a speech eine Rede halten IV • **make friends (with)** Freunde finden; sich anfreunden (mit) II
°**make it** es schaffen • °**make it out of sth.** etwas überleben
make love miteinander schlafen, sich lieben V 1 (16) • °**make one's way** sich begeben • **make sb. sth.** jn. zu etwas machen III • **make sb. do sth.** jn. zwingen, etwas zu tun; jn. dazu bringen, etwas zu tun V 3 (52) • °**make sb.'s life hell** jm. das Leben zur Hölle machen
make sth. up etwas bilden V 1 (10)
make sure sich vergewissern IV
make-up ['meɪkʌp] Make-up II
make-up artist Maskenbildner/in
male [meɪl] Männchen II
mall [mɔ:l, *BE auch* mæl] (großes) Einkaufszentrum III
man [mæn], *pl* **men** [men] Mann I
manager ['mænɪdʒə] Manager/in III
°**manatee** [,mænə'ti:] Seekuh
°**manufactured goods** *(pl)* [,mænju'fæktʃəd] Fertigprodukte
many ['meni] viele I • **how many?** wie viele? I
map [mæp] Landkarte, Stadtplan II
March [mɑ:tʃ] März I
march [mɑ:tʃ] Marsch, Demonstration IV
march [mɑ:tʃ] marschieren, demonstrieren V 3 (64)
°**marcher** ['mɑ:tʃə] Demonstrant/in
mark [mɑ:k] (Schul-)Note, Zensur IV
mark [mɑ:k]: **quotation marks** Anführungszeichen, -striche III
mark sth. (up) [,mɑ:k‿'ʌp] etwas markieren, kennzeichnen II
market ['mɑ:kɪt] Markt II
marmalade ['mɑ:məleɪd] Orangenmarmelade I
married (to) ['mærɪd] verheiratet (mit) I
marry ['mæri] heiraten III • °**get someone married** jn. verheiraten
mass [mæs] Messe *(Gottesdienst)* IV
massage ['mæsɑ:ʒ] Massage II
have a massage sich massieren lassen II
match [mætʃ] Spiel, Wettkampf I
°**match sth. (to sth.)** [mætʃ] etwas (zu etwas) zuordnen
mate [meɪt] *(infml)* Freund/in, Kumpel V 1 (6)
material [mə'tɪəriəl] Material, Stoff II • °**raw material** Rohstoff
maths [mæθs] Mathematik I
matter ['mætə]: **no matter what, who, etc.** ganz gleich, was, wer usw. V 3 (52) • **What's the matter?** Was ist los? / Was ist denn? II
mattress ['mætrəs] Matratze V 1 (17)
may [meɪ] dürfen I
May [meɪ] Mai I
maybe ['meɪbi] vielleicht I
mayor ['meə] Bürgermeister/in IV
maximum ['mæksɪməm] Maximum V 2 (47)
me [mi:] mir; mich I • **Me too.** Ich auch. I • **more than me** mehr als ich II • **That's me.** Das bin ich. I
Why me? Warum ich? I
meal [mi:l] Mahlzeit, Essen III **set meal** Menü III
mean [mi:n], **meant, meant**
1. bedeuten II
2. meinen, sagen wollen I
mean [mi:n] gemein IV
meaning ['mi:nɪŋ] Bedeutung I
°**meaningful** ['mi:nɪŋfʊl] aussagekräftig
meant [ment] *siehe* **mean**
meat [mi:t] Fleisch I
medal ['medl] Medaille III
media *(pl)* ['mi:diə] Medien III
mediate ['mi:dieɪt] vermitteln IV
mediation [,mi:di'eɪʃn] Vermittlung, Sprachmittlung, Mediation II
medical ['medɪkl] medizinisch V 3 (63)
medium ['mi:diəm] mittel-, mittlere(r, s); mittelgroß III
meet [mi:t], **met, met**
1. treffen; kennenlernen I
2. sich treffen I
meeting ['mi:tɪŋ] Versammlung, Besprechung IV
°**megaphone** ['megəfəʊn] Megafon
melting pot ['meltɪŋ ,pɒt] Schmelztiegel V 3 (66)
member ['membə]: **member of staff** *(BE)*, **staff member** *(AE)* Mitarbeiter/in IV
membership (of sth.) ['membəʃɪp] Mitgliedschaft (in etwas) V 2 (39)
men [men] *Plural von „man"* I
menu ['menju:] Speisekarte; Menü *(Computer)* III
mention sth. (to sb.) ['menʃn] etwas (jm. gegenüber) erwähnen V 3 (61)
merry-go-round ['merɪgəʊ,raʊnd] Karussel IV

mess [mes]**: make a mess** alles durcheinanderbringen, alles in Unordnung bringen I
°**message** ['mesɪdʒ] Botschaft, Aussage
message: instant message [ˌɪnstənt 'mesɪdʒ] *Nachricht, die man im Internet austauscht (in Echtzeit)* III
messy ['mesi] schmutzig, unordentlich V 3 (60)
met [met] *siehe* **meet**
metaphor ['metəfə, 'metəfɔ:] Metapher V 1 (25)
method ['meθəd] Methode IV
metre ['mi:tə] Meter II
mice [maɪs] *Plural von „mouse"* I
microphone ['maɪkrəfəʊn] Mikrofon III
middle (of) ['mɪdl] Mitte; Mittelteil I • **the middle of nowhere** *(infml) etwa:* das Ende der Welt V 1 (12/185)
middle school ['mɪdl ˌsku:l] *(USA) Schule für 11- bis 14-Jährige* IV
might [maɪt]**: you might need help** du könntest (vielleicht) Hilfe brauchen III
migrant worker [ˌmaɪgrənt 'wɜ:kə] Wanderarbeiter/in IV
mild [maɪld] mild III
mile [maɪl] Meile *(= ca. 1,6 km)* II **for miles** meilenweit II • **miles per hour** Meilen pro Stunde *(100 mph entspricht ca. 160 km/h)* V 4 (87) • **go at 50 mph** 50 Meilen pro Stunde fahren V 4 (87)
military ['mɪlətri] militärisch, Militär- V 4 (85) • **military-style fashion** Mode im Militärstil V 4 (85/207)
milk [mɪlk] melken IV
milk [mɪlk] Milch I
milkshake ['mɪlkʃeɪk] Milchshake I
million ['mɪljən] Million III
millionaire [ˌmɪljə'neə] Millionär/in IV
mime [maɪm] vorspielen, pantomimisch darstellen II
mind sth. [maɪnd]
1. etwas dagegen haben (etwas zu tun) V 2 (35) • **Do you mind?** Stört es dich/Sie? V 2 (35/191) • **I don't mind** Es macht mir nichts aus V 2 (35/191) • **if you don't mind** wenn Sie nichts dagegen haben V 2 (35/191) • **Would you mind ...?** Würden Sie bitte ...? V 2 (35/191)
► S.191 (to) mind
2. *(sich kümmern)* **Mind your own business.** Das geht dich nichts an! / Kümmere dich um deine eigenen Angelegenheiten! II
Never mind. Kümmere dich nicht drum. / Macht nichts. II
mind [maɪnd] Verstand, Kopf V 2 (42)
°have sth. on one's mind an etwas denken
mind map ['maɪnd mæp] Mindmap („Gedankenkarte", „Wissensnetz") I
mine [maɪn] meiner, meine, meins II
minimum ['mɪnɪməm] Minimum V 2 (47)
minister ['mɪnɪstə]
1. Minister/in IV • **prime minister** Premierminister/in IV
2. Pfarrer/in, Pastor/in IV
minority [maɪ'nɒrəti] Minderheit IV
mints *(pl)* [mɪnts] Pfefferminzbonbons I
minute ['mɪnɪt] Minute I • **Wait a minute.** Warte mal! / Moment mal! II • **a 30-minute ride** eine 30-minütige Fahrt III
Minuteman ['mɪnɪtˌmən] *Angehöriger der amerikanischen Miliz* IV
mirror ['mɪrə] Spiegel II
Miss White [mɪs] Frau White *(unverheiratet)* I
miss [mɪs]
1. vermissen II
2. verpassen II
Miss a turn. Einmal aussetzen. II
missing ['mɪsɪŋ]**: be missing** fehlen II
mistake [mɪ'steɪk] Fehler I • **by mistake** aus Versehen IV
mix [mɪks] mischen, mixen III
mixed-race [ˌmɪkst 'reɪs] gemischtrassig V 1 (17)
mixture ['mɪkstʃə] Mischung III
mobile (phone) ['məʊbaɪl] Mobiltelefon, Handy I
model ['mɒdl] Modell(-flugzeug, -schiff usw.) I; (Foto-)Modell II
mole [məʊl] Maulwurf II
mom [mɑ:m] *(AE)* Mutti, Mama; Mutter III
moment ['məʊmənt] Augenblick, Moment I • **at the moment** im Moment, gerade, zurzeit I • **for a moment** einen Moment lang II
monarch ['mɒnək] Monarch/in V 3 (53/200)
monarchy ['mɒnəki] Monarchie V 3 (53/200)
► S.200 Different forms of government
Monday ['mʌndeɪ, 'mʌndi] Montag I • **Monday morning** Montagmorgen I
money ['mʌni] Geld I • **Money doesn't grow on trees.** *Redensart:* Geld wächst nicht auf Bäumen; Geld liegt nicht auf der Straße. III
raise money (for) Geld sammeln (für) IV
monitor ['mɒnɪtə] Bildschirm, Monitor III
monk [mʌŋk] Mönch V 1 (17)
monkey ['mʌŋki] Affe II
monolingual [ˌmɒnə'lɪŋgwəl] einsprachig V 4 (90)
monster ['mɒnstə] Monster, Ungeheuer III
month [mʌnθ] Monat I
mood [mu:d] Laune V 4 (94) • **be in a good/bad mood** gute/schlechte Laune haben V 4 (94)
moon [mu:n] Mond II
moped ['məʊped] Moped V 4 (92)
°**moral** ['mɒrəl] Lehre, Moral
more [mɔ:] mehr I • **lots more** viel mehr I • **more boring (than)** langweiliger (als) II • **more or less** mehr oder weniger IV • **more quickly (than)** schneller (als) II **more than me** mehr als ich II **no more music** keine Musik mehr I • **not (...) any more** nicht mehr II • **one more** noch ein(e), ein(e) weitere(r, s) I
°**morn** [mɔ:n] *(gehoben)* Morgen
morning ['mɔ:nɪŋ] Morgen, Vormittag I • **in the morning** morgens, am Morgen I • **Monday morning** Montagmorgen I • **on Friday morning** freitagmorgens, am Freitagmorgen I
mosque [mɒsk] Moschee III
► S.198 Religions
most [məʊst] (der/die/das) meiste ...; am meisten II • **most people** die meisten Leute I • **(the) most boring ...** der/die/das langweiligste ...; am langweiligsten II
motel [məʊ'tel] Motel III
mother ['mʌðə] Mutter I
motorway ['məʊtəweɪ] *(BE)* Autobahn IV
mountain ['maʊntən] Berg II
mouse [maʊs]**,** *pl* **mice** [maɪs] Maus I
mouth [maʊθ] Mund I
move [mu:v]
1. bewegen; sich bewegen II
Move back one space. Geh ein Feld zurück. II • **Move on one space.** Geh ein Feld vor. II
2. move (to) umziehen (nach, in) II • **move in** einziehen II • **move out** ausziehen II
move [mu:v] Umzug IV
movement ['mu:vmənt] Bewegung II

movie ['mu:vi] Film IV
MP3 player [ˌempi:'θri: ˌpleɪə] MP3-Spieler I
mph (miles per hour) [ˌem pi: 'aɪtʃ] Meilen pro Stunde *(100 mph entspricht ca. 160 km/h)* V 4 (87) • **go at 50 mph** 50 Meilen pro Stunde fahren V 4 (87)
Mr, Mr. ... ['mɪstə] Herr ... I
Mrs, Mrs. ... ['mɪsɪz] Frau ... I
Ms, Ms. ... [mɪz, məz] Frau ... II
much [mʌtʃ] viel I • **how much?** wie viel? I • **How much is/are ...?** Was kostet/kosten ...? / Wie viel kostet/kosten ...? I • **like/love sth. very much** etwas sehr mögen/sehr lieben II • **Thanks very much!** Danke sehr! / Vielen Dank! II
mud [mʌd] Schlamm, Matsch V 4 (96/210)
muddy ['mʌdi] schlammig, matschig V 4 (96)
muesli ['mju:zli] Müsli I
mule [mju:l] Maultier IV • **mule train** Maultierkarawane IV
°**mulga-tree** ['mʌlgə] Mulgabaum
multi- ['mʌltɪ] viel-, mehr-; multi-, Multi- IV • **multi-coloured** mehrfarbig IV • **multi-millionaire** Multimillionär(in) IV
mum [mʌm], **mummy** ['mʌmi], Mama, Mutti; Mutter I
murderer ['mɜ:dərə] Mörder/in III
murder ['mɜ:də] (er)morden III
murder ['mɜ:də] Mord III
museum [mju'zi:əm] Museum I
music ['mju:zɪk]
1. Musik I • **Music is for dancing.** *etwa:* Musik ist zum Tanzen da. III
2. Noten III • **I can read music.** Ich kann Noten lesen. III
musical ['mju:zɪkl] Musical I
musician [mju:'zɪʃn] Musiker/in III
Muslim ['mʊzlɪm] Muslim/Muslima, Muslimin; muslimisch V 3 (50/198)
► S.198 Religions
must [mʌst] müssen I
mustard ['mʌstəd] Senf IV
mustn't do ['mʌsnt] nicht tun dürfen II
my [maɪ] mein/e I • **My name is ...** Ich heiße ... / Mein Name ist ... I
It's my turn. Ich bin dran / an der Reihe. I
myself [maɪ'self]
1. mir/mich III
2. selbst IV
mystery ['mɪstri] Rätsel, Geheimnis I

N

naked ['neɪkɪd] nackt V 1 (9) • **with the naked eye** mit dem bloßen Auge V 1 (9/184)
name [neɪm] Name I • **My name is ...** Ich heiße ... / Mein Name ist ... I • **What's your name?** Wie heißt du? I • **call sb. names** jn. mit Schimpfwörtern hänseln, jm. Schimpfwörter nachrufen III
put one's name on a list sich eintragen IV
name [neɪm] nennen; benennen II
narrator [nə'reɪtə] Erzähler/in IV
nation ['neɪʃn] Nation, Volk III
the First Nations die Ersten Nationen *(indianische Ureinwohner/innen Kanadas)* III
national ['næʃnəl] national III
national park Nationalpark IV
°**National Minimum Drinking Age Act** *entspricht ungefähr dem Jugendschutzgesetz*
nationality [ˌnæʃə'næləti] Staatsangehörigkeit, Nationalität V 2 (39)
Native American [ˌneɪtɪv_ə'merɪkən] amerikanische(r) Ureinwohner/in, Indianer/in IV
natural ['nætʃrəl] natürlich, Natur- II
near [nɪə] in der Nähe von, nahe (bei) I
nearby [ˌnɪə'baɪ] *(adj)* nahegelegen; *(adv)* in der Nähe V 1 (23)
nearly ['nɪəli] fast, beinahe IV
neat [ni:t]
1. gepflegt II • **neat and tidy** schön ordentlich II
2. *(AE, infml)* großartig, toll, klasse III
necessary ['nesəsri] notwendig, nötig V 2 (35)
neck [nek] Hals IV
need [ni:d] brauchen, benötigen I
needn't do ['ni:dnt] nicht tun müssen, nicht zu tun brauchen II
°**need** [ni:d]**: people in need** Notleidende
negative ['negətɪv] negativ V 2 (39)
neighbour ['neɪbə] Nachbar/in I
Neither. ['naɪðə, 'ni:ðə] Weder noch.; Keiner der beiden. V 2 (34)
► S.190 neither
nervous ['nɜ:vəs] nervös, aufgeregt I
network ['netwɜ:k] (Fernseh-/Radio-) Sendernetz IV
never ['nevə] nie, niemals I
Never mind. Kümmere dich nicht drum. / Macht nichts. II

new [nju:] neu I • °**the New World** die Neue Welt *(Amerika)*
news *(no pl)* [nju:z] Nachrichten I
news agency ['nju:z_ˌeɪdʒənsi] Nachrichtenagentur IV
newspaper ['nju:speɪpə] Zeitung I
do a (news)paper round Zeitungen austragen V 4 (92)
°**newsreader** ['nju:zri:də] Nachrichtensprecher
next [nekst]**: be next** der/die Nächste sein I • °**the boy next door** der Junge von nebenan
the next day am nächsten Tag I
the next photo das nächste Foto I
What have we got next? Was haben wir als Nächstes? I
next to [nekst] neben I
nice [naɪs] schön, nett I • **nice and cool/clean/...** schön kühl/sauber/... I • **Nice to meet you.** Nett, dich/euch/Sie kennenzulernen. III
night [naɪt] Nacht, später Abend I
at night nachts, in der Nacht I
late at night spät abends V 4 (84)
on Friday night freitagnachts, Freitagnacht I
nightclub ['naɪtklʌb] Nachtklub III
nil [nɪl] null III
no [nəʊ] nein I
no [nəʊ] kein, keine I • **no more music** keine Musik mehr I • **no people at all** überhaupt keine Menschen IV • **No way!** [ˌnəʊ 'weɪ] Auf keinen Fall! / Kommt nicht in Frage! II; Was du nicht sagst! / Das kann nicht dein Ernst sein! III
no., *pl* **nos.** ['nʌmbə] Nr. III
noble ['nəʊbl] ehrenhaft; adlig IV
nobody ['nəʊbədi] niemand II
nod (-dd-) [nɒd] nicken (mit) II
nod (one's head) (mit dem Kopf) nicken III
noise [nɔɪz] Geräusch; Lärm I
noisy ['nɔɪzi] laut, lärmend II
no one ['nəʊ wʌn] niemand III
°**not listening to no one** *(infml)* = **not listening to anyone**
non-fiction ['nɒnˌfɪkʃn] Sachliteratur IV
non-fictional text [ˌnɒn'fɪkʃənl] Sachtext V 3 (61)
non-violent [ˌnɒn 'vaɪələnt] gewaltlos, gewaltfrei IV
north [nɔ:θ] Norden; nach Norden; nördlich II • **northbound** ['nɔ:θbaʊnd] Richtung Norden III
north-east [ˌnɔ:θ'i:st] Nordosten; nach Nordosten; nordöstlich II
northern ['nɔ:ðən] nördlich, Nord- III • **north-west** [ˌnɔ:θ'west] Nord-

westen; nach Nordwesten; nordwestlich II
nose [nəʊz] Nase I
not [nɒt] nicht I • **not (...) any** kein, keine I • **not (...) any more** nicht mehr II • **not (...) anybody** niemand II • **not (...) anything** nichts II • **not (...) anywhere** nirgendwo(hin) II • **not at all** gar nicht, überhaupt nicht, überhaupt kein(e) IV • **not (...) either** auch nicht II • **not only ... but also ...** nicht nur ... sondern auch ... IV
not (...) yet noch nicht II
note [nəʊt]
1. Mitteilung, Notiz I • **take notes (on)** sich Notizen machen (über, zu) I
2. Ton III
3. *(BE)* (Geld-)Schein, Banknote V 4 (88)
°**note sth. down** [ˌnəʊt 'daʊn] (sich) etwas notieren
nothing ['nʌθɪŋ] nichts II
nothing at all gar nichts, überhaupt nichts IV
notice ['nəʊtɪs] (be)merken IV
notice board ['nəʊtɪs bɔːd] schwarzes Brett, Anschlagtafel IV
novel ['nɒvl] Roman IV
November [nəʊ'vembə] November I
now [naʊ] nun, jetzt I • **(and) now for ...** und jetzt ... *(kündigt ein neues Thema an)* III • **now and again** ab und zu, von Zeit zu Zeit III
nowadays ['naʊədeɪz] heutzutage IV
nowhere ['nəʊweə] nirgendwo(hin) V 1 (12) • **the middle of nowhere** *(infml)* *etwa:* das Ende der Welt V 1 (12/185)
number ['nʌmbə] Zahl, Ziffer, Nummer I
number plate ['nʌmbə ˌpleɪt] Nummernschild IV
nun [nʌn] Nonne V 1 (17)
nut [nʌt] Nuss III

O

o [əʊ] null I
obey [ə'beɪ] gehorchen; sich halten an IV
observatory [əb'zɜːvətri] Aussichtsplattform IV
ocean ['əʊʃn] Ozean IV
o'clock [ə'klɒk]: **eleven o'clock** elf Uhr I
October [ɒk'təʊbə] Oktober I
of [əv, ɒv] von I • **of the summer holidays** der Sommerferien I
a kilogram of oranges ein Kilogramm Orangen III
of course [əv 'kɔːs] natürlich, selbstverständlich I
off [ɒf]: °**she cleans the potatoes off her shirt** sie reinigt ihr Hemd von den Kartoffeln • **take 10 c off** 10 Cent abziehen I
offer ['ɒfə] (an)bieten IV
office ['ɒfɪs]
1. Amt V 3 (60) • **term of office** Amtsperiode V 3 (60)
2. Büro V 3 (60)
officer ['ɒfɪsə]: **police officer** Polizist/in V 3 (56)
official [ə'fɪʃl] Amts-, amtliche(r, s); offiziell V 3 (60)
often ['ɒfn] oft, häufig I
Oh dear! Oje! II
OHP [ˌəʊ_eɪtʃ 'piː] Tageslichtprojektor, Polylux V 2 (45)
Oh well ... [əʊ 'wel] Na ja ... / Na gut ... I
OK [əʊ'keɪ] okay, gut, in Ordnung I
old [əʊld] alt I • **How old are you?** Wie alt bist du? I • **I'm ... years old.** Ich bin ... Jahre alt. I • **old folks' home** *(infml)* Altenheim, Seniorenresidenz • **old people's home** Altenheim, Seniorenresidenz V 1 (17/187)
► S.209 the rich, the poor, etc.
old-fashioned [ˌəʊld'fæʃənd] altmodisch IV
oldie ['əʊldi] *(infml)* Oldie III
oligarchy [ˌɒlɪgɑːki] Oligarchie V 3 (53/201)
► S.200 Different forms of government
Olympic Games [əˌlɪmpɪk 'geɪmz] Olympische Spiele IV
on [ɒn]
1. auf I
2. weiter III
3. *(Radio, Licht usw.)* an, eingeschaltet II
be on *(in the cinema, theatre, etc.)* laufen *(im Kino, Theater, usw.)* V 1 (14)
go on angehen III • **on a/my shift** in einer/meiner Schicht IV • **on 13th June** am 13. Juni I • **on foot** zu Fuß III • **on Friday** am Freitag I • **on Friday afternoon** freitagnachmittags, am Freitagnachmittag I • **on Friday evening** freitagabends, am Freitagabend I • **on Friday morning** freitagmorgens, am Freitagmorgen I • **on Friday night** freitagnachts, Freitagnacht I • **on his street** in seiner Straße III • **on the beach** am Strand II
on the board an die Tafel I • **on the left** links, auf der linken Seite I
on the Missouri River am Missourifluss IV • **on the phone** am Telefon I • **on the plane** im Flugzeug II • **on the radio** im Radio I • **on the right** rechts, auf der rechten Seite I • **on the scene** vor Ort, zur Stelle IV • **on the second floor** im zweiten Stock *(BE)* / im ersten Stock *(AE)* IV • **on the train** im Zug I • **on their/your/the way (to)** unterwegs (nach) IV • **on the weekend** *(AE)* am Wochenende IV
on top of oben auf IV • **on TV** im Fernsehen I • **What page are we on?** Auf welcher Seite sind wir? I
be on holiday in Urlaub sein II
go on holiday in Urlaub fahren II
straight on geradeaus weiter II
once [wʌns] einmal III • **once/twice a week** (einmal/zweimal) pro Woche III • **at once** gleichzeitig, zugleich, auf einmal V 2 (35)
one ['wʌn] eins, ein, eine I • **one day** eines Tages I • **one more** noch ein/e, ein/e weitere(r, s) I
a new one ein neuer / eine neue / ein neues II • **my old ones** meine alten II • **one by one** eins nach dem anderen V 2 (45) • **one tough girl** *(AE, infml)* *etwa:* ein wirklich toughes Mädchen III
onion ['ʌnjən] Zwiebel III
online [ˌɒn'laɪn] online, Online- III
only ['əʊnli]
1. nur, bloß I • **not only ... but also ...** nicht nur ... sondern auch ... IV
2. erst II
3. the only guest der einzige Gast I
onto ['ɒntə, 'ɒntʊ] auf (... hinauf) III
°**Oops.** [uːps, ʊps] Upps.
open ['əʊpən]
1. öffnen, aufmachen I
2. sich öffnen I
open ['əʊpən] geöffnet, offen I
open-air concert [ˌəʊpən_'eə ˌkɒnsət] Open-Air-Konzert, Konzert im Freien II • **opening times** Öffnungszeiten IV
opera ['ɒprə] Oper III
opera house ['ɒprə haʊs] Oper, Opernhaus III
operation (on) [ˌɒpə'reɪʃn] Operation (an) III
opinion (on/of) [ə'pɪnjən] Meinung (zu/von) IV • **in my opinion** meiner Meinung nach IV
opponent [ə'pəʊnənt] Gegner/in IV

opportunity [ˌɒpəˈtjuːnəti] Gelegenheit, Chance, Möglichkeit V 2 (40)
► S.194 German „Möglichkeit"
oppose sb./sth. [əˈpəʊz] sich jm./etwas widersetzen; jn./etwas ablehnen V 3 (63)
opposite [ˈɒpəzɪt] gegenüber (von) II
opposite [ˈɒpəzɪt] entgegengesetzt; gegenüberliegende(r, s) V 4 (82)
opposite [ˈɒpəzɪt] Gegenteil IV
or [ɔː] oder I
oral [ˈɔːrəl] mündlich V 3 (65)
orange [ˈɒrɪndʒ] orange(farben) I
orange [ˈɒrɪndʒ] Orange, Apfelsine I • **orange juice** Orangensaft I
orchestra [ˈɔːkɪstrə] Orchester V 2 (41)
► S.196 Collective nouns
order [ˈɔːdə]
1. Befehl, Anweisung, Anordnung V 4 (84) • **break an order** gegen eine Anordnung verstoßen V 4 (84)
2. Reihenfolge V 3 (61)
3. Bestellung V 3 (66/205)
4. **out of order** außer Betrieb; *(infml)* nicht in Ordnung V 4 (80)
order [ˈɔːdə]
1. bestellen II
2. befehlen V 4 (84)
3. ordnen V 3 (66/205)
► S.205 Verbs & nouns with the same form
organization [ˌɔːɡənaɪˈzeɪʃn] Organisation IV
organize [ˈɔːɡənaɪz] organisieren, veranstalten III
organized [ˈɔːɡənaɪzd] (gut) organisiert V 2 (35)
origin [ˈɒrɪdʒɪn] Herkunft, Abstammung V 1 (9)
original *(n; adj)* [əˈrɪdʒənl] Original; Original-, ursprünglich IV
original version Originalfassung IV
orphan [ˈɔːfən] Waise, Waisenkind V 1 (17)
other [ˈʌðə] andere(r, s) I • **the others** die anderen I • **the other way round** anders herum II
otherwise [ˈʌðəwaɪz] sonst IV
Ouch! [aʊtʃ] Autsch! I
our [ˈaʊə] unser, unsere I
ours [ˈaʊəz] unsere(r, s) II
ourselves [aʊəˈselvz]
1. uns III
2. selbst IV
out [aʊt] heraus, hinaus; draußen II
be out weg sein, nicht da sein I
out of ... aus ... (heraus/hinaus) I
out of order außer Betrieb; *(infml)* nicht in Ordnung V 4 (80)
outback [ˈaʊtbæk]: **the outback** *(Australien)* das Hinterland V 1 (6)
°**outcast** [ˈaʊtkɑːst] Ausgestoßene(r)
outfit [ˈaʊtfɪt] Outfit *(Kleidung; Ausrüstung)* II
outdoor [ˈaʊtdɔː] im Freien, Außen- III
outline [ˈaʊtlaɪn] Gliederung IV
outside [ˌaʊtˈsaɪd]
1. draußen I; Außen- IV
2. nach draußen II
3. **outside the room** vor dem Zimmer; außerhalb des Zimmers I
oven [ˈʌvn] Ofen, Backofen IV
over [ˈəʊvə]
1. über, oberhalb von I • **all over the world** auf der ganzen Welt III **from all over the world** aus der ganzen Welt II • **over there** da drüben, dort drüben I • **over to ...** hinüber zu/nach ... II • **over time** [ˌəʊvə ˈtaɪm] im Laufe der Zeit IV
2. **be over** vorbei sein, zu Ende sein I
°**overfishing** [ˌəʊvəˈfɪʃɪŋ] Überfischung
overhead projector [ˌəʊvəhed prəˈdʒektə] Tageslichtprojektor, Polylux V 2 (45)
own [əʊn] besitzen IV
own [əʊn]: **our own pool** unser eigenes Schwimmbecken II • **of one's own** seine eigene V 3 (60)
on our/my/... own allein, selbstständig *(ohne Hilfe)* IV
owner [ˈəʊnə] Besitzer/in, Eigentümer/in IV
ozone hole [ˈəʊzəʊn həʊl] Ozonloch V 1 (9)

P

pack [pæk] packen, einpacken II
packet [ˈpækɪt] Päckchen, Packung, Schachtel I • **a packet of mints** ein Päckchen/eine Packung Pfefferminzbonbons I
paddle [ˈpædl] paddeln III
paddle [ˈpædl] Paddel III
pads [pædz] Knieschützer; Schulterpolster III
page [peɪdʒ] (Buch-, Heft-)Seite I
What page are we on? Auf welcher Seite sind wir? I
paid [peɪd] *siehe* **pay**
pain [peɪn] Schmerz(en) I • **cry in pain** vor Schmerzen schreien I
paint [peɪnt] (an)malen I; anstreichen II
paint [peɪnt] Farbe, Lack IV
painter [ˈpeɪntə] Maler/in II
painting [ˈpeɪntɪŋ] Gemälde, Bild; Malerei III
pair [peə]: **a pair (of)** ein Paar II
palace [ˈpæləs] Palast, Schloss III
panic [ˈpænɪk] in Panik geraten III
pants *(pl)* [pænts] *(AE)* Hose IV
paper [ˈpeɪpə]
1. Papier I
2. Zeitung V 4 (92)
do a paper round Zeitungen austragen V 4 (92)
parade [pəˈreɪd] Parade, Umzug IV
paradise [ˈpærədaɪs] Paradies III
paragraph [ˈpærəɡrɑːf] Absatz *(in einem Text)* II
Paralympics [ˌpærəˈlɪmpɪks] Paralympische Spiele *(Olympische Spiele für Sportler/innen mit körperlicher Behinderung)* III
paramedic [ˌpærəˈmedɪk] Sanitäter/in II
paraphrase [ˈpærəfreɪz] umschreiben, anders ausdrücken III
parcel [ˈpɑːsl] Paket I
pardon [ˈpɑːdn] begnadigen IV
parent [ˈpeərənt]: **a single parent** ein(e) Alleinerziehende(r) II
parents [ˈpeərənts] Eltern I
park [pɑːk] Park I • **car park** Parkplatz III • **national park** Nationalpark IV
parking lot [ˈpɑːkɪŋ lɒt] *(AE)* Parkplatz IV
parliament [ˈpɑːləmənt] Parlament III
°**parliamentary** [ˌpɑːləˈmentri]: **parliamentary procedure** Geschäftsordnung
parrot [ˈpærət] Papagei I
part [pɑːt] Teil I • **take part in sth.** teilnehmen an etwas III
participate (in) [pɑːˈtɪsɪpeɪt] teilnehmen (an) IV
particular [pəˈtɪkjələ] bestimmte(r, s), spezielle(r, s) V 2 (35)
partner [ˈpɑːtnə] Partner/in I
party [ˈpɑːti]
1. Party I
2. Partei V 3 (62)
pass [pɑːs]
1. (herüber)reichen, weitergeben I • **pass sth. on** etwas weiterleiten, -geben IV • **pass round** herumgeben I
2. bestehen *(Test, Prüfung usw.)* V 2 (32)
3. genehmigen, verabschieden *(Gesetz usw.)* V 3 (50)
passenger [ˈpæsɪndʒə] Passagier/in, Fahrgast III
passive [ˈpæsɪv] Passiv III
past [pɑːst] Vergangenheit II

past [pɑːst] vorbei (an), vorüber (an) II • **half past 11** halb zwölf (11.30 / 23.30) I • **quarter past 11** Viertel nach 11 (11.15 / 23.15) I
path [pɑːθ] Pfad, Weg II • **bridle path** ['braɪdl ˌpɑːθ] Reitweg III
patient ['peɪʃnt] geduldig V 4 (94)
patrol [pə'trəʊl] Streife, Patrouille IV
pavement ['peɪvmənt] Gehweg, Bürgersteig IV
pay (for) [peɪ], **paid, paid** bezahlen II • **pay (sb.) sth. back** etwas (jm.) zurückzahlen V 3 (50)
PE [ˌpiː‿'iː], **Physical Education** [ˌfɪzɪkəl‿edʒu'keɪʃn] Sportunterricht, Turnen I
peaceful ['piːsfl] friedlich V 3 (64)
pedestrian [pə'destriən] Fußgänger/in IV
pedestrian crossing [pəˌdestriən 'krɒsɪŋ] Fußgängerüberweg IV
pen [pen] Kugelschreiber, Füller I
penalty ['penəlti] Strafstoß; Elfmeter *(Fußball)* III
pence (p) *(pl)* [pens] Pence *(Plural von „penny")* I
pencil ['pensl] Bleistift I • **pencil case** ['pensl keɪs] Federmäppchen I • **pencil sharpener** ['pensl ʃɑːpnə] Bleistiftanspitzer I
penny ['peni] *kleinste britische Münze* I
people ['piːpl] Menschen, Leute I
°**people in need** Notleidende
old people's home Altenheim, Seniorenresidenz V 1 (17/187)
pepper ['pepə] Pfeffer V 1 (22)
per [pɜː, pə] pro III
per cent (%) [pə'sent] Prozent III
percentage [pə'sentɪdʒ] Prozentsatz, prozentualer Anteil V 1 (10)
perfect ['pɜːfɪkt] perfekt; ideal; vollkommen IV
performer: (street) performer [pə'fɔːmə] Straßenkünstler/in III
period ['pɪəriəd] (Unterrichts-/Schul-)Stunde IV
person ['pɜːsn] Person I
personal ['pɜːsənl] persönlich III
personality [ˌpɜːsə'næləti] Persönlichkeit V 2 (34)
persuade [pə'sweɪd] überreden V 3 (65)
pet [pet] Haustier I • **pet shop** Tierhandlung I
petrol ['petrəl] Benzin IV
petrol station ['petrəl ˌsteɪʃn] Tankstelle IV
phone [fəʊn] anrufen I
phone [fəʊn] Telefon I • **on the phone** am Telefon I • **phone number** Telefonnummer I • **pick up the phone** den Hörer abnehmen II
photo ['fəʊtəʊ] Foto I • **in the photo** auf dem Foto I • **take photos** Fotos machen, fotografieren I
photographer [fə'tɒgrəfə] Fotograf/in II
phrase [freɪz] Ausdruck, (Rede-)Wendung II
piano [pi'ænəʊ] Klavier, Piano I
play the piano Klavier spielen I
pick [pɪk]: **pick fruit/flowers** Obst/Blumen pflücken IV • **pick sb. up** jn. abholen III • **pick sth. up** etwas hochheben, aufheben III
pick up the phone den Hörer abnehmen II
picnic ['pɪknɪk] Picknick II
°**Picts** *(pl)* [pɪkt] die Pikten
picture ['pɪktʃə] Bild I • **in the picture** auf dem Bild I
pie [paɪ] Obstkuchen; Pastete II
pie chart ['paɪ tʃɑːt] Tortendiagramm V 1 (10)
piece [piːs]: **a piece of** ein Stück I
a piece of paper ein Stück Papier I
a piece of clothing Kleidungsstück IV
pilgrim ['pɪlgrɪm] Pilger/in IV
pilot ['paɪlət] Pilot/in IV
°**pinboard** ['pɪnbɔːd] Pinnwand
pink [pɪŋk] pink(farben), rosa I
pipe [paɪp] Pfeife III
pirate ['paɪrət] Pirat, Piratin I
pitch [pɪtʃ]: **football/hockey pitch** Fußball-/Hockeyplatz, -feld II
pity ['pɪti]: **It's a pity (that ...)** Es ist schade, dass ... II
pizza ['piːtsə] Pizza I
place [pleɪs] Ort, Platz I • **place of birth** Geburtsort IV • **take place** stattfinden II • **in other places** an anderen Orten, anderswo III
placement ['pleɪsmənt] Praktikum V 2 (38)
plain [pleɪn] einfach, schlicht IV
plan [plæn] Plan I
plan (-nn-) [plæn] planen II
plane [pleɪn] Flugzeug II • **on the plane** im Flugzeug II
planet ['plænɪt] Planet II
plant [plɑːnt] (ein-, aus-, be-)pflanzen IV
plant [plɑːnt] Pflanze IV
°**plantation** [plɑːn'teɪʃn] Plantage
plastic ['plæstɪk] Plastik, Kunststoff IV
plate [pleɪt] Teller I • **a plate of chips** ein Teller Pommes frites I
license plate *(AE)* Nummernschild IV • **number plate** Nummernschild IV
platform ['plætfɔːm] Bahnsteig, Gleis III
play [pleɪ] spielen I • **play a trick on sb.** jm. einen Streich spielen II
play football Fußball spielen I
play the drums Schlagzeug spielen III • **play the fiddle** Geige spielen III • **play the guitar** Gitarre spielen I • **play the piano** Klavier spielen I • **play the violin** Geige spielen III
play [pleɪ] Theaterstück I
°**play area** ['pleɪ‿ˌeəriə] Spielplatz
player ['pleɪə] Spieler/in I
please [pliːz] bitte *(in Fragen und Aufforderungen)* I
pleased [pliːzd]: **be pleased** sich freuen IV
plenty of ['plenti‿əv] reichlich, viel(e) IV
plot [plɒt] Handlung V 1 (24)
plug [plʌg] Stecker III
plutocracy [pluː'tɒkrəsi] Plutokratie V 3 (53/201)
► S.200 Different forms of government
pm [ˌpiː‿'em]: **7 pm** 7 Uhr abends/19 Uhr I
pocket ['pɒkɪt] Tasche *(an Kleidungsstück)* II • **pocket money** Taschengeld II
poem ['pəʊɪm] Gedicht I
point [pɔɪnt] Punkt II • **11.4 (eleven point four)** 11,4 (elf Komma vier) II • **point of view** Standpunkt II
from my point of view aus meiner Sicht; von meinem Standpunkt aus gesehen II • **That's a good point.** Das ist ein gutes Argument. V 4 (86) • **There was no point.** Es hatte keinen Sinn. III • **What's the point?** Was soll das? III
point (at/to sth.) [pɔɪnt] zeigen, deuten (auf etwas) II • **point sth. out (to sb.)** (jm.) etwas zeigen; (jn.) auf etwas hinweisen V 2 (47)
poison ['pɔɪzn] Gift V 1 (22)
poisonous ['pɔɪzənəs] giftig V 1 (22)
police *(pl)* [pə'liːs] Polizei I • **police officer** Polizist/in V 3 (56) • **police station** Polizeiwache, Polizeirevier II
policy (on sth.) ['pɒləsi] Politik *(in Bezug auf etwas)* V 3 (62)
polite [pə'laɪt] höflich IV
political [pə'lɪtɪkl] politisch V 3 (62)
politician [ˌpɒlə'tɪʃn] Politiker/in IV
politics ['pɒlətɪks] (die) Politik IV

pollution [pə'lu:ʃn] Verschmutzung IV
poltergeist ['pəʊltəgaɪst] Poltergeist I
ponytail ['pəʊniteɪl] Pferdeschwanz *(Frisur)* III
pool [pu:l] Schwimmbad, Schwimmbecken II
poor [pɔ:, pʊə] arm I • **poor Sophie** (die) arme Sophie I
► S.209 the rich, the poor, etc.
pop *siehe* **population**
pop (music) [pɒp] Pop(musik) III
popcorn ['pɒpkɔ:n] Popcorn II
popular ['pɒpjələ] populär, beliebt III
population [,pɒpju'leɪʃn] Bevölkerung, Einwohner(zahl) III
positive ['pɒzətɪv] positiv V 2 (39)
possess [pə'zes] (fml) besitzen, haben V 3 (63)
possibility [,pɒsə'bɪləti] Möglichkeit IV
► S.194 German „Möglichkeit"
possible ['pɒsəbl] möglich II
post [pəʊst] Post *(Briefe, Päckchen, ...)* III
post office ['pəʊst_ɒfɪs] Postamt II
postcard ['pəʊstkɑ:d] Postkarte II
poster ['pəʊstə] Poster I
postscript ['pəʊstskrɪpt] Postskript III
potato [pə'teɪtəʊ], *pl* **potatoes** Kartoffel I • °**couch potato** [kaʊtʃ] Dauerglotzer/in • **potato chips** *(AE)* Kartoffelchips IV
pound (£) [paʊnd] Pfund *(britische Währung)* I
pound [paʊnd] Pfund *(Gewichtseinheit)*: **a three-pound ball** ein drei Pfund schwerer Ball III
power ['paʊə] Macht; Stärke V 3 (53)
°**powerful** ['paʊəfl] mächtig, einflussreich
practical ['præktɪkl] praktisch; praxisnah, praxisbezogen V 2 (35)
practice ['præktɪs] *im Lehrwerk:* Übungsteil I
practice ['præktɪs] *(AE)* üben; trainieren IV
practise ['præktɪs] üben; trainieren I
pray [preɪ] beten IV
prayer [preə] Gebet IV
precinct ['pri:sɪŋkt]: **shopping precinct** Einkaufsviertel, Einkaufsstraße III
prefer sth. (to sth.) (-rr-) [prɪ'fɜ:] etwas (einer anderen Sache) vorziehen; etwas lieber tun (als etwas) IV
prefix ['pri:fɪks] Präfix III
prejudice (against) ['predʒudɪs] Voreingenommenheit (gegen), Vorurteil (gegenüber) IV
prejudiced: ['predʒudɪst]: **be prejudiced (against)** voreingenommen sein (gegen), Vorurteile haben (gegenüber) IV
prepare [prɪ'peə] vorbereiten; sich vorbereiten II • **prepare for** sich vorbereiten auf II
present ['preznt]
1. Gegenwart I
2. Geschenk I
present sth. (to sb.) [prɪ'zent] (jm.) etwas präsentieren, vorstellen I; überreichen III
presentation [,prezn'teɪʃn] Präsentation, Vorstellung I
present-day [,preznt 'deɪ] heutige(r, s) IV
presenter [prɪ'zentə] Moderator/in II
president ['prezɪdənt] Präsident/in IV
press [pres]: **the press** die Presse, Zeitungen V 3 (53)
pressure ['preʃə] Druck, Belastung V 3 (53)
pretend [prɪ'tend] so tun, als ob V 4 (95)
pretty ['prɪti]
1. hübsch I
► S.206 German „schön" etc.
2. pretty cool/good/... ziemlich cool/gut/... II
prevent sth. [prɪ'vent] etwas verhindern IV • **prevent sb./sth. from doing sth.** jn./etwas daran hindern, etwas zu tun IV
prewriting exercise [,pri:'raɪtɪŋ] Übung vor dem Schreiben III
price [praɪs] (Kauf-)Preis I
primary school ['praɪməri] *Grundschule in GB, von 4–5 bis 11 Jahren* V 2 (38)
prime minister [,praɪm 'mɪnɪstə] Premierminister/in IV
principal ['prɪnsəpl] *(bes. AE)* Schulleiter/in IV
print sth. out [,prɪnt_'aʊt] etwas ausdrucken II
prison ['prɪzn] Gefängnis IV • **in prison for murder** im Gefängnis wegen Mordes IV
prisoner ['prɪznə] Gefangene(r) IV
private ['praɪvət] privat V 1 (15)
privilege ['prɪvəlɪdʒ] Privileg V 4 (92)
prize [praɪz] Preis, Gewinn I
°**pro** [prəʊ]: **pros and cons** *(pl)* Vor- und Nachteile
probably ['prɒbəbli] wahrscheinlich II
problem ['prɒbləm] Problem II
°**face a problem** mit einem Problem konfrontiert sein
°**procedure** [prə'si:dʒə]: **parliamentary procedure** Geschäftsordnung
produce [prə'dju:s] produzieren, erzeugen, herstellen II
°**producer** [prə'dju:sə] Produzent/in
professional [prə'feʃənl] professionell IV
profile ['prəʊfaɪl] Profil; Beschreibung, Porträt V 1 (6)
program ['prəʊgræm] *(AE)* Programm IV
programme ['prəʊgræm] programmieren; planen IV
programme ['prəʊgræm]
1. Programm I
2. (Fernseh-/Radio-)Sendung IV
progress ['prəʊgres]: **in progress** im Gange V 2 (49)
project (about, on) ['prɒdʒekt] Projekt (über, zu) I • **do a project** ein Projekt machen, durchführen II
projector [prə'dʒektə]: **video projector** Videoprojektor, Beamer V 2 (45)
promise ['prɒmɪs] versprechen II
°**promo (video)** ['prəʊməʊ] Werbevideo
°**promotional** [prə'məʊʃənl] Werbe-
pronunciation [prə,nʌnsi'eɪʃn] Aussprache I
proof *(no pl)* [pru:f] Beweis(e) II
proposal [prə'pəʊzl] (offizieller) Vorschlag V 3 (60)
protect sb./sth. (from sb./sth.) [prə'tekt] jn./etwas (be)schützen (vor jm./etwas) IV
protective [prə'tektɪv] Schutz-, schützend V 1 (9)
protest (against/about) [prə'test] protestieren (gegen) IV
protest ['prəʊtest] Protest IV
protester [prə'tester] Demonstrant/in V 3 (64)
proud (of sb./sth.) [praʊd] stolz (auf jn./etwas) II
PS [,pi:_'es] (**postscript** ['pəʊstskrɪpt]) PS, Postskript *(Nachschrift unter Briefen)* III
pub [pʌb] Kneipe, Lokal II
public ['pʌblɪk] öffentlich IV; öffentlich bekannt V 3 (56) • **public transport** öffentlicher Verkehr IV
public ['pʌblɪk]: **the public** die Öffentlichkeit IV
publish ['pʌblɪʃ] veröffentlichen III
pull [pʊl] ziehen I
pullover ['pʊləʊvə] Pullover II

punctual ['pʌŋktʃuəl] pünktlich V 2 (35)
punish ['pʌnɪʃ] bestrafen V 4 (84)
punishment ['pʌnɪʃmənt] Bestrafung, Strafe V 4 (84)
punk [pʌŋk] Punker/in II
purple ['pɜːpl] violett; lila I
purse [pɜːs] Geldbörse II
push [pʊʃ] drücken, schieben, stoßen I
put (-tt-) [pʊt], **put, put** legen, stellen, (etwas wohin) tun I • **put sth. away** wegräumen IV • **put sth. in** etwas hineinstecken V 3 (50) • **put sth. in order** etwas in Ordnung bringen IV • **put sb. to bed** jn. ins Bett bringen III • **put sth. on** etwas anziehen *(Kleidung)*; etwas aufsetzen *(Hut, Helm)* II • **put out a fire** ein Feuer löschen IV • °**put one's hand up** sich melden • **put one's name on a list** sich eintragen IV • **You know how to put it.** Sie wissen, wie man es formuliert/ausdrückt. IV
puzzled ['pʌzld] verwirrt II
pyjamas *(pl)* [pəˈdʒɑːməz] Schlafanzug II

Q

qualifications [ˌkwɒlɪfɪ'keɪʃn] Abschluss, Qualifikation V 2 (32)
quality ['kwɒləti] Eigenschaft; Qualität IV
quarter ['kwɔːtə]: **quarter past 11** Viertel nach 11 (11.15 / 23.15) I **quarter to 12** Viertel vor 12 (11.45 / 23.45) I
quay [kiː] Kai III
queen [kwiːn] Königin III
question ['kwestʃn] Frage I • **ask questions** Fragen stellen I
questionnaire (on sth.) [ˌkwestʃə'neə] Fragebogen (zu etwas) V 4 (80)
queue [kjuː] Schlange, Reihe *(wartender Menschen)* IV
quick [kwɪk] schnell I
quiet ['kwaɪət] leise, still, ruhig I **keep quiet** still sein, leise sein IV
quite [kwaɪt] ziemlich; ganz III
quiz [kwɪz], *pl* **quizzes** ['kwɪzɪz] Quiz, Ratespiel I
quotation [kwəʊ'teɪʃn] Zitat V 4 (97)
quotation marks [kwəʊ'teɪʃn ˌmɑːks] Anführungszeichen, -striche III

R

rabbit ['ræbɪt] Kaninchen I
rabbitproof ['ræbɪtpruːf] kaninchensicher, kaninchen-fest V 1 (17)
race (sb./sth.) [reɪs] (mit jm./etwas) um die Wette laufen/schwimmen/fahren/... V 1 (12)
race [reɪs] Rennen, (Wett-)Lauf V 1 (12)
race [reɪs] Rasse V 1 (17) • **mixed-race** gemischtrassig V 1 (17) • °**race discrimination** Diskriminierung aufgrund der Rasse • °**race relations** *(pl)* Beziehungen zwischen den Rassen
racing ['reɪsɪŋ] (Pferde-)Rennsport V 1 (12)
racist ['reɪsɪst] Rassist/in; rassistisch V 1 (17)
racket ['rækɪt] Schläger *(Badminton, Tennis, Squash)* III
radio ['reɪdiəʊ] Radio I • **on the radio** im Radio I
raft [rɑːft] Schlauchboot, Floß IV
raft [rɑːft] mit einem Schlauchboot/Floß fahren IV
railway ['reɪlweɪ] Eisenbahn II
rain [reɪn] Regen II
rain [reɪn] regnen II
rainfall ['reɪnfɔːl] Niederschlag *(Regen)*; Regenfälle V 1 (11)
rainproof ['reɪnpruːf] regendicht V 1 (17/187)
rainy ['reɪni] regnerisch II • **rainy season** Regenzeit II
raise [reɪz]: **raise money (for)** Geld sammeln (für) IV • °**raise one's hand** sich melden
ran [ræn] *siehe* **run**
rang [ræŋ] *siehe* **ring**
ranger ['reɪndʒə] Ranger/in, Aufseher/in III
rap [ræp] Rap(musik) *(rhythmischer Sprechgesang)* I
rapids *(pl)* ['ræpɪdz] Stromschnellen III
rapper ['ræpə] Rapper/in IV
rat [ræt] Ratte III
rate [reɪt] Rate V 1 (9) • **birth rate** Geburtsrate V 1 (9/183) • **death rate** Sterberate V 1 (9/183)
rate [reɪt] bewerten, einschätzen V 4 (82)
°**rating** ['reɪtɪŋ] Einschätzung
°**raw material** [rɔː] Rohstoff
ray [reɪ] (Licht-)Strahl V 1 (9) **ultraviolet rays** *(pl)* ultraviolette Strahlen V 1 (9)
RE [ˌɑːr‿'iː], **Religious Education** [rɪˌlɪdʒəs‿edʒu'keɪʃn] Religion, Religionsunterricht I
reach [riːtʃ] erreichen III • **reach agreement** sich einigen V 3 (52/199)
react (to sth.) [ri'ækt] reagieren (auf/gegen etwas) V 1 (14)
reaction (to) [ri'ækʃn] Reaktion (auf) IV
read [riːd], **read, read** lesen I **read sth. aloud** [ə'laʊd] etwas vorlesen V 3 (69) • **easy-to-read** leicht zu lesende(r, s) V 2 (39)
reader ['riːdə] Leser/in II
°**reading** ['riːdɪŋ] Lesung
ready ['redi] bereit, fertig I • **get ready (for)** sich fertig machen (für), sich vorbereiten (auf) I • **get things ready** Dinge fertig machen, vorbereiten I
real [rɪəl] echt, wirklich I • **real late** *(AE, infml)* wirklich spät, echt spät III
realistic [ˌriːə'lɪstɪk] realistisch, wirklichkeitsnah III
reality [ri'æləti] Wirklichkeit, Realität IV • **reality show** Reality-Show IV
realize ['rɪəlaɪz] erkennen, merken I
really ['rɪəli] wirklich I
reason (for) ['riːzn] Grund (für), Begründung I • **the reason why** der Grund, warum IV • **for lots of reasons** aus vielen Gründen I
receive [rɪ'siːv] erhalten III
recent ['riːsnt] jüngst, aktuell V 2 (39)
recently ['riːsntli] vor kurzem, kürzlich, neulich; in letzter Zeit V 2 (39)
°**receptionist** [rɪ'sepʃənɪst] Empfangsmitarbeiter/in
recess ['riːses] *(AE)* Pause *(zwischen Schulstunden)* IV • **during recess** in der Pause IV
reef [riːf] Riff V 1 (9)
reference ['refrəns] Referenz, Empfehlung V 2 (38)
refuse to do sth. [rɪ'fjuːz] sich weigern, etwas zu tun V 3 (54)
recognize ['rekəgnaɪz] (an)erkennen IV
°**recommend sth./sb. (to sb.)** [ˌrekə'mend] (jm.) etwas/jn. empfehlen
record [rɪ'kɔːd] aufnehmen, aufzeichnen III
°**record** ['rekɔːd] Rekord, Rekord-
recorder [rɪ'kɔːdə] Blockflöte III
recording [rɪ'kɔːdɪŋ] Aufnahme, Aufzeichnung III
recover (from) [rɪ'kʌvə] sich erholen (von) II
recycled [ˌriː'saɪkld] wiederverwertet, wiederverwendet, recycelt II

recycling [ˌriːˈsaɪklɪŋ] Wiederverwertung, Recycling II
red [red] rot I
reddish [ˈredɪʃ] rötlich IV
reduce sth. (by) [rɪˈdʒuːs] etwas reduzieren (um) IV
referee [ˌrefəˈriː] Schiedsrichter/in III
reflex [ˈriːfleks] Reflex IV
register [ˈredʒɪstə] sich anmelden; sich eintragen *(z.B. in die Wahlliste)* V 3 (65)
regular [ˈregjələ] regelmäßig III
rehearsal [rɪˈhɜːsl] Probe *(am Theater)* I
rehearse [rɪˈhɜːs] proben *(am Theater)* I
relations *(pl)* [rɪˈleɪʃnz] Beziehungen IV • °**race relations** *(pl)* Beziehungen zwischen den Rassen
relationship [rɪˈleɪʃnʃɪp] Verhältnis, Beziehung V 4 (80) • **end a relationship** mit jm. Schluss machen V 4 (80/206)
relative [ˈrelətɪv] Verwandte(r) II
relax [rɪˈlæks] (sich) entspannen, sich ausruhen II
relaxed [rɪˈlækst] entspannt V 2 (44)
release [rɪˈliːs] *(CD, Film usw.)* herausbringen, auf den Markt bringen III
reliable [rɪˈlaɪəbl] zuverlässig IV
religion [rɪˈlɪdʒən] Religion IV
religious [rɪˈlɪdʒəs] gläubig, religiös IV
remember sth. [rɪˈmembə]
1. sich an etwas erinnern I
2. sich etwas merken I
► S.195 Same verb, different meaning
remove [rɪˈmuːv] entfernen, wegnehmen; herausnehmen V 3 (66)
repair [rɪˈpeə] reparieren, ausbessern III
repeat [rɪˈpiːt] wiederholen II
repetition [ˌrepəˈtɪʃn] Wiederholung V 4 (97)
replace sth. (with) [rɪˈpleɪs] etwas ersetzen (durch) III
reply (to) [rɪˈplaɪ] antworten (auf), beantworten; erwidern III
report (on) [rɪˈpɔːt] Bericht, Reportage (über) I
report (to sb.) [rɪˈpɔːt] jm. berichten, sich bei jm. melden II
reporter [rɪˈpɔːtə] Reporter/in II
represent [ˌreprɪˈzent] repräsentieren, vertreten III; *(stellvertretend)* für etwas stehen V 3 (59)
request [rɪˈkwest] Bitte, Wunsch V 2 (38) • **on request** auf Wunsch V 2 (38/193)

require sb. to do sth [rɪˈkwaɪə] vor jm. verlangen, etwas zu tun V 4 (89)
rescue [ˈreskjuː] Rettung, Rettungsdienst IV
research *(no pl)* [rɪˈsɜːtʃ, ˈriːsɜːtʃ] Recherche, Forschung(en) III
researcher [rɪˈsɜːtʃə, ˈriːsɜːtʃə] Rechercheur/in III
reservation [ˌrezəˈveɪʃn] Reservat IV
resources *(pl)* [rɪˈzɔːsɪs, rɪˈsɔːsɪz] Mittel, Ressourcen IV
respect (for) [rɪˈspekt] Achtung, Respekt (vor) V 1 (16) • **With respect, ...** Bei allem Respekt, ... V 1 (16/186)
respect sb./sth. (for sth.) [rɪˈspekt] jn./etwas (wegen einer Sache) achten, respektieren V 1 (16)
responsibility (for) [rɪˌspɒnsəˈbɪləti] Verantwortung (für) V 2 (39) • **take responsibility (for)** Verantwortung (für) übernehmen V 2 (39)
responsible (for) [rɪˈspɒnsəbl] verantwortlich (für) V 2 (39)
rest [rest] Rest II
restart [ˌriːˈstɑːt] neu starten *(Computer)* II
restaurant [ˈrestrɒnt] Restaurant II
restroom [ˈrestˌruːm] *(AE)* (öffentliche) Toilette IV
result [rɪˈzʌlt] Ergebnis, Resultat I
°**result in sth.** [rɪˈzʌlt] zu etwas führen
résumé [ˈrezəmeɪ] *(AE)* Lebenslauf V 2 (38)
°**retreat** [rɪˈtriːt] sich zurückziehen
°**return** [rɪˈtɜːn] zurückkehren
°**reverse** [rɪˈvɜːs] umgekehrte(r, s)
review [rɪˈvjuː] (Buch-, Film-)Besprechung, Rezension V 3 (54)
revise [rɪˈvaɪz] überarbeiten IV
revision [rɪˈvɪʒn] Wiederholung *(des Lernstoffs)* I
revolution [ˌrevəˈluːʃn] Revolution IV
°**rewrite** [ˌriːˈraɪt] neu schreiben, umschreiben
rhino [ˈraɪnəʊ] Nashorn II
rhythm [ˈrɪðəm] Rhythmus III
rich [rɪtʃ] reich II
► S.209 the rich, the poor, etc.
ridden [ˈrɪdn] *siehe* **ride**
riddle [ˈrɪdl] Rätsel, Scherzfrage III
ride [raɪd], **rode, ridden** reiten I
ride a (motor)bike (Motor-)Rad fahren I
ride [raɪd]: **(bike) ride** (Rad-)Fahrt, (Rad-)Tour II • **(bus) ride** (Bus-)Fahrt II • **take a ride** eine Spritztour/Fahrt machen III

riding [ˈraɪdɪŋ] Reiten, Reitsport I
go riding [ˈraɪdɪŋ] reiten gehen I
riding boots *(pl)* Reitstiefel III
riding hat Reitkappe, Reiterhelm III
right [raɪt] richtig I • **all right** gut, in Ordnung II • **be right** Recht haben I • **get sth. right** etwas richtig machen III • **That's right.** Das ist richtig. / Das stimmt. I
You need a school bag, right? Du brauchst eine Schultasche, stimmt's? / nicht wahr? I
right [raɪt] Recht IV • °**Bill of Rights** *Zusatzartikel 1–10 zu den Grundrechten der USA* • **civil rights** *(pl)* Bürgerrechte IV • **human rights** *(pl)* Menschenrechte V 3 (50)
right [raɪt] rechte(r, s) I • **look right** nach rechts schauen I • **on the right** rechts, auf der rechten Seite I • **to the right** nach rechts III • **turn right** (nach) rechts abbiegen II • **take a right** *(AE)* nach links/rechts abbiegen IV
right [raɪt]: **right behind you** direkt/genau hinter dir II • **right now** jetzt sofort; jetzt gerade I
rim [rɪm] Rand, Kante IV
ring [rɪŋ] Ring II
ring [rɪŋ], **rang, rung** klingeln, läuten II
ringtone [ˈrɪŋtəʊn] Klingelton III
riot [ˈraɪət] Aufruhr, Krawall IV
ripe [raɪp] reif IV
rise [raɪz], **rose, risen** (auf)steigen IV
risen [ˈrɪzn] *siehe* **rise**
°**rival** [ˈraɪvl] Rivale
river [ˈrɪvə] Fluss II
road [rəʊd] Straße I • **Park Road** Parkstraße I • **road sign** Verkehrszeichen V 4 (87)
rock [rɒk] Fels, Felsen III • **rock art** *(no pl)* Felsmalerei(en) V 1 (8)
rock (music) [rɒk] Rock(musik) III
°**rock** [rɒk]: **rock the vote** *Wortspiel auf die Redewendung* **rock the boat** *(wortwörtlich:* das Boot schaukeln; *figurativ:* Ärger machen*)*
rode [rəʊd] *siehe* **ride**
role [rəʊl] Rolle III
role model [ˈrəʊl ˌmɒdl] Vorbild V 2 (48)
roll [rəʊl] Brötchen II
°**roll call** [ˈrəʊl kɔːl] Namensaufruf
Roman [ˈrəʊmən] römisch; Römer, Römerin II
roof [ruːf] Dach II
room [ruːm, rʊm] Raum, Zimmer I
rope [rəʊp] Seil IV
rose [rəʊz] *siehe* **rise**

round [raʊnd] rund II • **round brackets** runde Klammern IV
round [raʊnd] um ... (herum); in ... umher II • **round here** hier (in der Gegend) IV • **the other way round** anders herum II
round [raʊnd]**: do a paper round** Zeitungen austragen V 4 (92)
route [ruːt] Strecke, Route IV
routine [ruːˈtiːn] Routine IV
row [rəʊ] Reihe IV
royal [ˈrɔɪəl] königlich, Königs II
rubber [ˈrʌbə] Radiergummi I
rubbish [ˈrʌbɪʃ] (Haus-)Müll, Abfall II • **rubbish collection** Müllabfuhr II
rucksack [ˈrʌksæk] Rucksack III
rude [ruːd] unhöflich, unverschämt II
rugby [ˈrʌgbi] Rugby III
ruin [ˈruːɪn] Ruine IV
ruin [ˈruːɪn] verderben; ruinieren V 4 (80)
rule [ruːl] Regel, Vorschrift III **break a rule** gegen eine Regel verstoßen IV • °**follow rules** sich an die Regeln halten • **set of rules** Regelwerk V 2 (47)
°**rule** [ruːl] regieren
ruler [ˈruːlə] Lineal I
run [rʌn] (Wett-)Lauf II • **go for a run** laufen gehen IV
run (-nn-) [rʌn]**, ran, run**
1. laufen *(auch Nase)*, rennen I **run away** weglaufen V 3 (64)
2. *(Auto)* fahren V 3 (60/202) • **run sb./sth. over** jn./etwas überfahren V 3 (60/202)
3. *(Fluß)* fließen V 3 (60/202)
4. run across sb. zufällig treffen V 3 (60/202)
5. run (for sth.) (als/für etwas) kandidieren V 3 (60)
6. verlaufen *(Straße; Grenze)* IV
7. run sth. etwas leiten *(Hotel, Firma usw.)* V 1 (17) • °**run one's own affairs** sich selbst verwalten
► S.202 (to) run
rung [rʌŋ] *siehe* **ring**
runner [ˈrʌnə] Läufer/in II
running shoes [ˈrʌnɪŋ ʃuːz] Laufschuhe III
running track [ˈrʌnɪŋ træk] Laufbahn *(Sport)* III

S

sad [sæd] traurig II
sadly [ˈsædli] leider; traurig V 1 (9)
saddle [ˈsædl] Sattel III
sadness [ˈsædnəs] Traurigkeit IV
safe [seɪf] Tresor, Safe IV
safe (from) [seɪf] sicher, in Sicherheit (vor) II
safety [ˈseɪfti] Sicherheit IV
said [sed]
1. *siehe* **say**
2. he is said to be rich er soll reich sein
► S.207 German „sollen"
sail [seɪl] (mit dem Schiff) fahren; segeln IV
saint [seɪnt] Heilige(r) IV
salad [ˈsæləd] Salat *(als Gericht oder Beilage)* I
sale [seɪl] (Aus-, Schluss-)Verkauf IV
salmon [ˈsæmən]**,** *pl* **salmon** Lachs III
salt [sɔːlt] Salz V 1 (22)
salty [ˈsɔːlti] salzig V 3 (66/205)
°**saltwater** [ˈsɔːltwɔːtə] Salzwasser-, Meereswasser- • **saltwater crocodile** Leisten- oder Salzwasserkrokodil
same [seɪm]**: the same ...** der-/die-/dasselbe ...; dieselben ... I • **be/look the same** gleich sein/aussehen I
°**sandbank** [ˈsændˌbæŋk] Sandbank
sandwich [ˈsænwɪtʃ, ˈsænwɪdʒ] Sandwich, *(zusammengeklapptes)* belegtes Brot I
sandy [ˈsændi] sandig IV
sang [sæŋ] *siehe* **sing**
sank [sæŋk] *siehe* **sink**
sat [sæt] *siehe* **sit**
Saturday [ˈsætədeɪ, ˈsætədi] Samstag, Sonnabend I
sauce [sɔːs] Soße III
sauna [ˈsɔːnə] Sauna II • **have a sauna** in die Sauna gehen II
sausage [ˈsɒsɪdʒ] (Brat-, Bock-) Würstchen, Wurst I
save [seɪv]
1. retten II
2. sparen II
saw [sɔː] *siehe* **see**
°**Saxons** *(pl)* [ˈsæksnz] die Sachsen
saxophone [ˈsæksəfəʊn] Saxophon III
say [seɪ]**, said, said** sagen I • **It says here: ...** Hier steht: ... / Es heißt hier: ... II • **say goodbye** sich verabschieden I • **Say hi to your parents for me.** Grüß deine Eltern von mir. I • **say sorry** sich entschuldigen II • **They say ...** Man sagt, ... III
scan (-nn-) [skæn]**: scan a text** einen Text schnell nach bestimmten Wörtern/Informationen absuchen II
°**scar** [skɑː] Narbe
scared [skeəd] verängstigt I • **be scared (of)** Angst haben (vor) I
scary [ˈskeəri] unheimlich; gruselig I • **kind of scary** *(infml)* irgendwie unheimlich III
scene [siːn] Szene I • **on the scene** vor Ort, zur Stelle IV
scenery [ˈsiːnəri] Landschaft III
schedule [*AE:* ˈskedʒuːl, *BE:* ˈʃedjuːl] *(bes. AE)* Stundenplan IV
school [skuːl] Schule I • **at school** in der Schule I • **from school** aus der Schule III • **in school** *(AE)* in der Schule IV • **school bag** Schultasche I • **school office** Sekretariat IV • **school subject** Schulfach I
science [ˈsaɪəns] Naturwissenschaft I
science fiction [ˌsaɪəns ˈfɪkʃn] Sciencefiction V 2 (34)
scientist [ˈsaɪəntɪst] Naturwissenschaftler/in V 2 (32)
score [skɔː] Spielstand; Punktestand III • **final score** Endstand *(beim Sport)* III • **What's the score?** Wie steht es? *(beim Sport)* III
score (a goal) [skɔː], [gəʊl] ein Tor schießen, einen Treffer erzielen III
Scottish [ˈskɒtɪʃ] schottisch III
scrapbook [ˈskræpbʊk] Sammelalbum IV
scream [skriːm] schreien IV
scream [skriːm] Schrei IV
screenplay [ˈskriːnpleɪ] Drehbuch V 3 (57)
°**screw up** [ˌskruː‿ˈʌp] *(infml)* Mist bauen; alles vermasseln
°**scrub** [skrʌb] Gebüsch, Gestrüpp
sea [siː] Meer, (die) See I • **at sea** auf See II
search sth./sb. (for sth./sb.) [sɜːtʃ] etwas/jn. (nach etwas/jm.) durchsuchen V 4 (94)
°**sea snake** [ˈsiː ˌsneɪk] Seeschlange
season [ˈsiːzn] Jahreszeit II • **rainy season** Regenzeit II
seat [siːt] Sitz, Platz IV
second [ˈsekənd] Sekunde • °**second hand** [ˈsekənd ˌhænd] Sekundenzeiger
second [ˈsekənd] zweite(r, s) I **second-hand** [ˌsekənd ˈhænd] gebraucht; aus zweiter Hand III **a second-half goal** ein Tor in der zweiten Hälfte/Halbzeit III
secondary school [ˈsekəndri] *weiterführende Schule* V 2 (38)
secret *(n)* [ˈsiːkrət] Geheimnis IV

secret *(adj)* ['si:krət] geheim IV
secretly ['si:krətli] heimlich, insgeheim V 4 (80)
section ['sekʃn] Abschnitt, Teil II; (Themen-)Bereich III
see [si:], **saw, seen**
1. sehen I
2. **see sb.** jn. besuchen, jn. aufsuchen II
See? Siehst du? I • **See you.** Bis bald. / Tschüs. I
seek [si:k], **sought, sought,** suchen V 1 (9)
seem (to be/to do) [si:m] (zu sein/tun) scheinen III
seen [si:n] *siehe* **see**
see-through ['si:θru:] durchsichtig IV
segregate ['segrɪgeɪt] trennen *(nach Rasse, Religion, Geschlecht)* IV
segregation [ˌsegrɪ'geɪʃn] Trennung *(nach Rasse, Religion, Geschlecht)* IV
selection (of) [sɪ'lekʃn] Auswahl (an) II
sell [sel], **sold, sold** verkaufen I
semester [sɪ'mestə] Semester *(Schulhalbjahr in den USA)* IV
semi-final [ˌsemi'faɪnl] Halbfinale III
send [send], **sent, sent** senden, schicken II • °**send sb. flying** jn. zu Boden schicken
senior ['si:niə]
1. **senior (to sb.)** (rang)höher (als jd.) IV
2. leitende(r, s) IV
senior ['si:niə] Rentner/in, Senior/in IV
sent [sent] *siehe* **send**
sentence sb. (to sth.) ['sentəns] jn. verurteilen (zu etwas) IV
sentence ['sentəns]
1. Satz I • **sentence for sentence** Satz um Satz III
2. Urteil, Strafe IV • **death sentence** Todesstrafe IV • **life sentence** lebenslängliche Haftstrafe IV
separate ['seprət] getrennt, separat, extra IV
September [sep'tembə] September I
series, *pl* **series** ['sɪəri:z] (Sende-)Reihe, Serie II
serious ['sɪəriəs] ernst(haft) V 1 (6)
seriously ['sɪəriəs] ernsthaft; *(infml)* sehr V 1 (6)
service ['sɜ:vɪs]
1. Dienst (am Kunden), Service II
social services Sozialeinrichtungen V 4 (89)
2. Gottesdienst IV
session ['seʃn]: **training session** Trainingsstunde, -einheit III
set (-tt-) [set], **set, set**
1. **set a trap (for sb.)** (jm.) eine Falle stellen II • **set sth. up** etwas aufstellen, aufbauen III • **set up a business** ein Unternehmen gründen V 2 (46)
2. **be set in** spielen in V 1 (25)
set [set] Reihe, Set, Satz V 2 (47)
set of rules Regelwerk V 2 (47)
set meal [ˌset 'mi:l] Menü III
setting ['setɪŋ] Schauplatz V 1 (25)
settle down [ˌsetl 'daʊn] zur Ruhe kommen, sesshaft werden V 2 (35)
settler ['setlə] Siedler/in IV
several ['sevrəl] mehrere, verschiedene IV
sew (on) [səʊ], **sewed, sewn** (an)nähen IV
sewn [səʊn] *siehe* **sew**
sex [seks]: **have sex** miteinander schlafen, sich lieben V 1 (16/186)
shade [ʃeɪd] Schatten *(von der Sonne geschützt)* V 1 (9)
shadow ['ʃædəʊ] Schatten *(Umriss)* III
shake [ʃeɪk], **shook, shaken** zittern; schütteln IV • **shake one's head** den Kopf schütteln III
Shall we ...? [ʃæl] Wollen wir ...? / Sollen wir ...? III
► S.207 German „sollen"
shape [ʃeɪp] Form, Gestalt II
share sth. (with sb.) [ʃeə]
1. sich etwas teilen (mit jm.) I; etwas gemeinsam (mit jm.) haben/nutzen IV
2. jm. etwas mitteilen IV
she [ʃi:] sie I
sheep, *pl* **sheep** [ʃi:p] Schaf II
°**sheep station** Schaffarm *(in Australien)*
sheet [ʃi:t] Blatt, Bogen *(Papier)* V 2 (44)
shelf [ʃelf], *pl* **shelves** [ʃelvz] Regal(brett) I
shell [ʃel] Muschel(schale) V 1 (8)
shift [ʃɪft] Schicht *(bei der Arbeit)* IV
shine [ʃaɪn], **shone, shone**
1. scheinen *(Sonne)* II
2. glänzen IV
ship [ʃɪp] Schiff I
shirt [ʃɜ:t] Hemd I • **football shirt** (Fußball-)Trikot III
shiver ['ʃɪvə] zittern II
shock [ʃɒk] Schock, Schreck V 1 (6)
shocked [ʃɒkt] schockiert III
shocking ['ʃɒkɪŋ] schockierend V 4 (85)
shoe [ʃu:] Schuh I
shone [ʃɒn, *AE* ʃəʊn] *siehe* **shine**
shoot [ʃu:t] **shot, shot**
1. (er)schießen IV
2. *(Film)* drehen; fotografieren IV
shop [ʃɒp] Laden, Geschäft I
shop assistant ['ʃɒp_əˌsɪstənt] Verkäufer/in I
shop (-pp-) [ʃɒp] einkaufen (gehen) I
shopping ['ʃɒpɪŋ] (das) Einkaufen I
go shopping einkaufen gehen I
shopping list Einkaufsliste I
shopping mall (großes) Einkaufszentrum III • **shopping precinct** Einkaufsviertel, -straße *(autofrei)* III
short [ʃɔ:t] kurz I • **a short time** kurz IV
shorts *(pl)* [ʃɔ:ts] Shorts, kurze Hose I
shot [ʃɒt] *siehe* **shoot**
shot [ʃɒt] Schuss III
should [ʃəd, ʃʊd]: **you should ...** du solltest ... / ihr solltet ... I • **you should have asked** du hättest fragen sollen IV
► S.207 German „sollen"
shoulder ['ʃəʊldə] Schulter I
shout [ʃaʊt] schreien, rufen I
shout at sb. jn. anschreien I
show [ʃəʊ] Show, Vorstellung I
show [ʃəʊ], **showed, shown** zeigen I • **show sb. around** jn. (in der Stadt/im Museum/... herumführen) III
show off [ˌʃəʊ_'ɒf], **showed off, shown off** angeben, prahlen IV
shower ['ʃaʊə] Dusche I • **have a shower** (sich) duschen I
shown [ʃəʊn] *siehe* **show**
shut up [ˌʃʌt_'ʌp], **shut, shut** den Mund halten II
shy [ʃaɪ] schüchtern, scheu II
sick [sɪk] krank IV • **I feel sick.** Mir ist schlecht. IV
side [saɪd] Seite II • **side door** Seitentür IV
sidetrack ['saɪdtræk]: **get sidetracked** abgelenkt werden V 2 (34)
sidewalk ['saɪdwɔ:k] *(AE)* Gehweg, Bürgersteig IV
sight [saɪt]: **Get out of my sight.** Geh mir aus den Augen. IV
sights *(pl)* [saɪts] Sehenswürdigkeiten II
sightseeing ['saɪtˌsi:ɪŋ] Sightseeing; das Anschauen von Sehenswürdigkeiten IV
sign [saɪn] unterschreiben III

sign [saɪn] Schild; Zeichen III
road sign Verkehrszeichen V 4 (87)
silence ['saɪləns] Stille, Schweigen V 3 (53)
silent letter [ˌsaɪlənt 'letə] „stummer" Buchstabe *(nicht gesprochener Buchstabe)* II
silly ['sɪli] albern, dumm II
°**Silures** [saɪ'lʊəri:z] die Silurer *(ein keltischer Stamm im frühen Britannien)*
°**similar** ['sɪmələ] ähnlich
simile ['sɪməli] Vergleich V 1 (25)
since September [sɪns] seit September III
Sincerely (yours) [sɪn'sɪəli] *(AE)* mit freundlichen Grüßen IV
sing [sɪŋ], **sang, sung** singen I
singer ['sɪŋə] Sänger/in II
°**singer-songwriter** [ˌsɪŋə'sɒŋraɪtə] Liedermacher
single ['sɪŋgl] ledig, alleinstehend I
a single parent ein(e) Alleinerziehende(r) II
sink [sɪŋk] Spüle, Spülbecken I
sink [sɪŋk], **sank, sunk** sinken V 1 (16)
sir [sɜ:] Sir *(höfliche Anrede, z. B. für Kunden, Vorgesetzte oder Lehrer)* IV • **Dear Sir or Madam ...** Sehr geehrte Damen und Herren IV
sister ['sɪstə] Schwester I
sister city ['sɪstə ˌsɪti] *(AE)* Partnerstadt IV
sit (-tt-) [sɪt], **sat, sat** sitzen; sich setzen I • **sit down** sich hinsetzen II • **sit up** sich aufsetzen II
Sit with me. Setz dich zu mir. / Setzt euch zu mir. I
site [saɪt] *siehe* **website**
situation [ˌsɪtju'eɪʃn] Situation IV
size [saɪz] Größe I
skate [skeɪt] Inliner/Skateboard fahren I
skateboard ['skeɪtbɔ:d] Skateboard I
skates *(pl)* [skeɪts] Inliner I
sketch [sketʃ] Sketch I
ski [ski:] Ski III • **ski slope** Skipiste III
ski [ski:] Ski laufen/fahren III
go skiing [ski:ɪŋ] Ski laufen/fahren III • **skiing instructor** Skilehrer/in V 1 (6/182)
skill [skɪl] Fähigkeit, Fertigkeit IV
skills file ['skɪlz faɪl] Anhang mit Lern- und Arbeitstechniken I
skim a text (-mm-) [skɪm] einen Text überfliegen *(um den Inhalt grob zu erfassen)* III
skin [skɪn] Haut IV
skirt [skɜ:t] Rock II
sky [skaɪ] Himmel II • **in the sky** am Himmel II
°**skydiving** ['skaɪˌdaɪvɪŋ] Fallschirmspringen, Skydiving
skyline ['skaɪˌlaɪn] Horizont, Skyline IV
skyscraper ['skaɪskreɪpə] Wolkenkratzer IV
°**slap on a hat** [ˌslæp‿'ɒn] einen Hut aufsetzen
slave [sleɪv] Sklave, Sklavin II
slavery ['sleɪvəri] Sklaverei IV
sledge [sledʒ] Schlitten III
sleep [sli:p], **slept, slept** schlafen I
sleep [sli:p] Schlaf III
sleepover ['sli:pəʊvə] Schlafparty III
slept [slept] *siehe* **sleep**
°**slid** [slɪd] *siehe* **slide**
slide [slaɪd] Folie *(bei Präsentationsprogrammen)* V 2 (45)
°**slide** [slaɪd], **slid, slid** rutschen
slide on some sunglasses eine Sonnenbrille aufsetzen
°**slip (-pp-)** [ˌslɪp]: **slip on some clothing** Kleidung überziehen
slogan ['sləʊgən] Slogan, Losung IV
°**slop (-pp-)** [ˌslɒp]: **slop on some sunscreen** Sonnenschutzmittel auftragen
slope: ski slope Skipiste III
slow [sləʊ] langsam II
small [smɔ:l] klein II • **small letters** Kleinbuchstaben III
smart [smɑ:t] schlau IV
smell [smel] riechen II
smell [smel] Geruch II
smile [smaɪl] lächeln I • **smile at sb.** jn. anlächeln II
smile [smaɪl] Lächeln II • **give (sb.) a smile** lächeln, jn. anlächeln IV
smoke [sməʊk] rauchen IV
smoke [sməʊk] Rauch IV • **There's no smoke without fire.** Wo Rauch ist, ist auch Feuer. IV
smoothie ['smu:ði] *dickflüssiger Fruchtshake mit Milch, Joghurt oder Eiscreme* II
smuggle ['smʌgl] schmuggeln IV
snack [snæk] Snack, Imbiss II
snake [sneɪk] Schlange I
°**snorkel (-ll-)** ['snɔ:kl] schnorcheln
snow [snəʊ] Schnee II
snowball ['snəʊbɔ:l] Schneeball IV
so [səʊ]
1. also; deshalb, daher I • **So?** Und? / Na und? II • **So what?** [səʊ 'wɒt] Und? / Na und? II
2. so sweet so süß I • **so far** bis jetzt, bis hierher III • **so (that)** sodass, damit III
3. I hope so. Ich hoffe es. II
I think so. Ich glaube (ja). I
I don't think so. Das finde/glaube ich nicht. I • **Do you really think so?** Meinst du wirklich? / Glaubst du das wirklich? II
soap [səʊp] Seife I
soap (opera) ['səʊp ˌɒprə] Seifenoper IV
social ['səʊʃl] sozial, Sozial-, gesellschaftlich V 4 (84) • **social services** Sozialeinrichtungen V 4 (89)
°**social networking site** [ˌsəʊʃl 'netwɜ:kɪŋ] *eine Website zur Bildung und Unterhaltung sozialer Netzwerke*
Social Studies [ˌsəʊʃl 'stʌdiz] Gemeinschaftskunde, Politische Bildung, Sozialkunde IV
sock [sɒk] Socke, Strumpf I
soda ['səʊdə] *(AE)* Limonade IV
sofa ['səʊfə] Sofa I
soft [sɒft] weich, sanft III • **soft drink** alkoholfreies Getränk IV
software ['sɒftweə] Software II
soil [sɔɪl] *(Erdreich)* Erde IV
sold [səʊld]
1. *siehe* **sell**
2. sold out [ˌsəʊld‿'aʊt]: **be sold out** ausverkauft/vergriffen sein III
soldier ['səʊldʒə] Soldat/in IV
solve [sɒlv] lösen IV
some [səm, sʌm] einige, ein paar I
some cheese/juice/money etwas Käse/Saft/Geld I
somebody ['sʌmbədi] jemand I
Find/Ask somebody who ... Finde/Frage jemanden, der ... II
somehow ['sʌmhaʊ] irgendwie IV
someone ['sʌmwʌn] jemand III
something ['sʌmθɪŋ] etwas I
sometimes ['sʌmtaɪmz] manchmal I
somewhere ['sʌmweə] irgendwo(hin) II
son [sʌn] Sohn I
song [sɒŋ] Lied, Song I
soon [su:n] bald I • **as soon as** sobald, sowie II
sore [sɔ:]: **be sore** wund sein, wehtun II • **have a sore throat** Halsschmerzen haben II
sorry ['sɒri]: **(I'm) sorry.** Entschuldigung. / Tut mir leid. I • **Sorry, I'm late.** Entschuldigung, dass ich zu spät bin/komme. I • **Sorry?** Wie bitte? I • **say sorry** sich entschuldigen II
sort [sɔ:t] einteilen; sortieren IV
sort (of) [sɔ:t] Art, Sorte II
°**SOS** [ˌes‿əʊ‿'es] SOS(-Ruf) (Notsignal)
sought [sɔ:t] *siehe* **seek**

soul [səʊl] Soul(musik) III
sound [saʊnd] klingen, sich (gut usw.) anhören I
sound [saʊnd] Laut; Klang I
sound file ['saʊnd faɪl] Tondatei, Soundfile III
soup [su:p] Suppe II
sour ['saʊə] sauer III
source [sɔ:s] Quelle *(Informationsquelle, Textquelle)* IV
south [saʊθ] Süden; nach Süden; südlich II • **southbound** ['saʊθbaʊnd] Richtung Süden III **south-east** [ˌsaʊθ'i:st] Südosten; nach Südosten; südöstlich II **southern** ['sʌðən] südlich, Süd- III • **south-west** [ˌsaʊθ'west] Südwesten; nach Südwesten; südwestlich II
souvenir [ˌsu:və'nɪə] Andenken, Souvenir III
space ['speɪs]
1. Weltraum II
2. **Move back one space.** Geh ein Feld zurück. II • **Move on one space.** Geh ein Feld vor. II
spaghetti [spə'geti] Spaghetti II
spark [spɑ:k] Funke IV
speak (to) [spi:k], **spoke, spoken** sprechen (mit), reden (mit) II
special ['speʃl] besondere(r, s) II **Did you do anything special?** Habt ihr irgendetwas Besonderes gemacht? I
species ['spi:ʃi:z] Art *(biologisch)*, Spezies V 1 (9)
specific [spə'sɪfɪk] bestimmte(r, s), spezifische(r, s) IV
spectacular [spek'tækjələ] spektakulär IV
speech [spi:tʃ] Rede IV • **make/ give a speech** eine Rede halten IV • **speech bubble** Sprechblase V 3 (50/199)
speed [spi:d] rasen, schnell fliegen III
speed [spi:d] Geschwindigkeit III **speed limit** Geschwindigkeitsbegrenzung, -beschränkung III
spell [spel] buchstabieren I
spelling ['spelɪŋ] Rechtschreibung V 2 (39)
spend [spend], **spent, spent: spend money (on)** Geld ausgeben (für) II • **spend time (on)** Zeit verbringen (mit) II
spent [spent] *siehe* **spend**
spice [spaɪs] Gewürz III
spicy ['spaɪsi] würzig, scharf gewürzt III
spill [spɪl] verschütten IV
spit (at sb.) (-tt-) [spɪt], **spat, spat** (jn. an)spucken IV
splash [splæʃ] spritzen IV
°**split (-tt-)** [splɪt], **split, split** spalten
spoke [spəʊk] *siehe* **speak**
spoken ['spəʊkən]
1. *siehe* **speak**
2. mündlich V 2 (38)
spoon [spu:n] Löffel III
sport [spɔ:t] Sport; Sportart I **do sport** Sport treiben I
sports gear *(no pl)* ['spɔ:ts gɪə] Sportausrüstung, Sportsachen II
sports hall ['spɔ:ts hɔ:l] Sporthalle III
spot (-tt-) [spɒt] entdecken III
spray [spreɪ] spritzen, (be)sprühen, sprayen IV
spray can ['spreɪ ˌkæn] Spraydose V 4 (84)
spread [spred], **spread, spread** (sich) ausbreiten, (sich) verbreiten IV
spring [sprɪŋ]
1. Frühling I
2. Quelle *(Wasser)* IV
spy [spaɪ] Spion/in I
square [skweə] Platz *(in der Stadt)* II
square km (sq km) [skweə] Quadratkilometer III
square brackets [ˌskweə 'brækɪts] eckige Klammern IV
squash [skwɒʃ], *pl* **squash** Kürbis IV
squeeze [skwi:z] drücken; (aus)pressen III
squirrel ['skwɪrəl] Eichhörnchen II
stadium ['steɪdiəm] Stadion III
staff [stɑ:f] Personal, Belegschaft; Lehrerkollegium IV • **member of staff** *(BE)* Mitarbeiter/in IV • **staff member** *(AE)* Mitarbeiter/in IV
► S.196 Collective nouns
stage [steɪdʒ] Bühne I
stairs *(pl)* [steəz] Treppe; Treppenstufen I
stamp [stæmp] Briefmarke I
stand [stænd], **stood, stood**
1. stehen; sich (hin)stellen II
2. ertragen, aushalten, ausstehen II • **I can't stand it.** Ich kann es nicht ertragen/aushalten/ausstehen. II
3. **stand up for sth./sb.** eintreten / sich einsetzen für etwas/jn. V 3 (50)
4. **stand (for sth.)** (für etwas) kandidieren V 3 (60)
star [stɑ:]
1. Stern II
2. (Film-, Pop-)Star I
stare (at sb./sth.) [steə] (jn./etwas an)starren V 3 (53)
°**starfish** ['stɑ:fɪʃ]: **crown-of-thorns starfish** [ˌkraʊn_əv 'θɔ:nz] Dornenkronenseestern
start [stɑ:t] starten, anfangen, beginnen (mit) I
start [stɑ:t] Anfang V 2 (46)
state [steɪt]
1. Staat III; die öffentliche Hand V 4 (89); Bundesstaat V 3 (53)
2. Zustand V 2 (49)
static (electricity) ['stætɪk, ˌstætɪk_ɪˌlek'trɪsəti] elektrische Aufladung IV
station ['steɪʃn]
1. Bahnhof I • **at the station** am Bahnhof I
2. **(radio/pop) station** (Radio-/ Pop-)Sender III
statistics *(pl)* [stə'tɪstɪks] Statistik V 1 (10)
statue ['stætʃu:] Statue II
status ['steɪtəs] Status, Stand V 4 (80)
stay [steɪ] bleiben; wohnen, übernachten II • **stay out** nicht nach Hause kommen, draußenbleiben III
steak [steɪk] (Rinder-)Steak IV
steal [sti:l], **stole, stolen** stehlen II
steel [sti:l] Stahl III
steel drum [ˌsti:l 'drʌm] Steeldrum III
steer [stɪə] lenken, steuern III
step [step]
1. Schritt I • **take steps** Schritte machen/unternehmen III • **take sth. a step at a time** etwas eins nach dem anderen tun; etwas Schritt für Schritt tun IV
2. Stufe IV
stereo ['steriəʊ] Stereoanlage III
stew [stju:] Eintopf(gericht) III
stick (on) [ˌstɪk_'ɒn], **stuck, stuck** (auf)kleben I • °**stick close to sb.** *(infml)* an jm. kleben
stick: (drum-)stick [stɪk] Trommelstock III
stick out of sth. [stɪk], **stuck, stuck** aus etwas herausragen, herausstehen III
still [stɪl]
1. (immer) noch I
2. trotzdem, dennoch II
still [stɪl] still *(bewegungslos)* IV
stole [stəʊl] *siehe* **steal**
stolen ['stəʊlən] *siehe* **steal**
stomach ['stʌmək] Magen II **stomach ache** Magenschmerzen, Bauchweh II
stone [stəʊn] Stein II
stood [stʊd] *siehe* **stand**

stop (-pp-) [stɒp]
1. aufhören I
2. anhalten I
Stop that! Hör auf damit! / Lass das! I • °**stop a danger** einer Gefahr Einhalt gebieten • **stop sb./sth. doing sth.** jn./etwas daran hindern, etwas zu tun V 4 (83)
► S.195 Same verb, different meaning
stop [stɒp] Halt, Anhalten IV
store *(AE)* [stɔ:] Laden V 4 (88)
store [stɔ:]: **hold in store** bereit halten
storm [stɔ:m] Sturm; Gewitter II
stormy ['stɔ:mi] stürmisch II
story ['stɔ:ri] Geschichte, Erzählung I • **crime story** Krimi IV
straight [streɪt] direkt IV
straight on [streɪt‿'ɒn] geradeaus weiter II
straightaway [ˌstreɪtə'weɪ] sofort, gleich III
straighten sth. up [ˌstreɪtn‿'ʌp] etwas aufräumen, etwas in Ordnung bringen V 4 (84)
strange [streɪndʒ]
1. seltsam, sonderbar I
2. fremd V 2 (34)
stranger ['streɪndʒə] Unbekannte(r), Fremde(r) V 2 (34)
strawberry ['strɔ:bəri] Erdbeere II
street [stri:t] Straße I • **at 7 Park Street** in der Parkstraße 7 I
street performer [pə'fɔ:mə] Straßenkünstler/in III
strength [streŋθ] Kraft, Stärke V 1 (23)
stress ['stres] Betonung III
stress [stres] betonen V 3 (65)
stressful ['stresfl] anstrengend, stressig V 2 (47)
stretch [stretʃ] sich (er)strecken IV
strict [strɪkt] streng III
strike [straɪk] Streik III • **be on strike** streiken, sich im Streik befinden III • **go on strike** streiken, in den Streik treten III
string [strɪŋ] Saite III
stripe [straɪp] Streifen V 3 (59)
strong [strɒŋ] stark II
structure ['strʌktʃə] strukturieren, aufbauen II
structure ['strʌktʃə] Struktur; Gliederung III
°**struggle** ['strʌgl] Kampf
stuck [stʌk] *siehe* **stick**
student ['stju:dənt] Schüler/in; Student/in I • **exchange student** Austauschschüler/in III
studio ['stju:diəʊ] Studio I
study ['stʌdi] lernen; studieren III
study hall ['stʌdi hɔ:l] *Zeit zum selbstständigen Lernen in der Schule* IV
study skills *(pl)* ['stʌdi skɪlz] Lern- und Arbeitstechniken I
stuff [stʌf] Zeug, Kram I
stupid ['stju:pɪd] blöd, dämlich V 1 (25)
style [staɪl] Stil III • **military-style fashion** Mode im Militärstil V 4 (85/207)
sub-heading ['sʌbˌhedɪŋ] Zwischenüberschrift IV
subject ['sʌbdʒɪkt]
1. Subjekt I
2. Schulfach I
3. Thema IV
4. Untertan/in; Staatsangehörige(r) *(in einer Monarchie)* IV
subscribe (to sth.) [səb'skraɪb] etwas abonnieren; etwas abonniert haben V 1 (6)
subway ['sʌbweɪ]: **the subway** *(AE)* die U-Bahn II
succeed (in sth.) [sək'si:d] Erfolg haben, erfolgreich sein (mit etwas, bei etwas) IV
success [sək'ses] Erfolg III
successful [sək'sesfəl] erfolgreich V 2 (39)
such [sʌtʃ]: **such a nice person** so ein netter Mensch III • **such good books** so gute Bücher III • **such as** wie zum Beispiel III
°**suck** [sʌk]: **That sucks!** Das ist Mist!
°**suck-up** ['sʌk‿ʌp] Streber/in, Schleimer/in
sudden ['sʌdn] plötzlich IV
suddenly ['sʌdnli] plötzlich, auf einmal I
suffer (from) ['sʌfə] leiden (an) IV
°**suffering** ['sʌfərɪŋ] Leiden, Leid
suffix ['sʌfɪks] Suffix, Nachsilbe IV
sugar ['ʃʊgə] Zucker II
°**suggestion** [sə'dʒestʃən] Vorschlag
suitable ['su:təbl] geeignet, passend V 2 (39)
sum sth. up (-mm-) [ˌsʌm‿'ʌp] (etwas) zusammenfassen V 4 (82)
summarize ['sʌməraɪz] zusammenfassen V 3 (61)
summary ['sʌməri] Zusammenfassung IV
summer ['sʌmə] Sommer I
sun [sʌn] Sonne II
Sunday ['sʌndeɪ, 'sʌndi] Sonntag I
sung [sʌŋ] *siehe* **sing**
sunk [sʌŋk] *siehe* **sink**
sunglasses *(pl)* ['sʌnglɑ:sɪz] (eine) Sonnenbrille I
sunny ['sʌni] sonnig II
sunrise ['sʌnraɪz] Sonnenaufgang IV
sunscreen ['sʌnskri:n] Sonnenschutzmittel V 1 (9)
sunset ['sʌnset] Sonnenuntergang IV
sunshine ['sʌnʃaɪn] Sonnenschein IV
°**sunsmart** ['sʌnˌsmɑ:t]: **Be sunsmart.** *etwa:* Schütze dich intelligent gegen die Sonne.
suntan ['sʌntæn] Sonnenbräune V 1 (9) • **have a suntan** sonnengebräunt sein III
supermarket ['su:pəmɑ:kɪt] Supermarkt I
supper ['sʌpə] Abendessen, Abendbrot IV
support [sə'pɔ:t]: **support a team** eine Mannschaft unterstützen; Fan einer Mannschaft sein III
support [sə'pɔ:t] Unterstützung IV
supporter [sə'pɔ:tə] Anhänger/in, Fan III
suppose [sə'pəʊz] annehmen, vermuten I • **be supposed to do sth.** etwas tun sollen V 4 (84)
► S.207 German „sollen"
sure [ʃʊə, ʃɔ:] sicher I • **make sure** sich vergewissern IV
surf [sɜ:f] surfen V 1 (6) • **go surfing** wellenreiten gehen, surfen gehen II • **surf the internet** im Internet surfen II • **surf instructor** Surflehrer/in V 1 (6)
surfboard ['sɜ:fbɔ:d] Surfbrett II
surprise (for/to) [sə'praɪz] Überraschung (für) III
surprise sb. [sə'praɪz] jn. überraschen III
surprised (at sth.) [sə'praɪzd] überrascht (über etwas) III
surprising [sə'praɪzɪŋ] überraschend V 1 (15)
surround [sə'raʊnd]: **be surrounded** umgeben sein IV
survey (on) ['sɜ:veɪ] Umfrage, Untersuchung (über) II
survival [sə'vaɪvl] Überleben II
survive [sə'vaɪv] überleben II
suspense [sə'spens] Spannung V 4 (97)
swam [swæm] *siehe* **swim**
swap (-pp-) [swɒp] tauschen I
swap sth. (for sth.) etwas (ein)tauschen (für/gegen etwas) IV
sweat [swet] schwitzen IV
sweat [swet] Schweiß IV
sweatshirt ['swetʃɜ:t] Sweatshirt I
sweep [swi:p], **swept, swept** fegen, kehren IV
sweet [swi:t] süß I

sweetheart ['swi:thɑ:t] Liebling, Schatz II
sweets *(pl)* Süßigkeiten I
swept [swept] *siehe* sweep
swim (-mm-) [swɪm], **swam, swum** schwimmen I
swimmer ['swɪmə] Schwimmer/in II
swimming ['swɪmɪŋ] Schwimmen I • **go swimming** schwimmen gehen I • **swimming instructor** Schwimmlehrer/in V 1 (6/182)
swimming pool ['swɪmɪŋ pu:l] Schwimmbad, -becken II
swimming trunks [trʌŋks] Badehose III
swimsuit ['swɪmsu:t] Badeanzug III
swum [swʌm] *siehe* **swim**
syllable ['sɪləbl] Silbe I
symbol ['sɪmbəl] Symbol V 3 (50)
sympathetic [ˌsɪmpə'θetɪk] mitfühlend, verständnisvoll, wohlwollend V 3 (52)
synagogue ['sɪnəgɒg] Synagoge III ► S.198 Religions
synonym ['sɪnənɪm] Synonym *(Wort mit gleicher oder sehr ähnlicher Bedeutung)* IV
system ['sɪstəm] System IV

T

table ['teɪbl]
1. Tisch I • **table tennis** ['teɪbl tenɪs] Tischtennis I • **table tennis bat** Tischtennisschläger III
2. Tabelle V 1 (10) • **table of contents** Inhaltsverzeichnis V 2 (43)
tablecloth ['teɪblklɒθ] Tischdecke IV
take [teɪk], **took, taken**
1. nehmen I • **I'll take it.** *(beim Einkaufen)* Ich werde es (ihn, sie) nehmen. / Ich nehme es (ihn, sie). I
2. (weg-, hin)bringen I
3. dauern, *(Zeit)* brauchen III
I can take it. Ich halt's aus. / Ich kann's aushalten. IV • **take a break** eine Pause machen IV
take a left/right *(AE)* nach links/rechts abbiegen IV • **take a trip** *(AE)* einen Ausflug/eine Reise machen IV • **Take another turn.** *(beim Spielen)* Würfel noch einmal. II • **take care of sth./sb.** sich um etwas/jn. kümmern III • **take notes** sich Notizen machen I
take sth. off etwas ausziehen *(Kleidung)*; etwas absetzen *(Hut, Helm)* II • **take 10 c off** 10 Cent abziehen I • **take sth. out** etwas herausnehmen I; *(Geld)* abheben V 3 (50) • **take sth. over** etwas übernehmen; etwas in seine Macht bringen IV • **take part in sth.** teilnehmen an etwas III
take photos Fotos machen, fotografieren I • **take place** stattfinden II • **take responsibility (for)** Verantwortung (für) übernehmen V 2 (39) • **take a ride** eine Spritztour/Fahrt machen III • **take sth. a step at a time** etwas eins nach dem anderen tun; etwas Schritt für Schritt tun IV • **take steps** Schritte machen/unternehmen III
take turns to do sth. sich abwechseln, etwas zu tun IV • **take sth. up** etwas in Anspruch nehmen V 3 (60)
takeaway ['teɪkəweɪ] *Restaurant, das auch Essen zum Mitnehmen verkauft; Essen zum Mitnehmen* III
taken ['teɪkən] *siehe* **take**
talent ['tælənt] Talent, Begabung III
talk [tɔ:k]: **talk (about)** reden (über), sich unterhalten (über) I
talk (to) reden (mit), sich unterhalten (mit) I
talk [tɔ:k] Rede, Gespräch; Vortrag, Referat IV
talk show ['tɔ:k ˌʃəʊ] Talkshow V 2 (32)
tall [tɔ:l]
1. groß *(Person)* III
2. hoch *(Gebäude, Baum)* IV
taste [teɪst] schmecken; kosten, probieren IV
taste [teɪst] Geschmack IV • **be in good/bad taste** geschmackvoll/-los sein IV
taught [tɔ:t] *siehe* **teach**
tavern ['tævən] Schenke, Gastwirtschaft IV
tax (on) [tæks] Steuer (auf) V 3 (52)
tax [tæks] besteuern V 3 (66/205) ► S.205 Verbs & nouns with the same form
taxi ['tæksi] Taxi III
tea [ti:] Tee; (auch:) leichte Nachmittags- oder Abendmahlzeit I
tea bag Teebeutel IV
teach [ti:tʃ], **taught, taught** unterrichten, lehren I
teacher ['ti:tʃə] Lehrer/in I • **head teacher** Schulleiter/in III
team [ti:m] Team, Mannschaft I ► S.196 Collective nouns
tear [teə], **tore, torn** (zer)reißen IV
tear [tɪə] Träne II
tease [ti:z] necken, auf den Arm nehmen III
teaspoon ['ti:spu:n] Teelöffel III
technique [tek'ni:k] (Arbeits-)Verfahren, Technik, Methode IV
technology [tek'nɒlədʒi] Technologie V 2 (35)
teddy bear ['tedi beə] Teddybär III
teen *(bes. AE)* [ti:n]
1. Teenager- III
2. Teenager/in V 4 (84)
teenage ['ti:neɪdʒ] Teenage- V 2 (46)
teenager ['ti:neɪdʒə] Teenager, Jugendliche(r) II
teeth [ti:θ] *Plural von „tooth"* I
telephone ['telɪfəʊn] Telefon I
telephone number Telefonnummer I
television ['telɪvɪʒn] Fernsehen I
tell (about) [tel], **told, told** erzählen (von), berichten (über) I • **Tell me your names.** Sagt mir eure Namen. I • **tell sb. the way** jm. den Weg beschreiben II
temperature ['temprətʃə] Temperatur II • **have a temperature** Fieber haben II
temple ['templ] Tempel V 3 (50/198) ► S.198 Religions
tennis ['tenɪs] Tennis I
tense [tens] (grammatische) Zeit, Tempus III
tent [tent] Zelt IV
term [tɜ:m]
1. Trimester II
2. **term (of office)** Amtsperiode V 3 (60)
terrible ['terəbl] schrecklich, furchtbar I
terrified ['terɪfaɪd]: **be terrified (of)** schreckliche Angst haben (vor) IV
terrorism ['terərɪzm] Terrorismus IV
test [test] Klassenarbeit, Test, Prüfung II
text [tekst] Text I
text (message) ['tekst ˌmesɪdʒ] SMS II
text sb. [tekst] jm. eine SMS schicken II
than [ðæn, ðən] als II • **more than me** mehr als ich II
thank [θæŋk]: **Thank God.** Gott sei Dank. IV • **Thank you.** Danke (schön). I • **Thanks.** Danke. I
Thanks a lot! Vielen Dank! I
Thanks very much! Danke sehr! / Vielen Dank! II • **give thanks** danken, feierlich danksagen IV
that [ðət, ðæt]
1. das (dort) I
2. jene(r, s) I • **that day** an jenem Tag III • **That's me.** Das bin ich. I
That's right. Das ist richtig. / Das stimmt. I • **That's up to you.** Das liegt bei dir. / Das kannst/musst du

(selbst) entscheiden. III • **that's why** deshalb, darum I
that [ðət, ðæt] dass I
that [ðət, ðæt] der, die, das; die *(Relativpronomen)* III
the [ðə, ði] der, die, das; die I
theatre ['θɪətə] Theater II
their [ðeə]
1. ihr, ihre *(Plural)* I
2. sein oder ihr (= his or her) IV
theirs [ðeəz] ihrer, ihre, ihrs II
them [ðəm, ðem]
1. sie; ihnen I • **the two of them** die beiden; alle beide II
2. ihn oder sie (= him or her) IV
theme park ['θi:m pɑ:k] Themenpark II
themselves [ðəm'selvz]
1. sich III
2. selbst IV
then [ðen]
1. dann, danach I
2. damals II
Then what? Was dann? II • **just then** genau in dem Moment; gerade dann II
theocracy [θi'ɒkrəsi] Theokratie V 3 (53/201)
► S.200 Different forms of government
there [ðeə]
1. da, dort I
2. dahin, dorthin I
down there (nach) dort unten II
in there dort drinnen I • **over there** da drüben, dort drüben I
up there dort oben III • **there are** es sind (vorhanden); es gibt I
there's es ist (vorhanden); es gibt I • **there isn't a ...** es ist kein/e ...; es gibt kein/e ... I
thermometer [θə'mɒmɪtə] Thermometer II
°**thesaurus** [θɪ'sɔ:rəs] Synonymwörterbuch
these [ði:z] diese, die (hier) I
they [ðeɪ]
1. sie *(Plural)* I • **They say ...** Man sagt, ... III
2. er oder sie (= he or she) IV
thief [θi:f], *pl* **thieves** [θi:vz] Dieb/in II
thing [θɪŋ] Ding, Sache I • **What was the best thing about ...?** Was war das Beste an ...? II
think [θɪŋk], **thought, thought** glauben, meinen, denken I • **Do you really think so?** Meinst du wirklich? / Glaubst du das wirklich? II • **I think so.** Ich glaube (ja). I • **I don't think so.** Das finde/glaube ich nicht. I • **think about 1.** nachdenken über II;
2. denken über, halten von II
think of 1. denken über, halten von II **2.** denken an; sich ausdenken II
third [θɜ:d]
1. dritte(r, s) I
°2. Drittel
thirsty ['θɜ:sti] durstig I • **be thirsty** Durst haben, durstig sein I
this [ðɪs]
1. dies (hier) I
2. diese(r, s) I
This is Isabel. Hier spricht Isabel. / Hier ist Isabel. *(am Telefon)* II
this morning/afternoon/evening heute Morgen/Nachmittag/Abend I • **this way** hier entlang, in diese Richtung II
those [ðəʊz] die (da), jene (dort) I
thought [θɔ:t] *siehe* think
thought [θɔ:t] Gedanke IV
thought bubble Denkblase V 3 (50/199)
thousand ['θaʊznd] tausend, Tausend I
threw [θru:] *siehe* throw
throat Hals, Kehle II • **have a sore throat** [sɔ: 'θrəʊt] Halsschmerzen haben II
through [θru:] durch II
throughout October [θru:'aʊt] den ganzen Oktober hindurch IV
throw [θrəʊ], **threw, thrown** werfen I • **throw the dice** würfeln II
throw up sich übergeben IV
thrown [θrəʊn] *siehe* throw
Thursday ['θɜ:zdeɪ, 'θɜ:zdi] Donnerstag I
ticket ['tɪkɪt]
1. Eintrittskarte I
2. Fahrkarte III
ticket machine ['tɪkɪt mə‚ʃi:n] Fahrkartenautomat III
ticket office ['tɪkɪt_ɒfɪs] Kasse *(für den Verkauf von Eintrittskarten)*; Fahrkartenschalter IV
tide [taɪd] Gezeiten, Ebbe und Flut II • **the tide is in** es ist Flut II
the tide is out es ist Ebbe II
tidy ['taɪdi] aufräumen I
tidy ['taɪdi] ordentlich, aufgeräumt II
tie *(-ing form:* **tying***)* [taɪ] (fest)binden IV
°**tie** [taɪ] Schlips, Krawatte
tiger ['taɪgə] Tiger II
tight [taɪt] eng; fest IV
tights *(pl)* [taɪts] Strumpfhose III
till [tɪl] bis *(zeitlich)* I
time [taɪm] Zeit; Uhrzeit I • **in time** rechtzeitig II • **What's the time?** Wie spät ist es? I • **a long time** lange III • **a short time** kurz IV • **time zone** Zeitzone IV
time(s) [taɪmz] Mal(e); -mal II • **for the first time** zum ersten Mal II
timeline ['taɪmlaɪn] Zeitstrahl, Zeitleiste IV
timetable ['taɪmteɪbl] Stundenplan I
timing ['taɪmɪŋ]: **bad timing** schlechtes Timing, schlechte Wahl des Zeitpunkts III
tin [tɪn] Dose V 1 (21)
tip [tɪp]
1. Tipp III
2. Spitze IV
tired ['taɪəd] müde I • **be tired of sth.** genug von etwas haben, etwas satt haben IV • **get tired of sth.** einer Sache überdrüssig werden, die Lust an etwas verlieren IV
title ['taɪtl] Titel, Überschrift I
to [tə, tu]
1. zu, nach I • **an e-mail to** eine E-Mail an I • **to Jenny's** zu Jenny I • **to the doctor's** zum Arzt III
to the front nach vorn I • **I've never been to Bath.** Ich bin noch nie in Bath gewesen. II • **write to** schreiben an I
2. **quarter to 12** Viertel vor 12 (11.45 / 23.45) I • **from Monday to Friday** von Montag bis Freitag III
3. **try to do** versuchen, zu tun I
4. um zu I
toast [təʊst] Toast(brot) I
today [tə'deɪ] heute I
toe [təʊ] Zeh I
together [tə'geðə] zusammen I
toilet ['tɔɪlət] Toilette I
told [təʊld] *siehe* tell
tomato [tə'mɑ:təʊ], *pl* **tomatoes** Tomate II
tomorrow [tə'mɒrəʊ] morgen I
tone of voice [təʊn] Ton(fall) V 3 (65)
tonight [tə'naɪt] heute Nacht, heute Abend I
too [tu:]: **from Bristol too** auch aus Bristol I • **Me too.** Ich auch. I
too much/big/... [tu:] zu viel/groß/... I
took [tʊk] *siehe* take
tool [tu:l] Werkzeug IV
tooth [tu:θ], *pl* **teeth** [ti:θ] Zahn I
toothache ['tu:θeɪk] Zahnschmerzen II
top [tɒp]
1. Spitze, oberes Ende I • **at the top (of)** oben, am oberen Ende, an der Spitze (von) I
2. Top, Oberteil I

top [tɒp] *(adj)* Spitzen-, oberste(r, s) III
topic ['tɒpɪk] Thema, Themenbereich I • **topic sentence** *Satz, der in das Thema eines Absatzes einführt* II
tore [tɔː] *siehe* **tear**
torn [tɔːn] *siehe* **tear**
tortoise ['tɔːtəs] Schildkröte I
touch [tʌtʃ] berühren, anfassen I
touch [tʌtʃ]: **keep in touch** in Verbindung bleiben, Kontakt halten II
tough [tʌf] tough, selbstsicher, zäh III; schwierig, hart IV
tour (of the house) [tʊə] Rundgang, Tour (durch das Haus) I
tourist ['tʊərɪst] Tourist/in II
tourist information Fremdenverkehrsamt II
toward [tə'wɔːd] *(AE) siehe* **towards**
towards Mr Green [tə'wɔːdz] auf Mr Green zu, in Mr Greens Richtung I
towel ['taʊəl] Handtuch II
tower ['taʊə] Turm I
town [taʊn] Stadt I • **the centre of town** die Mitte der Stadt III • **in town** in der Stadt III • **into town** in die Stadt III
°**town hall** [ˌtaʊn 'hɔːl] Rathaus
track [træk]
1. Stück, Titel, Track *(auf einer CD)* III
2. Spur, Fährte; Pfad, Weg V 1 (16)
trade [treɪd] Handel II
°**trade** [treɪd] Handel treiben
tradition [trə'dɪʃn] Tradition IV
traditional [trə'dɪʃənl] traditionell III
traffic ['træfɪk] Verkehr II
trail [treɪl] (Lehr-)Pfad IV
train [treɪn] Zug I • **on the train** im Zug I • **mule train** Maultierkarawane IV
train [treɪn]
1. trainieren III
2. train as ... eine Ausbildung machen zu ... V 4 (84)
trained [treɪnd] ausgebildet V 4 (88)
trainers *(pl)* ['treɪnəz] Turnschuhe II
training session ['seʃn] Trainingsstunde, -einheit III
tram [træm] Straßenbahn III
translate (from ... into) [træns'leɪt] übersetzen (aus ... in) III
translation [træns'leɪʃn] Übersetzung III
transparency [træns'pærənsi] Folie V 2 (45)
transport *(no pl)* ['trænspɔːt] Transport(wesen) III • **public transport** öffentlicher Verkehr IV
trap [træp] Falle II
trap (-pp-) [træp] (mit einer Falle) fangen III
trash [træʃ] *(AE)* Abfall, Müll V 4 (88)
travel (-ll-) ['trævl] reisen II
Travelcard ['trævlkɑːd] Tages-/Wochen-/Monatsfahrkarte *(der Londoner Verkehrsbetriebe)* III
treason ['triːzn] Hochverrat IV
treat [triːt] behandeln V 3 (66)
tree [triː] Baum I • **Christmas tree** Christ-, Weihnachtsbaum V 2 (34/190)
trendy ['trendi] modisch, schick III
tribal ['traɪbl] Stammes- IV
tribe [traɪb] (Volks-)Stamm IV
trick [trɪk]
1. (Zauber-)Kunststück, Trick I
do tricks (Zauber-)Kunststücke machen I
2. Streich II • **play a trick on sb.** jm. einen Streich spielen II
trick sb. [trɪk] jn. austricksen, reinlegen V 1 (17)
trick sb. into doing sth. [trɪk] jn. mit einer List / einem Trick dazu bringen, etwas zu tun V 1 (17)
tricky ['trɪki] verzwickt, heikel V 1 (15)
trip [trɪp] Reise; Ausflug I • **go on a trip** einen Ausflug/eine Reise machen II • **take a trip** *(AE)* einen Ausflug/eine Reise machen IV
trombone [trɒm'bəʊn] Posaune III
trouble ['trʌbl] Schwierigkeiten, Ärger II • **be in trouble** in Schwierigkeiten sein; Ärger kriegen II
troublemaker ['trʌblˌmeɪkə] Unruhestifter/in V 4 (84)
trousers *(pl)* ['traʊzəz] Hose II
truck [trʌk] Lastwagen, LKW V 1 (17)
true [truː] wahr II • **come true** wahr werden II
truly ['truːli]: **Yours truly** *(AE)* mit freundlichen Grüßen IV
trumpet ['trʌmpɪt] Trompete III
°**trunk** [trʌŋk] Baumstamm
trust [trʌst] trauen, vertrauen V 2 (47)
trust (in) [trʌst] Vertrauen (zu) V 3 (66/205)
► S.205 Verbs & nouns with the same form
try [traɪ]
1. versuchen I
2. probieren, kosten I
try and do sth. / try to do sth. versuchen, etwas zu tun I • **try sth. on** etwas anprobieren *(Kleidung)* I
► S.195 Same verb, different meaning
tsunami [tsuː'nɑːmi] Tsunami III
T-shirt ['tiːʃɜːt] T-Shirt I
tube [tjuːb]: **the Tube** *(no pl) (BE)* die Londoner U-Bahn III
Tuesday ['tjuːzdeɪ, -di] Dienstag I
tune [tjuːn]: **tune a radio to a station** ein Radio auf einen Sender einstellen IV • **You're tuned to Radio Bristol.** Sie hören gerade Radio Bristol. IV
tune [tjuːn] Melodie III
tunnel ['tʌnl] Tunnel II
turkey ['tɜːki] Pute, Truthahn IV
turn [tɜːn]
1. sich umdrehen II • **turn around** sich umdrehen IV • **turn left/right** (nach) links/rechts abbiegen II
turn to sb. sich jm. zuwenden; sich an jn. wenden II
2. turn sth. off/on etwas aus-/einschalten I • **turn sth. down/up** etwas leiser/lauter stellen III
3. turn sb./sth. into sth. jn./etwas in etwas verwandeln V 3 (53)
turn [tɜːn]: **(It's) my turn.** Ich bin dran / an der Reihe. I • **Miss a turn.** Einmal aussetzen. II • **Take another turn.** *(beim Spielen)* Würfel noch einmal. II • **take turns to do sth.** sich abwechseln IV
turtle ['tɜːtl] Wasserschildkröte V 4 (88)
TV [tiː'viː] Fernsehen I • **on TV** im Fernsehen I • **watch TV** fernsehen I
twice [twaɪs] zweimal III
twin [twɪn]: **twin brother** Zwillingsbruder I • **twins** *(pl)* Zwillinge I
twin town Partnerstadt I
°**type** [taɪp] Typ
typical (of) ['tɪpɪkl] typisch (für) V 2 (40)

U

ugly ['ʌgli] hässlich V 4 (94)
ultimate ['ʌltɪmət] ultimativ, perfekt IV
ultraviolet rays *(pl)* [ˌʌltrəˌvaɪələt 'reɪz] ultraviolette Strahlen V 1 (9)
unable [ʌn'eɪbl]: **be unable to do sth.** etwas nicht können V 2 (37/192)
unafraid [ˌʌnə'freɪd]: **be unafraid** keine Angst haben V 2 (37/192)
unanswered [ˌʌn'ɑːnsəd] unbeantwortet IV
unavailable [ˌʌnə'veɪləbl] nicht erhältlich, nicht vorrätig V 2 (37/192)
uncle ['ʌŋkl] Onkel I
unclear [ˌʌn'klɪə] unklar, undeutlich II
uncomfortable [ʌn'kʌmftəbl] unbequem II

unconscious [ʌn'kɒnʃəs] bewusstlos II
uncool [ˌʌn'ku:l] *(infml)* uncool III
under ['ʌndə] unter I
under age [ˌʌndər_'eɪdʒ] minderjährig V 4 (84)
under control [kən'trəʊl] unter Kontrolle IV
underground ['ʌndəgraʊnd]: **the underground** die U-Bahn II
underground [ˌʌndə'graʊnd] unterirdisch IV
°**underline** [ˌʌndə'laɪn] unterstreichen
understand [ˌʌndə'stænd], **understood, understood** verstehen, begreifen I
understanding [ˌʌndə'stændɪŋ] verständnisvoll IV
understanding [ˌʌndə'stændɪŋ] Verständnis, Verständigung V 3 (66)
understood [ˌʌndə'stʊd] *siehe* **understand**
unequal [ʌn'i:kwəl] ungleich V 2 (37/192)
unexpected [ˌʌnɪk'spektɪd] unerwartet, überraschend V 4 (97)
unfair [ˌʌn'feə] unfair, ungerecht II
unfriendly [ʌn'frendli] unfreundlich II
unhappy [ʌn'hæpi] unglücklich II
unhealthy [ʌn'helθi] ungesund III
uniform ['ju:nɪfɔ:m] Uniform I
unimportant [ˌʌnɪm'pɔ:tnt] unwichtig III
uninteresting [ʌn'ɪntrəstɪŋ] uninteressant II
unique [ju'ni:k] einzigartig, einmalig V 1 (9)
unit ['ju:nɪt] Kapitel, Lektion I
united: **the United Kingdom (UK)** [juˌnaɪtɪd 'kɪŋdəm], [ˌju: 'keɪ] das Vereinigte Königreich *(Großbritannien und Nordirland)* III • **the United States (US)** [juˌnaɪtɪd 'steɪts], [ˌju:_'es] die Vereinigten Staaten (von Amerika) III
unity ['ju:nəti] Einheit V 3 (66)
°**universal declaration** [ju:nɪˌvɜ:sl ˌdeklə'reɪʃn] Allgemeine Erklärung
university [ˌju:nɪ'vɜ:səti] Universität, Hochschule V 2 (32) • **go to university** mit dem Studium anfangen V 2 (43)
unknown [ˌʌn'nəʊn] unbekannt IV
unless [ən'les] es sei denn; außer (wenn) V 4 (86)
unlike [ˌʌn'laɪk] im Gegensatz zu III
unload [ʌn'ləʊd] entladen III
unlucky [ʌn'lʌki]: **be unlucky** Pech haben V 2 (37/192)
unpopular [ʌn'pɒpjələ] unpopulär, unbeliebt V 2 (37/192)
unreal [ˌʌn'rɪəl] unwirklich V 2 (37/192)
unrealistic [ˌʌnrɪə'lɪstɪk] unrealistisch V 2 (37/192)
unreliable [ˌʌnrɪ'laɪəbl] unzuverlässig V 2 (37/192)
unsafe [ʌn'seɪf] nicht sicher, gefährlich III
unsure [ˌʌn'ʃʊə, ˌʌn'ʃɔ:] unsicher II
untidy [ʌn'taɪdi] unordentlich III
until [ən'tɪl] bis III
unwanted [ˌʌn'wɒntɪd] unerwünscht, ungewollt V 4 (80)
up [ʌp] hinauf, herauf, nach oben I
up the hill den Hügel hinauf II
up there dort oben III • **That's up to you.** Das liegt bei dir. / Das kannst/musst du (selbst) entscheiden. III • **What's up?** Was ist los? IV
upset (about) [ˌʌp'set] aufgebracht, gekränkt, mitgenommen (wegen) III
upset sb. **(-tt-)** [ʌp'set], **upset, upset** jn. ärgern, kränken, aus der Fassung bringen III
upstairs [ˌʌp'steəz] oben; nach oben I
us [əs, ʌs] uns I
US [ˌju:_es] US-amerikanische(r, s) IV
use [ju:z] benutzen, verwenden I
use [ju:s] Gebrauch III
used [ju:st]: **get used to sth./sb.** sich gewöhnen an jn./etwas IV
I used to be Früher war ich (immer) ... V 1 (6/182)
► S.182 ... used to be/do ...
useful ['ju:sfl] nützlich V 1 (10)
useless ['ju:sləs] nutzlos, unfähig IV
usual ['ju:ʒuəl] gewöhnlich, üblich IV
usually ['ju:ʒuəli] meistens, gewöhnlich, normalerweise I
UV rays *(pl)* [ˌju: 'vi: reɪz] ultraviolette Strahlen V 1 (9)

V

vacation [və'keɪʃn, *AE:* veɪ'keɪʃn] *(AE)* Urlaub, Ferien III
valley ['væli] Tal II • **valley floor** Talboden II
valuable ['væljuəbl] wertvoll, nützlich V 2 (38)
value ['vælju:] Wert IV
vandalism ['vændəlɪzəm] Vandalismus, Zerstörungswut V 4 (84)
vandalize ['vændəlaɪz] mutwillig beschädigen, mutwillig zerstören V 4 (84)
vegetable ['vedʒtəbl] (ein) Gemüse III
verse [vɜ:s] Vers *(von der Bibel)*; Strophe IV
version ['vɜ:ʃn] Fassung IV • **original version** Originalfassung IV
°**vertical** ['vɜ:tɪkl] senkrecht
very ['veri] sehr I • **like/love sth. very much** etwas sehr mögen/lieben II • **Thanks very much!** Danke sehr! / Vielen Dank! II
victim ['vɪktɪm] Opfer III
victory ['vɪktəri] Sieg IV
video ['vɪdiəʊ] Video III • **video projector** Videoprojektor, Beamer V 2 (45)
view (of) [vju:]
1. Aussicht, Blick (auf) II
2. Ansicht, Meinung III
in my view meiner Ansicht nach III • **point of view** [ˌpɔɪnt_əv 'vju:] Standpunkt II • **from my point of view** aus meiner Sicht; von meinem Standpunkt aus gesehen II
°**view** [vju:] betrachten, sehen; im Fernsehen/Kino anschauen
villa ['vɪlə] Ferienhaus; Villa II
village ['vɪlɪdʒ] Dorf I
°**villager** ['vɪlɪdʒə] Dorfbewohner/in
vineyard ['vɪnjəd] Weinberg IV
violence ['vaɪələns] Gewalt, Gewalttätigkeit IV
violent ['vaɪələnt] gewalttätig, gewaltsam IV
violin [ˌvaɪə'lɪn] Violine, Geige III
play the violin Geige spielen III
visibility [ˌvɪzə'bɪləti] Sicht(weite) IV
visit ['vɪzɪt] besuchen, aufsuchen II
visit ['vɪzɪt] Besuch II
visitor ['vɪzɪtə] Besucher/in, Gast I
visual aids *(pl)* [ˌvɪʒuəl_'eɪdz] Anschauungsmaterialien V 2 (45)
vocabulary [və'kæbjələri] Vokabelverzeichnis, Wörterverzeichnis I
voice [vɔɪs] Stimme I • **tone of voice** Ton(fall) V 3 (65)
volleyball ['vɒlibɔ:l] Volleyball I
°**voluntary** ['vɒləntri] freiwillig
volunteer [ˌvɒlən'tɪə] sich freiwillig melden, sich bereit erklären IV; ehrenamtliche Arbeit leisten für/bei V 4 (84)
volunteer work [ˌvɒlən'tɪə] Arbeit als Freiwillige(r) III
vote [vəʊt]
1. (for/against sb./sth.) für/gegen jn./etwas stimmen IV
2. zur Wahl gehen, wählen V 2 (46)

vote [vəʊt] Stimme; die Stimmen; Stimmrecht III
vowel sound ['vaʊəl saʊnd] Vokallaut II

W

°**wages** *(pl)* ['weɪdʒɪz] (Wochen-)Lohn
wait (for) ['weɪt fɔː] warten (auf) I
I can't wait to see ... ich kann es kaum erwarten, ... zu sehen I
Wait a minute. Warte mal! / Moment mal! II • **Wait and see!** Wart's ab! III • °**wait in line (for sth.)** sich (nach etwas) anstellen
wake [weɪk], **woke, woken:**
1. wake sb. (up) jn. (auf)wecken III
2. wake up aufwachen III
walk [wɔːk] (zu Fuß) gehen, laufen I; spazieren gehen III • **walk on** weiterlaufen III • **walk around** herumlaufen III • **walk the dog** den Hund ausführen V 4 (92)
walk [wɔːk] Spaziergang II • **go for a walk** spazieren gehen, einen Spaziergang machen II
wall [wɔːl] Wand; Mauer II
wander ['wɒndə] schlendern, herumirren IV
want [wɒnt] (haben) wollen I
want to do tun wollen I • **They want me to say something.** Sie möchten, dass ich etwas sage IV
war [wɔː] Krieg III • °**fight a war** einen Krieg führen
wardrobe ['wɔːdrəʊb] Kleiderschrank I
warm [wɔːm] warm II
warn sb. (about/of sth.) [wɔːn] jn. vor etwas warnen IV
warning ['wɔːnɪŋ] Warnung IV
was [wəz, wɒz] *siehe* **be**
wash [wɒʃ] waschen I • **I wash my hands.** Ich wasche mir die Hände. I
washing machine ['wɒʃɪŋ məˌʃiːn] Waschmaschine II
waste sth. (on) [weɪst] etwas verschwenden, vergeuden (für) III
waste [weɪst] Verschwendung IV
watch [wɒtʃ] beobachten, sich etwas ansehen; zusehen I
watch TV fernsehen I
watch [wɒtʃ] Armbanduhr I
water ['wɔːtə] Wasser I • °**drinking water** Trinkwasser
waterproof ['wɔːtəpruːf] wasserdicht, -fest V 1 (17/187)
waterfall ['wɔːtəfɔːl] Wasserfall III
wave [weɪv] winken II • **wave at sb.** jm. zuwinken V 4 (94)
wave [weɪv] Welle IV
way [weɪ]
1. Weg; Strecke II • **a long way (from)** weit entfernt (von) I • **ask sb. the way** jn. nach dem Weg fragen II • **in the way** im Weg V 3 (64) • **on the way (to)** auf dem Weg (zu/nach) II • **tell sb. the way** jm. den Weg beschreiben II
What's the best way to get there? Wie komme ich am besten dahin? III • **I'm on my way.** Ich bin (schon) unterwegs. IV
2. Richtung II • **the other way round** anders herum II • **the wrong way** in die falsche Richtung II • **this way** hier entlang, in diese Richtung II • **which way?** in welche Richtung? / wohin? II
3. No way! [ˌnəʊ 'weɪ] Auf keinen Fall! / Kommt nicht in Frage! II; Was du nicht sagst! / Das kann nicht dein Ernst sein! III
4. by the way übrigens, nebenbei (bemerkt) III
5. Art und Weise • **way of life** Lebensart III • **the way you ...** so wie du ..., auf dieselbe Weise wie du ... IV
► S.194 German „Möglichkeit"
we [wiː] wir I
weak [wiːk] schwach II
weakness ['wiːknəs] Schwäche, Schwachpunkt V 2 (44)
wealth [welθ] Reichtum IV
wealthy ['welθi] reich IV
wear [weə], **wore, worn** tragen, anhaben (Kleidung) I
weather ['weðə] Wetter II
weatherproof ['weðəpruːf] wetterbeständig, -fest V 1 (17/187)
°**web address** [web] Webadresse
webcam ['webkæm] Webcam, Internetkamera II
web design ['webdɪˌzaɪn] Webgestaltung V 2 (38)
website ['websaɪt] Website II
Wednesday ['wenzdeɪ, 'wenzdi] Mittwoch I
week [wiːk] Woche I • **days of the week** Wochentage I • **a three-week holiday** ein dreiwöchiger Urlaub III • **once a week** einmal pro Woche III
weekend [ˌwiːk'end] Wochenende I
at the weekend am Wochenende I • **on the weekend** *(AE)* am Wochenende IV
weigh [weɪ] wiegen III
weight [weɪt] Gewicht IV
weird [wɪəd] seltsam III
welcome ['welkəm]
1. Welcome (to Bristol). Willkommen (in Bristol). I
2. You're welcome. Gern geschehen. / Nichts zu danken. I
welcome sb. (to) ['welkəm] jn. begrüßen, willkommen heißen (in) I
They welcome you to ... Sie heißen dich in ... willkommen I
well [wel] *(gesundheitlich)* gut; gesund, wohlauf II
well [wel] gut II • **go well** gut (ver)laufen, gutgehen II • **You looked after them well.** Du hast dich gut um sie gekümmert. II
Oh well ... Na ja ... / Na gut ... I
Well, ... Nun, ... / Also, ... I • **well-structured** gut aufgebaut, gut strukturiert V 2 (45) • **well-written** gut geschriebene(r, s) V 3 (54)
°**well** [wel] *(adv, infml)* richtig, sehr, „voll"
Welsh [welʃ] walisisch; Walisisch II
went [went] *siehe* **go**
were [wə, wɜː]: **(we/you/they) were** *siehe* **be**
west [west] Westen; nach Westen; westlich II • **westbound** ['westbaʊnd] Richtung Westen III
western ['westən] westlich, West- III
wet [wet] feucht, nass II
wetsuit ['wetsuːt] Nassanzug *(Tauch- oder Surfanzug)* V 1 (15)
whale [weɪl] Wal V 1 (9)
what [wɒt]
1. was I
2. welche(r, s) I
like what? wie zum Beispiel? IV
So what? [səʊ 'wɒt] Und? / Na und? II • **Then what?** Was dann? II • **they didn't know what to do** sie wussten nicht, was sie tun sollten; sie wussten nicht, was zu tun war III • °**What a ...!** Was für ein(e) ... • **What a bummer!** *(infml)* So ein Mist! / Wie schade! III • **What about ...? 1.** Was ist mit ...? / Und ...? I; **2.** Wie wär's mit ...? I
What are you talking about? Wovon redest du? I • **What can I get you?** Was kann/darf ich euch/Ihnen bringen? II • **What colour is ...?** Welche Farbe hat ...? I • **What for?** [ˌwɒt 'fɔː] Wofür? II • **What have we got next?** Was haben wir als Nächstes? I • **What kind of car ...?** Was für ein Auto ...? III • **What page are we on?** Auf welcher Seite sind wir? I • **What's for homework?** Was haben wir als Haus-

aufgabe auf? I • **What's the best way to get there?** Wie komme ich am besten dahin? III • **What's the point?** Was soll das? III • **What's the time?** Wie spät ist es? I
What's the matter? Was ist los? / Was ist denn? II • **What's up?** Was ist los? IV • **What's wrong with you?** Was fehlt dir? II
What's your name? Wie heißt du? I • **What was the weather like?** Wie war das Wetter? II
whatever [ˌwɒtˈevə] egal; wie dem auch sei; was (auch) immer IV
whatever the movie egal, in welchem Film IV
wheel [wiːl] Rad III • **big wheel** Riesenrad III
wheelchair [ˈwiːltʃeə] Rollstuhl I
when [wen] wann I • **When's your birthday?** Wann hast du Geburtstag? I
when [wen]
1. wenn I
2. als I
whenever [ˌwenˈevə] wann (auch) immer; egal, wann IV
where [weə]
1. wo I
2. wohin I
Where are you from? Wo kommst du her? I • **He had no idea where to go.** Er hatte keine Ahnung, wo er gehen sollte. IV
wherever [ˌwerˈevə] wo(hin) (auch) immer; egal, wo(hin) IV
whether [ˈweðə] ob IV
which [wɪtʃ] welche(r, s) I • **Which picture ...?** Welches Bild ...? I
which way? in welche Richtung? / wohin? II
which [wɪtʃ] der, die, das; die *(Relativpronomen)* III
while [waɪl]
1. *(conj)* während III
2. *(n)* **(for) a while** eine Weile, einige Zeit IV
whisper [ˈwɪspə] flüstern I
whistle [ˈwɪsl] pfeifen II
whistle [ˈwɪsl] Pfiff; (Triller-)Pfeife II
white [waɪt] weiß I
°**white** [waɪt] Weiße(r)
who [huː]
1. wer I
2. wen / wem II
Who did she talk to? Mit wem hat sie geredet? II • **He had no idea who to ask.** Er hatte keine Ahnung, wen er fragen sollte. IV
who [huː] der, die, das; die *(Relativpronomen)* III
whoever [ˌhuːˈevə] wer/wen/wem (auch) immer; egal, wer/wen/wem IV
whole [həʊl] ganze(r, s), gesamte(r, s) II • **the whole of 2006** das ganze Jahr 2006 II • °**on the whole** im Großen und Ganzen
whom [huːm]**: To whom it may concern** *(bes. AE)* Sehr geehrte Damen und Herren IV
whose [huːz] wessen II • **Whose are these?** Wem gehören diese? II
whose [huːz]**: the man whose statue ...** der Mann, dessen Statue ... II
why [waɪ] warum I • **Why me?** Warum ich? I • **that's why** deshalb, darum I
wide [waɪd] weit, breit III • **far and wide** weit und breit IV • °**widely-used** weit verbreitet
wife [waɪf], *pl* **wives** [waɪvz] Ehefrau II
wild [waɪld] wild II
wildfire [ˈwaɪldfaɪə] Waldbrand, Buschbrand IV
wildlife [ˈwaɪldlaɪf] Tierwelt, frei lebende Tiere IV
will [wɪl]**: you'll be cold (= you will be cold)** du wirst frieren; ihr werdet frieren II • **you'll have travelled** du wirst gereist sein III
win (-nn-) [wɪn], **won, won** gewinnen I
win [wɪn] Sieg III
wind [wɪnd] Wind I
windproof [ˈwɪndpruːf] winddicht V 1 (17/187)
window [ˈwɪndəʊ] Fenster I
windy [ˈwɪndi] windig I
wine [waɪn] Wein IV
winemaker [ˈwaɪnmeɪkə] Winzer/in IV
winemaking [ˈwaɪnmeɪkɪŋ] Weinherstellung IV
wing [wɪŋ] Flügel IV
winner [ˈwɪnə] Gewinner/in, Sieger/in II
winter [ˈwɪntə] Winter I
°**winter's day** Wintertag
wipe [waɪp] (ab)wischen IV
wisdom *(no pl)* [ˈwɪzdəm] Weisheit, Klugheit V 3 (69)
wish [wɪʃ] sich etwas wünschen III • **You wish!** *etwa:* Das hättest du wohl gerne! III
wish [wɪʃ]**: Best wishes** Viele Grüße IV
with [wɪð]
1. mit I
2. bei I
Sit with me. Setz dich zu mir. / Setzt euch zu mir. I • **be with sb.** mit jm. zusammen sein IV
°**withdrawn** [wɪðˈdrɔːn] verschlossen, zurückhaltend
within [wɪˈðɪn] innerhalb (von) V 2 (46)
without [wɪˈðaʊt] ohne I
wives [waɪvz] *pl von „wife"* II
woke [wəʊk] *siehe* **wake**
woken [wəʊkn] *siehe* **wake**
wolf [wʊlf], *pl* **wolves** [wʊlvz] Wolf II
woman [ˈwʊmən], *pl* **women** [ˈwɪmɪn] Frau I
won [wʌn] *siehe* **win**
wonder [ˈwʌndə] sich fragen, gern wissen wollen II
wonderful [ˈwʌndəfəl] wunderbar II
won't [wəʊnt]**: you won't be cold (= you will not be cold)** du wirst nicht frieren; ihr werdet nicht frieren II
wood [wʊd] Holz II • **woods** *(pl)* Wald, Wälder II
woodpecker [ˈwʊdpekə] Specht II
woods *(pl)* [wʊdz] Wald, Wälder II
word [wɜːd] Wort I • **word building** Wortbildung II • **word field** Wortfeld III
wore [wɔː] *siehe* **wear**
work [wɜːk]
1. arbeiten I • **work hard** hart arbeiten II • **work on sb./sth.** an jn./etwas arbeiten I • **work out** klappen, gutgehen IV • **work sth. out** etwas herausfinden, etwas herausarbeiten IV
2. funktionieren III
work [wɜːk] Arbeit I • **at work** bei der Arbeit / am Arbeitsplatz I
be in a line of work einen Beruf ausüben IV • **volunteer work** Arbeit als Freiwillige(r) III • **work experience** *(no pl)* Arbeits-, Praxiserfahrung(en) V 2 (38)
worker [ˈwɜːkə] Arbeiter/in II
workplace [ˈwɜːkpleɪs] Arbeitsplatz *(Ort)* IV
worksheet [ˈwɜːkʃiːt] Arbeitsblatt I
workshop [ˈwɜːkʃɒp] Workshop, Lehrgang III
world [wɜːld] Welt I • **all over the world** auf der ganzen Welt III
from all over the world aus der ganzen Welt II • **in the world** auf der Welt II • °**the New World** die Neue Welt *(Amerika)* • **world music** Weltmusik III • °**world war** Weltkrieg
world-famous [ˌwɜːld ˈfeɪməs] weltberühmt IV

worldwide [ˌwɜːld'waɪd] weltweit IV
worn [wɔːn] *siehe* **wear**
worried ['wʌrid]: **be worried (about)** beunruhigt sein, besorgt sein (wegen) I
worry ['wʌri] Sorge, Kummer II
No worries! *(bes. Australisches E)* Kein Problem! V 1 (6)
worry (about) ['wʌri] sich Sorgen machen (wegen, um) I • **Don't worry.** Mach dir keine Sorgen. I
worse (than) [wɜːs] schlechter, schlimmer (als) II
worst [wɜːst]: **(the) worst** am schlechtesten, schlimmsten; der/die/das schlechteste, schlimmste ... II
worth [wɜːθ]: **it is worth doing sth.** es lohnt sich, etwas zu tun IV
It's worth it. Es lohnt sich. IV
It isn't worth it. Es lohnt sich nicht. IV
would [wəd, wʊd] würde, würdest, würden II • **I'd like ... (= I would like ...)** Ich hätte gern ... / Ich möchte gern ... I • **Would you like ...?** Möchtest du ...? / Möchten Sie ...? I • **I'd like to go (= I would like to go)** Ich würde gern gehen / Ich möchte gehen I • **I wouldn't like to go** ich würde nicht gern gehen / ich möchte nicht gehen I
wrist [rɪst] Handgelenk IV
write [raɪt], **wrote, written** schreiben I • **write down** aufschreiben I • **write to** schreiben an I
writer ['raɪtə] Schreiber/in; Schriftsteller/in II
written ['rɪtn]
1. *siehe* **write**
2. schriftlich V 2 (38)
wrong [rɒŋ] falsch, verkehrt I • **do sth. wrong** etwas Verbotenes tun V 4 (87) • **get sth. wrong** etwas falsch machen III • **the wrong way** in die falsche Richtung II
What's wrong with you? Was fehlt dir? II
wrote [rəʊt] *siehe* **write**

X

xenophobic [ˌzenə'fəʊbɪk] fremdenfeindlich, xenophob V 3 (53)

Y

yard [jɑːd]
1. Hof II • **in the yard** auf dem Hof II
2. Yard *(Längenmaß, 0,91 m)* IV
yawn [jɔːn] gähnen II
°**Yay!** [jeɪ] ja
year [jɪə]
1. Jahr I • **a 70-year-old teacher** ein 70-jähriger Lehrer III • **an 18-year-old** ein(e) 18-Jährige(r) V 3 (60)
2. Jahrgangsstufe I
yellow ['jeləʊ] gelb I
yes [jes] ja I
yesterday ['jestədeɪ, 'jestədi] gestern I • **the day before yesterday** vorgestern II • **yesterday morning/afternoon/evening** gestern Morgen/Nachmittag/Abend I
yet [jet]: **not (...) yet** noch nicht II
yet? schon? II
°**YMCA** [ˌwaɪ‿em siː‿'eɪ] *(Young Men's Christian Association) dem CVJM (Christlicher Verein Junger Menschen) vergleichbare Organisation*
yoga ['jəʊgə] Yoga I
yogurt ['jɒgət] Jogurt III
you [juː]
1. du; Sie I
2. ihr I
3. dir; dich; euch I
4. man III
How are you? Wie geht es dir/Ihnen/euch? II • **You're welcome.** Gern geschehen. / Nichts zu danken. I • **you two** ihr zwei I • **You wish!** *etwa:* Das hättest du wohl gerne! III
young [jʌŋ] jung I
► S.209 the rich, the poor, etc.
your [jɔː]
1. dein/e I
2. Ihr I
3. euer/eure I
yours [jɔːz]
1. deiner, deine, deins II
2. eurer, eure, eures II
Yours faithfully mit freundlichen Grüßen IV • **Yours sincerely** *(BE)* mit freundlichen Grüßen IV
Yours truly *(AE)* mit freundlichen Grüßen IV
yourself [jə'self, jɔː'self]
1. dir/dich III • **about yourself** über dich selbst III
2. selbst IV
yourselves [jə'selvz, jɔː'selvz]
1. euch/sich III
2. selbst IV
youth [juːθ] Jugend III
youth group ['juːθ ˌgruːp] Jugendgruppe IV
youth hostel ['juːθ ˌhɒstəl] Jugendherberge III
yummy ['jʌmi] *(infml)* lecker III

Z

zebra ['zebrə] Zebra II
zero ['zɪərəʊ] null I
zone [zəʊn] Zone, Bereich III
time zone Zeitzone IV
zoo [zuː] Zoo, Tierpark I

First names
(Vornamen)

Aggie ['ægi]
Albert ['ælbət]
Ali ['æli]
Anna ['ænə]
Arthur ['ɑ:θə]
Ashley ['æʃli]
Benjamin ['bendʒəmɪn]
Betsy ['betsi]
Bill [bɪl]
Bob [bɒb]
Brian ['braɪən]
Britney ['brɪtni]
Candice ['kændɪs]
Cath [kæθ]
Charles [tʃɑ:lz]
Chris [krɪs]
Colm [kɒlm, 'kɒləm]
Darren ['dærən]
Dave [deɪv]
David ['deɪvɪd]
Delaney [dɪ'leɪni]
Duane [dweɪn]
Ella ['elə]
Emmeline ['eməli:n]
George [dʒɔ:dʒ]
Gerard ['dʒerɑ:d, dʒə'rɑ:d]
Henry ['henri]
Ishmael ['ɪʃmeɪl]
Jacob ['dʒeɪkəb]
James [dʒeɪmz]
Jeannie ['dʒi:ni]
Jemma ['dʒemə]
Jenny ['dʒeni]
Jeremy ['dʒerəmi]
Jessica ['dʒesɪkə]
Jill [dʒɪl]
John [dʒɒn]
Jon [dʒɒn]
Jude [dʒu:d]
Judith ['dʒu:dɪθ]
Judy ['dʒu:di]
Julia ['dʒu:liə]
Keira [kɪərə]
Kelly ['keli]
Kevin ['kevɪn]
Kirsty ['kɜ:sti]
Langston ['læŋstən]
Laurie ['lɒri]
Lea ['liə]
Leo [liəʊ]
Lindsay ['lɪnzi]
Lucy ['lu:si]
Luke [lu:k]
Mani ['mæni]
Margaret ['mɑ:grət]
Maria [mə'riə]
Mary ['meəri]
Matt [mæt]
Melinda [mə'lɪndə]
Michael ['maɪkl]
Missy ['mɪsi]
Noelle [ˌnəʊ'el]
Orazio [ɔ'ræziəʊ]
Paris ['pærɪs]
Phil [fɪl]
Reece [ri:s]
Richard ['rɪtʃəd]
Riley ['raɪli]
Rita ['ri:tə]
Rob [rɒb]
Robert ['rɒbət]
Sally ['sæli]
Sam [sæm]
Scobie ['skəʊbi]
Shane [ʃeɪn]
Simon ['saɪmən]
Stella ['stelə]
Victoria [vɪk'tɔ:ria]
William ['wɪliəm]
Yates [jeɪts]
Zita [zi:tə]
Zoe [zəʊi]

Family names
(Familiennamen)

Anderson ['ændəsən]
Armstrong ['ɑ:mstrɒŋ]
Aylen ['eɪlən]
Bauer [baʊə]
Bird [bɜ:d]
Canny ['kæni]
Cook [kʊk]
Faulkner [fɔ:lknə]
Freeman ['fri:mən]
Gubbins ['gʌbɪnz]
Halse [hæls]
Hilton ['hɪltn]
Hornblower ['hɔ:nbləʊə]
Hughes [hju:z]
Juhl [dʒu:l]
Le Gallienne [ləˌgæli'en]
Leseur [lə'zɜ:]
Mackintosh ['mækɪntɒʃ]
Marley ['mɑ:li]
McQueen [mə'kwi:n]
Murray ['mʌri]
Nalick ['nælɪk]
Neck [nek]
Newton ['nju:tən]
Pankhurst ['pæŋkhɜ:st]
Preston ['prestən]
Qualls [kwɒlz, kwɔ:lz]
Ross [rɒs]
Rudd [rʌd]
San Souci [ˌsæn sə'si]
Saunders ['sɔ:ndəz]
Sheen [ʃi:n]
Smith [smɪθ]
Sordino [sɔ:'di:nəʊ]
Spears [spɪəz]
Wallace ['wɒlɪs]
Walters ['wɔ:ltəz]
Washington ['wɒʃɪŋtən]
White [waɪt]
Wilson ['wɪlsn]
Wright [raɪt]
Zephaniah [ˌzefə'naɪə]
Zorzotto [zɔ:'zɒtəʊ]

Place names
(Ortsnamen)

Adelaide ['ædəleɪd]
Alice Springs [ˌælɪs 'sprɪŋz]
Ames [eɪmz]
the **Antarctic** [æn'tɑ:ktɪk]
Bangor ['bæŋgə]
Brownville ['braʊnwɪl]
Cairns [keənz, kænz]
Canberra ['kænbərə]
the **Caribbean** ['kærə'bi:ən]
Ceduna [sə'du:nə]
Cologne [kə'ləʊn], *Köln*
Colorado [ˌkɒlə'rɑ:dəʊ]
Darlington ['dɑ:lɪŋtən]
Darwin ['dɑ:wɪn]
Detroit [di'trɔɪt]
El Paso [el 'pæsəʊ]
Ellis Island [ˌelɪs 'aɪlənd]
Fountain Valley [ˌfaʊntn 'væli]
the **Great Barrier Reef** [ˌgreɪt 'bæriə ri:f]
the **Great Victoria Desert** [ˌgreɪt vɪkˌtɔ:riə 'dezət]
Hamburg ['hæmbɜ:g]
Haybrook ['heɪbrʊk]
Hickory ['hɪkəri]
Hobart ['həʊbɑ:t]
Hong Kong [ˌhɒŋ 'kɒŋ]
Illinois [ˌɪlə 'nɔɪ]
Iowa ['aɪəwə]
Katherine ['kæθrɪn]
Kurdistan [ˌkɜ:dɪ'stɑ:n]
Lincoln Park [ˌlɪnkən 'pɑ:k]
London ['lʌndən]
Los Angeles [lɒs 'ændʒəli:z]
Melbourne ['melbən, 'melbɔ:n]
Onslow ['ɒnzləʊ]
Orange ['ɒrɪndʒ]
Palestine ['pæləstaɪn]
Philadelphia [ˌfɪlə'delfiə]
Plimoth ['plɪməθ]
Provincetown ['prɒvɪnstaʊn]
Queensland ['kwi:nzlænd]
Roland ['rəʊlənd]
Roland-Story [ˌrəʊlənd 'stɔ:ri]
Sydney ['sɪdni]
Tara Downs [ˌtɑ:rə 'daʊnz]
Tasmania [ˌtæz'meɪniə]
Uluru [ˌu:lə'ru:, 'u:ləru:]
Uluru-Kata Tjuta [ˌu:ləru: ˌkætə 'tju:tə]
Ur [ɜ:]
Victoria [vɪk'tɔ:riə]
Weeki Wachee Springs [ˌwi:ki ˌwɑ:tʃi 'sprɪŋz]
Wellington ['welɪŋtən]
Worita [wə'ri:tə]
Yarra ['jærə]

Other names
(Andere Namen)

Ashmead's Kernel [ˌæʃmi:dz 'kɜ:nəl]
Batman ['bætmæn]
Capitol ['kæpɪtl]
the **Champions League** ['tʃæmpiənz li:g]
Charles Ross [ˌtʃɑ:lz 'rɒs]
Conservative [kən'sɜ:vətɪv]
Cupid ['kju:pɪd]
Discovery [dɪs'kʌvəri]
the **European Union** [jʊərəˌpiən 'ju:nɪən]
Excalibur [ek'skælɪbə]
Ffordd Deiniol [ˌfɔ:ð 'deɪnɪɒl]
Gascoyne's Scarlet [ˌgæskɔɪnz 'skɑ:lət]
Gateway School ['geɪtweɪ]
Hogwarts ['hɒgwɔ:ts]
Human Rights Watch [ˌhju:mən 'raɪts ˌwɒtʃ]
Ida Red [ˌaɪdə 'red]
Jonathan ['dʒɒnəθən]
Labour ['leɪbə]
Magna Carta [ˌmægnə 'kɑ:tə]
McIntosh ['mækɪntɒʃ]
Moorfield High School ['mʊəfi:ld]
Northern Spy [ˌnɔ:ðən 'spaɪ]
Orange Pippin [ˌɒrɪndʒ 'pipin]
Oscar ['ɒskə]
Oz [ɒz]
Russett ['rʌsɪt]
Rusty ['rʌsti]
Tasmanian Devil [tæzˌmeɪniən 'devəl]
Tatji ['tætʃi]
Tin Annie [ˌtɪn 'æni]
The **Tribune** ['tribju:n]
the **United Nations** [juˌnaɪtɪd 'neɪʃənz]
the **White House** ['waɪt haʊs]
Worcester ['wʊstə]

Country/Continent	Adjective	Person	People
Afghanistan [æf'gænɪstæn] *Afghanistan*	Afghan ['æfgæn]	an Afghan	the Afghans
Africa ['æfrɪkə] *Afrika*	African ['æfrɪkən]	an African	the Africans
America [ə'merɪkə] *Amerika*	American [ə'merɪkən]	an American	the Americans
Asia ['eɪʃə, 'eɪʒə] *Asien*	Asian ['eɪʃn, 'eɪʒn]	an Asian	the Asians
Australia [ɒ'streɪliə] *Australien*	Australian [ɒ'streɪliən]	an Australian	the Australians
Austria ['ɒstriə] *Österreich*	Austrian ['ɒstriən]	an Austrian	the Austrians
Bangladesh [ˌbæŋglə'deʃ] *Bangladesch*	Bangladeshi [ˌbæŋglə'deʃi]	a Bangladeshi	the Bangladeshis
Barbados [bɑː'beɪdɒs] *Barbados*	Barbadian [bɑː'beidɪən], Bajan ['beɪdʒn]	a Barbadian a Bajan	the Barbadians the Bajans
Belgium ['beldʒəm] *Belgien*	Belgian ['beldʒən]	a Belgian	the Belgians
Bosnia ['bɒznɪə] *Bosnien*	Bosnian ['bɒznɪən]	a Bosnian	the Bosnians
Canada ['kænədə] *Kanada*	Canadian [kə'neɪdiən]	a Canadian	the Canadians
Chile ['tʃɪli] *Chile*	Chilean ['tʃɪliən]	a Chilean	the Chileans
China ['tʃaɪnə] *China*	Chinese [ˌtʃaɪ'niːz]	a Chinese	the Chinese
Croatia [krəʊ'eɪʃə] *Kroatien*	Croatian [krəʊ'eɪʃn]	a Croatian	the Croatians
Cuba ['kjuːbə] *Kuba*	Cuban ['kjuːbən]	a Cuban	the Cubans
the Czech Republic [ˌtʃek rɪ'pʌblɪk] *Tschechien, die Tschechische Republik*	Czech [tʃek]	a Czech	the Czechs
Denmark ['denmɑːk] *Dänemark*	Danish ['deɪnɪʃ]	a Dane [deɪn]	the Danes
Dominica [ˌdɒ'mɪ'niːkə] *Dominica*	Dominican [ˌdɒ'mɪ'niːkən]	a Dominican	the Dominicans
England ['ɪŋglənd] *England*	English ['ɪŋglɪʃ]	an Englishman/-woman	the English
Ethiopia [ˌiːθi'əʊpɪə] *Äthiopien*	Ethiopian [ˌiːθi'əʊpɪən]	an Ethiopian	the Ethiopians
Europe ['jʊərəp] *Europa*	European [ˌjʊərə'piːən]	a European	the Europeans
Finland ['fɪnlənd] *Finnland*	Finnish ['fɪnɪʃ]	a Finn [fɪn]	the Finns
France [frɑːns] *Frankreich*	French [frentʃ]	a Frenchman/-woman	the French
Georgia ['dʒɔːdʒə] *Georgien*	Georgian ['dʒɔːdʒən]	a Georgian	the Georgians
Germany ['dʒɜːməni] *Deutschland*	German ['dʒɜːmən]	a German	the Germans
(Great) Britain ['brɪtn] *Großbritannien*	British ['brɪtɪʃ]	a Briton ['brɪtn]	the British
Greece [griːs] *Griechenland*	Greek [griːk]	a Greek	the Greeks
Guyana [gaɪ'ænə] *Guyana*	Guyanese [ˌgaɪə'niːz]	a Guyanese	the Guyanese
Holland ['hɒlənd] *Holland, die Niederlande*	Dutch [dʌtʃ]	a Dutchman/-woman	the Dutch
Hungary ['hʌŋgəri] *Ungarn*	Hungarian [hʌŋ'geəriən]	a Hungarian	the Hungarians
India ['ɪndiə] *Indien*	Indian ['ɪndiən]	an Indian	the Indians
Iraq [ɪ'rɑːk] *Irak*	Iraqi [ɪ'rɑːki]	an Iraqi	the Iraqis
Ireland ['aɪələnd] *Irland*	Irish ['aɪrɪʃ]	an Irishman/-woman	the Irish
Italy ['ɪtəli] *Italien*	Italian [ɪ'tæliən]	an Italian	the Italians
Jamaica [dʒə'meɪkə] *Jamaika*	Jamaican [dʒə'meɪkən]	a Jamaican	the Jamaicans
Japan [dʒə'pæn] *Japan*	Japanese [ˌdʒæpə'niːz]	a Japanese	the Japanese
Korea [kə'riə] *Korea*	Korean [kə'riən]	a Korean	the Koreans
Malaysia [mə'leɪʒə, mə'leɪziə] *Malaysia*	Malaysian [mə'leɪʒən, mə'leɪziən]	a Malaysian	the Malaysians
Mexico ['meksɪkəʊ] *Mexiko*	Mexican [kə'riən]	a Mexican	the Mexicans
the Netherlands ['neðələndz] *die Niederlande, Holland*	Dutch [dʌtʃ]	a Dutchman/-woman	the Dutch
New Zealand [ˌnjuː 'ziːlənd] *Neuseeland*	New Zealand [ˌnjuː 'ziːlənd]	a New Zealander	the New Zealanders
Nigeria [naɪ'dʒɪəriə] *Nigeria*	Nigerian [naɪ'dʒɪəriən]	a Nigerian	the Nigerians
Norway ['nɔːweɪ] *Norwegen*	Norwegian [nɔː'wiːdʒən]	a Norwegian	the Norwegians
Pakistan [ˌpækɪ'stæn, ˌpɑːkɪ'stɑːn] *Pakistan*	Pakistani [ˌpækɪ'stæni, ˌpɑːkɪ'stɑːni]	a Pakistani	the Pakistanis
the Philippines ['fɪlɪpiːnz] *die Philippinen*	Philippine ['fɪlɪpiːn]	a Filipino [ˌfɪlɪ'piːnəʊ]/ Filipina [ˌfɪlɪ'piːnə]	the Filipinos/ Filipinas
Poland ['pəʊlənd] *Polen*	Polish ['pəʊlɪʃ]	a Pole [pəʊl]	the Poles
Portugal ['pɔːtʃʊgl] *Portugal*	Portuguese [ˌpɔːtʃu'giːz]	a Portuguese	the Portuguese
Russia ['rʌʃə] *Russland*	Russian ['rʌʃn]	a Russian	the Russians
Scotland ['skɒtlənd] *Schottland*	Scottish ['skɒtɪʃ]	a Scotsman/-woman, a Scot [skɒt]	the Scots, the Scottish
Slovakia [sləʊ'vɑːkiə, sləʊ'vækiə] *die Slowakei*	Slovak ['sləʊvæk]	a Slovak	the Slovaks

Country/Continent	Adjective	Person	People
Slovenia [sləʊ'vi:niə] *Slowenien*	Slovenian [sləʊ'vi:niən], Slovene ['sləʊvi:n]	a Slovene, a Slovenian	the Slovenes, the Slovenians
Somalia [sə'mɑ:liə] *Somalia*	Somali [sə'mɑ:li]	a Somali	the Somalis
Spain [speɪn] *Spanien*	Spanish ['spænɪʃ]	a Spaniard ['spænɪəd]	the Spaniards
Sri Lanka [ˌsri 'læŋkə] *Sri Lanka*	Sri Lankan [ˌsri 'læŋkən]	a Sri Lankan	the Sri Lankans
Sudan [su'dɑ:n] *Sudan*	Sudanese [ˌsudə'ni:z]	a Sudanese	the Sudanese
Sweden ['swi:dn] *Schweden*	Swedish ['swi:dɪʃ]	a Swede [swi:d]	the Swedes
Switzerland ['swɪtsələnd] *die Schweiz*	Swiss [swɪs]	a Swiss	the Swiss
Trinidad and Tobago [ˌtrɪnɪdæd ən tə'beɪgəʊ] *Trinidad und Tobago*	Trinidadian [ˌtrɪnɪ'dædiən] Tobagan [tə'beɪgən]	a Trinidadian a Tobagan	the Trinidadians the Tobagans
Turkey ['tɜ:ki] *die Türkei*	Turkish ['tɜ:kɪʃ]	a Turk [tɜ:k]	the Turks
the United Kingdom (the UK) [juˌnaɪtɪd 'kɪŋdəm, ju:'keɪ] *das Vereinigte Königreich (Großbritannien und Nordirland)*	British ['brɪtɪʃ]	a Briton ['brɪtn]	the British
the United States of America (the USA) [juˌnaɪtɪd ˌsteɪts‿əv‿ə'merɪkə, ju:‿es‿'eɪ] *die Vereinigten Staaten von Amerika*	American [ə'merɪkən]	an American	the Americans
Vietnam [ˌvjet'næm] *Vietnam*	Vietnamese [ˌvjetnə'mi:z]	a Vietnamese	the Vietnamese
Wales [weɪlz] *Wales*	Welsh [welʃ]	a Welshman/-woman	the Welsh

English sounds (Englische Laute)

Die Lautschrift in den eckigen Klammern zeigt dir, wie ein Wort ausgesprochen wird.
In der folgenden Übersicht findest du alle Lautzeichen.

Vokale (Selbstlaute)

[i:]	green	[ʊ]	book	[ɪə]	here
[i]	happy	[ʌ]	mum	[eə]	where
[ɪ]	in	[ɜ:]	T-shirt	[ʊə]	tour
[e]	yes	[ə]	a partner		
[æ]	black	[eɪ]	skate		
[ɑ:]	park	[aɪ]	time		
[ɒ]	song	[ɔɪ]	boy		
[ɔ:]	morning	[əʊ]	old		
[u:]	blue	[aʊ]	now		

Konsonanten (Mitlaute)

[b]	box	[l]	hello	[ʒ]	television
[p]	play	[r]	red	[tʃ]	teacher
[d]	dad	[w]	we	[dʒ]	Germany
[t]	ten	[j]	you	[θ]	thanks
[g]	good	[f]	full	[ð]	this
[k]	cat	[v]	very	[h]	he
[m]	mum	[s]	sister	[x]	loch
[n]	no	[z]	please		
[ŋ]	sing	[ʃ]	shop		

The English alphabet (Das englische Alphabet)

a	[eɪ]	**h**	[eɪtʃ]	**o**	[əʊ]	**v**	[vi:]
b	[bi:]	**i**	[aɪ]	**p**	[pi:]	**w**	['dʌblju:]
c	[si:]	**j**	[dʒeɪ]	**q**	[kju:]	**x**	[eks]
d	[di:]	**k**	[keɪ]	**r**	[ɑ:]	**y**	[waɪ]
e	[i:]	**l**	[el]	**s**	[es]	**z**	[zed]
f	[ef]	**m**	[em]	**t**	[ti:]		
g	[dʒi:]	**n**	[en]	**u**	[ju:]		

Infinitive	Simple past form	Past participle	
(to) **be**	**was/were**	**been**	sein
(to) **beat**	**beat**	**beaten**	schlagen; besiegen
(to) **become**	**became**	**become**	werden
(to) **begin**	**began**	**begun**	beginnen, anfangen (mit)
(to) **bleed** [iː]	**bled** [e]	**bled** [e]	bluten
(to) **blow**	**blew**	**blown**	wehen, blasen, pusten
(to) **break**	**broke**	**broken**	zerbrechen, kaputt machen
(to) **bring**	**brought**	**brought**	(mit-, her)bringen
(to) **broadcast**	**broadcast**	**broadcast**	ausstrahlen; senden
(to) **build**	**built**	**built**	bauen
(to) **buy**	**bought**	**bought**	kaufen
(to) **catch**	**caught**	**caught**	fangen; erwischen
(to) **choose** [uː]	**chose** [əʊ]	**chosen** [əʊ]	(aus)wählen; (sich) aussuchen
(to) **come**	**came**	**come**	kommen
(to) **cut**	**cut**	**cut**	schneiden
(to) **deal** with [iː]	**dealt** [e]	**dealt** [e]	sich beschäftigen mit
(to) **do**	**did**	**done** [ʌ]	tun, machen
(to) **draw**	**drew**	**drawn**	zeichnen
(to) **drink**	**drank**	**drunk**	trinken
(to) **drive** [aɪ]	**drove**	**driven** [ɪ]	*(ein Auto)* fahren
(to) **eat**	**ate** [et, eɪt]	**eaten**	essen
(to) **fall**	**fell**	**fallen**	(hin)fallen, stürzen
(to) **feed**	**fed**	**fed**	füttern
(to) **feel**	**felt**	**felt**	(sich) fühlen; sich anfühlen
(to) **fight**	**fought**	**fought**	kämpfen
(to) **find**	**found**	**found**	finden
(to) **fly**	**flew**	**flown**	fliegen
(to) **forget**	**forgot**	**forgotten**	vergessen
(to) **forgive**	**forgave**	**forgiven**	vergeben, verzeihen
(to) **get**	**got**	**got**	bekommen; holen; werden; (hin) kommen
(to) **give**	**gave**	**given**	geben
(to) **go**	**went**	**gone** [ɒ]	gehen, fahren
(to) **grow**	**grew**	**grown**	wachsen; anbauen, anpflanzen
(to) **hang**	**hung**	**hung**	(etwas) aufhängen
(to) **have (have got)**	**had**	**had**	haben, besitzen
(to) **hear** [ɪə]	**heard** [ɜː]	**heard** [ɜː]	hören
(to) **hide** [aɪ]	**hid** [ɪ]	**hidden** [ɪ]	(sich) verstecken
(to) **hit**	**hit**	**hit**	treffen; schlagen
(to) **hold**	**held**	**held**	halten
(to) **hurt**	**hurt**	**hurt**	wehtun; verletzen
(to) **keep**	**kept**	**kept**	(be)halten; aufbewahren
(to) **kneel** [niːl]	**knelt** [nelt]	**knelt**	sich hinknien
(to) **know** [nəʊ]	**knew** [njuː]	**known** [nəʊn]	wissen; kennen
(to) **lay** the table	**laid**	**laid**	den Tisch decken
(to) **lead** [iː]	**led** [e]	**led** [e]	führen
(to) **leave**	**left**	**left**	(weg)gehen; abfahren; verlassen; zurücklassen
(to) **lend**	**lent**	**lent**	leihen
(to) **let**	**let**	**let**	lassen

Infinitive	Simple past form	Past participle	
(to) **lie**	**lay**	**lain**	liegen
(to) **lose** [uː]	**lost** [ɒ]	**lost** [ɒ]	verlieren
(to) **make**	**made**	**made**	machen; bauen; bilden
(to) **mean** [iː]	**meant** [e]	**meant** [e]	bedeuten; meinen
(to) **meet**	**met**	**met**	(sich) treffen
(to) **pay**	**paid**	**paid**	bezahlen
(to) **put**	**put**	**put**	legen, stellen, *(wohin)* tun
(to) **read** [iː]	**read** [e]	**read** [e]	lesen
(to) **ride** [aɪ]	**rode**	**ridden** [ɪ]	reiten; *(Rad)* fahren
(to) **ring**	**rang**	**rung**	klingeln, läuten
(to) **rise** [aɪ]	**rose**	**risen** [ɪ]	(auf)steigen
(to) **run**	**ran**	**run**	rennen, (ver)laufen
(to) **say** [eɪ]	**said** [e]	**said** [e]	sagen
(to) **see**	**saw**	**seen**	sehen; besuchen, aufsuchen
(to) **seek** [iː]	**sought** [ɔː]	**sought**	suchen
(to) **sell**	**sold**	**sold**	verkaufen
(to) **send**	**sent**	**sent**	schicken, senden
(to) **set** a trap	**set**	**set**	eine Falle stellen
(to) **sew**	**sewed**	**sewn**	(an)nähen
(to) **shake**	**shook**	**shaken**	schütteln
(to) **shine**	**shone** [ɒ, *AE* əʊ]	**shone** [ɒ]	scheinen *(Sonne)*
(to) **shoot** [uː]	**shot** [ɒ]	**shot** [ɒ]	(er)schießen
(to) **show**	**showed**	**shown**	zeigen
(to) **shut up**	**shut**	**shut**	den Mund halten
(to) **sing**	**sang**	**sung**	singen
(to) **sink**	**sank**	**sunk**	sinken
(to) **sit**	**sat**	**sat**	sitzen; sich setzen
(to) **sleep**	**slept**	**slept**	schlafen
(to) **speak**	**spoke**	**spoken**	sprechen
(to) **spend**	**spent**	**spent**	*(Zeit)* verbringen; *(Geld)* ausgeben
(to) **spit**	**spat**	**spat**	spucken
(to) **spread** [e]	**spread** [e]	**spread** [e]	(sich) ausbreiten, (sich) verbreiten
(to) **stand**	**stood**	**stood**	stehen; sich (hin)stellen
(to) **steal**	**stole**	**stolen**	stehlen
(to) **stick**	**stuck**	**stuck**	herausragen, herausstehen; (auf)kleben
(to) **sweep** [iː]	**swept** [e]	**swept** [e]	fegen, kehren
(to) **swim**	**swam**	**swum**	schwimmen
(to) **take**	**took**	**taken**	nehmen; (weg-, hin)bringen; dauern, *(Zeit)* brauchen
(to) **teach**	**taught**	**taught**	unterrichten, lehren
(to) **tear** [eə]	**tore** [ɔː]	**torn** [ɔː]	(zer)reißen
(to) **tell**	**told**	**told**	erzählen, berichten
(to) **think**	**thought**	**thought**	denken, glauben, meinen
(to) **throw**	**threw**	**thrown**	werfen
(to) **understand**	**understood**	**understood**	verstehen
(to) **upset**	**upset**	**upset**	ärgern, kränken, aus der Fassung bringen
(to) **wake** up	**woke**	**woken**	aufwachen; wecken
(to) **wear** [eə]	**wore** [ɔː]	**worn** [ɔː]	tragen *(Kleidung)*
(to) **win**	**won** [ʌ]	**won** [ʌ]	gewinnen
(to) **write**	**wrote**	**written**	schreiben

Was DU im Klassenzimmer sagen kannst / What YOU can say in the classroom

Du brauchst Hilfe	You need help
Tut mir leid, ich habe das nicht verstanden.	**Sorry, I don't understand.**
Können Sie/Kannst du das bitte noch einmal sagen?	**Can you say that again, please?**
Können Sie/Kannst du bitte lauter sprechen?	**Can you speak louder, please?**
Kann ich eine Frage stellen?	**Can I ask a question, please?**
Können Sie/Kannst du mir bitte helfen?	**Can you help me, please?**
Was bedeutet ...?	**What does ... mean?**
Ich habe ... – ist das auch richtig?	**I've got ... – is that right too?**
Können Sie ... bitte buchstabieren?	**Can you spell ..., please?**
Wie spricht man das erste Wort in Zeile 2 aus?	**How do you say the first word in line 2?**
Können Sie es bitte an die Tafel schreiben?	**Can you write that on the board, please?**
Tut mir leid, ich finde es nicht. Auf welcher Seite sind wir?	**Sorry, I can't find it. What page are we on?**
Was haben wir (als Hausaufgabe) auf?	**What's for homework?**

Du hast ein Problem	You're in trouble
Entschuldigung, dass ich zu spät komme/meine Hausaufgaben nicht gemacht habe, Herr .../Frau ...	**Sorry, I'm late/ I haven't done my homework, Mr/Mrs/Ms/Miss ...**
Tut mir leid, dass ich mein Schulheft vergessen habe.	**Sorry, I've forgotten my exercise book.**
Ich bin noch nicht fertig.	**I haven't finished yet.**
Entschuldigung, ich habe nicht zugehört/ das weiß ich nicht.	**Sorry, I wasn't listening / I don't know.**
Ich kann Nummer 3 nicht lösen.	**I can't do number 3.**

Über Texte reden	Talking about texts
Die Geschichte/Das Theaterstück/Das Gedicht/ Das Lied/ Der Film handelt von ...	**The story/play/poem/ song/ film is about ...**
Die Handlung spielt während/in ...	**The action takes place during/in ...**
In Zeile 15–20 steht, dass ...	**In lines 15–20 it says that ...**
Die Hauptfigur ist ...	**The main character is ...**
Der Mann/Die Frau/... scheint sehr einsam/zornig/ traurig/... zu sein.	**The man/woman/... seems to be very lonely/ angry/ sad/...**
Die Beziehung zwischen ... und ... ist sonderbar/...	**The relationship between ... and ... is strange/...**
Es war lustig/unheimlich/langweilig/..., als ...	**It was funny/scary/boring/... when ...**
Ich fand es gut/nicht gut, als ...,	**I liked it/didn't like it when ...**
Ich fand den Schluss überraschend/blöd/... , weil ...	**I found the ending surprising/stupid/... because ...**
Ich finde die Geschichte ist lustig/aufregend/..., weil ...	**I think the story is funny/exciting/...because ...**
Die Geschichte hat mich glücklich/wütend/... gemacht.	**The story made me (feel) happy/angry/...**

In einer Diskussion	In a discussion
Meiner Meinung nach ...	**In my opinion ...**
Ich will dir ein Beispiel geben: ...	**Let me give you an example: ...**
Erstens ... / Zweitens ... / Und schließlich ...	**First ... / Second ... / And finally ...**
Ich stimme (...) zu/nicht zu, weil ...	**I agree/disagree with ... because ...**
Ja, du hast Recht. / Genau!	**Yes, you're right. / Exactly!**
Was Tim sagt, ist richtig/falsch.	**What Tim says is right/wrong.**
Du sagst ..., aber ...	**You say ..., but ...**
Was genau meinst du?	**What do you mean exactly?**
Du könntest Recht haben, aber ...	**You may be right, but ...**
Ich bin mir nicht sicher. Vielleicht ...	**I'm not so sure. Maybe/Perhaps ...**
Was meinst du (zu ...)?	**What do you think (about ...)?**

Bei der Partner- oder Gruppenarbeit	Working with a partner or in a group
Kann ich mit ... arbeiten?	**Can I work with ...?**

Was machen wir als Erstes?	**What are we going to do first?**
Lass/Lasst uns die Aufgabe noch einmal lesen.	**Let's read the task again.**
Wer ist dran? – Ich bin/Du bist dran, das zu schreiben/ die Fragen zu stellen.	**Whose turn is it? – It's my/your turn to write/ ask questions.**
Ich finde, wir sollten/könnten ...	**I think we should/could ...**
Hast du eine Idee/einen Vorschlag?	**Have you got any ideas?**
Mir gefällt deine Idee sehr gut. / Das klingt gut.	**I really like your idea. / That sounds good.**
Wo können wir etwas zu ... finden?	**Where can we find out about ...?**
Was hast du im Internet gefunden?	**What did you find on the internet?**
Was hältst du von meinem Text/Bild/...?	**What do you think of my text/picture/...?**
Ich verstehe nicht, was du meinst. / Ich bin mir da nicht sicher.	**I don't understand what you mean./I'm not sure about that.**
Lass/Lasst uns ... auf unser Poster schreiben.	**Let's write ... on our poster.**
Lass/Lasst uns das Bild hier hinsetzen/-kleben.	**Let's put the picture here.**
Wie viel Zeit haben wir (noch)?	**How much (more) time do we have?**
Wir haben nur noch ... Minuten Zeit.	**We've only got ... minutes left.**
Lass/Lasst uns ... schnell machen und dann mit ... fortfahren.	**Let's do ... quickly and then go on to ...**
Vielleicht sollten wir ... weglassen / etwas zu ... sagen.	**Maybe we should leave out ... / say something about ...**
Wir sind fast fertig. Ich denke, wir sollten ... weglassen.	**We've nearly finished. I think we should leave out ...**

Bei einer Präsentation / Giving a talk / presentation

Das Thema meines Vortrags ist ...	**The topic of my talk/presentation is ...**
Ich werde meinen Vortrag in ... Teile gliedern.	**I'm going to divide my talk into ... parts.**
Erstens/Als nächstes/... würde ich gern ...	**First/Next/... I would like to ...**
Zum Schluss werde ich etwas über ... erzählen.	**Finally, I'll tell you something about ...**
Auf der ersten Folie links/rechts könnt ihr sehen ...	**On the first slide on the left/right you can see ...**
Zusammenfassend möchte ich sagen, ...	**To sum things up I'd like to say ...**
Gibt es/Habt ihr Fragen oder Kommentare dazu?	**Are there any questions or comments?**

What YOUR TEACHER says / Was DEIN/E LEHRER/IN sagt

Copy/Fill in the chart/form.	Kopiert/Füllt die Tabelle/das Formular aus.
Correct the mistakes.	Verbessert die Fehler.
Don't forget to check your spelling.	Vergesst nicht die Rechtschreibung zu überprüfen.
Be careful with the word order.	Achtet auf die Satzstellung.
Write it on the board, please.	Schreibe es bitte an die Tafel.
Compare your sentences/answers/... with your partner.	Vergleiche deine Sätze/Antworten/... mit deinem Partner/deiner Partnerin.
Discuss ... with your partner/ in your group.	Diskutiert ... mit einem Partner/einer Partnerin/ in der Gruppe.
Practise/Act out the dialogue with a partner, please.	Bitte übe/spiele den Dialog mit deinem Partner/deiner Partnerin.
Walk around the class and ask other students.	Geht durch die Klasse und fragt andere Schüler/innen.
Take notes.	Macht euch Notizen.
Imagine you are ...	Stellt euch vor, ihr seid ...
What do you think of ...?	Was haltet ihr von ...?
Have you got any other ideas?	Habt ihr andere/sonstige Ideen?
Give three reasons.	Nenne drei Gründe.
Have you finished?	Seid ihr/Bist du fertig?
Present your talk/poster/... to the class.	Präsentiere dein Referat/Poster/... vor der Klasse.
Do exercise 3 for homework, please.	Macht bitte Übung 3 als Hausaufgabe.

Illustrationen

Silke Bachmann, Hamburg (S. 14; 25; 114; 119; 120 unten (u. 101 2. v. unten); 121 oben (u. 101 unten); **Roland Beier**, Berlin (S. 9 oben; 56; 58; 108 (u. 101 5. v. oben); 123 – 126; 129 – 210); **Carlos Borrell**, Berlin (vordere und hintere Umschlaginnenseite; S. 9 unten; 10; 11; 102/103 Hintergrund); **Dylan Gibson**, Pitlochry (S. 36; 42; 92); **Christian Görke**, Berlin (S. 105; 120 oben; 127 oben); **Graham-Cameron Illustration**, UK: **Eoin Coveney** (S. 95 – 96); **Alfred Schüssler**, Frankfurt/Main (S. 93 oben re.; 104 Vignetten (M))

Bildquellen

Alamy, Abingdon (S. 12 Bild B (u. 126): photocay; S. 13 Mitte li.: Buzz Pictures; S. 19 unten: Susanna Bennett; S. 30 unten re.: Brownstock Inc. (RF); S. 32 unten li.: BlueMoon Stock (RF), unten 2. v. re.: Rob Walls; S. 33 Mitte li.: keith morris; S. 37: SHOUT; S. 64 unten: UpperCut Images (RF); S. 78 Bild A: Photofusion Picture Library, Bild D: Steve Skjold; S. 79 Bild G: JJ pixs (RF); S. 84: Janine Wiedel Photolibrary; S. 88 tin (M): FB-StockPhoto; S. 89 oben kids: Steve Skjold (RF), unten li.: Jim West, Mitte: Bubbles Photolibrary, unten re.: PhotoAlto (RF); S. 106 Bild 3: David Page, unten: Alex Maddox; S. 139 „Kit's Wilderness" teenager: BananaStock (RF), „The Australian Connection" man: StockImage/Pixland (RF)); **Argus**, Hamburg (S. 75: Peter Frischmuth); **Associated Press**, Frankfurt/Main (S. 33 unten 2. v. li.; S. 50 Bild B; S. 103 unten re.); **Australia Post** (S. 139 „From Prison to Prosperity" stamp); **Chuck Braverman. Art and Design ©2004 New Video Group, Inc.** (S. 85 film still taken from "High school boot camp"); **CartoonStock**, Bath (S. 39: Ralph Hagen; S. 82: Dave Carpenter; S. 83 (u. 100): W. B. Park; S. 90: Ham –Khan-; S. 121 unten: KES); **Cinetext**, Frankfurt/Main (S. 17 unten: Arsenal/Cinetext); **Corbis**, Düsseldorf (Inhaltsverz. Bob Marley (u. 51): Jeff Albertson; S. 6 Bild 1: Dennis Degnan; S. 7 Bild 2: Aurora Open/Lars Schneider (RF); S. 12 Bild C: Hannah Mason (RF); S. 16 oben re.: Charles & Josette Lenars; S. 32 unten re.: Lawrence Manning; S. 51 Bild E: Sygma/JP Laffont; S. 63: Howard Pyle); **Corel Library** (S. 41; S. 139 "Kit's Wilderness" landscape, "Pick a Poem" scrabble tiles, LOVE sign, "The Australian Connection" fish, "From Prison to Prosperity" sea); **Cornelsen Verlag**, Berlin (S. 44 oben; S. 45 oben: Michael Weihrauch); **ECHO BRIDGE ENTERTAINMENT LLC**, Needham, USA (S. 54; S. 57); **Gareth Evans**, Berlin (S. 40); **Das Fotoarchiv**, Essen (S. 78 Bild B: Yavuz Arslan); **Fotosearch**, Waukesha (Inhaltsverz. young couple (u. 32 Mitte re.): WestEnd61 (RF)); **Fountain Valley School of Colorado**, Colorado Springs (S. 89 oben website, logo (M)); **Deneen Frost**, Roland (S. 60); **Getty Images**, München (Inhaltsverz. teens with mobiles (u. 80): Per-Anders Pettersson; S. 6/7 Uluru: Ted Mead; S. 7 Bild 3: Bec Parsons, Bild 6: Doug Armand; S. 9: Jeff Hunter; S. 12 oben girl (M): Jack Hollingsworth (RF); S. 13 oben: Anthony Ong (RF), unten li.: James Knowler, unten re.: Tony Lewis; S. 16 oben li.: AFP; S. 22: Ian Waldie; S. 28 Bild 5: UpperCut Images (RF); S. 29 oben: Annie Griffiths Belt; S. 32 unten 2. v. li.: Sean Ellis; S. 33 oben li.: Daly & Newton, unten li.: Image Source (RF), unten re.: John Kelly; S. 51 Bild D: AFP; S. 52 book cover crouching girl (M): Terry Vine; S. 67 oben li.; S. 68 unten: Popperfoto; S. 78 Bild C: Rubberball (RF); S. 101 2. v. oben (u. 105); S. 110 oben: AFP/ARTHUR EDWARDS); **Bonnie Glänzer**, Berlin (S. 46 unten); **Guardian News & Media Ltd 2008** (S. 17 oben: Barbara McMahon); **The Hickory Daily Record**, Hickory (S. 88 unten website, logo, unten li.: Robert Reed); © **Human Rights Watch** (S. 56 oben); **iStockphoto**, Calgary (Inhaltsverz. scientists (u. 33 oben re.): LajosRepasi; S. 6 oben: Renee Lee; S. 12 Bild A: John Simmons; S. 20 re.: Timothy Ball; S. 26 unten li.: Gene Chutka, re.: Jeffrey Smith; S. 27 (u. 103 Mitte re.): susan flashman; S. 29 unten: Chuck Babbitt; S. 30 oben: Pali Rao, unten li. monitor (M): zak, question mark (M): Zeffss1; S. 32 oben li.: Lisa Klumpp; S. 33 unten 2. v. re.: Rich Legg; S. 44 unten: dawn liljenquist; S. 59: Justin Horrocks; S. 64 oben li.: Christine Glade, re.: Johnny Greig; S. 68 oben: Rebecca Ellis; S. 70 unten re.: Diane White Rosier; S. 71: Chris Schmidt; S. 74 li.: Søren Sielemann, 2. v. li.: Rich Legg, Mitte: Chris Schmidt, 2. v. re.: ronen, re.: Suzanne Tucker; S. 79 Bild I lipstick kiss (M): konstantin32; S. 101 3. v. oben (u. 106 Bild 2): James Bowyer, 3. v. unten: (u. 111 li.): Jolande Gerritsen; S. 102 Mitte: KJA; S. 104 lake (M): Paul Morton; S. 106 Bild 1: Linda & Colin McKie, Bild 4 u. Bild 5: david franklin; S. 137 unten: james steidl); **http://manateens.blogspot.com** (S. 88 oben website, background, logo (M): used with permission of Volunteer Manatee. Volunteer Services of Manatee County, Inc. (Stand 15.06.2009)); **mauritius images**, Mittenwald (S. 89 Mitte: Cultura Images Ltd. (RF)); © **Ewa Nogiec/iamprovincetown.com** (S. 93 oben li.); **Okapia**, Frankfurt/Main (S. 23: Hans Reinhard); **Onslow College**, Johnsonville (S. 99 logo, students: James Gilberd); **Photofusion Picture Library**, London (Inhaltsverz. nursing aide (u. 79 unten li.): Ulrike Preuss); Photolibrary, London (S. 78 Bild E (u. 79 Hintergrund): Cultura/Britt Erlanson); **Picture-Alliance**,

Frankfurt/Main (S. 13 Mitte re.: dpa – Report; S. 28 Bild 3: dpa-Report/ZB/Martin Schutt; S. 32 Mitte li.: dpa – Fotoreport; S. 50 Hintergrund child: dpa – Report, Bild A: dpa; S. 51 Bild C: Godong; S. 67 unten: akg; S. 72: empics; S. 86: Sander; S. 102 unten: KPA; S. 103 oben re: NHPA/photoshot, unten li.: dpa-Report; S. 110 unten: dpa_Bildarchiv; S. 111 re.: empics); **The Picture Desk**, London (S. 73 li. u. re.: Film 4/Celador Films/Pathe International/The Kobal Collection; S. 76 Mitte li.: EON/DANJAQ/SONY/The Kobal Collection, Mitte re.: New Line Cinema/The Kobal Collection, unten li.: LUCASFILM/20TH CENTURY FOX/The Kobal Collection, unten Mitte: 20TH CENTURY FOX/The Kobal Collection, unten re.: 20TH CENTURY FOX/The Kobal Collection); **Rex Features**, London (S. 66: Stuart Clarke); **Rock the Vote**, Washington, D. C. (S. 65 oben logo); **Shooting Jozi, a project of Global Studio 2007 and the individuals who participated** (S. 128); **Shutterstock**, New York (Inhaltsverz. dirt road (u. 21 unten): ILYA GENKIN, Uluru: Ronald Sumners, UN logo (u. 50): keellla; S. 7 Bild 4: Sharyn Young, Bild 5: BlueSoul Photography; S. 8 li.: Dimitrios Kaisaris, re.: Andrei Marincas; S. 11: Susan Law Cain; S. 12 oben trees (M): aliciahh; S. 16 unten: Kaspars Grinvalds; S. 19 oben: Carsten Reisinger; S. 20 li.: Ashley Whitworth; S. 21 oben: aliciahh; S. 26 oben: Rob Wilson; S. 28 Bild 1: Rob Wilson, Bild 2: Gregory Gerber; S. 32/33 Hintergrund: javarman; S. 32 oben re.: Shmeliova Natalia; S. 45 2. v. unten: Tracy Whiteside, unten: Jeff Banke; S. 52 book cover leaves (M): debra hughes, face (M): Doreen Salcher, tree (M): Alexei Novikov; S. 53: Hudyma Natallia; S. 65 unten re.: Gelpi; S. 70 oben li.: Robert Ranson, oben re.: Rick Becker-Leckrone, unten li.: Amy Myers; S. 76 oben li.: Marina Krasnorutskaya, oben re.: Valeria73; S. 79 Bild I mobile (M): Tatiana Popova; S. 87 li., re., 2. v. re., 3. v. li.: designalldone, 2. v. li.: E. Sweet, 3. v. re.: John Rawsterne; S. 93 unten: Andresr; S. 97: Alex Staroseltsev; S. 101 oben: Patsy A. Jacks, 4. v. oben (u. 107): Serg64, 4. v. unten (u. 109 unten re.): Gary Blakeley; S. 102 oben: oksana.perkins; S. 109 oben: Condor 36, unten li.: Jonathan Larsen; S. 135: Holger Mette; S. 137 oben: Tatiana Popova); **Benjamin Singer, SMG Entertainment**, Santa Monica (S. 65 unten li. film still); **Superbild Bildagentur**, Taufkirchen (S. 103 Mitte li.: JTB); **The Tribune**, Ames, Iowa. Reprinted by permission (S. 61); **ullstein bild**, Berlin (S. 55: Granger Collection; S. 67 oben re.: Heritage); **Universal Press Syndicate** © 2009, reprinted by permission (S. 79 Bild F); **vario-images**, Bonn (S. 88 oben snorkeling (M)); **Fotoagentur VISUM**, Hamburg (S. 28 Bild 4:Wildlight); **Martynka Wawrzyniak**, New York (S. 46 oben; S. 47); **Wellington High School**, Wellington (S. 43)

Titelbild

Corbis, Düsseldorf (Monorail (M): Mark Karrass (RF)); **Corel Library** (flag Hintergrund (M)); **Getty Images**, München (Sydney (M): Michelangelo Gratton (RF))

Textquellen

S. 17 *Children were stolen for a racist ideal. Now a nation says sorry*. Adapted from "Snatched from home for a racist ideal. Now a nation says sorry" by Barbara McMahon, 11.2.2008. http://www.guardian.co.uk/world/2008/feb/11/australia. Copyright Guardian News & Media Ltd 2008; **S. 20 – 24** (u. 138) *In the outback*. Abridged and adapted from „Children of the Wind - A Prayer for Blue Delaney" by Kirsty Murray. Allen & Unwin, Crows Nest, Australia, 2005 (www.allenandunwin.com); **S. 43** *Wellington High School* article printed by permission; **S. 52 – 53** *First Amendment*. From SPEAK by Laurie Halse Anderson. Copyright © 1999 by Laurie Halse Anderson. Reprinted by permission of Farrar, Straus and Giroux, LLC; **S. 60** *Eighteen-year-old mayor may be youngest in US* by Jeff Raasch. Adapted from: http://www.midiowanews.com/site/index.cfm?newsid=15900970&BRD=2700&PAG=461&dept_id=554188&rfi=8 (1.10.2006). Copyright The Tribune, Ames, Iowa. Reprinted by Permission; **S. 63** *Discobesuche, Alkohol*. Auszug von "Das darf ich!" von Dominik Endres, www.deine-rechte.de; **S. 66** *The British* u. **S. 69** *Whosland* by Benjamin Zephaniah. (Copyright © Benjamin Zephaniah) is reproduced by permission of United Agents (www.unitedagents.co.uk) on behalf of Benjamin Zephaniah; **S. 81** *14: a txt msg pom*. Taken from "The message is the medium" by Victor Keegan, 3.5.2001, http://www.guardian.co.uk/technology/2001/may/03/internet.poetry Poem © Julia Bird, 2001/www.juliabird.wordpress.com; **S. 84** *'ASBO has helped me'*
Adapted from "ASBO made me give up life as a yob". http://www.mirror.co.uk/news/top-stories/2007/11/13/asbo-made-me-give-up-life-as-a-yob-115875-20099323/ by Jeremy Armstrong, 13.11.2007. Mirror Syndication International, London; **S. 88** *Springs Clean-up*. Text adapted from http://manateens.blogspot.com/ (Stand 15.06.2009) used with permission of Volunteer Manatee. Volunteer Services of Manatee County, Inc., Hickory Soup Kitchen. Adapted from "Students soup up kitchen" by Sarah Newell Williamson, 6.8.2008.

http://www2.hickoryrecord.com/content/2008/aug/06/students-soup-kitchen/. Used with permission of The Hickory Daily Record, Hickory; **S. 89** *Community Service.* Adapted from http://www.fvs.edu/podium/default.aspx?t=39763. Used with permission of Fountain Valley School of Colorado, Colorado Springs; **S. 93** *Ein Beitrag für sich und die Gesellschaft* Auszug aus der Informationsbroschüre "Für mich und für andere" http://www.bmfsfj.de/bmfsfj/generator/RedaktionBMFSFJ/Broschuerenstelle/Pdf-Anlagen/Fuer-mich-und-fuer-andere-FSJ-FOEJ-GFD,property=pdf,bereich=bmfsfj,sprache=de,rwb=true.pdf. Herausgegeben vom Bundesministerium für Familie, Senioren, Frauen und Jugend. Berlin, 2008; **S. 94–96** *The caller* by Robert D. San Souci. Reprinted by permission of Carus Publishing Company, from DARE TO BE SCARED: THIRTEEN STORIES TO CHILL AND THRILL by Daniel D. San Souci, text © 2003 by Robert D. San Souci; **S. 99** *Onslow.* Used by permission of Onslow College, Wellington, NZ; **S. 107** (u. 138) *Dreams* by Langston Hughes. Copyright © 1994 by the Estate of Langston Hughes. Abdruck mit Genehmigung der Liepman AG, Zürich, *Somewhere in the sky.* Copyright © Leo Aylen. First published in "Rhymoceros: poems by Leo Aylen" (Macmillan London 1989) subsequently published as title poem in "Somewhere in the Sky" (Nelson 1996) and also in four other anthologies. It was selected as one of the poems to be performed in the 2008 Hong Kong Festival of Speech; **S. 112–113** *Luuurve debate.* From "Don't Call Me Ishmael" by Michael Gerard Bauer. Text copyright © Michael Gerard Bauer, 2006. Cover and text illustrations © Joe Bauer, 2006. First published by Omnibus Books, a division of Scholastic Australia Pty Ltd, 2006. Published in Germany by Carl Hanser Verlag München, 2008. Reproduced by permission of Scholastic Australia Pty Limited; **S. 114–118** (u. 139) *Who's guilty?* Abridged and adapted from "Just", taken from a collection of plays: Shell Connections 2005, New plays for young people, Faber & Faber, 2005. JUST © 2004, Ali Smith. All rights reserved; **S. 120–122** *Bus attack Part 1, Bus attack Part 2.* Abridged and adapted from case study 4, taken from http://www.restorativejustice.org.uk/Media/pdf/Case%20Study%20-%20Bus%20Co.pdf (30.06.2009). Used by permission of Restorative Justice Consortium, London; **S. 124** Auszug v. S. 516 aus „English G 2000 Wörterbuch – Das Wörterbuch zum Lehrwerk". Herausgegeben von der Langenscheidt-Redaktion Wörterbücher und der Cornelsen-Redaktion Englisch. © 2002 Cornelsen Verlag GmbH & Co. OHG, Berlin und Langenscheidt KG, Berlin und München.

Liedquellen:

S. 51 *Get up, stand up.* Words and Music by Bob Marley and Peter Tosh © 1974 FSMGI (IMRO), Embassy Music Corporation, Fity-six Hope Road Music, Ltd. and Odnil Music, Ltd. All Rights for FSMGI (IMRO). Administered by State One Music America (BMI). All Rights for Fity-six Hope Road Music, Ltd. and Odnil Music, Ltd. Administered in North America by Fairwood Music USA. On behalf of Blue Mountain Music Ltd. All Rights Reserved. Used by Permission. 3.125% administered by Alfred Music Publishing Co., Inc. Special thanks to Alfred Music Publishing for their consideration in providing the use of these lyrics and their publication. Alfred Music Publishing – Learn · Teach · Play – www.alfred.com and Blue Mountain Limited (93.75%)/Campbell Connelly & Company Limited (3.12%) **S. 107** *Breathe* Words and Music by Anna Christine Nalick. © 2004 Annibonna Music/Shapiro Bernstein & Co Limited. Reproduced by permission of Faber Music Ltd. All Rights Reserved. [Lyrics only].

Getting ready for a test 1

1 LISTENING Travelling to Australia

1 (Gate) 17
2 pasta (with tomato sauce); fruit juice, water, cola
3 passport office
4 2.50; 52.50
5 227; 7 (o'clock)/10:30 (a.m.)

2 LISTENING Shark attack!

Part 1: *1* C; *2* A; *3* B; *4* D
Part 2: *1* C, *2* D, *3* C, *4* B, *5* C

3 LISTENING Young Australians and the internet

Student 1: E
Student 2: C
Student 3: A
Student 4: F
Student 5: G
Student 6: D

Getting ready for a test 2

1 READING Dev Patel

1 C; *2* C; *3* D; *4* A; *5* B; *6* D; *7* C; *8* A

2 READING Choosing a book

Student A: 7
Student B: 5
Student C: 1
Student D: 4
Student E: 3

Country	Area (km²)	Population (2008 estimate)	Pop./km²	English as first language (est.)*	English as additional language (est.)**
Australia	7,691,951	20,951,000	3	15,581,329	2,591,660
Bahamas	13,878	335,000	24	260,000	28,000
Barbados	416	295,000	709	262,000	13,000
Belize	22,965	294,000	13	190,000	56,000
Bermuda	50	65,000	1294	63,000	***
Botswana	581,730	1,906,000	3	***	630,000
Cameroon	475,650	18,920,000	40	***	7,700,000
Canada	9,984,670	33,170,000	3	17,694,830	7,551,390
Dominica	751	67,000	89	3,000	60,000
Fiji Islands	18,333	844,000	46	4,930	14,900
Gambia	10,689	1,754,000	164	***	40,000
Ghana	238,537	24,947,000	100	***	1,400,000
Guyana	214,970	736,000	3	650,000	30,000
India	3,287,263	1,186,186,000	361	320,000	90,000,000
Ireland	70,273	4,380,000	62	4,123,000	257,000
Jamaica	10,991	2,728,000	248	2,600,000	50,00
Kenya	582,646	38,550,000	66	***	2,700,000
Lesotho	30,355	2,020,000	67	***	500,000
Liberia	97,754	3,942,000	40	600,000	2,500,000
Madagascar	587,295	20,215,000	34	***	***
Malawi	118,500	14,288,000	121	209	540,000
Malta	316	408,000	1292	2,400	370,000
Marshall Islands	181	61,000	335	***	60,000
Mauritius	2040	1,272,000	623	2,000	200,000
Micronesia	700	112,000	159	3,540	***
Namibia	824,268	2,102,000	3	14,000	300,000
Nauru	21	10,000	485	800	9,200
New Zealand	268,680	4,215,000	16	3,700,000	***
Nigeria	923,768	151,478,000	164	4,000,000	75,000,000
Pakistan	796,095	166,961,000	210	***	17,000,000
Palau	490	20,000	42	500	18,000
Papua New Guinea	462,840	6,458,000	14	150,000	3,000,000
Philippines	300,016	89,651,000	299	3,427,000	45,373,000
Puerto Rico	8,870	4,012,000	452	100,000	1,840,000
Rwanda	26,340	10,009,000	380	***	20,000
Seychelles	455	87,000	191	3,000	30,000
Sierra Leone	71,740	5,969,000	83	500,000	4,400,000
Singapore	704	4,490,000	6378	665,087	1,128,158
Solomon Islands	28,896	536,000	19	10,000	165,000
South Africa	1,219,090	48,832,000	40	3,673,203	10,000,000
Swaziland	17,363	1,148,000	66	***	50,000
Tanzania	883,749	41,464,000	47	***	4,000,000
Trinidad and Tobago	5,128	1,338,000	261	1,145,000	***
Uganda	241,548	31,903,000	132	***	2,500,000
United Kingdom	242,495	61,019,000	253	58,100,000	1,500,000
United States of America	9,826,675	308,798,000	31	215,423,557	35,964,744
Vanuatu	12,190	232,000	19	60,000	120,000
Zambia	752,612	12,154,000	16	110,000	1,800,000
Zimbabwe	390,757	13,481,000	35	250,000	5,300,000

* People who learned English as a child and prefer English in a multi-lingual environment
** People whose first language is not English but who may have to regularly use English in daily life
*** No reliable data
(Population and area: Statistisches Bundesamt, Statistisches Jahrbuch 2008; English as first or additional language: various sources)